John Myre

The Book of Common Prayer compared with the first prayer book of Edward the Sixth

John Myre

The Book of Common Prayer compared with the first prayer book of Edward the Sixth

ISBN/EAN: 9783337200879

Printed in Europe, USA, Canada, Australia, Japan

Cover: Foto ©Lupo / pixelio.de

More available books at **www.hansebooks.com**

THE BOOK OF COMMON PRAYER:

1549. 1886.

THE BOOK OF

COMMON PRAYER,

A.D. 1886,

Compared with

THE FIRST PRAYER BOOK

OF

KING EDWARD THE SIXTH,

A.D. 1549.

EDITED, WITH INTRODUCTION,

BY

W. MILES MYRES, M.A.

VICAR OF SWANBOURNE, BUCKS, AND RURAL DEAN.

With PREFACE by the LORD BISHOP OF OXFORD.

LONDON:

THOMAS BAKER, 1, SOHO SQUARE, W.

MDCCCLXXXVII.

TO

THE RIGHT REVEREND FATHER IN GOD,

JOHN FIELDER,

LORD BISHOP OF OXFORD,

THIS VOLUME

IS,

WITH HIS LORDSHIP'S PERMISSION,

DUTIFULLY DEDICATED

BY

THE EDITOR.

Whitsuntide, 1887.

PREFACE.

I am asked to say a few words by way of preface to this volume. In doing so I desire only to insist on a very obvious truth, that all who pronounce an opinion on the merits of the First Prayer Book of Edward the Sixth ought to be well acquainted with it. For my own part, I believe that some of the changes made by the Second Book were changes for the worse, others much for the better. I should deprecate the return to an Office-Book, now long disused, for better for worse. Such as desire to restore it may do well to remember Bishop Burnet's reflection on the refusal of the Convocation to accept alterations in the way of comprehension, which he had strongly favoured. "By all the "judgments we could afterwards make, if we had carried a majority "in the Convocation for alterations, they would have done us more "hurt than good." Now, as then, there are very good reasons for not furnishing "pretences for separation" to those who perhaps might not be sorry to find them.

J. F. OXON.

TABLE OF CONTENTS.

PAGE.

Preface
Introduction ... vii.

The Preface ... 5
Concerning the Service of the Church ... 10
Of Ceremonies... 14
Order how the Psalter is appointed to be read ... 18
Order how the rest of Holy Scripture is appointed to be read... 20
Proper Lessons for Sundays and Holy-days ... 22
Calendar and Table of Lessons ... 26
Table and Rules... 39
Notes for decent ministration (1549) ... 51
Ornaments Rubric ... 51
Order for Morning Prayer ... 52
Order for Evening Prayer... 66
Athanasian Creed ... 76
Litany ... 79
Prayers and Thanksgivings ... 86
Introits, Collects, Epistles, and Gospels ... 95
Holy Communion ... 154
Public Baptism of Infants... 198
Private Baptism of Infants ... 210
Baptism of such as are of Riper Years ... 220
Catechism ... 231
Confirmation ... 239
Matrimony ... 243
Visitation of the Sick... 254
Communion of the Sick... 268
Burial of the Dead ... 272
Communion at Burial ... 286
Churching of Women ... 290
A Commination ... 294

PAGE.
Form of making of Deacons 310
Form of ordering of Priests 325
Form of consecrating of Bishops 346
Table of Kindred and Affinity 360

APPENDIX i. Tabular View of Morning and Evening Prayer. 365
" ii. Tabular View of Office for Holy Communion. 367
" iii. Exhortations to Holy Communion compared. 370
" iv. Prayer of Consecration compared. 376

Index 381

INTRODUCTION.

IT is not the object of this work to trace the various steps by which the Book of Common Prayer has come to its present state, or to point out the movements, progressive or retrograde, which have influenced its form. It has a definite aim, to compare the Prayer Book as we have it now, in the main sanctioned by Convocation in 1661, and by Parliament in 1662, with the first Reformed Prayer Book, commonly called the First Prayer Book of King Edward VI., printed and published at Whitsuntide, 1549, by authority of Parliament. It is right to observe that it is doubtful whether this Prayer Book of Edward had the sanction of Convocation. Before the Reformation the sanction of Convocation was not necessary. Each Bishop put forth his own form. There was the use of Sarum, the use of York, Bangor, Lincoln, and so forth.

The reasons which have led to the course here adopted are briefly these.

There has been for some years a tendency to introduce into our public services some of the customs which were prescribed in Edward's Book, but which find no place in the Book to which all the Clergy have given assent, either in the older and more stringent form of declaration, or in the more lax form of the Clerical Subscription Act of 1865.

There is, moreover, a growing inclination on the part of many to bring forward, as the Rites and Ceremonies, the Doctrines and Precepts, of the Church of England, what may have some support from Edward's Book, though there be no recognition of them in the Prayer Book as it now stands.

It is not the intention to press the fact that subsequent Revisions established the exclusion or insertion of these rites or practices; or to enforce the dictum that what the Book does not prescribe, it forbids; or rather, that what it deliberately, upon opportunity given, refuses to enact, it implicitly excludes, and that what it does enact, it intends to make binding. It is easy, though scarcely straightforward, to read into any revision something from a former copy, which has been left out, and to take as included everything which is not specially in plain words forbidden. This, however, need not be further noticed here.

But there is one reason for this work which must be put prominently forward.

At the Church Congress at Derby in 1882, a proposition was made as a kind of Eirenicon by a prominent churchman—the president of the English Church Union—to legalize the use of the First Prayer Book of Edward VI. as alternative with the use of our present Book, in Churches where it might be preferred. And this proposition has been pressed in many quarters since that time.

But how many, either laymen or clergy, can give a clear account of the difference between the two?

THIS volume will be a help to some. It places the two books side by side—as was well done by Dr. Cardwell, in the case of the First and Second Prayer Books of King Edward—that the strong points of each, the weak points of each, may be the better known, and a calm and candid judgment be formed, as to the expediency—not to say the right or wrong—of legalizing the use of the first reformed Prayer Book as alternative with the last.

It may be worth while to record the fact that between the two there have been three Revisions with several Conferences at which alterations were suggested. The First Book of Edward had a short life: it was superseded by the great revision of 1552, which gave us the Second Prayer Book of Edward; then followed the revision of 1559 under the authority of Elizabeth, the revision of James I. in 1604, the changes proposed but not carried in 1641 under Charles I., the final revision in 1662 under Charles II., which gave the Book as in the main it stands now, notwithstanding the attempted revision in the reign of William III. in 1689.

Perhaps allusion ought to be made, by the way, to the Scottish Liturgy, which was drawn up in 1637, and to the Nonjurors' New Communion Office put forth in 1718, and to the American Prayer Book arranged in 1789.

A writer in the 'Nineteenth Century,' a short time ago (September, 1885), advocating the revival of the practice of reserving the elements at Holy Communion, uses the words 'the legalised use of the first reformed Prayer Book would meet our want; and Parliament in that case need only be asked to legalize a document which they legalized once before.' (Dr. T. W. Belcher.)

AMONG customs which are supported by retrogression to the First Prayer Book of Edward (without any adequate authority, so far as appears, from our present Book), may be mentioned the following,—

The use of albes and tunicles, the use of the vestment, the use of corporas, and of round unleavened bread, the use of the pastoral staff, the mixing pure clean water with the wine, the permission of crossing, knocking on the breast and other gestures;

The name 'Altar' as applied to the Holy Table, and 'Mass' as meaning the office of Holy Communion;

The term 'Matins and Evensong' rather than Morning and Evening Prayer;

The ascription of praise before the reading of the Holy Gospel. The use of the three clauses of the Lesser Litany by the choir—(no change in type for the second clause appearing in Edward's Morning Prayer).

The practice, (which may, like the last, have been confirmed by musical composers), of leaving to the Priest alone the introductory words of the angelic hymn, 'Therefore with angels and archangels,' while the choir and people keep silence till the burst of the Ter Sanctus—'Holy, Holy, Holy'—seems to have its origin in the division of the paragraph in Edward's Book, and possibly (though this is somewhat ambiguous), in the rubric which follows in the same.

The custom of allowing the minister alone to say the opening words of the Lord's prayer, while the people only join in at the words 'Which art in heaven,' is based possibly on the direction in First Prayer Book of Edward that the people only respond, 'Deliver us from evil: Amen.'

The similar practice of the priest alone beginning the Nicene Creed (and in some places the same use obtains in the case of the Apostles' Creed), with the words 'I believe in one God,' the people not joining in this individual confession of faith, has its foundation in the direction of Edward's Book.

The use, again, of Benedicite instead of Te Deum in Lent, the omission of Doxology from the Lord's prayer, the singing of the sentences at the offertory or the saying of one sentence only before the collection is made, the singing of the Agnus Dei at Communion time, the use of the first clause of the Gloria in Excelsis by the priest alone—have their origin in Edward's Book.

The omission at times of portions of the office for Holy Communion, especially of the Ten Commandments;

The omission of the manual acts of breaking the bread, and of laying the hand upon the bread and on the cup in the Prayer of Consecration;

The introduction of the sign of the cross over the bread and wine in the Prayer of Consecration in the Communion office, and the similar sign over the water in the Prayer of Consecration at Holy Baptism;

The practice of trine immersion, or trine aspersion (as a substitute);

The provision of weekly Communions in Parish Churches, even with one communicant at least;

The exhortation to private and secret confession, and the provision of a form of absolution to be used in private at other times than with the sick;

The reservation of the consecrated elements, allowed by the absence of any order to consume them in church, and prescribed for the Communion of the Sick;

The separation of the men from the women in church at Communion;

The non-withdrawal of non-communicants from the church, although they are directed to withdraw from the quire;—

These are rites and ceremonies, in themselves, it may be, godly and edifying, and not contrary to Holy Scripture, which are prescribed in the First Book of Edward, which the Second Book of Edward seems to have abrogated, and of which the Book of Common Prayer as it now stands appears to know nothing, but which have been revived, and are more or less in use in these latter days. Ought they to be legalized and be in use by authority of Parliament?

The vexed question of the Ornaments Rubric may receive some light when the fact is recognized that the words shall 'be retained and be in use' were substitued for the simpler words 'shall use,' which had been in the rubric of Queen Elizabeth. The words as they now stand were incorporated in the rubric of 1662 from Elizabeth's Act of Uniformity, where, however, they had been qualified by the remarkable addition which has been brought into prominence in our day, 'until other order shall be therein taken by authority of the Queen's Majesty with the advice of her Commissioners, appointed and authorized under the great Seal of England for causes ecclesiastical, or of the Metropolitan of this realm,'—that 'other order' being taken by Queen Elizabeth and Archbishop Parker in the Injunctions and Interpretations and further considerations of 1559.

Now to find out what could be 'retained,' it is necessary to ascertain what was at the time 'in use,' that is, what ornaments and so forth, which were prescribed in the second year of King Edward, i.e., in the Prayer Book of 1549, were actually in use in the Church of England, by authority, in 1662, the year of the last revision. To 'retain' is not to re-introduce.

A careful examination of the visitation articles of the Bishops between the time of Elizabeth and the time of the revision of Charles II. (as recorded in Cardwell's 'Documentary Annals'), will shew that the vestments of the rubrics of Edward's First Prayer Book for the parochial clergy (with the exception of the surplice), having been abolished by the Second Book of Edward, had fallen into disuse. They are not recognised; and therefore to talk about 'retaining' them would be a mistake. Moreover, the only garment about which there had been any dispute at the Savoy Conference, which had come at all into question in regard to the parochial clergy in their ministrations, was the surplice, which the extreme puritan party desired to have cast away, but which the main body of the Church decided should 'be retained and be in use,' as it had been in the second year of Edward VI.

But the two books must be compared in detail. It is assumed that all are accurately acquainted with the Prayer Book as it now stands. It will be well, therefore, first to examine the Order for Matins, the Litany, and the Occasional Offices, according to the Book of Edward, reserving to the end of this introduction the Order for Holy Communion, as being that in which the most important points of contrast are to be found.

THE FIRST PRAYER BOOK OF EDWARD VI.

MATINS.

The priest in the quire, vested in surplice, begins the service, saying alone the Lord's prayer, followed by the Versicles with the singular pronoun, and by the invitation 'Praise ye the Lord' after the Gloria Patri without a respond, 'Alleluia' being added from Easter to Trinity. After the Venite and the Psalms, the Lessons are to be read, and 'in places where they sing to the end that people may the better hear, they shall be sung in a plain tune, after the manner of distinct reading;' the first Lesson according to the Kalendar.

Then shall follow Te Deum, except in Lent, when Benedicite shall be used.

After the second Lesson, Benedictus only. Then the lesser Litany, to be said by all, devoutly kneeling, and the Creed and the Lord's prayer by the minister, still kneeling, the people responding 'But deliver us from evil. Amen.'

The Suffrages follow; then the priest, standing up, says, 'Let us pray,' and the Collect for the day, and the two Collects for peace and for grace, said by the priest standing, close the service.

EVENSONG

Follows the Order for Matins.

Magnificat and Nunc Dimittis stand alone.

And the Collects for peace and aid against perils close the service.

THE ATHANASIAN CREED

Is to be used immediately after Benedictus, apparently as well as the Apostles' Creed, in the feasts of Christmas, the Epiphany, Easter, the Ascension, Pentecost, and upon Trinity Sunday.

THE LITANY AND SUFFRAGES

Stand as we have them now, with the exceptions that the

deprecation from 'all sedition and privy conspiracy' does not mention 'rebellion and schism,' but inserts 'from the tyranny of the Bishop of Rome and all his detestable enormities'; and that the suffrage for the King is only 'to keep'; and that the intercession for the Clergy runs 'that it may please Thee to illuminate all Bishops, Pastors, and Ministers of the Church with true knowledge,' &c.

There is no Apostolic Benediction at the close.

THE PSALTER

Was printed separately, and not as part of the First Prayer Book.

PUBLIC BAPTISM.

The former part of the service is to be used at the Church door, unless there be many to be baptised, and the congregation great.

The First Prayer is longer, having the petition 'that by this wholesome laver of regeneration, whatsoever sin is in them may be washed clean away.'

The Name is to be asked at the beginning of the service, and the sign of the Cross to be made on forehead and breast 'in token &c.'

After the prayer 'Almighty and immortal God,' there follows the exorcism of unclean spirit;

The Lord's Prayer and Creed are to be recited by minister, sponsors, and people, the priest adding the prayer 'Almighty and everlasting God, heavenly Father.'

Then one of the children is taken by hand, the rest following, and brought into the Church towards the font.

The questions are more full.

Change and Consecration of water once a month at least, with special prayers and sign of cross over water. (See Office for private Baptism.)

Trine immersion, dipping right side, left side, face.

The putting on of Chrisom or white vesture, and laying on of hands of Godfathers and Godmothers, and the anointing upon forehead of child, are prescribed.

The Chrisom is to be brought to priest at purification of mother.

CONFIRMATION.

The Catechism appears as introduction.

The second and fourth Commandments are shortened.

There is no section on 'Sacraments.'

Confirmation is a shorter service.

Sign of cross is to be made on forehead, and hand is to be laid on head of each.

A General blessing—'The peace of the Lord abide with you. Answer—And with thy spirit.'

MATRIMONY.

The Man gives ring, and 'other tokens of spousage,' as gold or silver, laying the same upon the book.

First benediction is fuller, and the sign of the cross is made.

Historical references are fuller,—

'As thou didst send thy angel Raphael to Thobie and Sara, the daughter of Raguel, to their great comfort.'

'Loving and amiable to her husband, as Rachel, wise as Rebecca, faithful and obedient as Sara.'

Sign of cross is prescribed in last benediction.

'Must receive the Holy Communion the same day of their marriage.'

VISITATION OF SICK.

Coming in to the sick's man's presence, the priest shall say Ps. cxliii.

In the prayer 'Hear us Almighty and most merciful,' there is the clause,

'Visit him, O Lord, as thou didst visit Peter's wife's mother and the captain's servant; and as thou preservedst Thobie and Sara by thy angel from danger, so restore unto this sick person his former health.'

After special confession, 'The priest shall absolve after this form.'

'And the same form of absolution shall be used in all private confessions.'

Ps. lxxi. is to be said throughout.

'If the sick person desire to be annointed, then shall the priest anoint him upon the forehead or breast only, making the sign of the cross,' saying prayer for anointing and Ps. xiii.

COMMUNION OF SICK.

If it be a day of open Communion in Church, there is provided a reservation of elements in Church for sick on that day; and there are said with sick person, before distribution, the general confession, absolution, and comfortable words, and, after communion, the collect 'Almighty and everlasting God we most heartily thank thee.'

If not a day of open communion, there is a full service to be used with the sick, with special introit and versicles before collect.

Provision is made for reservation of the sacrament for other sick, to be immediately ministered to them.

BURIAL.

Earth is to be cast on corpse by priest.

There is Commendation of the soul of departed brother by name.

The Psalm and Lesson in Church may be used either before or after the burial.

Ps. cxvi. and cxlvi. and cxxxix.

There is definite Prayer for departed.

Celebration of Holy Communion with Collect ('O merciful God, the Father of our Lord') and Epistle and Gospel.

PURIFICATION OF WOMEN.

Woman to kneel in some convenient place nigh unto the quire door.

Ps. cxxi.

The Chrisom to be offered.

COMMINATION.

No concluding blessing.

THE ORDINAL

Was not published with the First Prayer Book, but after it, in 1550.

It was superseded in 1552 by the Second Book, and by the new Ordinal which is in the present book. It seems to be more than probable that this second Ordinal is that which is referred to in Art. xxxvi.

DEACONS.

The Candidate, not under 21 years, to be presented, 'having on him a plain albe.'

The oath of King's supremacy, and against usurped power and authority of Bishop of Rome, to be ministered (as before 1865) in the service, with concluding words,—

'So help me God, all saints and the holy evangelist.'

Tunicle to be put on by the deacon who reads the gospel.

PRIESTS.

Candidate to be 24 years at least.

Introit.

No special Collect.

Epistle, Acts xx., or 1 Tim., iii.

Gospel, Matt. xxviii., or John x., or John xx. (as in Consecration of Bishops, 1662.)

Veni Creator ('Come Holy Ghost, eternal God') is to be said or sung immediately after Gospel.

Priests to be presented, 'having on a plain albe.'

The Chalice, or Cup, with the Bread, as well as Bible to be delivered to each ordained.

BISHOP.

Introit (as in Ordination of Priests.)

No special Collect.

The Bishop to be presented, 'having on surplice and cope.'

Presenting Bishops to have surplices, copes, and pastoral staves.

The oath of due obedience ends—'So help me God and his holy gospel.'

The Archbishop is to lay the Bible upon the neck of the

consecrated Bishop, and to put into his hand the pastoral staff.

Ceremonies and Notes.

Bishop celebrating Holy Communion, or executing any other public ministration, to have upon him, besides his rochette, a surplice or albe, and a cope or vestment, and also his pastoral staff in his hand, or else borne or holden by his chaplain.

Kneeling, crossing, holding up of hands, knocking upon breast and other gestures, may be used or left, as every man's devotion serveth, without blame.

At Holy Communion.

Introits are provided (with special Lessons on certain days) with the Collects, Epistles and Gospels for each Sunday and Holy day.

There is no direction as to the Collect at 'evening service next before;'

No direction as to use of Advent collect with the other Sunday collects in Advent;

No direction as to use of Ash Wednesday collect in Lent.

There is a variation in the Collects for—

3rd Sunday in Advent;
St. Stephen's Day, which is shorter also;
St. John Evangelist's Day;
Innocents' Day;
1st Sunday after Epiphany;
4th „ „ .

There are variations in the Easter Anthem;

In Collects for—

4th Sunday after Easter;
Trinity Sunday;
2nd Sunday after Trinity, and use of 'congregation' instead of 'Church' (1662);
8th Sunday after Trinity;
18th „ „ ;

There is no collect for 6th Sunday after Epiphany, or for Easter Even.

No rubric as to greater number of Sundays after Trinity.

There is a provision for 2nd Communion with second introit, collect, epistle and gospel on Christmas Day; and on Easter Day (with special anthems.)

There is a different collect for St. Andrew's Day.

" special collect for St. Mary Magdalene's.

There are variations in the collect—

for St. Paul's Day;

for St. Mark's;

for St. Philip's and St. James';

for St. Luke's.

All the Epistles and Gospels are from the older translation of 1539, called the Great Bible (Cranmer's.)

THE SUPPER OF THE LORD AND THE HOLY COMMUNION, COMMONLY CALLED THE MASS.

Notice of intention to partake may be given as late as after Matins.

The priest that shall execute the holy mystery shall put upon him the vesture appointed for that ministration, that is to say, a white albe, plain, with a vestment or cope. The other priests and deacons shall have upon them albes with tunicles.

The clerks shall sing for the Introit a Psalm appointed for the day.

The priest 'standing humbly afore the midst of the altar' shall say the Lord's prayer with the Collect for purity.

Then shall he say a Psalm appointed for the Introit, which Psalm ended, the priest shall say, or else the clerks shall sing, 'Lord have mercy upon us, Christ have mercy, &c.'

Then the priest, 'standing at God's board,' shall begin 'Glory be to God on high.'

The clerks, 'And in earth peace, goodwill towards men,' and the rest.

The Salutation and the Collects for the King follow.

The Epistle is to be read in a place assigned for the purpose.

After the epistle ended, the Holy Gospel is announced, and

the answer made by clerks and people, 'Glory be to thee, O Lord.'

After the gospel ended the priest shall begin—

'I believe in one God.'

The clerks shall sing the rest (omitting, 'whose kingdom shall have no end').

The exhortation, 'Dearly beloved in the Lord,' is to be read (in cathedrals, or where daily communion), once a month, if no sermon on Holy Communion;

If people negligent, then a longer exhortation (in part similar to the first exhortation of 1662, but) with invitation to secret confession, and justification of auricular confession.

Then follows the offertory, one or more sentences being sung whilst the people offer, or one of them being said by the minister immediately after the offering.

Communicants to tarry in the quire, men on one side and women on the other; others to depart out of the quire.

Of the elements sufficient to be taken, the bread to be laid on the corporas or the paten, or some other comely thing prepared; the wine to be put into the chalice or cup, the priest putting thereto a little pure and clean water; and 'setting both the bread and wine upon the altar, then the priest shall say'—

The Salutation.

Sursum Corda.

The proper Preface.

Introduction.

Ter Sanctus (by the clerks), which is longer than at present.

Then a priest or deacon shall turn him to the people and say—

'Let us pray for the whole state of Christ's Church.'

'Then the priest turning him to the altar shall say, or sing, plainly and distinctly, this prayer following':—

The Consecration Prayer, in which we observe—

(*a*) The substance of the three prayers—the prayer for Church militant, the prayer of consecration, and the first post-communion prayer—of our present book.

(*b*) The commemoration of the Virgin and saints.

(*c*) The commendation of the departed, and prayer for the departed.

(*d*) The invocation of the Holy Spirit on the elements, the sign of the cross, the petition 'that they may be unto us the body and blood of Thy most dearly beloved Son.'

(*e*) The making of memorial with the holy gifts.

(*f*) The intervention of angels in prayer.

(*g*) The bread and the cup are to be taken into the hands, but there is no manual—breaking of bread, or laying on of hands.

(*h*) No elevation is allowed, or shewing of the sacrament.

Then follows the Lord's prayer, by priest, with response, 'But deliver us,' &c.

The commemoration of the Sacrifice of Christ as the Paschal Lamb.

The invitation to communicants.

Confession by one of communicants in name of all,
or by one of ministers,
or by priest himself.

The Absolution by priest, turning to people.

The Comfortable Words.

The Prayer of humble access.

The Communion of priest in both kinds—
" of other ministers, 'that they may be ready to help.'

The delivery of 'Sacrament of body,' (rubric at end of office, 'into mouth'), with the words, 'The body—everlasting life.'

The delivery of the 'Sacrament of the blood,' giving everyone to drink once, and no more, with the words, 'The blood—everlasting life.'

Deacon (if any) or other priest, to follow with the Chalice.

The singing of the Agnus Dei by clerks in the Communion time.

The singing of the Post Communion sentences of Holy Scripture.

The thanksgiving by the priest, with salutation, and the

prayer 'Almighty and everliving God we most heartily thank.'

The blessing, 'turning to people.'

On week-days or in private houses—

Gloria in Excelsis, Homily, Creed, and Exhortation ('Dearly beloved in the Lord') may be omitted.

Collects after offertory when no communion—every day one.

Additional Collects for rain, for fair weather.

RUBRICS.

On Wednesdays and Fridays the Litany to be said or sung in all places. And 'though there be none to communicate with the priest, yet these days (after the Litany ended) the priest shall put on him a plain albe or surplice, with a cope, and say all things at the altar, until after the offertory, and then shall add one or two of the collects, and let the people depart with the blessing.'

The bread is to be unleavened and round, but 'without all manner of print, something more larger and thicker than it was,' to be aptly divided, into two pieces at the least.

'And men must not think less to be received in part than in the whole, but in each of them the whole body of our Saviour Jesus Christ.'

Each parishioner to communicate once a year.

Some one at least of the house, whose turn it is to provide in course the charges for Holy Communion, shall communicate weekly with the priest.

The people to 'receive the sacrament of Christ's body in their mouths at the hands of the priest.'

IT would be interesting to point out the resemblances and differences between our present Prayer Book and the Second Prayer Book of King Edward, but this not within the scope of the present work.

IT remains to mention some of the special marks of distinction which characterize the Prayer Book as it is now in contrast with the Book which has just been reviewed.

THE BOOK OF COMMON PRAYER.

PREFACE.

First, there is the valuable Preface ('It hath been the wisdom') which was added by Bishop Sanderson in 1662.

MORNING AND EVENING PRAYER.

There are the Introductory Sentences of Holy Scripture, the Exhortation, the Confession and the Absolution at the beginning of Morning and Evening prayer (1552.)

There is the use of the Hundredth Psalm as alternative with the Benedictus in the morning; and the 98th Psalm with the Magnificat, and the 67th with Nunc Dimittis, in the evening.

The Creed is to be said throughout by both minister and people, standing; and the Lord's prayer, with a loud voice, by all, devoutly kneeling.

There are the prayers for the Queen (1559), for the Royal Family (1604), and for the clergy (1559), with the prayer of St. Chrysostom, brought from the Litany into morning and evening prayer, and the Apostolic Benediction prayer (1559).

THE LITANY.

There are the words, 'rebellion and schism' in the litany (1662), and the longer suffrages for the Queen (1559), while the Clergy are spoken of by Orders, as Bishops, Priests, and Deacons (1662.)

There are the prayers and thanksgivings upon several occasions: in Ember-week, for Parliament, for all conditions of men, the General Thanksgiving (1662), and others, of which only two—for rain and for fair weather—are found in the First Prayer Book of Edward.

THE ORDER FOR THE ADMINISTRATION OF THE LORD'S SUPPER OR HOLY COMMUNION.

There are no Introits.

The Epistles and Gospels are from the authorized version of 1604, and the Collects, where altered, are generally more full.

Notice is to be given of intention to communicate, at least sometime the day before.

In the office for Holy Communion there is no mention of Mass, or Altar; there is no vestment rubric, but there is a direction as to the position of the Holy Table, and an order as to its fair linen covering.

The priest, 'standing at the north side of the Table,' shall say the Lord's Prayer.

The Ten Commandments are ordered to be recited, with a petition for mercy and for grace to follow each (1552).

The elements are to be placed upon the Holy Table, after the alms have been presented.

The Prayer 'for the whole state of Christ's Church militant here on earth' (1552), has the clause for acceptance of alms and oblations, (1662), and the thanksgiving for departed, and prayer for grace to imitate (1662), but no prayer for the departed, no commemoration of the saints by name.

The Prayer of Consecration follows the Confession, the Absolution, the Comfortable Words, and the Prayer of humble access.

The Introduction of the 'Ter Sanctus' is to be said, or sung, as well as the hymn itself.

The Bread and Wine are to be so ordered by the priest, 'standing before the table' (1662), that he may with the more readiness and decency break the bread before the people, and take the cup into his hands.

The Prayer of Consecration has no invocation of the Holy Ghost upon the bread and wine; no sign of the cross, no making of memorial; but it has the taking and the breaking of the bread, and the blessing of the bread by the laying on of the hand, and the blessing of the cup by the laying on of the hand (1662.)

There is a second clause in the words at the delivery of the bread and wine: 'Take and eat—thanksgiving.'
'Drink—thankful.'

The bread is to be delivered to the people 'into their hands,' and not their mouths.

Provision is made for the consecration of additional bread

or wine (1662), and for the reverent covering with a fair linen cloth of any consecrated which may remain unused (1662).

The Lord's prayer repeated by the people after the priest, with one of two Thanksgiving Prayers (the first having formed part of the prayer of consecration in the Book of Edward), followed by the Gloria in Excelsis, said or sung, and by the Benediction pronounced by Priest or Bishop (if he be present), closes the office.

'It shall suffice that the bread be such as is usual to be eaten, but the best and purest wheaten bread that conveniently may be gotten.'

Any consecrated Bread or Wine remaining shall not be carried out of the Church, but shall be reverently eaten and drunk by the priest and such other communicants as he shall then call unto him, immediately after the Blessing (1662.)

Every parishioner shall communicate three times a year, of which Easter shall be one.

The rubric on kneeling, and on the presence of the Lord (1662.)

Baptismal Services.

The filling of the font each time (1662), and the consecration of the water at each service is ordered.

The declaration as to the use of the cross in Baptism.

The Service for Baptism of those of Riper Years (1662.)

Catechism.

In the Catechism, the latter part of the second and fourth commandments (1552), the part relating to the Sacraments (1604.)

Confirmation.

The Preface, the Ratification of promises, and the last Collect in Confirmation (1662.)

The words, 'ready and desirous to be confirmed' (1662.)

VISITATION.

The special prayers in Visitation of the Sick for child, for troubled in mind, &c. (1662.)

THE FORM OF PRAYER TO BE USED AT SEA (1662.)

THE PSALTER as a part of the Book of Common Prayer (1662.)

THE ARTICLES OF RELIGION.

THE ORDINAL as a part of Book of Common Prayer (1552).

The special Gospel in ordination of Deacons.

The special Collect in Priests' and Bishops' ordination.

The words in Priests' ordination, 'The Holy Ghost for the Office and Work of a Priest in the Church of God now committed unto thee by imposition of our hands.'

The words in Bishops' consecration, 'for the Office and Work of a Bishop in the Church of God now committed, &c.'

THE two books have now been carefully compared. The loss or the gain to be effected by the return to the first reformed Prayer Book, may be estimated.

There is no doubt that the earlier book is more sacerdotal, that it is more closely allied to the Mediæval uses, it is more complicated, and its ceremonial is greater, but it was a vast step to true and simple teaching and worship from the ante-reformation service-books. It retains many ancient usages, not necessarily superstitious or unscriptural, though there are practices and expressions which have ministered to superstition and false doctrine.

Every Particular or National Church has the power and the authority to alter its ceremonies, to abrogate old customs, if it shall judge them unedifying, to enact new rites, provided they be not contrary to Holy Scripture; and it is within the province of the Church of England to revise her service book, and to change or remodel it.

But it must not be forgotten that there are proposals on the other hand to carry the reaction from mediævalism to a much greater extent than was done in 1662 or in 1552, as may be seen in the changes recommended by the Prayer Book Revision Society. And the age in which our lot is cast is somewhat impatient of ecclesiastical disputes.

Is it wise to unsettle the minds of Churchmen, to provoke the antagonism of Parliament, to run the risk of the disruption of the Church of England, by urging the legalisation of the use of the First Prayer Book of Edward VI., in congregations where it may be desired? Is it expedient to force out, at the will of a possible majority in any individual Parish or Congregation, the use of the Book of Common Prayer, which has been for 220, if not for 330 years, the heritage, the treasure, the support and stay of the members of the Church? Is England willing to lay aside the Prayer Book, of Hooker, Jewell, Andrewes, Hall, Sanderson, Bull, and Waterland, of Cranmer, Parker, Bancroft, Laud, Juxon, Sancroft, Tillotson, Tenison, Secker, Sumner, Longley, Tait?

A LOYAL AND HISTORIC CHURCHMAN, PRIMITIVE AND MODERATE, WILL SURELY ANSWER 'NO!'

N.B.—In this volume the text of the First Prayer Book of Edward VI. is from the edition of Edward Whitechurch, March 1549. The text of the Book of Common Prayer is from S.P.C.K., Oxford, 1886.

CORRECTIONS AND ADDITIONS.

Page viii., line 36, *add* and the Common Prayer Book of the Church of Ireland revised in 1871.

Page x., line 6, *add* may be traced to the same source.

Page x., line 14, *for* aspersion *read* affusion.

Page x., line 30, *for* which the Second Book of Edward seems to have abrogated;

read which are omitted in the Second Book of Edward, which are not enjoined by any subsequent revision (of Elizabeth, or James i, or Charles ii),

THE

BOOK OF THE COMMON PRAYER AND ADMINISTRATION OF THE SACRAMENTS, AND OTHER RITES AND CEREMONIES OF THE CHURCH: AFTER THE USE OF THE CHURCH OF ENGLAND.

Londini in Officina
Edouardi Whitchurche
Cum privilegio ad imprimendum solum.
Anno Do. 1549, *Mense* Martii.

THE BOOK OF

COMMON PRAYER,

AND

ADMINISTRATION OF THE SACRAMENTS,
AND OTHER RITES AND CEREMONIES
OF THE CHURCH,

ACCORDING TO THE USE OF

THE CHURCH OF ENGLAND:

TOGETHER WITH

The Psalter or Psalms of David,

POINTED AS THEY ARE TO BE SUNG OR SAID
IN CHURCHES;

AND THE FORM AND MANNER OF MAKING,
ORDAINING AND CONSECRATING OF

BISHOPS, PRIESTS, AND DEACONS.

OXFORD:
PRINTED AT THE UNIVERSITY PRESS,
FOR THE
SOCIETY FOR PROMOTING CHRISTIAN KNOWLEDGE.

M.DCCC.LXXXVI.

THE

CONTENTS OF THIS BOOK.

- i. A Preface.
- ii. A Table and Kalendar for Psalms and Lessons, with necessary rules pertaining to the same.
- iii. The Order for Matins and Evensong, throughout the year.
- iv. The Introits, Collects, Epistles and Gospels, to be used at the celebration of the Lord's Supper and holy Communion through the year, with proper Psalms and Lessons, for divers feasts and days.
- v. The Supper of the Lord and holy Communion, commonly called the Mass.
- vi. The Litany and Suffrages.
- vii. Of Baptism, both public and private.
- viii. Of Confirmation, where also is a Catechism for children.
- ix. Of Matrimony.
- x. Of Visitation of the Sick, and Communion of the same.
- xi. Of Burial.
- xii. The purification of women.
- xiii. A declaration of Scripture, with certain prayers to be used the first day of Lent, commonly called Ashwednesday.
- xiv. Of Ceremonies omitted or retained.
- xv. Certain notes for the more plain explication and decent ministration of things contained in this book.

THE

CONTENTS OF THIS BOOK.

1. The Preface.
2. Concerning the Service of the Church.
3. Concerning Ceremonies, why some be abolished, and some retained.
4. The Order how the Psalter is appointed to be read.
5. The Order how the rest of the holy Scripture is appointed to be read.
6. A Table of Proper Lessons and Psalms.
7. The Calendar, with the Table of Lessons.
8. Tables and Rules for the Feasts and Fasts through the whole year.
9. The Order for Morning Prayer.
10. The Order for Evening Prayer.
11. The Creed of Saint Athanasius.
12. The Litany.
13. Prayers and Thanksgivings upon several Occasions.
14. The Collects, Epistles, and Gospels, to be used at the Ministration of the holy Communion, throughout the year.
15. The Order of the Ministration of the holy Communion.
16. The Order of Baptism both Publick and Private.
17. The Order of Baptism for those of Riper Years.
18. The Catechism.
19. The Order of Confirmation.
20. The Form of Solemnization of Matrimony.
21. The Order for the Visitation of the Sick, and the Communion of the Sick.
22. The Order for the Burial of the Dead.
23. The Thanksgiving of Women after Childbirth.
24. A Commination, or denouncing of God's anger and judgements against Sinners.
25. The Psalter
26. Forms of Prayer to be used at Sea.
27. The Form and Manner of Making, Ordaining, and Consecrating of Bishops, Priests, and Deacons.
28. A form of Prayer for the Twentieth Day of June.
29. Articles of Religion.

THE PREFACE.

IT hath been the wisdom of the Church of *England*, ever since the first compiling of her Publick Liturgy, to keep the mean between the two extremes, of too much stiffness in refusing, and of too much easiness in admitting any variation from it. For, as on the one side common experience sheweth, that where a change hath been made of things advisedly established (no evident necessity so requiring) sundry inconveniences have thereupon ensued; and those many times more and greater than the evils, that were intended to be remedied by such change: So on the other side, the particular Forms of Divine worship, and the Rites and Ceremonies appointed to be used therein, being things in their own nature indifferent, and alterable, and so acknowledged; it is but reasonable, that upon weighty and important considerations, according to the various exigency of times and occasions, such changes and alterations should be made therein, as to those that are in place of Authority should from time to time seem either necessary or expedient. Accordingly we find, that in the Reigns of several Princes of blessed memory since the Reformation, the Church, upon just and weighty considerations her thereunto moving, hath yielded to make such alterations in some particulars, as in their respective times were thought convenient: Yet so, as that the main Body and Essentials of it (as well in the chiefest materials, as in the frame and order thereof) have still continued the same unto this day, and do yet stand firm and unshaken, notwithstanding all the vain attemps and impetuous assaults made against it, by such men as are given to change, and have always discovered a greater regard to their own private fancies and interests, than to that duty they owe to the publick.

By what undue means, and for what mischievous purposes, the use of the Liturgy (though enjoined by the Laws of the Land, and those Laws never yet repealed) came, during the late unhappy confusions, to be discontinued, is too well known to the world, and we are not willing here to remember. But when, upon His Majesty's happy Restoration, it seemed probable, that, amongst other things, the use of the Liturgy would also return of course (the same having never been legally abolished) unless some timely means were used to prevent it; those men who under the late usurped powers had made it a great part of their business to render the people disaffected thereunto, saw themselves in point of reputation and interest concerned (unless they would freely acknowledge themselves to have erred, which such men are very hardly brought to do) with their utmost endeavours to hinder the restitution thereof. In order whereunto divers Pamphlets were published against the Book of *Common Prayer*, the old objections mustered up, with the addition of some new ones, more than formerly had been made, to make the number swell. In fine, great importunities were used to his Sacred Majesty, that the said Book might be revised, and such Alterations therein, and Additions thereunto made, as should be thought requisite for the ease of tender Consciences: whereunto His Majesty, out of his pious inclination to give satisfaction (so far as could be reasonably expected) to all his subjects of what persuasion soever, did graciously condescend.

In which review we have endeavoured to observe the like moderation, as we find to have been used in the like case in former times. And therefore of the sundry alterations proposed unto us, we have rejected all such as were either of dangerous consequence (as secretly striking at some established Doctrine, or laudable practice of the Church of *England*, or indeed of the whole Catholic Church of Christ) or else of no consequence at all, but utterly frivolous and vain. But such alterations as were tendered to us (by what persons, under what pretences, or to what purpose soever tendered) as seemed to us in any degree requisite or expedient, we have willingly, and of our own accord, assented unto: not enforced so to do by any strength of Argument, convincing us of the necessity of making the said Alterations: For we are fully persuaded in our judgments (and we here profess it to the world) that the Book, as it stood before established by Law, doth not contain in it anything contrary to the Word of God, or to sound Doctrine, or which a godly man may not with a good Conscience use and submit unto, or which is not fairly defensible against any that shall oppose the same; if it shall be allowed such just and favourable construction as in common equity ought to be allowed to all human Writings, especially such as are set forth by Authority, and even to the very best translations of the holy Scripture itself.

Our general aim therefore in this undertaking was, not to gratify this or that party in any their unreasonable demands; but to do that, which to our best understandings we conceived might most tend to the preservation of Peace and Unity in the Church; the procuring of Reverence, and exciting of Piety and Devotion in the publick Worship of God; and the cutting off occasion from them that seek occasion of cavil or quarrel against the Liturgy of the Church. And as to the several variations from the former Book, whether by Alteration, Addition, or otherwise, it shall suffice to give this general account, That most of the Alterations were made, either first, for the better direction of them that are to officiate in any part of Divine Service; which is chiefly done in the Calendars and Rubricks: Or secondly, for the more proper expressing of some words or phrases of ancient usage in terms more suitable to the language of the present times, and the clearer explanation of some other words and phrases, that were either of doubtful signification, or otherwise liable to misconstruction: Or thirdly, for a more perfect rendering of such portions of holy Scripture, as are inserted into the Liturgy; which, in the Epistles and Gospels especially, and in sundry other places, are now ordered to be read according to the last Translation: and that it was thought convenient, that some Prayers and Thanksgivings, fitted to special occasions, should be added in their due places; particularly for those at Sea, together with an Office for the Baptism of such as are of riper years: which, although not so necessary when the former Book was compiled, yet by the growth of Anabaptism, through the licentiousness of the late times crept in amongst us, is now become necessary, and may be always useful for the baptising of Natives in our Plantations, and others converted to the Faith. If any man, who shall desire a more particular account of the several

Alterations in any part of the Liturgy, shall take the pains to compare the present Book with the former; we doubt not but the reason of the change may easily appear.

And having thus endeavoured to discharge our duties in this weighty affair, as in the sight of God, and to approve our sincerity therein (so far as lay in us) to the consciences of all men; although we know it impossible (in such variety of apprehensions, humours, and interests, as are in the world) to please all; nor can expect that men of factious, peevish, and perverse spirits should be satisfied with any thing that can be done in this kind by any other than themselves; Yet we have good hope, that what is here presented, and hath been by the Convocations of both Provinces with great diligence examined and approved, will be also well accepted and approved by all sober, peaceable, and truly conscientious Sons of the Church of *England*.

THE PREFACE.

THERE was never any thing by the wit of man so well devised, or so surely established, which (in continuance of time) hath not been corrupted: as (among other things) it may plainly appear by the common prayers in the Church, commonly called divine service: the first original and ground whereof if a man would search out by the ancient fathers, he shall find that the same was not ordained, but of a good purpose, and for a great advancement of godliness: for they so ordered the matter, that all the whole Bible (or the greatest part thereof) should be read over once in the year, intending thereby, that the Clergy, and specially such as were Ministers of the congregation, should (by often reading and meditation of God's word) be stirred up to godliness themselves, and be more able also to exhort other by wholesome doctrine, and to confute them that were adversaries to the truth. And further, that the people (by daily hearing of holy scripture read in the Church) should continually profit more and more in the knowledge of God, and be the more inflamed with the love of his true religion. But these many years passed, this godly and decent order of the ancient fathers hath been so altered, broken, and neglected, by planting in uncertain stories, Legends, Responds, Verses, vain repetitions, Commemorations, and Synodals, that commonly when any book of the Bible was begun, before three or four chapters were read out, all the rest were unread. And in this sort, the book of Esaie was begun in Advent, and the book of Genesis in Septuagesima: but

CONCERNING THE SERVICE OF THE CHURCH.

THERE was never any thing by the wit of man so well devised, or so sure established which in continuance of time hath not been corrupted: As, among other things, it may plainly appear by the Common Prayers in the Church, commonly called *Divine Service*. The first original and ground whereof if a man would search out by the ancient Fathers, he shall find, that the same was not ordained but of a good purpose, and for a great advancement of godliness. For they so ordered the matter, that all the whole Bible (or the greatest part thereof) should be read over once every year; intending thereby, that the Clergy, and especially such as were Ministers in the congregation, should (by often reading and meditation in God's word) be stirred up to godliness themselves, and be more able to exhort others by wholesome Doctrine, and to confute them that were adversaries to the Truth; and further, that the people (by daily hearing of holy Scripture read in the Church) might continually profit more and more in the knowledge of God, and be the more inflamed with the love of his true Religion.

But these many years passed, this godly and decent order of the ancient Fathers hath been so altered, broken, and neglected, by planting in uncertain Stories, and Legends, with multitude of Responds, Verses, vain Repetitions, Commemorations, and Synodals; that commonly when any Book of the Bible was begun, after three or four Chapters were read out, all the rest were unread. And in this sort the Book of *Isaiah* was begun

they were only begun, and never read through. After a like sort were other books of holy scripture used. And moreover, whereas St. Paul would have such language spoken to the people in the church, as they might understand and have profit by hearing the same; the service in this Church of England (these many years) hath been read in Latin to the people, which they understood not; so that they have heard with their ears only; and their hearts, spirit, and mind, have not been edified thereby. And furthermore, notwithstanding that the ancient fathers had divided the Psalms into seven portions, whereof every one was called a nocturn; now of late time a few of them have been daily said (and oft repeated) and the rest utterly omitted. Moreover, the number and hardness of the rules called the Pie, and the manifold changings of the service, was the cause, that to turn the book only was so hard and intricate a matter, that many times there was more business to find out what should be read, than to read it when it was found out.

These inconveniences therefore considered, here is set forth such an order, whereby the same shall be redressed. And for a readiness in this matter, here is drawn out a Kalendar for that purpose, which is plain and easy to be understanded; wherein (so much as may be) the reading of holy scripture is so set forth, that all things shall be done in order, without breaking one piece thereof from another. For this cause be cut off Anthems, Responds, Invitatories, and such like things, as did break the continual course of the reading of the scripture. Yet because there is no remedy, but that of necessity there must be some rules: therefore certain rules are here set forth, which as they be few in number, so they

in *Advent*, and the Book of *Genesis* in *Septuagesima*; but they were only begun, and never read through: After like sort were other Books of holy Scripture used. And moreover, whereas *St. Paul* would have such language spoken to the people in the Church, as they might understand, and have profit by hearing the same; The service in this Church of *England* these many years hath been read in Latin to the people, which they understand not: so that they have heard with their ears only, and their heart, spirit, and mind, have not been edified thereby. And furthermore, notwithstanding that the ancient Fathers have divided the *Psalms* into seven portions, whereof every one was called a *Nocturn*: Now of late time a few of them have been daily said, and the rest utterly omitted. Moreover, the number and hardness of the Rules called the *Pie*, and the manifold changings of the Service, was the cause, that to turn the Book only was so hard and intricate a matter, that many times there was more business to find out what should be read, than to read it when it was found out.

These inconveniences therefore considered, here is set forth such an Order, whereby the same shall be redressed. And for a readiness in this matter, here is drawn out a Calendar for that purpose, which is plain and easy to be understood; wherein (so much as may be) the reading of holy Scripture is so set forth, that all things shall be done in order, without breaking one piece from another. For this cause be cut off Anthems, Responds, Invitatories, and such like things as did break the continual course of the reading of the Scripture.

Yet, because there is no remedy, but that of necessity there must be some Rules; therefore certain Rules

be plain and easy to be understanded. So that here you have an order for prayer (as touching the reading of holy scripture) much agreeable to the mind and purpose of the old fathers, and a great deal more profitable and commodious, than that which of late was used. It is more profitable, because here are left out many things, whereof some be untrue, some uncertain, some vain and superstitious: and is ordained nothing to be read, but the very pure word of God, the holy scriptures, or that which is evidently grounded upon the same; and that in such a language and order, as is most easy and plain for the understanding, both of the readers and hearers. It is also more commodious, both for the shortness thereof, and for the plainness of the order, and for that the rules be few and easy. Futhermore, by this order, the curates shall need none other books for their public service, but this book and the Bible: by the means whereof, the people shall not be at so great charge for books, as in time past they have been.

And where heretofore there hath been great diversity in saying and singing in churches within this realm: some following Salisbury use, some Hereford use, some the use of Bangor, some of York, and some of Lincoln: Now from henceforth, all the whole realm shall have but one use. And if any would judge this way more painful, because that all things must be read upon the book, whereas before, by the reason of so often repetition, they could say many things by heart: if those men will weigh their labour, with the profit in knowledge, which daily they shall obtain by reading upon the book, they will not refuse the pain, in consideration of the great profit that shall ensue thereof.

are here set forth; which, as they are few in number, so they are plain and easy to be understood. So that here you have an Order for Prayer, and for the reading of the holy Scripture, much agreeable to the mind and purpose of the old Fathers, and a great deal more profitable and commodious, than that which of late was used. It is more profitable, because here are left out many things, whereof some are untrue, some uncertain, some vain and superstitious; and nothing is ordained to be read, but the very pure Word of God, the holy Scriptures, or that which is agreeable to the same; and that in such a Language and Order as is most easy and plain for the understanding both of the Readers and Hearers. It is also more commodious, both for the shortness thereof, and for the plainness of the Order, and for that the Rules be few and easy.

And whereas heretofore there hath been great diversity in saying and singing in Churches within this Realm; some following *Salisbury* Use, some *Hereford* Use, and some the Use of *Bangor*, some of *York*, some of *Lincoln;* now from henceforth all the whole Realm shall have but one Use.

And forsomuch as nothing can, almost, be so plainly set forth, but doubts may rise in the use and practising of the same: to appease all such diversity (if any arise), and for the resolution of all doubts, concerning the manner how to understand, do, and execute the things contained in this book, the parties that so doubt, or diversely take any thing, shall always resort to the Bishop of the Diocese, who by his discretion shall take order for the quieting and appeasing of the same: so that the same order be not contrary to any thing contained in this book.

And forasmuch as nothing can be so plainly set forth, but doubts may arise in the use and practice of the same; to appease all such diversity (if any arise) and for the resolution of all doubts, concerning the manner how to understand, do, and execute the things contained in this Book; the parties that so doubt, or diversely take any thing, shall alway resort to the Bishop of the Diocese, who by his discretion shall take order for the quieting and appeasing of the same; so that the same order be not contrary to any thing contained in this Book. And if the Bishop of the Diocese be in doubt, then he may send for the resolution thereof to the Archbishop.

¶ Though it be appointed in the afore written preface, that all things shall be read and sung in the church, in the English tongue, to the end that the congregation may be thereby edified: yet it is not meant, but when men say Matins and Evensong privately, they may say the same in any language that they themselves do understand. Neither that any man shall be bound to the saying of them, but such as from time to time, in Cathedral and Collegiate Churches, Parish Churches, and Chapels to the same annexed, shall serve the congregation.

THOUGH it be appointed, that all things shall be read and sung in the Church in the *English* Tongue, to the end that the congregation may be thereby edified; yet it is not meant, but that when men say Morning and Evening Prayer privately, they may say the same in any language that they themselves do understand.

And all Priests and Deacons are to say daily the Morning and Evening Prayer either privately or openly, not being let by sickness, or some other urgent cause.

And the Curate that ministereth in every Parish-Church or Chapel, being at home, and not being otherwise reasonably hindered, shall say the same in the Parish-Church or Chapel where he ministereth, and shall cause a Bell to be tolled, thereunto a convenient time before he begin, that the people may come to hear God's Word, and to pray with him.

OF CEREMONIES,

WHY SOME BE ABOLISHED AND SOME RETAINED. (a)

OF such ceremonies as be used in the Church, and have had their beginning by the institution of man: Some at the first were of Godly intent and purpose devised, and yet at length turned to vanity and superstition: Some entered into the Church by undiscreet devotion, and such a zeal as was without knowledge; and for because they were winked at in the beginning, they grew daily to more and more abuses, which not only for their unprofitableness, but also because they have much blinded the people, and obscured the glory of God, are worthy to be cut away, and clean rejected. Other there be, which although they have been devised by man, yet it is thought good to reserve them still, as well for a decent order in the Church (for the which they were first devised) as because they pertain to edification, whereunto all things done in the church (as the Apostle teacheth) ought to be referred. And although the keeping or omitting of a ceremony (in itself considered) is but a small thing: yet the wilful and contemptuous transgression, and breaking of a common order, and discipline, is no small offence before God. Let all things be done among you (saith St. Paul) in a seemly and due order. The appointment of the which order pertaineth not to private men: Therefore no man ought to take in hand, nor presume to appoint or alter any public or common order in Christ's Church, except he be lawfully called and authorised thereunto. And where-

(a) This follows the Commination Service in 1549.

OF CEREMONIES,

WHY SOME BE ABOLISHED AND SOME RETAINED.

OF such ceremonies as be used in the Church, and have had their beginning by the institution of man, some at the first were of godly intent and purpose devised, and yet at length turned to vanity and superstition: some entered into the Church by undiscreet devotion, and such a zeal as was without knowledge; and for because they were winked at in the beginning, they grew daily to more and more abuses, which not only for their unprofitableness, but also because they have much blinded the people, and obscured the glory of God, are worthy to be cut away, and clean rejected: other there be, which although they have been devised by man, yet it is thought good to reserve them still, as well for a decent order in the Church, (for the which they were first devised) as because they pertain to edification, whereunto all things done in the church (as the Apostle teacheth) ought to be referred.

And although the keeping or omitting of a Ceremony, in itself considered, is but a small thing, yet the wilful and contemptuous transgression and breaking of a common order and discipline is no small offence before God, *Let all things be done among you*, saith St. *Paul, in a seemly and due order:* The appointment of the which order pertaineth not to private men; therefore no man ought to take in hand, nor presume to appoint or alter any publick or common Order in Christ's Church, except he be lawfully called and authorized thereunto.

And whereas in this our time,

as, in this our time, the minds of men be so diverse, that some think it a great matter of conscience to depart from a piece of the least of their ceremonies (they be so addicted to their old customs), and again on the other side, some be so new fangle that they would innovate all thing, and so do despise the old that nothing can like them, but that is new: It was thought expedient not so much to have respect how to please and satisfy either of these parties, as how to please God, and profit them both. And yet lest any man should be offended (whom good reason might satisfy), here be certain causes rendered why some of the accustomed ceremonies be put away, and some be retained and kept still.

Some are put away, because the great excess and multitude of them hath so increased in these latter days, that the burden of them was intolerable: whereof St. Augustine in his time complained, that they were grown to such a number, that the state of Christian people was in worse case (concerning that matter) than were the Jews. And he counselled that such yoke and burden should be taken away, as time would serve quietly to do it. But what would St. Augustine have said, if he had seen the ceremonies of late days used among us, whereunto the multitude used in his time was not to be compared? This our excessive multitude of ceremonies was so great, and many of them so dark, that they did more confound and darken, than declare and set forth Christ's benefits unto us. And besides this, Christ's Gospel is not a ceremonial law (as much of Moses' law was); but it is a religion to serve God, not in bondage of the figure or shadow, but in the freedom of spirit, being content only with those ceremonies which do serve to a decent order

the minds of men are so diverse, that some think it a great matter of conscience to depart from a piece of the least of their Ceremonies, they be so addicted to their old customs: and again on the other side, some be so new-fangled, that they would innovate all things, and so despise the old, that nothing can like them, but that is new: it was thought expedient, not so much to have respect how to please and satisfy either of these parties, as how to please God, and profit them both. And yet lest any man should be offended, whom good reason might satisfy, here be certain causes rendered why some of the accustomed Ceremonies be put away, and some retained and kept still.

Some are put away, because the great excess and multitude of them hath so increased in these latter days, that the burden of them was intolerable; whereof St. *Augustine* in his time complained, that they were grown to such a number, that the estate of Christian people was in worse case concerning that matter, than were the Jews. And he counselled that such yoke and burden should be taken away, as time would serve quietly to do it. But what would St. *Augustine* have said, if he had seen the Ceremonies of late days used among us; whereunto the multitude used in his time was not to be compared? This our excessive multitude of Ceremonies was so great, and many of them so dark, that they did more confound and darken, than declare and set forth Christ's benefits unto us. And besides this, Christ's Gospel is not a Ceremonial Law, (as much of *Moses*' Law was) but it is a Religion to serve God, not in bondage of the figure or shadow, but in the freedom of the Spirit; being content only with those Ceremonies which do serve to a decent and godly discipline, and such as be apt to stir up the dull mind of man, to the remembrance of his duty to God, by some notable and special signification, whereby he might be edified.

¶ Furthermore, the most weighty cause of the abolishment of certain ceremonies was, that they were so far abused, partly by the superstitious blindness of the rude and unlearned, and partly by the unsatiable avarice of such as sought more their own lucre than the glory of God; that the abuses could not well be taken away, the thing remaining still. But now as concerning those persons, which peradventure will be offended for that some of the old ceremonies are retained still: if they consider, that without some ceremonies it is not possible to keep any order or quiet discipline in the church, they shall easily perceive just cause to reform their judgments. And if they think much that any of the old do remain, and would rather have all devised anew: then such men (granting some ceremonies convenient to be had) surely where the old may be well used, there they cannot reasonably reprove the old (only for their age) without bewraying of their own folly. For in such a case they ought rather to have reverence unto them for their antiquity, if they will declare themselves to be more studious of unity and concord, than of innovations and newfangleness, which (as much as may be with the true setting forth of Christ's religion) is always to be eschewed. Furthermore, such shall have no just cause with the ceremonies reserved to be offended: for as those be taken away which were most abused, and did burden men's consciences without any cause; so the other that remain are retained for a discipline and order, which (upon just causes)

Order and godly Discipline, and such as be apt to stir up the dull mind of man to the remembrance of his duty to God, by some notable and special signification, whereby he might be edified. Furthermore, the most weighty cause of the abolishment of certain Ceremonies was, That they were so far abused, partly by the superstitious blindness of the rude and unlearned, and partly by the unsatiable avarice of such as sought more their own lucre, than the glory of God, that the abuses could not well be taken away, the thing remaining still.

But now as concerning those persons, which peradventure will be offended, for that some of the old Ceremonies are retained still: If they consider that without some Ceremonies it is not possible to keep any Order, or quiet Discipline in the Church, they shall easily perceive just cause to reform their judgements. And if they think much, that any of the old do remain, and would rather have all devised anew, then such men granting some Ceremonies convenient to be had, surely where the old may be well used, there they cannot reasonably reprove the old only for their age, without bewraying of their own folly. For in such a case they ought rather to have reverence unto them for their antiquity, if they will declare themselves to be more studious of unity and concord, than of innovations and new-fangleness, which (as much as may be with true setting forth of Christ's Religion) is always to be eschewed. Furthermore, such shall have no just cause with the Ceremonies reserved to be offended. For as those be taken away which were most abused, and did burden men's consciences without any cause; so the other that remain, are retained for a discipline and order, which upon just causes may

may be altered and changed, and therefore are not to be esteemed equal with God's law. And moreover they be neither dark nor dumb ceremonies, but are so set forth that every man may understand what they do mean, and to what use they do serve. So that it is not like that they, in time to come, should be abused as the other have been. And in these all our doings we condemn no other nations, nor prescribe any thing, but to our own people only. For we think it convenient that every country should use such ceremonies, as they shall think best to the setting forth of God's honour and glory, and to the reducing of the people to a most perfect and godly living, without error or superstition; and that they should put away other things, which from time to time they perceive to be most abused, as in men's ordinances it often chanceth diversely in divers countries.

be altered and changed, and therefore are not to be esteemed equal with God's Law. And moreover, they be neither dark nor dumb Ceremonies, but are so set forth, that every man may understand what they do mean, and to what use they do serve. So that it is not like that they in time to come should be abused as other have been. And in these our doings we condemn no other Nations, nor prescribe any thing but to our own people only: For we think it convenient that every country should use such Ceremonies as they shall think best to the setting forth of God's honour and glory, and to the reducing of the people to a most perfect and godly living, without error or superstition; and that they should put away other things, which from time to time they perceive to be most abused, as in men's ordinances it often chanceth diversly in divers countries.

THE TABLE AND

KALENDAR EXPRESSING THE ORDER OF THE PSALMS AND LESSONS TO BE SAID AT MATINS AND EVENSONG, THROUGHOUT THE YEAR, EXCEPT CERTAIN PROPER FEASTS, AS THE RULES FOLLOWING MORE PLAINLY DECLARE.

THE ORDER HOW THE PSALTER IS APPOINTED TO BE READ.

THE Psalter shall be read through once every month: and because that some months be longer than some other be, it is thought good to make them even by this means.

To every month, as concerning this purpose, shall be appointed just xxx days.

And because January and March hath one day above the said number, and February, which is placed between them both, hath only xxviii days, February shall borrow of either of the months of January and March one day, and so the Psalter which shall be read in February, must be begun the last day of January, and ended the first day of March.

And whereas May, July, August, October and December hath xxxi days apiece, it is ordered that the said Psalms shall be read the last day of the said month[s], which were read the day before: so that the Psalter may be begun again the first day of the next months ensuing.

Now to know what Psalms shall be read every day, look in the Kalendar the number that is appointed for the Psalms, and then find the same number in this Table, and upon that number shall you see, what Psalms shall be said at Matins, and Evensong.

¶ THE ORDER HOW THE PSALTER IS APPOINTED TO BE READ.

THE Psalter shall be read through once every Month, as it is there appointed, both for Morning and Evening Prayer. But in *February* it shall be read only to the twenty-eighth, or twenty-ninth day of the Month.

And, whereas *January*, *March*, *May*, *July*, *August*, *October and December* have One-and-thirty days apiece; It is ordered, that the same Psalms shall be read the last day of the said Months, which were read the day before: So that the Psalter may begin again the first day of the next Month ensuing.

And, whereas the 119th Psalm is divided into twenty-two portions, and is over-long to be read at one time; It is so ordered, that at one time shall not be read above four or five of the said portions.

And at the end of every Psalm, and of every such part of the 119th Psalm, shall be repeated this Hymn,

Glory be to the Father, and to the Son: and to the Holy Ghost;

As it was in the beginning, is now and ever shall be: world without end. Amen.

Note, that the Psalter followeth the Division of the Hebrews, and the Translation of the great English Bible, set forth and used in the time of King *Henry* the Eighth, and *Edward* the Sixth.

And where the cxix Psalm is divided into xxii portions, and is over long to be read at one time: it is so ordered, that at one time shall not be read above iv or v of the said portions, as you shall perceive to be noted in this Table.

And here is also to be noted, that in this Table, and in all other parts of the service, where any Psalms are appointed, the number is expressed after the great English Bible, which from the ixth Psalm unto the cxlviiith Psalm (following the division of the Ebrues) doth vary in numbers from the common Latin translation.

A TABLE FOR

The Order of the Psalms, to be said at Matins and Evensong.

	Matins	Evensong.
i.	i, ii, iii, iv. v.	vi. vii, viii.
ii.	ix, x, xi.	xii, xiii, xiv.
iii.	xv, xvi, xvii.	xviii.
iv.	xix, xx, xxi.	xxii, xxiii.
v.	xxiv, xxv, xxvi.	xxvii, xxviii, xxix.
vi.	xxx, xxxi.	xxxii, xxxiii, xxxiv.
vii.	xxxv, xxxvi.	xxxvii.
viii.	xxxviii, xxxix, xl.	xli, xlii, xliii.
ix.	xliv, xlv, xlvi.	xlvii, xlviii, xlix.
x.	l, li, lii.	liii, liv, lv.
xi.	lvi, lvii, lviii.	lix, lx, lxi.
xii.	lxii, lxiii, lxiv.	lxv, lxvi, lxvii.
xiii.	lxviii.	lxix, lxx.
xiv.	lxi, lxii.	lxiii, lxiv.
xv.	lxxv, lxxvi, lxxvii,	lxxviii.
xvi.	lxxix, lxxx, lxxxi.	lxxxii, lxxxiii. lxxxiv, lxxxv.
xvii.	lxxxvi, lxxxvii, lxxxviii	lxxxix.
xviii.	xc, xci, xcii.	xciii, xciv.
xix	xcv, xcvi, xcvii.	xcviii, xcix, c, ci.
xx.	cii, ciii.	civ.
xxi.	cv.	cvi,
xxii.	cvii.	cviii, cix.
xxiii.	cx, cxi, cxii, cxiii,	cxiv, cxv.
xxiv.	cxvi, cxvii, cxviii.	cxix, Inde. iv.
xxv.	Inde. v.	Inde. iv.
xxvi.	Inde. v,	Inde. iv.
xxvii.	cxx. cxxi, cxxii, cxxiii, cxxiv, cxxv,	cxxvi, cxxvii, cxxviii, cxxix, cxxx, cxxxi.
xxviii.	cxxxii, cxxxiii, cxxxiv. cxxxv,	cxxxvi, cxxxvii, cxxxviii.
xxix.	cxxxix, cxl, cxli.	cxlii, cxliii.
xxx.	cxliv, cxlv, cxlvi.	cxlvii, cxlviii, cxlix, cl.

THE ORDER

HOW THE REST OF HOLY SCRIPTURE (BESIDES THE PSALTER) IS APPOINTED TO BE READ.

The Old Testament. The Old Testament is appointed for the first Lessons, at Matins and Evensong, and shall be read through every year once, except certain books and chapters, which be least edifying, and might best be spared, and therefore are left unread.

The New Testament. The New Testament is appointed for the Second Lessons, at Matins and Evensong, and shall be read over orderly every year thrice, beside the Epistles and Gospels; except the Apocalypse, out of which there be only certain Lessons appointed upon divers proper feasts.

Lessons. And to know what Lessons shall be read every day: find the day of the month in the Kalendar following: and there ye shall perceive the books and chapters, that shall be read for the Lessons, both at Matins and Evensong.

¶ THE ORDER HOW THE REST OF HOLY SCRIPTURE IS APPOINTED TO BE READ.

THE Old Testament is appointed for the first Lessons at Morning and Evening Prayer, so as the most part thereof will be read every year once, as in the Calendar is appointed.

The New Testament is appointed for the second Lessons at Morning and Evening Prayer, and shall be read over orderly every year twice, once in the Morning and once in the Evening, besides the Epistles and Gospels, except the Apocalypse, out of which there are only certain Lessons appointed at the end of the year, and certain Proper Lessons appointed upon divers Feasts.

And to know what Lessons shall be read every day, look for the day of the Month in the Calendar following, and there ye shall find the Chapters and portions of Chapters that shall be read for the Lessons, both at Morning and Evening Prayer, except only the Moveable Feasts, which are not in the Calendar, and the Immoveable, where there is a blank left in the Column of Lessons, the Proper Lessons for all which days are to be found in the Table of Proper Lessons.

If Evening Prayer is said at two different times in the same place of worship on any Sunday (except a Sunday for which Alternative second Lessons are specially appointed in the Table,) the second Lesson at the second time may, at the discretion of the minister, be any Chapter from the four Gospels, or any Lesson appointed in the Table of Lessons from the four Gospels.

Proper Psalms. And here is to be noted, that whensoever there be any proper Psalms or Lessons appointed for any feasts moveable or unmoveable; then the Psalms and Lessons appointed in the Kalendar shall be omitted for that time.

Ye must note also, that the Collect, Epistle, and Gospel, appointed for the Sunday, shall serve all the week after, except there fall some feast that hath his proper.

The Leap-year. This is also to be noted, concerning the leap-years, that the xxvth day of February, which in leap-years is counted for two days, shall in those two days alter neither Psalm nor Lesson: but the same Psalms and Lessons, which be said the first day, shall serve also for the second day.

Also, wheresoever the beginning of any Lesson, Epistle, or Gospel is not expressed, there ye must begin at the beginning of the chapter.

Upon occasions to be approved by the ordinary, other Lessons may, with his consent, be substituted for those which are appointed in the Calendar.

And note, that whensoever Proper Psalms or Lessons are appointed, then the Psalms and Lessons of ordinary course appointed in the Psalter and Calendar (if they be different) shall be omitted for that time.

Note also, that upon occasions to be appointed by the Ordinary, other Psalms may, with his consent, be substituted for those appointed in the Psalter.

If any of the Holy-days for which Proper Lessons are appointed in the Table fall upon a Snnday which is the first Sunday in Advent, Easter-day, Whit-Sunday, or Trinity-Sunday, the Lessons appointed for such Sunday shall be read, but if it fall upon any other Sunday, the Lessons appointed either for the Sunday or for the Holy-day may be read at the discretion of the Minister.

Note also, that the Collect, Epistle, and Gospel appointed for the Sunday shall serve all the week after, where it is not in this Book otherwise ordered.

In the First Prayer Book of Edward, the Lessons Proper for Sundays and Holy-days are found with the Collects, Epistles and Gospels.

PROPER LESSONS

TO BE READ AT MORNING AND EVENING PRAYER, ON THE SUNDAYS, AND OTHER HOLY-DAYS THROUGHOUT THE YEAR.

¶ LESSONS PROPER FOR SUNDAYS.

	MATTINS.	EVENSONG.
Sundays of Advent.		
The First..........	Isaiah—— i.	Isaiah—— ii. or Isaiah iv *v.* 2.
Second........	—— v.	——xi *to v.* 11 „ ——xxiv.
Third.........	—— xxv.	—— xxvi. „ — xxviii. *v.* 5 (*to v.* 19.
Fourth........	-xxx. *to v.* 27.	—— xxxii. „ — xxxiii. *v.* 2 (*to v.* 23.
Sundays after Christmas.		
The First	—— xxxv.	——xxxviii. „ ——xl.
Second........	—— xlii.	—— xliii. „ —— xliv.
Sundays after the Epiphany.		
The First	—— li.	lii. *v.* 13 & liii. „ —— liv.
Second	—— lv.	—— lvii. „ —— lxi.
Third........... ..	—— lxii.	—— lxv. „ —— lxvi.
Fourth	Job——xxvii.	Job——xxviii. „ Job—— xxix.
Fifth	Proverbs —i.	Proverbs—— iii. „ Proverbs viii.
Sixth	—— ix.	—— xi. „ ——xv.
Septuagesima.		
1 Lesson.	Genesis i. & ii (*to v.* 4.	Gen.—— ii. *v.* 4 „ Job—xxxviii.
2 Lesson.	Revel. xxi. *to* (*v.* 9.	Rev. xxi. *v.* 9 *to* (xxii. *v.* 6 „ ——
Sexagesima	Genesis— iii.	Genesis——vi. „ Genesis—viii.
Quinquagesima ..	— ix *to v.* 20.	—— xii. „ —— xiii.
Sundays in LENT.		
The First	—— xix *v.* 12 (*to v.* 30.	——xxii. *to v.* 20 „ —— xxiii.
Second..........	xxvii. *to v.* 41.	—— xxviii. „ —— xxxii.
Third	——xxxvii.	—— xxxix. „ ——xl.
Fourth	—— xlii.	—— xliii. „ —— xlv.
Fifth.............	Exodus— iii.	Exodus—— v. „ Exodus vi. *to* (*v.* 14
Sixth—		
1 Lesson	——ix.	—— x. „ ——xi.
2 Lesson	Matth.—xxvi.	Luke xix. *v.* 28 „ Luke xx. *v.* 9 (*to v.* 21
Easter Day.		
1 Lesson.	Ex. xii *to v* 29	Ex.——xii. *v.* 29 „ Exodus—xiv.
2 Lesson.	Revel. i. *v.* 10 (*to v.* 19	John-- xx. *v.* 11 (to *v.* 19 „ Revelation v.
Sundays after Easter		
The First—		
1 Lesson.	Num.—xvi *to* (*v.* 26	Num. xvi. *v.* 26 „ Num.——xvii. (*to v.* 12
2 Lesson.	1 Cor. xv. *to* (*v.* 29	John— xx. *v.* 24 (*to v.* 30 „ ——
Second	Num.—xx. *to* (*v.* 14	Num. xx. *v.* 14 (to xxi. *v.* 10 „ ——xxi. *v.* 10
Third	——xxii.	—— xxiii. „ —— xxiv.
Fourth	Deut.— iv. *to* (*v.* 23	Deut.— iv. *v.* 23 (*to v.* 41 „ Deut.——v.
Fifth	—— vi.	—— ix. „ —— x.
Sunday after Ascension Day..	Deut.— xxx.	Deut.—— xxxiv. „ Joshua—— i.
Whitsunday.		
1 Lesson.	-xvi. *to v.* 18.	Isaiah—— xi. „ Ezek. xxxvi. (*v.* 25
2 Lesson.	Rom.—viii. *to* (*v.* 18	Galat.— v. *v.* 16 „ Acts xviii. (*v.* 24 *to* xix. *v.* 21
Trinity-Sunday.		
1 Lesson.	Isaiah—vi. *to* (*v.* 11	Genesis— xviii. „ Gen. i. & ii. (*to v.* 4.
2 Lesson.	Rev. i. *to v.* 9	Eph. iv. *to v.* 17 „ Matthew iii.

In the First Prayer Book of Edward, the Lessons Proper for Sundays and Holy-days are found with the Collects, Epistles and Gospels.

	MATTINS.	EVENSONG.
Sundays after Trinity.		
The First	Josh. iii. *v.* 7 (to iv. *v.* 15	Josh. v. *v.* 13 *to* (vi. *v.* 21 „ Joshua xxiv.
Second	Judges——iv.	Judges—— v. „ Judg. vi. *v.* 11
Third	1 Sam.—ii. *to* (*v.* 27	1 Sam.—— iii. „ 1 Sam. iv. *to* (*v.* 19
Fourth	—— xii.	——xiii. „ Ruth——i.
Fifth	—xv. *to v.* 24	—— xvi „ 1 Sam.—xvii.
Sixth	2 Samuel— i.	2 Sam.——xii. *to* (*v.* 24 „ 2 Sam. xviii.
Seventh	1 Chron.-xxi.	1 Chron.— xxii. „ 1 Chron. xxviii (*to v.* 21
Eighth	——xxix *v.* 9 (to *v.* 29	2 Chron.—— i. „ 1 Kings— iii.
Ninth	1 Kings-x. *to* (*v.* 25	1 Kings— xi. *to* [*v.* 15 „ —— xi. *v.* 26
Tenth	—— xii.	——xiii. „ —— xvii.
Eleventh	—— ——xviii.	—— xix „ —— xxi.
Twelfth	-xxii. to *v.* 41	2 Kings—— ii *to* (*v.* 16 „ 2 Kings iv *v.* 8 *to v.* 38
Thirteenth	2 Kings—— v.	——vi. to *v.* 24 „ ——vii
Fourteenth	——ix.	—— x. *to v.* 32 „ —— xiii.
Fifteenth	——xviii.	——xix. „ xxiii. *to v.* 31
Sixteenth	2 Chron. xxxvi.	Neh.— i. & ii. *to* (*v.* 9 „ Nehem. viii.
Seventeenth	Jeremiah— v.	Jerem.—— xxii. „ Jerem. xxxv.
Eighteenth	—— xxxvi.	Exekiel—— ii. „ Ezek. xiii *to* (*v.* 17
Nineteenth	Ezekiel—xiv.	—— xviii „ — xxiv. *v.* 15
Twentieth	—— xxxiv.	—— xxxvii. „ Daniel—— i.
Twenty-first	Daniel——iii,	Daniel—— iv. „ —— v.
Twenty-second	——vi.	—— vii. *v* 9 „ —— xii.
Twenty-third	Hosea— xiv.	Joel—— ii. *v.* 21 „ Joel iii. *v.* 9
Twenty-fourth	Amos—— iii.	Amos—— v. „ Amos—— ix.
Twenty-fifth	Micah iv. & v (*to v.* 8	Micah—— vi. „ Micah——vii.
Twenty-sixth	Habakkuk ii.	Habakkuk— iii. „ Zephan.— iii.
Twenty-seventh	Eccles.- xi. & (xii.	Haggai—— ii. *to* (*v.* 10 „ Mal. iii. & iv.

Note.—That the Lessons appointed in the above Table for the Twenty-seventh Sunday after Trinity shall always be read on the Sunday next before Advent.

If there be a third Service on Sundays, the Second Lesson for that Service may be any Chapter from the four Gospels, or any Lesson appointed in the Calendar from the four Gospels, at the discretion of the Minister, except on those Sundays for which alternative Second Lessons are specially appointed in the above Table.

In the First Prayer Book of Edward, the Proper Lessons for Sundays and Holy-days are found with the Collects, Epistles and Gospels.

	MATTINS.	EVENSONG.
St. Andrew.		
First Lesson	Isaiah—— liv.	Isaiah— lxv. *to v.* 17
Second Lesson	John—i. *v.* 35 *to v.* 43	John xii. *v.* 20 *to v.* 42
St. Thomas.		
First Lesson	Job—— xlii. *to v.* 7	Isaiah—— xxxv.
Second Lesson	John xx. *v.* 19 *to v.* 24	John—— xiv. *to v.* 8
Nativity of Christ.		
First Lesson	Isaiah—— ix. *to v.* 8	Isaiah vii. *v.* 10 *to v.* 17
Second Lesson	Luke——ii. *to v.* 15	Titus—iii. *v.* 4 *to v.* 9
St. Stephen.		
First Lesson	Genesis— iv. *to v.* 11	2Chr.xxiv. *v* 15 *to v* 23
Second Lesson	Acts—— vi.	Acts——viii. *to v.* 9
St. John Evangelist.		
First Lesson	Exodus— xxxiii. *v.* 9	Isaiah——vi.
Second Lesson	John xiii. *v.* 23 *to v.* 36	Revelation—— i.
Innocents' Day..........	Jeremiah xxxi. *to v* 18	Baruch iv. *v* 21 *to v* 31
Circumcision.		
First Lesson	Genesis——xvii, *v.* 9	Deuteronomy x. *v* 12.
Second Lesson	Romans—— ii. *v.* 17	Colos. ii *v.* 8 to *v.* 18
Epiphany.		
First Lesson	Isaiah——lx.	Isa. xlix. *v.* 13 *to v.* 24
Second Lesson	Luke iii. *v.* 15 *to v.* 23	John——ii. to *v.* 12
Conversion of St. Paul.		
First Lesson	Isaiah— xlix *to v.* 13	Jeremiah—i. *to v.* 11
Second Lesson	Galatians—— i. *v.* 11	Acts——xxvi. *to v.* 21
Purification of the Virgin Mary	Exodus—xiii. *to v.* 17	Haggai——ii. *to v.* 10
St. Matthias	1 Sam. ii. *v.* 27 *to v.* 36	Isaiah—— xxii. *v.* 15
Annunciation of our Lady	Genesis— iii. *to v.* 16	Isaiah lii. *v.* 7 *to v.* 13
Ash-Wednesday.		
First Lesson	Isaiah— lviii. *to v.* 13	Jonah——iii.
Second Lesson	Mark ii. *v.* 13 *to v.* 23	Heb. xii. *v.* 3 *to v.* 18
Monday before Easter.		
First Lesson	Lamentat.— i. *to v.* 15	Lamentations ii. *v.* 13
Second Lesson	John—— xiv. *to v.* 15	John—— xiv. *v.* 15
Tuesday before Easter		
First Lesson	Lamentat. iii. to *v.* 34	Lamentations iii. *v.* 34
Second Lesson	John—— xv. *to v.* 14	John—— xv. *v.* 14
Wednesday before Easter.		
First Lesson	Lament.— iv. *to v.* 21	Daniel—— ix. *v.* 20
Second Lesson	John—— xvi. *to v.* 16	John—— xvi. *v.* 16
Thursday before Easter.		
First Lesson	Hosea— xiii. *to v.* 15	Hosea—— xiv.
Second Lesson	John—— xvii.	John—— xiii to *v.* 36
Good Friday		
First Lesson	Genesis xxii. *to v.* 20	Isaiah lii. *v.* 13 & liii
Second Lesson	John—— xviii.	1 Peter ——ii.
Easter Even.		
First Lesson	Zechariah—— ix.	Hosea v. *v.* 8 *to* vi. *v.* 4
Second Lesson	Luke—— xxiii. *v.* 50	Romans— vi. *to v.* 14
Monday in Easter-Week.		
First Lesson	Exodus— xv. *to v.* 22	Canticles—— ii. *v.* 10
Second Lesson	Luke——xxiv. *to v.* 13	Matt.—xxviii to *v.* 10
Tuesday in Easter-Week		
First Lesson	2 Kgs. xiii. *v* 14 *to v* 22	Ezekiel xxxvii *to v* 15
Second Lesson	John—— xxi. *to v.* 15	John—— xxi. *v.* 15
St. Mark	Isaiah——lxii. *v.* 6.	Ezekiel—— i. *to v.* 15
St. Philip and *St. James.*		
First Lesson	Isaiah—— lxi.	Zechariah ——iv.
Second Lesson	John—— i. *v.* 43	

In the First Prayer Book of Edward, the Lessons Proper for Sundays and Holy-days are found with the Collects, Epistles and Gospels.

	MATTINS.	EVENSONG.
Ascension Day.		
First Lesson	Daniel vii *v.* 9 *to v.* 15	2 Kings——ii. *to v.* 16
Second Lesson	Luke——; xxiv. *v.* 44	Hebrews—— iv.
Monday in Whitsun-Week		
First Lesson	Genesis— xi. *to v.* 10	Num. xi. *v.* 16 *to v.* 31
Second Lesson	1 Cor.——xii. to *v.* 14	1 Cor. xii. *v.* 27 & xiii.
Tuesday in Whitsun-Week		
First Lesson	Joel—— ii. *v.* 21	Micah—— iv. *to v.* 8
Second Lesson	1 Thes. v. *v* 12 *to v* 24	1 John——iv. *to v.* 14
St. Barnabas.		
First Lesson	Deut. —xxxiii. *to v.* 12	Nahum—— i.
Second Lesson	Acts ——iv. *v.* 31	Acts—— xiv. *v.* 8
St. John Baptist.		
First Lesson	Malachi— iii. *to v.* 7	Malachi ——iv.
Second Lesson	Matthew—— iii.	Matthew xiv. to *v.* 13
St. Peter.		
First Lesson	Ezek. iii. *v.* 4 *to v.* 15	Zechariah——iii.
Second Lesson	John xxi. *v.* 15 *to v.* 23	Acts— iv. *v.* 8 *to v* 23
St. James.		
First Lesson	2 Kings——i. *to v.* 16	Jer. xxvi. *v.* 8 *to v.* 16
Second Lesson	Luke ix. *v.* 51 *to v.* 57	
St. Bartholomew	Gen.xxviii. *v* 10 *to v* 18	Deuteron. xviii. *v.* 15
St. Matthew	1 Kings——xix. *v.* 15	1 Chron. xxix. *to v.* 20
St. Michael.		
First Lesson	Genesis—— xxxii.	Daniel——x. *v.* 4
Second Lesson	Acts xii. *v.* 5 *to v.* 18	Revelation xiv. *v.* 14
St. Luke	Isaiah—— lv.	Ecclus.xxxviii. *to v* 15
St. Simon and *St. Jude* ...	— xxviii. *v.* 9 *to v.* 17.	Jer. iii. *v.* 12 *to v.* 19
All Saints.		
First Lesson	Wisdom— iii. *to v.* 10	Wisdom— v. *to v.* 17
Second Lesson	Heb.xi.*v.*33&xii.*to v.*7	Revelation xix. *to v.*17

¶ PROPER PSALMS FOR CERTAIN DAYS.

In the First Prayer Book of Edward, the Proper Psalms are found with the Collects, Epistles, and Gospels.

	Mattins.	*Evensong.*
Christmas Day	Psalm 19	Psalm 89
	— 45	—110
	— 85	—132
Ash-Wednesday	— 6	—102
	— 32	—130
	— 38	—143
Good Friday	— 22	— 69
	— 40	— 88
	— 54	—
Easter-Day	— 2	—113
	— 57	—114
	—111	—118
Ascension Day........	— 8	— 24
	— 15	— 47
	— 21	—108
Whit-Sunday	— 48	—104
	— 68	—145

JANUARY.

	JANUARY.			Psalms.	MATINS.		EVENSONG.	
					1 Lesson.	*2 Lesson.*	*1 Lesson.*	*2 Lesson.*
A	*Kalend.*	1	*Circumci.*	1	Gene. 17	Roma. 2	Deut. 10	Collos. 2
b	4 No.	2		2	Gene. 1	Math. 1	Gene. 2	Roma. 1
c	3 No.	3		3	3	2	4	2
d	Prid. No.	4		4	5	3	6	3
e	*Nonas.*	5		5	7	4	8	4
f	8 Id.	6	*Epiphani.*	6	Esai. 60	Luke 3	Esai. 49	John 2
g	7 Id.	7		7	Gene. 9	Math. 5	Gene. 11	Roma. 5
A	6 Id.	8		8	12	6	13	6
b	5 Id.	9		9	14	7	15	7
c	4 Id.	10		10	16	8	17	8
d	3 Id.	11		11	18	9	19	9
e	Prid. Id.	12		12	20	10	21	10
f	*Idus.*	13		13	22	11	23	11
g	19 kl.	14		14	24	12	25	12
A	18 kl.	15		15	26	13	27	13
b	17 kl.	16		16	28	14	29	14
c	16 kl.	17		17	30	15	31	15
d	15 kl.	18		18	32	16	33	16
e	14 kl.	19		19	34	17	35	1 Cor. 1
f	13 kl.	20		20	36	18	37	2
g	12 kl.	21		21	38	19	39	3
A	11 kl.	22		22	40	20	41	4
b	10 kl.	23		23	42	21	43	5
c	9 kl.	24		24	44	22	45	6
d	8 kl.	25	*Con. Pauli.*	25	46	Act. 22	47	Act. 26
e	7 kl.	26		26	48	Mat. 23	49	1 Cor. 7
f	6 kl.	27		27	50	24	Exod. 1	8
g	5 kl.	28		28	Exod. 2	25	3	9
A	4 kl.	29		29	4	26	5	10
b	3 kl.	30		30	6	27	7	11
c	*Prid.* kl.	31		1	8	28	9	12

JANUARY hath XXXI Days.

		MORNING PRAYER.		EVENING PRAYER.	
		FIRST LESSON.	SECOND LESSON.	FIRST LESSON.	SECOND LESSON.
1	A	*Circumcision.*	—	—	—
2	b	Genesis—i. *to v.* 20	Matt.— i. *v.* 18	Gen. i *v.* 20 *to* ii. *v.* 4	Acts— i.
3	c	— ii *v.* 4	— ii.	— iii *to v.* 20	— ii *to v.* 22
4	d	iii. *v.* 20 *to* iv. *v.* 16	— iii.	— iv. *v.* 16	— ii. *v.* 22
5	e	— v. *to v.* 28	—iv. *to v.* 23	—v. *v.* 28 *to* vi. *v.* 9	— iii.
6	f	*Epiphany.*	—	—	—
7	g	Genesis— vi. *v.* 9	iv. *v.* 23 *to* v. *v.* 13	— vii.	— iv. *to v.* 32
8	A	Lucian, P. & M.			
		Genesis— viii.	—v. *v.* 13 *to v.* 33	—ix. *to v.* 20	iv. *v.* 32 *to* v. *v.* 17
9	b	— xi. *to v.* 10	— v. *v.* 33	— xii.	— v. *v.* 17
10	c	— xiii.	— vi. *to v.* 19	— xiv.	— vi.
11	d	— xv.	vi. *v.* 19 *to* vii. *v.* 7	— xvi.	—vii. *to v.* 35
12	e	— xvii. *to v.* 23	— vii. *v.* 7	—xviii. *to v.* 17	vii. *v.* 35 *to* viii. *v.* 5
13	f	Hilary, B. & C.			
		Genesis xviii. *v.* 17	— viii. *to v.* 18	—xix. *v.* 12 *to v.* 30	—viii. *v.* 5 *to v.* 26
14	g	— xx.	—viii. *v.* 18	— xxi. *to v.* 22	— viii. *v.* 26
15	A	— xxi. *v.* 33 *to* (xxii. *v.* 20	—ix. *to v.* 18	— xxiii.	—ix. *to v.* 23
16	b	—xxiv. *to v.* 29	— ix. *v.* 18	xxiv. *v.* 29 *to v.* 52	— ix. *v.* 23
17	c	— xxiv. *v.* 52	— x. *to v.* 24	— xxv. *v.* 5 *to v.* 19	— x. *to v.* 24
18	d	Prisca, V. & M.			
		Genesis—xxv. *v.* 19	— x. *v.* 24	—xxvi. *to v.* 18	— x. *v.* 24
19	e	— xxvi. *v.* 18	— xi.	—xxvii. *to v.* 30	— xi.
20	f	Fabian, B. & M.			
		Genesis xxvii. *v.* 30	— xii. *to v.* 22	— xxviii.	— xii.
21	g	Agnes, V. & M.			
		Gen. xxix. *to v.* 21	—xii. *v.* 22	—xxxi. *to v.* 25	— xiii. *to v.* 26
22	A	Vincent, D. & M.			
		Genesis xxxi. *v.* 36	— xiii. *to v.* 24	— xxxii. *to v.* 22	— xiii. *v.* 26
23	b	—xxxii *v.* 22	—xiii. *v.* 24 *to v.* 53	— xxxiii	— xiv.
24	c	— xxxv. *to v.* 21	xiii. *v* 53 *to* xiv *v* 13	—xxxvii. *to v.* 12	— xv. *to v.* 30
25	d	*Conv. of St. Paul.*	—	—	—
26	e	Gen.—xxxvii. *v.* 12	— xiv. *v.* 13	—xxxix.	xv. *v.* 30 *to* xvi. *v.* 16
27	f	— xl.	— xv. *to v.* 21	— xli. *to v.* 17	— xvi. *v.* 16
28	g	— xli. *v.* 17 *to v.* 53	— xv. *v.* 21	xli. *v.* 53 *to* xlii. *v.* 25	— xvii *to v.* 16
29	A	— xlii. *v.* 25	— xvi *to v.* 24	—xliii. *to v.* 25	— xvii. *v.* 16
30	b	— xliii. *v.* 25 *to* (xliv. *v.* 14	xvi. *v.* 24 *to* xvii *v* 14	— xliv. *v.* 14	— xviii. *to v.* 24
31	c	— xlv. *to v* 25	— xvii. *v.* 14	— xlv. *v.* 25 *to* (xlvi. *v.* 8	—xviii. *v.* 24 *to* (xix. *v.* 21

FEBRUARY.

FEBRUARY.				Psalms.	MATINS.		EVENSONG.	
					1 *Lesson.*	2 *Lesson.*	1 *Lesson.*	2 *Lesson.*
d	*Kalend.*	1		2	Exod. 10	Mark 1	Exod. 11	1 Cor. 13
e	4 No.	2	*Puri. Ma.*	3	12	2	13	14
f	3 No.	3		4	14	3	15	15
g	Prid. No.	4		5	16	4	17	16
A	*Nonas.*	5		6	18	5	19	2 Cor. 1
b	8 Id.	6		7	20	6	21	2
c	7 Id.	7		8	22	7	23	3
d	6 Id.	8		9	24	8	32	4
e	5 Id.	9		10	33	9	34	5
f	4 Id.	10		11	35	10	40	6
g	3 Id.	11		12	Leui. 18	11	Leui. 19	7
A	Prid. Id.	12		13	20	12	Nume. 10	8
b	*Idus.*	13		14	Num. 11	13	12	9
c	16 kl.	14		15	13	14	14	10
d	15 kl.	15		16	15	15	16	11
e	14 kl.	16		17	17	16	18	12
f	13 kl.	17		18	19	Luk. di. 1.	20	13
g	12 kl.	18		19	21	di. 1	22	Galath. 1
A	11 kl.	19		20	23	2	24	2
b	10 kl.	20		21	25	3	26	3
c	9 kl.	21		22	27	4	28	4
d	8 kl.	22		23	29	5	30	5
e	7 kl.	23		24	31	6	32	6
f	6 kl.	24	*Mathias.*	25	33	7	34	Ephes. 1
g	5 kl.	25		26	35	8	36	2
A	4 kl.	26		27	Deut. 1	9	Deut. 2	3
b	3 kl.	27		28	3	10	4	4
c	*Prid.* kl.	28		29	5	11	6	5

FEBRUARY hath XXVIII Days, and in every Leap-year XXIX Days.

		MORNING PRAYER.		EVENING PRAYER.	
		FIRST LESSON.	SECOND LESSON.	FIRST LESSON.	SECOND LESSON.
1	d	—Fast Gen. xlvi. *v.* 26 *to* (xlvii. *v.* 13	Matt.— xviii. *to* (*v.* 21	Gen.—xlvii. *v.* 13	Acts— xix *v.* 21
2	e	*Purific. of V. M.*	— xviii. *v.* 21	—	— xx *to v* 17
3	f	Blasius, B. & M. Genesis— xlviii.	(*to* xix. *v.* 3 — xix. *v* 3 *to v.* 27	— xlix.	— xx. *v.* 17
4	g	— l.	xix. *v.* 27 *to* xx. *v.* 17	Exodus— i.	— xxi. *to v.* 17
5	A	Agatha, V. & M. Exodus— ii.	— xx. *v.* 17	— iii.	—xxi. *v.* 17 *to v.* 37
6	b	— iv. *to v.* 24	— xxi. *to v.* 23	— iv. *v.* 27 *to* v. (*v.* 15	— xxi. *v.* 37 *to* (xxii. *v.* 23
7	c	— v. *v.* 15 *to* vi. (*v.* 14	— xxi. *v.* 23	— vi. *v.* 28 *to* (vii. *v.* 14	— xxii. *v.* 23 (*to* xxiii. *v.* 12
8	d	— vii. *v.* 14	— xxii. *to v.* 15	— viii. *to v.* 20	— xxiii. *v.* 12
9	e	— viii. *v.* 20 *to* (ix. *v.* 13	xxii. *v.* 15 *to v.* 41	— ix. *v.* 13	— xxiv.
10	f	— x. *to v.* 21	— xxii. *v.* 41 (*to* xxiii *v.* 13	— x. *v.* 21 & xi.	— xxv.
11	g	— xii. *to v.* 21	— xxiii. *v.* 13	— xii. *v.* 21 *to v.* 43	— xxvi.
12	A	— xii. *v.* 43 *to* (xiii. *v.* 17	— xxiv. *to v.* 29	— xiii. *v.* 17 *to* (xiv. *v.* 10	— xxvii. *to v.* 18
13	b	— xiv. *v.* 10	— xxiv. *v.* 29	— xv. *to v.* 22	— xxvii. *v.* 18
14	c	Valentine, Bp. Exodus xv. *v.* 22 *to* (xvi. *v.* 11	— xxv. *to v.* 31	— xvi. *v.* 11	— xxviii. *to v.* 17
15	d	— xvii.	— xxv. *v.* 31	— xviii.	— xxviii. *v.* 17
16	e	— xix.	— xxvi. *to v.* 31	— xx. to *v.* 22	Romans— i.
17	f	— xxi. *to v.* 18	xxvi. *v.* 31 *to v.* 57	— xxii. *v.* 21 (*to* xxiii. *v.* 10	— ii. *to v.* 17
18	g	— xxiii. *v.* 14	— xxvi. *v.* 57	— xxiv	— ii. *v.* 17
19	A	— xxv. *to v.* 23	— xxvii. *to v.* 27	— xxviii. *to v.* 13	— iii.
20	b	— xxviii *v.* 29 (*to v.* 42	— xxvii. *v.* 27 (*to v.* 57	— xxix. *v.* 35 (*to* xxx *v.* 11	— iv.
21	c	— xxxi.	— xxvii. *v.* 57	— xxxii. *to v.* 15	— v.
22	d	— xxxii. *v.* 15	— xxviii.	— xxxiii. *to v.* 12	— vi.
23	e	— Fast. — xxxiii. *v.* 12 (*to* xxxiv. *v.* 10	Mark—i. *to v.* 21	— xxxiv. *v.* 10 (*to v.* 27	— vii.
24	f	*St. Matthias*, Ap.	— i. *v.* 21	—	— viii. *to v.* 18
25	g	Exodus xxxiv. *v.* 27	— ii. *to v.* 23	— xxxv. *v.* 29 *to* (xxxvi. *v.* 8	— viii. *v.* 18
26	A	— xxxix. *v.* 30	ii. *v.* 23 *to* iii. *v.* 13	— xl. *to v.* 17	— ix. *to v.* 19
27	b	— xl. *v.* 17	— iii. *v.* 13	Lev.—ix. *v.* 22 *to* (x. *v.* 12	— ix. *v.* 19
28	c	Lev.— xiv. *to v.* 23	— iv. *to v.* 35	— xvi. *to v.* 23	— x.
29	—	— xix. *to v.* 19	Matt.— vii.	xix. *v.* 30 *to* xx. *v.* 9	— xii.

MARCH.

MARCH.				Psalms.	MATINS.		EVENSONG.	
					1 *Lesson.*	2 *Lesson.*	1 *Lesson.*	2 *Lesson.*
d	*Kalend.*	1		30	Deu. 7	Luke 12	Deu. 8	Ephe. 6
e	6 No.	2		1	9	13	10	Philip. 1
f	5 No.	3		2	11	14	12	2
g	4 No.	4		3	13	15	14	3
A	3 No.	5		4	15	16	16	4
b	Prid. No.	6		5	17	17	18	Collos. 1.
c	*Nonas.*	7		6	19	18	20	2
d	8 Id.	8		7	21	19	22	3
e	7 Id.	9		8	23	20	24	4
f	6 Id.	10		9	25	21	26	1 Thes. 1
g	5 Id.	11		10	27	22	28	2
A	4 Id.	12		11	29	23	30	3
b	3 Id.	13		12	31	24	32	4
c	Prid. Id.	14		13	33	John. 1	34	5
d	*Idus.*	15		14	Josue. 1	2	Josue. 2	2 Thes. 1
e	17 kl.	16		15	3	3	4	2
f	16 kl.	17		16	5	4	6	3
g	15 kl.	18		17	7	5	8	1 Timo. 1
A	14 kl.	19		18	9	6	10	2. 3
b	13 kl.	20		19	11	7	12	4
c	12 kl.	21		20	13	8	14	5
d	11 kl.	22		21	15	9	16	6
e	10 kl.	23		22	17	10	18	2 Tim. 1
f	9 kl.	24		23	19	11	20	2
g	8 kl.	25	*Annuncia.*	24	21	12	22	3
A	7 kl.	26		25	23	13	24	4
b	6 kl.	27		26	Judic. 1	14	Judic. 2	Titus 1
c	5 kl.	28		27	3	15	4	2. 3
d	4 kl.	29		28	5	16	6	Phile. 1
e	3 kl.	30		29	7	17	8.	Hebre. 1
f	*Prid.* kl.	31		30	9	18	10	2

MARCH hath XXXI Days.

			MORNING PRAYER.		EVENING PRAYER.	
			FIRST LESSON.	SECOND LESSON.	FIRST LESSON.	SECOND LESSON.
	1	d	David, Abp.			
			Lev.— xxv. *to v.* 18	Mark—— iv. *v.* 35 *to* (v. *v.* 21	Lev. xxv *v* 18 *to v* 44	Rom.—— xi. *to v.* 25
	2	e	Chad. Bishop			
			Lev.—xxvi. *to v.* 21	—— v. *v.* 21	——xxvi. *v.* 21	—— xi. *v.* 25
	3	f	Numbers—— vi.	——vi. *to v.* 14	Numb.—ix. *v.* 15 *to* (x. *v.* 11	——xii.
	4	g	—— x. *v.* 11	——vi. *v.* 14 *to v.* 30	——xi. *to v.* 24	——xiii.
	5	A	—— xi. *v.* 24	—— vi. *v.* 30	—— xii.	—xiv. & xv. *to v.* 8
	6	b	—— xiii. *v.* 17	—— vii. *to v.* 24	—— xiv. *to v.* 26	—— xv. *v.* 8
	7	c	Perpetua, M.			
			Numbers xiv. *v.* 26	vii. *v.* 24 *to* viii. *v.* 10	—— xvi. *to v.* 23	——xvi.
	8	d	——xvi. *v.* 23	viii. *v.* 10 *to* ix. *v.* 2	——xvii.	1 Cor.——i. *to v.* 26
	9	e	——xx. *to v.* 14	——ix. *v.* 2 *to v.* 30	——xx. *v.* 14	—— i. *v.* 26 & ii
	10	f	—— xxi. *to v.* 10	—— ix. *v.* 30	—xxi. *v.* 10 *to v.* 32	—— iii.
	11	g	—— xxii. *to v.* 22	—— x. *to v.* 32	—— xxii. *v.* 22	——iv. *to v.* 18
	12	A	Gregory, M. B.			
			Numbers—— xxiii.	—— x. *v.* 32	—— xxiv.	——iv. *v.* 18 & v.
	13	b	——xxv.	——xi. *to v.* 27	—— xxvii. *v.* 12	—— vi.
	14	c	Deuter.— i. *to v.* 19	——xi. *v.* 27 *to* xii. *v.* 13	Deuter.—— i. *v.* 19	—— vii. *to v.* 25
	15	d	—— ii. *to v.* 26	— xii. *v.* 13 *to v.* 35	-ii. *v.* 26 *to* iii. *v.* 18	—— vii. *v.* 25
	16	c	—— iii. *v.* 18	xii. *v.* 35 *to* xiii. *v.* 14	—— iv. *to v.* 25	——viii.
	17	f	—iv. *v.* 25 *to v.* 41	—— xiii. *v.* 14	—— v. *to v.* 22	—— ix.
	18	g	Edward, King.			
			Deut.......... v. *v.* 22	—— xiv. *to v.* 27	—— vi.	—— x. & xi. *v.* 1
	19	A	——vii. *to v.* 12	—xiv. *v.* 27 *to v.* 53	——vii. *v.* 12	— xi. *v.* 2 *to v.* 17
	20	b	—— viii.	——xiv. *v.* 53	——x. *v.* 8	—— xi. *v.* 17
14	21	c	Benedict, Abb.			
			Deut.— xi. *to v.* 18	—— xv. *to v.* 42	—— xi. *v.* 18	—— xii. *to v.* 28
3	22	d	——xv. *to v.* 16	... xv. *v.* 42 & xvi.	——xvii. *v.* 8	— xii. *v.* 28 & xiii.
	23	e	—— xviii. *v.* 9	Luke ——i. *to v.* 26	—— xxiv. *v.* 5	——xiv *to v.* 20
11	24	f	—— Fast.			
			—— xxvi.	—i. *v.* 26 *to v.* 46	—— xxvii.	—— xiv. *v.* 20
	25	g	*Annun. V. Mary.*	—— i. *v.* 46	——	——xv. *to* v. 35
19	26	A	Deut. xxviii. *to v* 15	—— ii. *to v.* 21	xxviii. *v.* 15 *to v.* 47	——xv. *v.* 35
8	27	b	—— xxviii. *v.* 47	—— ii. *v.* 21	—— xxix. *v.* 9	—— xvi.
	28	c	——xxx.	——iii. *to v.* 23	——xxxi. *to v.* 14	2 Cor.——i. *to v.* 23
16	29	d	-xxxi. *v.* 14 *to v.* 30	——iv. *to v.* 16	——xxxi. *v.* 30 *to* (xxxii. *v.* 44	—i. *v.* 23 *to* ii. *v.* 14
5	30	e	——xxxii. *v.* 44	—— iv. *v.* 16	——xxxiii.	— ii. *v.* 14 & iii.
	31	f	—— xxxiv.	—— v. *to v.* 17	Joshua—— i.	—— iv.

APRIL.

APRIL.				Psalms.	MATINS. 1 Lesson	MATINS. 2 Lesson.	EVENSONG. 1 Lesson.	EVENSONG. 2 Lesson.
g	Kalend.	1		1	Judi. 11	John 19	Judi. 12	Hebre. 3
A	4 No.	2		2	13	20	14	4
b	3 No.	3		3	15	21	16	5
c	Prid. No.	4		4	17	Acts 1	18	6
d	*Nonas.*	5		5	19	2	20	7
e	8 Id.	6		6	21		Ruth 1	8
f	7 Id.	7		7	Ruth 2	4	3	9
g	6 Id.	8		8	4	5	1 Regum 1	10
A	5 Id.	9		9	1 Regum 2	6	3	11
b	4 Id.	10		10	4	7	5	12
c	3 Id.	11		11	6	8	7	13
d	Prid Id.	12		12	8	9	9	Jacob 1
e	*Idus.*	13		13	10	10	11	2
f	18 kl.	14		14	12	11	13	3
g	17 kl.	15		15	14	12	15	4
A	16 kl.	16		16	16	13	17	5
b	15 kl.	17		17	18	14	19	1 Peter 1
c	14 kl.	18		18	20	15	21	2
d	13 kl.	19		19	22	16	23	3
e	12 kl.	20		20	24	17	25	4
f	11 kl.	21		21	26	18	27	5
g	10 kl.	22		22	28	19	29	2 Peter. 1
A	9 kl.	23		23	30	20	31	2
b	8 kl.	24		24	2 Reg 1	21	2 Reg. 2	3
c	7 kl.	25	*Mar. Evan*	25	3	22	4	1 John 1
d	6 kl.	26		26	5	23	6	2
e	5 kl.	27		27	7	24	8	3
f	4 kl.	28		28	9	25	10	4
g	3 kl.	29		29	11	26	12	5
A	*Prid* kl.	30		30	13	27	14	2. 3. Joh.

APRIL hath XXX Days.

			MORNING PRAYER. FIRST LESSON.	MORNING PRAYER. SECOND LESSON.	EVENING PRAYER. FIRST LESSON.	EVENING PRAYER. SECOND LESSON.
13	1	g	Joshua—ii.	Luke—v. *v.* 17	Joshua—iii.	2—Corinthians v
2	2	A	—iv.	—vi. *to v.* 20	—v.	—vi. & vii. *v.* 1
	3	b	Richard Bp.			
			Joshua—vi.	—vi *v.* 20	—vii.	—vii. *v.* 2.
10	4	c	St. Ambrose, B.			
			Joshua—ix. *v.* 3	—vii. *to v.* 24	—x. *to v.* 16	—viii.
	5	d	—xxi. *v.* 43 *to* (xxii. *v.* 11	—vii. *v.* 24	—xxii. *v.* 11	—ix.
18	6	e	—xxiii.	—viii. *to v.* 26	—xxiv.	—x.
7	7	f	Judges—ii.	—viii. *v.* 26	Judges—iv.	—xi. *to v.* 30
	8	g	—v.	—ix. *to v.* 28	—vi. *to v.* 24	—xi. *v.* 30 *to* (xii. *v.* 14
15	9	A	—vi. *v.* 24	—ix. *v.* 28 *to v.* 51	—vii.	—xii. *v.* 14 & xiii.
4	10	b	—viii. *v.* 32 *to* (ix. *v.* 25	—ix. *v.* 51 *to* x. *v.* 17	—x.	Galatians—i.
	11	c	—xi. *to v.* 29	—x. *v.* 17	—xi. *v.* 29	—ii.
12	12	d	—xiii.	—xi. *to v.* 29	—xiv.	—iii.
1	13	e	—xv.	—xi. *v.* 29	—xvi.	—iv. *to v.* 21
	14	f	Ruth—i.	—xii. *to v.* 35	Ruth—ii.	—iv. *v.* 21 *to* v. *v.* 13
9	15	g	—iii.	—xii. *v.* 35	—iv.	—v. *v.* 13
	16	A	1 Samuel—i.	—xiii. *to v.* 18	1 Sam. ii. *to v.* 21	—vi.
17	17	b	—ii. *v.* 21.	—xiii. *v.* 18	—iii.	Ephesians—i.
6	18	c	—iv.	—xiv. *to v.* 25	—v.	—ii.
	19	d	Alphege, Abp.			
			1 Sam.—vi.	—xiv. *v.* 25 *to* (xv. *v* 11	—vii.	—iii.
	20	e	—viii.	—xv. *v.* 11	—ix.	—iv. *to v.* 25.
	21	f	—x.	—xvi.	—xi.	—iv. *v* 25 *to* v. *v.* 22
	22	g	—xii.	—xvii. *to v.* 20	—xiii.	v. *v.* 22 *to* vi. *v.* 10
	23	A	St. George, M.			
			1 Sam. xiv. *to v.* 24	—xvii. *v.* 20	—xiv. *v.* 24 *to v.* 47	—vi. *v.* 10.
	24	b	—xv.	—xviii. *to v.* 31	—xvi.	Philippians—i.
	25	c	*St. Mark*, Evang.	xviii. *v.* 31 *to* (xix *v.* 11	—	—ii.
	26	d	1 Sam. xvii. *to v.* 31	—xix. *v.* 11 *to v.* 28	xvii. *v.* 31 *to v.* 55	—iii.
	27	e	—xvii. *v.* 55 *to* (xviii. *v.* 17	—xix. *v.* 28	—xix.	—iv.
	28	f	—xx. *to v*, 18	—xx. *to v.* 27	—xx. *v.* 18	Coloss. i. *to v.* 21
	29	g	—xxi.	—xx, *v.* 27 *to* (xxi. *v.* 5	—xxii.	i. *v.* 21 *to* ii. *v.* 8
	30	A	—xxiii.	—xxi. *v.* 5	—xxiv. & xxv. *v.* 1	—ii. *v* 8.

MAY.				Psalms.	MATINS.		EVENSONG.	
					1 Lesson.	*2 Lesson.*	*1 Lesson.*	*2 Lesson.*
b	*Kalend.*	1	*Phil. & Ja.*	1	2 Re. 15	Acts 8	2 Re. 16	Judas. 1
c	6 No.	2		2	17	28	18	Roma. 1
d	5 No.	3		3	19	Math. 1	20	2
e	4 No.	4		4	21	2	22	3
f	3 No.	5		5	23	3	24	4
g	Prid. No.	6		6	3 Reg. 1	4	3 Reg. 2	5
A	*Nonas.*	7		7	3	5	4	6
b	8 Id.	8		8	5	6	6	7
c	7 Id.	9		9	7	7	8	8
d	6 Id.	10		10	9	8	10	9
e	5 Id.	11		11	11	9	12	10
f	4 Id.	12		12	13	10	14	11
g	3 Id.	13		13	15	11	16	12
A	Prid. Id.	14		14	17	12	18	13
b	*Idus.*	15		15	19	13	20	14
c	17 kl.	16		16	21	14	22	15
d	16 kl.	17		17	4 Reg. 1	15	4 Reg. 2	16
e	15 kl.	18		18	3	16	4	1 Cor. 1
f	14 kl.	19		19	5	17	6	2
g	13 kl.	20		20	7	18	8	3
A	12 kl.	21		21	9	19	10	4
b	11 kl.	22		22	11	20	12	5
c	10 kl.	23		23	13	21	14	6
d	9 kl,	24		24	15	22	16	7
e	8 kl.	25		25	17	23	18	8
f	7 kl.	26		26	19	24	20	9
g	6 kl.	27		27	21	25	22	10
A	5 kl.	28		28	23	26	24	11
b	4 kl.	29		29	25	27	1 Esd. 1	12
c	3 kl.	30		30	1 Esd. 2	28	3	13
d	*Prid.* kl.	31		30	4	Mark 1	5	14

MAY hath XXXI Days.

		MORNING PRAYER.		EVENING PRAYER.	
		FIRST LESSON.	SECOND LESSON.	FIRST LESSON.	SECOND LESSON.
1	b	*St. Philip* and *St. James*, App.		—	Colos. iii. *to v.* 18
2	c	1 Samuel — xxvi.	Luke — xxii *to v.* 31	1 Samuel xxviii. *v.* 3	— iii. *v.* 18 *to* iv. *v.* 7
3	d	Invent. of Cross. 1 Samuel — xxxi.	— xxii *v.* 31 *to v.* 54	2 Samuel — i.	— iv. *v.* 7
4	e	2 Sam. — iii. *v.* 17	— xxii. *v.* 54	— iv.	1 Thess. — i.
5	f	— vi.	— xxiii. *to v* 26	— vii. *to v.* 18	— ii.
6	g	St. John Evan. 2 Sam. — vii. *v.* 18	xxiii. *v.* 26 *to v.* 50	— ix.	— iii.
7	A	— xi.	— xxiii. *v.* 50 *to* (xxiv. *v.* 13	— xii. *to v.* 24	— iv.
8	b	xiii. *v.* 38 *to* xiv. *v* 26	— xxiv. *v.* 13	— xv. *to v.* 16	— v.
9	c	— xv. *v.* 16	John — i. *to v.* 29	— xvi. *to v.* 15	2 Thess. — i.
10	d	— xvi. *v* 15 *to* (xvii. *v.* 24	— i. *v.* 29	— xvii. *v.* 24 (*to* xviii. *v.* 18	— ii.
11	e	— xviii. *v* 18	— ii.	— xix. *to v.* 24	— iii.
12	f	— xix. *v.* 24	— iii. *to v.* 22	— xxi. *to v.* 15	1 Tim —. i. *to v.* 18
13	g	— xxiii. *to v.* 24	— iii. *v.* 22	— xxiv.	— i. *v.* 18 & ii.
14	A	1 Kings — i. *to v.* 28	— iv. *to v.* 31	1 Kings — i. *v.* 28 *to* (*v.* 49	— iii.
15	b	1 Chron. xxix. *v.* 10	— iv. *v.* 31	— iii.	— iv.
16	c	1 Kings — iv. *v* 20	— v. *to v.* 24	— v.	— v.
17	d	— vi. *to v.* 15	— v. *v.* 24	— viii. *to v.* 22	— vi.
18	e	— viii. *v.* 22 *to v.* 54	— vi. *to v.* 22	viii. *v.* 54 *to* ix. *v.* 10	2 Tim. — i.
19	f	Dunstan. Abp. 1 Kings — x.	— vi. *v.* 22 *to v.* 41	— xi. *to v.* 26	— ii.
20	g	— xi. *v.* 26	— vi. *v.* 41	— xii. *to v.* 25	— iii.
21	A	— xii. *v.* 25 *to* (xiii. *v.* 11	— vii. *to v.* 25	— xiii. *v.* 11	— iv.
22	b	— xiv. *to v.* 21	— vii. *v.* 25	xv. *v.* 25 *to* xvi. *v.* 8	Titus — i.
23	c	— xvi. *v.* 8	— viii. *to v.* 31	— xvii.	— ii.
24	d	— xviii. *to v.* 17	— viii. *v.* 31	— xviii. *v.* 17	— iii.
25	e	— xix.	— ix. *to v.* 39	— xxi.	Philemon. —
26	f	Augustine, Abp. — xxii. *to v.* 41	— ix. *v.* 39 *to* x. *v.* 22	2 Kings — i.	Hebrews — i.
27	g	Ven. Bede, Pr. 2 Kings — ii.	— x. *v.* 22	— iv. *v.* 8	— ii. & iii. *to v.* 7
28	A	— v.	— xi. *to v.* 17	— vi. *to v.* 24	— iii. *v.* 7 *to* iv. *v.* 14
29	b	— vi. *v.* 24	— xi. *v.* 17 *to v.* 47	— vii.	— iv. *v.* 14 & v.
30	c	— viii. *to v.* 16	xi. *v.* 47 *to* xii. *v.* 20	— ix.	— vi.
31	d	— x. *to v.* 18	— xii. *v.* 20	— x. *v.* 18	— vii.

JUNE.				Psalms.	MATINS.		EVENSONG.	
					1 *Lesson.*	2 *Lesson.*	1 *Lesson.*	2 *Lesson.*
e	*Kalend.*	1		1	1 Esd. 6	Mark. 2	1 Esd. 7	1 Cor. 15
f	4 No.	2		2	8	3	9	16
g	3 No.	3		3	10	4	2 Esd. 1	2 Cor. 1
A	Prid. No.	4		4	2 Esd. 2	5	3	2
b	*Nonas.*	5		5	4	6	5	3
c	8 Id.	6		6	6	7	7	4
d	7 Id.	7		7	8	8	9	5
e	6 Id.	8		8	10	9	11	6
f	5 Id.	9		9	12	10	13	7
g	4 Id.	10		10	Hester 1	11	Hester 2	8
A	3 Id.	11	*Barna. apo*	11	3	Act. 14	4	Acts 15
b	Prid. Id.	12		12	5	Mar. 12	6	2 Cor. 9
c	*Idus.*	13		13	7	13	8	10
d	18 kl.	14		14	9	14	Job 1	11
e	17 kl.	15		15	Job 2	15	3	12
f	16 kl.	16		16	4	16	5	13
g	15 kl.	17		17	6	Luke 1	7	Gala. 1.
A	14 kl.	18		18	8	2	9	2
b	13 kl.	19		19	10	3	11	3
c	12 kl.	20		20	12	4	13	4
d	11 kl.	21		21	14	5	15	5
e	10 kl.	22		22	16	6	17. 18	6
f	9 kl.	23		23	19	7	20	Ephe. 1.
g	8 kl.	24	*Na. Jo. Ba.*	24	Mala. 3	Mat. 3.	Mal. 3.	Math. 14.
A	7 kl.	25		25	Job 21	Lu. 8.	Job 22	Ephe. 2
b	6 kl.	26		26	23	9	24. 25	3
c	5 kl.	27		27	26. 27	10	28	4
d	4 kl.	28		28	29	11	30	5
e	3 kl.	29	*S. Peter.*	29	31	Acts 3	32	Acts 4
f	*Prid.* kl.	30		30	33	Luke 12	34	Ephe. 6

JUNE hath XXX Days.

		MORNING PRAYER.		EVENING PRAYER.	
		FIRST LESSON.	SECOND LESSON.	FIRST LESSON.	SECOND LESSON.
1	e	Niocomede, P. 2 Kings — xiii.	John xiii. *to v.* 21	2 Kings xvii. *to v* 24	Hebrews — viii.
2	f	— xvii. *v.* 24	— xiii. *v.* 21	2 Chron. — xii.	— ix.
3	g	2 Chron — xiii.	— xiv.	— xiv.	— x. *to v.* 19.
4	A	— xv.	— xv.	xvi. & xvii. *to v.* 14.	— x. *v.* 19.
5	b	Boniface, Bp. 2 Chron. — xix.	— xvi. *to v.* 16	— xx. *to v.* 31	— xi. *to v.* 17
6	c	— xx. *v.* 31 & xxi.	— xvi. *v.* 16	— xxii.	— xi. *v.* 17
7	d	— xxiii.	— xvii.	— xxiv.	— xii.
8	e	— xxv.	— xviii. *to v.* 28	— xxvi. & xxvii.	— xiii.
9	f	— xxviii.	— xviii. *v.* 28	2 Kings xviii. *to v.* 9	James — i.
10	g	xxix *v.* 3. *to v.* 21.	— xix *to v.* 25	— 2 Chron. xxx. & (xxxi. *v.* i.	— ii.
11	A	*St. Barnabas*, A.			
12	b	2 Kin. xviii. *v.* 13	— xix. *v.* 25	2 Kings xix *to v.* 20	— iii.
13	c	— xix *v.* 20	— xx. *to v.* 19	— xx.	— iv.
14	d	Isaiah — xxxviii. (*v.* 9 *to v.* 21.	— xx. *v.* 19	2 Chron — xxxiii.	— v.
15	e	2 Kings — xxii.	— xxi.	2 Kings xxiii. *to v* 21	1 Peter i. *to v.* 22
16	f	xxiii. *v.* 21 *to* xxiv *v* 8	Acts — i.	xxiv. *v.* 8 *to* xxv. *v.* 8	i. *v.* 22 *to* ii. *v.* 11
17	g	St. Alban, M. 2 Kin. — xxv. *v.* 8	— ii. *to v.* 22	Ezra — i. & iii.	— ii. *v.* 11 *to* iii. *v.* 8
18	A	Ezra — iv.	— ii. *v.* 22	— v.	— iii. *v.* 8 *to* iv. *v.* 7
19	b	— vii.	— iii.	— viii. *v.* 15	— iv. *v.* 7
20	c	Tr. of K. Edw. Ezra — ix.	— iv. *to v.* 32	— x. *to v.* 20	— v.
21	d	Nehemiah — i.	iv. *v.* 32 *to* v. *v.* 17	Nehemiah — ii.	2 Peter — i.
22	e	— iv.	— v. *v.* 17	— v.	— ii.
23	f	— Fast. — vi. & vii. *to v.* 5	— vi.	— vii. *v.* 73 & viii.	— iii.
24	g	*St. John Baptist.*			
25	A	Neh. — xiii. *to v.* 15	— vii. *to v.* 35	— xiii. *v.* 15	1 John — i.
26	b	Esther — i.	vii. *v.* 35 *to* viii. *v.* 5	Esther ii. *v.* 15 & iii.	— ii. *to v.* 15
27	c	— iv.	— viii. *v.* 5 *to v.* 26	— v.	— ii. *v.* 15
28	d	— Fast. — vi.	— viii. *v.* 26	— vii.	— iii. *to v.* 16
29	e	*St. Peter*, Apos.			
30	f	Job — i.	— ix. *to v.* 23	Job — ii.	iii. *v.* 16 *to* iv. *v.* 7

	JULY,			Psalms.	MATINS. 1 Lesson.	MATINS. 2 Lesson.	EVENSONG. 1 Lesson.	EVENSONG. 2 Lesson.
g	*Kalend.*	1		1	Job 35	Luk. 13	Job 36	Philip. 1
A	6 No.	2		2	37	14	38	2
b	5 No.	3		3	39	15	40	3
c	4 No.	4		4	41	16	42	4
d	3 No.	5		5	Prover. 1	17	Prov. 2	Collos. 1
e	Prid. No.	6		6	3	18	4	2
f	*Nonas.*	7		7	5	19	6	3
g	8 Id.	8		8	7	20	8	4
A	7 Id.	9		9	9	21	10	1 Thes. 1
b	6 Id.	10		10	11	22	12	2
c	5 Id.	11		11	13	23	14	3
d	4 Id.	12		12	15	24	16	4
e	3 Id.	13		13	17	John 1	18	5
f	Prid. Id.	14		14	19	2	20	2 Thes. 1
g	*Idus.*	15		15	21	3	22	2
A	17 kl.	16		16	23	4	24	3
b	16 kl.	17		17	25	5	26	1 Timo. 1
c	15 kl.	18		18	27	6	28	2. 3
d	14 kl.	19		19	29	7	30	4
e	13 kl.	20		20	31	8	Eccles. 1	5
f	12 kl.	21		21	Eccles. 2	9	3	6
g	11 kl.	22	*Magdalen.*	22	4	10	5	2 Tim. 1
A	10 kl.	23		23	6	11	7	2
b	9 kl.	24		24	8	12	9	3
c	8 kl.	25	*James Ap.*	25	10	13	11	4
d	7 kl.	26		26	12	14	Jere. 1	Titus. 1
e	6 kl.	27		27	Jere. 2	15	3	2. 3
f	5 kl.	28		28	4	16	5	Phile. 1
g	4 kl.	29		29	6	17	7	Hebre. 1
A	3 kl.	30		30	8	18	9	2
b	*Prid.* kl.	31		30	10	19	11	3

JULY hath XXXI. Days.

		MORNING PRAYER. First Lesson.	MORNING PRAYER. Second Lesson.	EVENING PRAYER. First Lesson.	EVENING PRAYER. Second Lesson.
1	g	Job iii.	Acts ix. *v.* 23	Job iv.	1 John iv. *v.* 7
2	A	Visit. of V. M.			
		Job v.	x. *to v.* 24	vi.	v.
3	b	vii.	x. *v.* 24	ix.	2 John —
4	c	Tr. of St. Mart.			
		Job x.	xi.	xi.	3 John —
5	d	xii.	xii.	xiii.	Jude —
6	e	xiv.	xiii. *to v.* 26	xvi.	Matthew i. *v.* 18
7	f	xvii.	xiii. *v.* 26	xix.	ii.
8	g	xxi.	xiv.	xxii. *v.* 12 *to v.* 29	iii.
9	A	xxiii.	xv. *to v.* 30	xxiv.	iv. *to v.* 23
10	b	xxv. & xxvi.	xv. *v.* 30 *to* xvi. *v.* 16	xxvii.	iv. *v.* 23 *to* v. *v.* 13
11	c	xxviii.	xvi. *v.* 16	xxix. & xxx. *v.* 1	v. *v.* 13 *to v.* 33
12	d	xxx. *v.* 12 *to v.* 27	xvii. *to v.* 16	xxxi. *v.* 13	v. *v.* 33
13	e	xxxii.	xvii. *v.* 16	xxxviii. *to v.* 39	vi. *to v* 19
14	f	xxxviii. *v.* 39 (& xxxix.	xviii. *to v.* 24	xl.	vi. *v.* 19 *to* (vii. *v.* 7
15	g	Swithun, Bp.			
		Job xli.	xviii. *v.* 24 *to* (xix. *v.* 21	xlii.	vii. *v.* 7
16	A	Prov. i. *to v.* 20	xix. *v.* 21	Proverbs i. *v.* 20	viii. *to v.* 18
17	b	ii.	xx. *to v.* 17	iii. *to v.* 27	viii. *v.* 18
18	c	iii. *v.* 27 *to* iv. *v.* 20	xx. *v.* 17	iv. *v.* 20 *to* v. *v.* 15	ix. *to v.* 18
19	d	v. *v.* 15	xxi. *to v.* 17	vi. *to v.* 20	ix. *v.* 18
20	e	Marg. V. & M.			
		Prov. vii.	xxi. *v.* 17 *to v.* 37	viii.	x. *to v.* 24
21	f	ix.	xxi. *v.* 37 *to* (xxii. *v.* 23	x. *v.* 16	x. *v.* 24
22	g	St. Mary Magd.			
		Prov. xi. *to v.* 15	xxii. *v.* 23 *to* (xxiii. *v.* 12	xi. *v.* 15	xi.
23	A	xii. *v.* 10	xxiii. *v.* 12	xiii.	xii. *to v.* 22
24	b	Fast.			
		xiv. *v.* 9 *to v.* 28	xxiv.	xiv. *v.* 28 *to* xv. *v.* 18	xii. *v.* 22
25	c	*St James*, Apos.	—	—	xiii. *to v.* 24
26	d	St. Anne.			
		Prov. xv. *v.* 18	xxv.	xvi *to v.* 20	xiii. *v.* 24 *to v.* 53
27	e	xvi. *v* 31 *to* xvii. *v* 18	xxvi.	xviii. *v.* 10	xiii. *v.* 53 *to* (xiv. *v.* 13
28	f	xix. *v.* 13	xxvii.	xx. *to v.* 23	xiv. *v.* 13
29	g	xxi. *to v.* 17	xxviii. *to v.* 17	xxii. *to v.* 17	xv. *to v.* 21
30	A	xxiii. *v.* 10	xxviii. *v.* 17	xxiv. *v.* 21	xv. *v.* 21

AUGUST.

	AUGUST.			Psalms.	MATINS.		EVENSONG.	
					1 *Lesson.*	2 *Lesson.*	1 *Lesson.*	2 *Lesson.*
c	*Kalend.*	1		1	Jere. 12	John. 20	Jere. 13	Hebr. 4
d	4 No.	2		2	14	21	15	5
e	3 No.	3		3	16	Acts 1	17	6
f	Prid. No.	4		4	18	2	19	7
g	*Nonas.*	5		5	20	3	21	8
A	8 Id.	6		6	22	4	23	9
b	7 Id.	7		7	24	5	25	10
c	6 Id.	8		8	26	6	27	11
d	5 Id.	9		9	28	7	29	12
e	4 Id.	10		10	30	8	31	13
f	3 Id.	11		11	32	9	33	Jacob. 1
g	Prid. Id.	12		12	34	10	35	2
A	*Idus.*	13		13	36	11	37	3
b	19 kl.	14		14	38	12	39	4
c	18 kl.	15		15	40	13	41	5
d	17 kl.	16		16	42	14	43	Peter. 1
e	16 kl.	17		17	44	15	45-46	2
f	15 kl.	18		18	47	16	48	3
g	14 kl.	19		19	49	17	50	4
A	13 kl.	20		20	51	18	52	5
b	12 kl.	21		21	Lament. 1	19	Lamen. 2	2 Peter 1
c	11 kl.	22		22	3	20	4	2
d	10 kl.	23		23	5	21	Ezech. 2	3
e	9 kl.	24	*Bart. Apost.*	24	Ezech. 3	22	6	1 John 1
f	8 kl.	25		25	7	23	13	2
g	7 kl.	26		26	14	24	18	3
A	6 kl.	27		27	33	25	34	4
b	5 kl.	28		28	Dani. 1	26	Dani. 2	5
c	4 kl.	29		29	3	27	4	2. 3 John
d	3 kl.	30		30	5	28	6	Jude 1
e	*Prid.* kl.	31		30	7	Math. 1	8	Roma. 1

AUGUST hath XXXI. Days.

		MORNING PRAYER.		EVENING PRAYER.	
		FIRST LESSON.	SECOND LESSON.	FIRST LESSON.	SECOND LESSON.
1	c	Lammas Day. Proverbs xxvii. *to* (*v.* 23	Romans—ii. *to v.* 17	Proverbs xxviii. *to* (*v.* 15	Matt.—xvi. *v.* 24 *to* (xvii. *v.* 14
2	d	—— xxx. *to v.* 18	—— ii. *v.* 17	—— xxxi. *v.* 10	—— xvii. *v.* 14
3	e	Ecclesiastes—— i.	—— iii.	Eccles.—ii. *to v.* 12	—— xviii. *to v.* 21
4	f	—— iii.	—— iv.	—— iv	—— xviii. *v.* 21 *to* (xix. *v.* 3
5	g	—— v.	—— v.	—— vi.	—— xix. *v.* 3 *to v.* 27
6	A	Transfigurat. Eccles. —— vii.	—— vi.	—— viii.	xix. *v.* 27 *to* xx. *v.* 17
7	b	Name of Jesus. Eccles. —— ix.	—— vii.	—— xi.	—— xx. *v.* 17
8	c	—— xii.	—— viii. *to v.* 18	Jeremiah—— i.	—— xxi. *to v.* 23
9	d	Jerem.— ii. *to v.* 14	—— viii. *v.* 18	—— v. *to v.* 19	—— xxi. *v.* 23
10	e	St. Lawrence. Jerem. —— v. *v.* 19	—— ix. *to v.* 19	—— vi. *to v.* 22	—— xxii. *to v.* 15
11	f	—— vii. *to v.* 17	—— ix. *v.* 19	—— viii. *v.* 4	—— xxii. *v.* 15 *to v.* 41
12	g	—— ix. *to v* 17	—— x.	— xiii. *v.* 8 *to v.* 24	—— xxii. *v.* 41 *to* (xxiii. *v.* 13
13	A	—— xv.	—— xi. *to v.* 25	—— xvii. *to v.* 19	—— xxiii. *v.* 13
14	b	—— xviii. *to v.* 18	—— xi. *v.* 25	—— xix.	—— xxiv. *to v.* 29
15	c	—— xxi.	—— xii.	—— xxii. *to v.* 13	—— xxiv. *v.* 29
16	d	—— xxii. *v.* 13	—— xiii.	—— xxiii. *to v.* 16	—— xxv. *to v.* 31
17	e	—— xxiv.	— xiv. & xv. *to v.* 8	—— xxv. *to v.* 15	—— xxv. *v.* 31
18	f	—— xxvi.	—— xv. *v.* 8	—— xxviii.	—— xxvi. *to v.* 31
19	g	—xxix. *v.* 4 *to v.* 20	—— xvi.	—— xxx.	—xxvi. *v.* 31 *to v.* 57
20	A	—— xxxi. *to v.* 15	1 Cor.—i. *to v.* 26	—xxxi. *v.* 15 *to v.* 38	—— xxvi. *v.* 57
21	b	—— xxxiii. *to v.* 14	—— i. *v.* 26 & ii.	—— xxxiii. *v.* 14	—— xxvii. *to v.* 27
22	c	—— xxxv.	—— iii.	—— xxxvi. *to v.* 14	xxvii. *v.* 27 *to v.* 57
23	d	—— Fast. —— xxxvi. *v.* 14	—— iv. *to v.* 18	— xxxviii. *to v.* 14	—— xxvii. *v.* 57
24	e	*St. Barthol.* Ap.	—— iv. *v.* 18 & v.		—— xxviii.
25	f	Jer.— xxxviii. *v.* 14	—— vi.	—— xxxix.	Mark—i. *to v.* 21
26	g	—— l. *to v.* 21	—— vii. *to v.* 25	—— li. *v.* 54	—— i. *v.* 21
27	A	Ezekiel—i. *to v.* 15	—— vii. *v.* 25	Ezekiel—— i. *v.* 15	—— ii. *to v.* 23
28	b	St. Augustine, B. Ezekiel—— ii.	—— viii.	—— iii. *to v.* 15	ii. *v.* 23 *to* iii. *v.* 13
29	c	Beheading of St. John Baptist. Ezekiel— iii. *v.* 15	—— ix.	—— viii.	—— iii. *v.* 13
30	d	—— ix.	—— x. & xi. *v.* 1	—— xi. *v* 14	—— iv. *to v.* 35
31	e	—— xii. *v.* 17	—— xi. *v.* 2 *to v.* 17	—— xiii. *to v.* 17	—iv. *v.* 35 *to* v. *v.* 21

	SEPTEMBER.			Psalms.	MATINS. 1 Lesson.	MATINS. 2 Lesson.	EVENSONG. 1 Lesson.	EVENSONG. 1 Lesson.
f	*Kalend.*	1		1	Dani. 9	Math. 2	Dani. 10	Roma. 2
g	4 No.	2		2	11	3	12	3
A	3 No.	3		3	13	4	14	4
b	Prid. No.	4		4	Ose. 1	5	Ose. 2. 3	5
c	*Nonas.*	5		5	4	6	5. 6	6
d	8 Id.	6		6	7	7	8	7
e	7 Id.	7		7	9	8	10	8
f	6 Id.	8		8	11	9	12	9
g	5 Id.	9		9	13	10	14	10
A	4 Id.	10		10	Joel 1	11	Joel 2	11
b	3 Id.	11		11	3	12	Amos 1	12
c	Prid. Id.	12		12	Amos 2	13	3	13
d	*Idus.*	13		13	4	14	5	14
e	18 kl.	14		14	6	15	7	15
f	17 kl.	15		15	8	16	9	16
g	16 kl.	16		16	Abdias. 1	17	Jonas 1	1 Cor. 1
A	15 kl.	17		17	Jon. 2. 3	18	4	2
b	14 kl.	18		18	Miche. 1.	19	Miche. 2	3
c	13 kl.	19		19	3	20	4	4
d	12 kl.	20		20	5	21	6	5
e	11 kl.	21	*Mathewe*	21	7	22	Naum. 1	6
f	10 kl.	22		22	Naum. 2	23	3	7
g	9 kl.	23		23	Abacuc. 1	24	Abacu. 2	8
A	8 kl.	24		24	3	25	Sopho. 1	9
b	7 kl.	25		25	Soph. 2	26	3	10
c	6 kl.	26		26	Agge. 1	27	Agge. 2	11
d	5 kl.	27		27	Zech. 1	28	Zech. 2. 3	12
e	4 kl.	28		28	4. 5	Marke 1	6	13
f	3 kl.	29	*Michael.*	29	7	2	8	14
g	*Prid.* kl.	30		30	9	3	10	15

SEPTEMBER hath XXX Days.

		MORNING PRAYER. First Lesson.	MORNING PRAYER. Second Lesson.	EVENING PRAYER. First Lesson.	EVENING PRAYER. Second Lesson.
1	f	Giles, Abbot. Ezekiel— xiii. v. 17	1 Cor.— xi. v. 17	Ezek. xiv. *to* v. 12	Mark— v. v. 21
2	g	— xiv. v. 12	— xii. *to* v. 28	— xvi. v. 44	— vi. *to* v. 14
3	A	— xviii. *to* v. 19	— xii. v. 28 & xiii.	— xviii. v. 19	— vi. v. 14 *to* v. 30
4	b	— xx. *to* v. 18	— xiv. *to* v. 20	— xx. v. 18 *to* v. 33	— vi. v. 30
5	c	— xx. v. 33. *to* v. 44	— xiv. v. 20	— xxii. v. 23	— vii. *to* v. 24
6	d	— xxiv. v. 15	— xv. *to* v. 35	— xxvi.	vii. v. 24 *to* viii. v. 10
7	e	Enurchus, Bp. Ezekiel xxvii. *to* v. 26	— xv. v 35	— xxvii. v. 26	viii. v. 10 *to* ix. v. 2
8	f	Nat. of V. Mary — xxviii. *to* v. 20	— xvi.	— xxxi.	— ix. v. 2 *to* v. 30
9	g	— xxxii. *to* v. 17	2 Cor.— i *to* v. 23	— xxxiii. *to* v. 21	— ix v. 30
10	A	— xxxiii. v. 21	— i. v. 23 *to* ii. v. 14	— xxxiv. *to* v. 17	— x. *to* v. 32
11	b	— xxxiv. v. 17	— ii. v. 14 & iii.	xxxvi. v. 16 *to* v. 33	— x. v. 32
12	c	— xxxvii. *to* v. 15	— iv.	— xxxvii. v. 15	— xi. *to* v. 27
13	d	— xlvii. to v. 13	— v.	Daniel— i.	xi. v. 27 *to* xii. v. 13
14	e	Holy-Cross Day Daniel— ii. *to* v. 24	— vi. & vii. v. 1	— ii. v. 24	— xii. v. 13 *to* v. 35
15	f	— iii.	— vii. v. 2	— iv. to v. 19	xii. v. 35 *to* xiii. v. 14
16	g	— iv. v. 19	— viii.	— v. *to* v. 17	— xiii. v. 14
17	A	Lambert, Bp. Daniel— v. v. 17	— ix.	— vi.	— xiv. *to* v. 27
18	b	— vii. *to* v. 15	— x.	— vii. v. 15	— xiv. v. 27 *to* v. 53
19	c	— ix. *to* v. 20	— xi. *to* v. 30	— ix. v. 20	— xiv. v. 53
20	d	— Fast. — x. *to* v. 20	xi. v. 30 *to* xii. v. 14	— xii.	— xv. *to* v. 42
21	e	*St. Matthew*, Ap.	— xii. v. 14 & xiii.		— xv. v. 42 & xvi.
22	f	Hosea— ii. v. 14	Galatians— i.	Hosea— iv. *to* v. 13	Luke— i. *to* v. 26
23	g	— v. v. 8 *to* vi. v. 7	— ii.	— vii. v. 8	— i. v. 26 *to* v. 57
24	A	— viii.	— iii.	— ix.	— i. v. 57
25	b	— x.	— iv *to* v. 21	— xi. & xii. *to* v. 7	— ii. *to* v. 21
26	c	S. Cyprian, Abp. Hos.— xiii. *to* v. 15	iv. v. 21 *to* v. v. 13	— xiv.	— ii. v. 21
27	d	Joel— i.	— v. v. 13	Joel— ii. to v. 15	— iii. *to* v. 23
28	e	— ii. v. 15 *to* v. 28	— vi.	— ii. v. 28 *to* iii. v. 9	— iv. *to* v. 16
29	f	*St. Michael & all Angels.*			
30	g	St. Jerom. Joel— iii. v. 9	Ephesians— i.	Amos i. & ii. *to* v. 4	— iv. v. 16

OCTOBER.				Psalms.	MATINS. 1 Lesson	MATINS. 2 Lesson	EVENSONG. 1 Lesson	EVENSONG. 2 Lesson
A	*Kalend.*	1		1	Zacha. 11	Mark 4	Zacha. 12	1 Cor. 16
b	6 No.	2		2	13	5	14	2 Cor. 1
c	5 No.	3		3	Mala. 1	6	Mala. 2	2
d	4 No.	4		4	3	7	4	3
e	3 No.	5		5	Toby. 1	8	Toby. 2	4
f	Prid. No.	6		6	3	9	4	5
g	*Nonas.*	7		7	5	10	6	6
A	8 Id.	8		8	7	11	8	7
b	7 Id.	9		9	9	12	10	8
c	6 Id.	10		10	11	13	12	9
d	5 Id.	11		11	13	14	14	10
e	4 Id.	12		12	Judith 1	15	Judit. 2	11
f	3 Id.	13		13	3	16	4	12
g	Prid Id.	14		14	5	Lu. di. 1	6	13
A	*Idus.*	15		15	7	di. 1	8	Gala. 1
b	17 kl.	16		16	9	2	10	2
c	16 kl.	17		17	11	3	12	3
d	15 kl.	18	*Luc. Evan.*	18	13	4	14	4
e	14 kl.	19		19	15	5	16	5
f	13 kl.	20		20	Sap. 1	6	Sapi. 2	6
g	12 kl.	21		21	3	7	4	Ephe. 1
A	11 kl.	22		22	5	8	6	2
b	10 kl.	23		23	7	9	8	3
c	9 kl.	24		24	9	10	10	4
d	8 kl.	25		25	11	11	12	5
e	7 kl.	26		26	13	12	14	6
f	6 kl.	27		27	15	13	16	Philip 1
g	5 kl.	28	*Sy. & Ju.*	28	17	14	18	2
A	4 kl.	29		29	19	15	Eccls. 1	3
b	3 kl.	30		30	Eccls. 2	16	3	4
c	*Prid* kl.	31		30	4	17	5	Collos. 1

OCTOBER hath XXXI Days.

		MORNING PRAYER. First Lesson.	MORNING PRAYER. Second Lesson.	EVENING PRAYER. First Lesson.	EVENING PRAYER. Second Lesson.
1	A	Remigius, Bp. Amos—ii. *v.* 4 *to* iii. (*v.* 9	Ephesians—— ii.	Amos—— iv. *v.* 4	Luke—v. *to v.* 17
2	b	——v. *to v.* 18	—— iii.	—v. *v.* 18 *to* vi. *v.* 9	—— v. *v.* 17
3	c	—— vii.	——iv. *to v.* 25	——viii.	——vi. *to v.* 20
4	d	—— ix.	iv. *v.* 25 *to* v. *v.* 22	Obadiah.	—— vi. *v.* 20
5	e	Jonah—— i.	v. *v.* 22 *to* vi. *v.* 10	Jonah—— ii.	——vii. *to v.* 24
6	f	Faith, V. & M. Jonah—— iii.	—— vi. *v.* 10	—— iv.	—— vii. *v.* 24
7	g	Micah—i, *to v.* 10	Philippians—— i.	Micah——ii.	—— viii. *to v.* 26
8	A	—— iii.	——ii.	—— iv.	—— viii. *v.* 26
9	b	St. Denys. Bp. Micah—— v.	—— iii.	—— vi.	——ix. *to v.* 28
10	c	—— vii.	—— iv.	Nahum ——.i	— ix. *v.* 28 *to v.* 51
11	d	Nahum—— ii.	Colossians i. *to v.* 21	—— ii.i	ix. *v.* 51 *to* x. *v.* 17
12	e	Habakkuk—— i.	— i. *v.* 21 *to* ii. *v.* 8	Habakkuk—— ii.	—— x. *v.* 17
13	f	Trans. K. Edw. Habakkuk——iii.	——ii. *v.* 8	Zeph.—i. *to v.* 14	——xi. *to v.* 29
14	g	Zephaniah i. *v.* 14 (*to* ii. *v.* 4	——iii. *to v.* 18	——ii. *v.* 4	—— xi. *v.* 29
15	A	—— iii.	—iii. *v.* 18 & iv.	Haggai—— i.	—— xii. *to v.* 35
16	b	Haggai—ii. *to v.* 10	1 Thess.—— i.	—— ii. *v.* 10	——xii. *v.* 35
17	c	Etheldreda, V. Zech.— i. *to v.* 18	——ii.	Zech.—i. *v.* 18 & ii.	—— xiii. *to v.* 18
18	d	*St Luke*, Evan.	——iii.	——	——xiii. *v* 18
19	e	Zechariah—— iii.	—— iv.	—— iv.	—— xiv. *to v.* 25
20	f	—— v.	—— v.	—— vi.	xiv. *v.* 25 *to* xv. *v.* 11
21	g	—— vii	2 Thess.—— i.	——viii. *to v.* 14	——xv. *v.* 11
22	A	——viii. *v.* 14	——ii.	——ix *v.* 9	—— xvi.
23	b	—— x.	—— iii.	—— xi.	—— xvii. *to v.* 20
24	c	—— xii.	1 Tim.— i. *to v.* 18	——xiii.	—— xvii. *v.* 20
25	d	Crispin, Mart. Zechariah— xiv.	—— i. *v* 18 & ii.	Malachi—— i.	——xviii. *to v.* 31
26	e	Malachi—— ii.	—— iii.	——iii. *to v.* 13	xviii. *v.* 31 *to* xix. (*v.* 11
27	f	—— Fast. — iii. *v.* 13 & iv.	—— iv.	Wisdom—— i.	—xix. *v.* 11 *to v.* 28
28	g	*St. Simon & St. Jude*, App.	——v.	—— ——	—— xix. *v.* 28
29	A	Wisdom—— ii.	—— vi.	—— iv. *v.* 7	——xx. *to v.* 27
30	b	—— vi, *to v.* 22	2 Timothy—— i.	vi. *v.* 22 *to* vii. *v.* 15	xx. *v.* 27 *to* xxi. *v.* 5
31	c	—— Fast. ——vii. *v.* 15	——ii.	—— viii. *to v.* 19	—— xxi. *v.* 5

NOVEMBER.				Psalms.	MATINS.		EVENSONG.	
					1 *Lesson.*	2 *Lesson.*	1 *Lesson.*	2 *Lesson.*
d	*Kalend.*	1	*All Saints.*	1	Sap. 3	He. 11.12	Sap. 5	Apoc. 19
e	4 No.	2		2	Eccle. 6	Lu. 18	Eccle. 7	Collos. 2
f	3 No.	3		3	8	19	9	3
g	Prid.	4		4	10	20	11	4
A	*Nonas.*	5		5	12	21	13	1 Thes. 1
b	8 Id.	6		6	14	22	15	2
c	7 Id.	7		7	16	23	17	3
d	6 Id.	8		8	18	24	19	4
e	5 Id.	9		9	20	John 1	21	5
f	4 Id.	10		10	22	2	23	2 Thes. 1
g	3 Id.	11		11	24	3	25	2
A	Prid. Id.	12		12	26	4	27	3
b	*Idus.*	13		13	28	5	29	1 Timo. 1
c	18 kl.	14		14	30	6	31	2. 3
d	17 kl.	15		15	32	7	33	4
e	16 kl.	16		16	34	8	35	5
f	15 kl.	17		17	36	9	37	6
g	14 kl.	18		18	38	10	39	2 Tim. 1
A	13 kl.	19		19	40	11	41	2
b	12 kl.	20		20	42	12	43	3
c	11 kl.	21		21	44	13	45	4
d	10 kl.	22		22	46	14	47	Titus. 1
e	9 kl.	23		23	48	15	49	2. 3
f	8 kl.	24		24	50	16	51	Phile. 1
g	7 kl.	25		25	Baruc. 1	17	Baruc. 2	Hebre. 1
A	6 kl.	26		26	3	18	4	2
b	5 kl.	27		27	5	19	6	3
c	4 kl.	28		28	Esay. 1	20	Esay. 2	4
d	3 kl.	29		29	3	21	4	5
e	*Prid.* kl.	30	*Andre Apo*	30	5	Acts 1	6	6

NOVEMBER hath XXX. Days.

		MORNING PRAYER.		EVENING PRAYER.	
		FIRST LESSON.	SECOND LESSON.	FIRST LESSON.	SECOND LESSON.
1	d	*All Saints' Day.*			
2	e	Wisdom——ix.	2 Timothy—— iii.	Wisd.— xi. *to v.* 15	Luke xxii. *to v.* 31
3	f	—xi. *v.* 15 *to* xii. *v.* 3	—— iv.	——xvii.	—xxii. *v.* 31 *to v.* 54
4	g	—Ecclus. i. *to v.* 14	Titus——i.	Ecclus.—— ii.	—— xxii. *v.* 54
5	A	— iii. *v.* 17 *to v.* 30	——ii.	—— iv. *v.* 10	——xxiii. *to v.* 26
6	b	Leonard, Conf.			
		Ecclus. ——v.	—— iii.	——vii. *v.* 27	—xxiii *v.* 26 *to v.* 50
7	c	—— x. *v.* 18	Philemon.	—— xiv. *to v.* 20	——xxiii. *v.* 50 *to* (xxiv. *v.* 13
8	d	—— xv. *v.* 9	Hebrews—— i.	—— xvi. v. 17	—— xxiv. *v.* 13
9	e	——xviii. *to v.* 15	—ii. & iii. *to v.* 7	——xviii. *v.* 15	John—i. *to v.* 29
10	f	——xix. *v.* 13	–iii. *v.* 7 *to* iv. *v.* 14	— xxii. *v.* 6 *to v.* 24	—— i. *v.* 29
11	g	Martin, Bp.			
		Ecclus. xxiv. *to v* 24	——iv. *v.* 14 & v.	—— xxiv. *v.* 24	——ii.
12	A	–xxxiii. *v.* 7 *to v.* 23	——vi.	—— xxxiv. *v.* 15	——iii. *to v.* 22
13	b	Britius, Bp.			
		Ecclus—— xxxv.	—— vii.	xxxvii *v.* 8 *to v.* 19	—— iii. *v.* 22
14	c	—xxxix. *to v.* 13	——viii.	—— xxxix. *v*, 13	—— iv. *to v.* 31
15	d	Machutus, Bp.			
		Ecclus.–xli. *to v.* 14	—— ix.	—— xlii. *v.* 15	—— iv. *v.* 31
16	e	—— xliv. *to v.* 16	—— x. *to v.* 19	—— l. *to v.* 25	—— v. *to v.* 24
17	f	Hugh, Bp.			
		Ecclus.—— li. *v.* 10	—— x. *v.* 19	Baruch. iv. *to v.* 21	—— v. *v.* 24
18	g	Baruch. iv. *v.* 36 & v.	——xi. *to v.* 17	Isaiah— i. *to v.* 21	——vi. *to v.* 22
19	A	Isaiah ——i. *v.* 21	—— xi. *v.* 17	——ii.	— vi. *v.* 22 *to v.* 41
20	b	Edmund, K.			
		——iii. *to v.* 16	—— xii.	—— iv. *v.* 2	—— vi. *v.* 41
21	c	—— v. *to v.* 18	——xiii.	—— v. *v.* 18	—— vii. *to v.* 25
22	d	Cecilia, V. & M.			
		Isaiah——vi.	James—— i.	—— vii. *to v.* 17	——vii. *v.* 25
23	e	St. Clement, Bp.			
		Isaiah viii. *v* 5 *to v* 18	——ii.	viii. *v.* 18 *to* ix. *v.* 8	—— viii. *to v.* 31
24	f	— ix. *v.* 8 *to* x. *v.* 5	—— iii.	— x. *v.* 5 *to v*, 20	——viii. *v.* 31
25	g	Catherine, V.			
		Isaiah——x. *v.* 20	—— iv.	—— xi. *to v.* 10	——ix. *to v.* 39
26	A	—— xi. *v.* 10	——v.	—— xii.	ix. *v.* 39 *to* x. *v.* 22
27	b	——xiii.	1 Peter— i. *to v.* 22	—— xiv. *to v.* 24	—— x. *v.* 22
28	c	——xvii.	—i. *v*, 22 *to* ii. *v.* 11	—— xviii.	——xi. *to v.* 17
29	d	—— Fast.			
		—— xix. *to v.* 16	—ii. *v*, 11 *to* iii. *v.* 8	—— xix. *v.* 16.	— xi. *v.* 17 *to v.* 47
30	e	*St. Andrew*, Ap.			

DECEMBER.

DECEMBER.				Psalms.	MATINS.		EVENSONG.	
					1 Lesson.	*2 Lesson.*	*1 Lesson.*	*2 Lesson.*
f	*Kalend.*	1		1	Esai: 7	Actes 2	Esai. 8	Hebr. 7
g	4 No.	2		2	9	3	10	8
A	3 No.	3		3	11	4	12	9
b	Prid. No.	4		4	13	5	14	10
c	*Nonas.*	5		5	15	6	16	11
d	8 Id.	6		6	17	di. 7	18	12
e	7 Id.	7		7	19	di. 7	20. 21	13
f	6 Id.	8		8	22	8	23	Jacob 1
g	5 Id.	9		9	24	9	25	2
A	4 Id.	10		10	26	10	27	3
b	3 Id.	11		11	28	11	29	4
c	Prid. Id.	12		12	30	12	31	5
d	*Idus.*	13		13	32	13	33	1 Peter. 1
e	19 kl.	14		14	34	14	35	2
f	18 kl.	15		15	36	15	37	3
g	17 kl.	16		16	38	16	39	4
A	16 kl.	17		17	40	17	41	5
b	15 kl.	18		18	42	18	43	2 Peter 1
c	14 kl.	19		19	44	19	45	2
d	13 kl.	20		20	46	20	47	3
e	12 kl.	21	*Tho. Apost.*	21	48	21	49	1 John 1
f	11 kl.	22		22	50	22	51	2
g	10 kl.	23		23	52	23	53	3
A	9 kl.	24	[*mini.*	24	54	24	55	4
b	8 kl.	25	*Nati. Do-*	25	Esay. 9	Math. 1	Esay. 7	Tit. 3
c	7 kl.	26	*Stephan.*	26	56	Act. 6. 7	57	Actes 7
d	6 kl.	27	*John Evan.*	27	58	Apoc. 1	59	Apo. 22
e	5 kl.	28	*Innocen.*	28	Jer. 31	Acte 25	60	1 John 5
f	4 kl.	29		29	Esay. 61	26	62	2 John 1
g	3 kl.	30		30	63	27	64	3 John 1
A	*Prid.* kl.	31		30	65	28	66	Jude 1

The Calendar, with the Table of Lessons.

DECEMBER hath XXXI. Days.

		MORNING PRAYER.		EVENING PRAYER.	
		FIRST LESSON.	SECOND LESSON.	FIRST LESSON.	SECOND LESSON.
1	f	Isaiah—xxi. *to v.* 13	1 Peter— iii. *v.* 8 *to* iv. *v.* 7	Isaiah xxii. *to v.* 15	John— xi. *v.* 47 *to* xii. *v.* 20
2	g	—— xxii. *v.* 15	——iv. *v.* 7	—— xxiii.	——xii. *v.* 20
3	A	—— xxiv.	——v.	—— xxv.	—— xiii. *to v.* 21
4	b	—— xxvi. *to v.* 20	2 Peter——i.	xxvi. *v.* 20 & xxvii.	—— xiii. *v.* 21
5	c	—— xxviii. *to v.* 14	——ii.	—— xxviii. *v* 14	——xiv.
6	d	Nicolas, Bp.			
		Isaiah xxix. *to v.* 9	—— iii.	—— xxix. *v.* 9	—— xv.
7	e	—— xxx. *to v.* 18	1 John—— i.	—— xxx. *v.* 18	—— xvi. *to v.* 16
8	f	Concept. V. M.			
		Isaiah—— xxxi.	—— ii. *to v.* 15	——xxxii.	—— xvi. *v.* 16
9	g	—— xxxiii.	—— ii. *v.* 15	——xxxiv.	—— xvii.
10	A	—— xxxv.	——iii. *to v.* 16	——xl. *to v.* 12	——xviii. *to v.* 28
11	b	—— xl. *v.* 12	iii. *v.* 16 *to* iv. *v.* 7	—— xli. *to v.* 17	——xviii. *v.* 28
12	c	——xli. *v.* 17	—— iv. *v.* 7	—— xlii. *to v.* 18	—— xix. *to v.* 25
13	d	Lucy, V. & M.			
		Isaiah xlii. *v.* 18 *to* (xliii. *v.* 8	——v.	—— xliii. *v.* 8	—— xix. *v.* 25
14	e	—— xliv. *to v.* 21	2 John.	——xliv. *v.* 21 *to* (xlv. *v.* 8	—— xx. *to v.* 19
15	f	—— xlv. *v.* 8	3 John.	—— xlvi	——xx. *v.* 19
16	g	O Sapientia.			
		Isaiah—— xlvii.	Jude.	—— xlviii.	——xxi.
17	A	—— xlix. *to v.* 13	Revelation—— i.	—— xlix. *v.* 13	Revel.— ii. *to v.* 18
18	b	—— l.	—ii. *v.* 18 *to* iii. *v.* 7	—— li. *to v.* 9	—— iii. *v.* 7
19	c	——li. *v.* 9	—— iv.	——lii. *to v.* 13	——v.
20	d	—— Fast.			
		—— lii. *v.* 13 & liii.	—— vi.	—— liv.	—— vii.
21	e	*St. Thomas*, Ap.	——	——	——
22	f	Isaiah——lv.	—— viii.	—— lvi.	—— x.
23	g	—— lvii	—— xi.	——lviii.	—— xii.
24	A	—— Fast			
		—— lix.	—— xiv.	—— lx.	—— xv
25	b	*Christmas-Day.*	——	——	——
26	c	*St. Stephen*, M.	——	——	——
27	d	*St. John*, Evang.	——	——	——
28	e	*Innocents' Day.*	—— xvi.	——	—— xviii.
29	f	Isaiah—— lxi.	—— xix. *to v.* 11	——lxii.	—— xix. *v.* 11
30	g	—— lxiii.	—— xx.	lxiv. & lxv. *to v.* 8	—— xxi. *to v.* 15
31	A	Silvester, Bp,			
		Isaiah—— lxv. *v.* 8	xxi *v.* 15 *to* xxii. *v.* 6	—— lxvi.	—— xxii. *v.* 6.

Note *(c)*.

The TABLES AND RULES do not appear in the First Prayer Book of Edward VI.

TABLES AND RULES

FOR THE MOVEABLE AND IMMOVEABLE FEASTS; TOGETHER WITH THE DAYS OF FASTING AND ABSTINENCE, THROUGH THE WHOLE YEAR. (*c*)

RULES to know when the Moveable Feasts and Holy-days begin.

EASTER DAY (on which the rest depend) is always the First *Sunday* after the Full moon which happens upon, or next after the Twenty-first day of *March;* and if the Full Moon happens upon a *Sunday*, *Easter Day* is the *Sunday* after.

Advent Sunday is always the nearest *Sunday* to the Feast of *Saint Andrew*, whether before or after.

Septuagesima	*Sunday* is	Nine	Weeks before *Easter.*
Sexagesima		Eight	
Quinquagesima		Seven	
Quadragesima		Six	
Rogation Sunday	*is*	Five Weeks	after Easter
Ascension Day		Forty Days	
Whit Sunday		Seven Weeks	
Trinity Sunday		Eight Weeks	

A TABLE

OF ALL THE FEASTS THAT ARE TO BE OBSERVED IN THE CHURCH OF ENGLAND THROUGHOUT THE YEAR.

All Sundays in the Year.

The Days of the Feasts of

The Circumcision of our Lord JESUS CHRIST.
The Epiphany.—The Conversion of *St. Paul.*
The Purification of the Blessed Virgin.
St. Matthias the Apostle.
The Annunciation of the Blessed Virgin.
St. Mark the Evangelist.
St. Philip and *St. James* the Apostles.
The Ascension of our Lord JESUS CHRIST.
St. Barnabas.—The Nativity of *St. John* Baptist.
St. Peter the Apostle—*St. James* the Apostle.
St. Bartholemew the Apostle.
St. Matthew the Apostle.
St. Michael and all Angels.
St. Luke the Evangelist.
St. Simon and *St. Jude* the Apostles.
All Saints.—*St. Andrew* the Apostle.
St. Thomas the Apostle.—The Nativity of our Lord.
St. Stephen the Martyr.—*St. John* the Evangelist.
The Holy Innocents.

Monday and *Tuesday* in *Easter-Week.*
Monday and *Tuesday* in *Whitsun-Week.*

A TABLE

OF THE

VIGILS, FASTS, AND DAYS OF ABSTINENCE,

TO BE OBSERVED IN THE YEAR.

The Evens or Vigils before

The Nativity of our Lord.
The Purification of the Blessed Virgin *Mary*.
The Annunciation of the Blessed Virgin.
Easter Day.
Ascension Day.
Pentecost.
St. Matthias.
St. John Baptist.
St. Peter.
St. James.
St. Bartholomew.
St. Matthew.
St. Simon and *St. Jude.*
St. Andrew.
St. Thomas.
All Saints.

Note, that if any of these Feast Days fall upon a *Monday*, then the Vigil or Fast-Day shall be kept upon the *Saturday*, and not upon the *Sunday* next before it.

Days of Fasting, or Abstinence.

I. The Forty Days of Lent.

II. The Ember Days at the Four Seasons, being the *Wednesday*, *Friday*, and *Saturday* after ....
The First *Sunday* in Lent.
The Feast of *Pentecost.*
September 14.
December 13.

III. The Three *Rogation Days* being the *Monday*, *Tuesday*, and *Wednesday* before *Holy Thursday*, or the *Ascension* of our LORD.

IV. All the *Fridays* in the Year, except CHRISTMAS DAY.

A SOLEMN DAY FOR WHICH A PARTICULAR SERVICE IS APPOINTED.

The Twentieth Day of *June*
being the Day on which Her Majesty began Her happy Reign.

A TABLE TO FIND EASTER DAY.

FROM THE PRESENT TIME TILL THE YEAR 1899 INCLUSIVE, ACCORDING TO THE FOREGOING CALENDAR.

Golden Number.	Days of the Month.	Sunday Letters.
14	Mar. 21	C
3	——22	D
	——23	E
11	——24	F
	——25	G
19	——26	A
8	——27	B
	——28	C
16	——29	D
5	——30	E
	——31	F
13	April 1	G
2	—— 2	A
	—— 3	B
10	—— 4	C
	—— 5	D
18	—— 6	E
7	—— 7	F
	—— 8	G
15	—— 9	A
4	——10	B
	——11	C
12	——12	D
1	——13	E
	——14	F
9	——15	G
	——16	A
17	——17	B
6	——18	C
	——19	D
	——20	E
	——21	F
	——22	G
	——23	A
	——24	B
	——25	C

THIS Table contains so much of the Calendar as is necessary for the determining of *Easter*; to find which, look for the Golden Number of the Year in the First Column of the Table, against which stands the Day of the Paschal Full Moon; then look in the Third Column for the Sunday Letter, next after the Day of the Full Moon, and the Day of the Month standing against that Sunday Letter is *Easter Day*. If the Full Moon happens upon a Sunday, then (according to the First Rule) the next Sunday after is *Easter Day*.

To find the Golden Number, or Prime, add 1 to the Year of our Lord, and then divide by 19; the Remainder, if any, is the Golden Number; but if nothing remaineth, then 19 is the Golden Number.

To find the Dominical or Sunday Letter, according to the Calendar, until the Year 1799 inclusive, add to the Year of our Lord its Fourth Part, omitting Fractions; and also the Number 1; Divide the Sum by 7; and if there is no Remainder, then A is the Sunday Letter: But if any Number remaineth, then the Letter standing against that Number in the small annexed table, is the Sunday Letter.

0	A
1	G
2	F
3	E
4	D
5	C
6	B

For the next Century, that is, from the Year 1800 till the Year 1899 inclusive, add to the current Year only its Fourth Part, and then divide by 7, and proceed as in the last Rule.

Note, that in all Bissextile or Leap-Years, the Letter found as above will be the Sunday Letter, from the intercalated Day exclusive to the End of the Year.

ANOTHER TABLE TO FIND EASTER TILL THE YEAR 1899 INCLUSIVE.

Golden Number	SUNDAY LETTERS.						
	A	B	C	D	E	F	G
I.	April 16	——17	——18	——19	——20	——14	——15
II.	April 9	—— 3	—— 4	—— 5	—— 6	—— 7	—— 8
III.	Mar. 26	——27	——28	——29	——23	——24	——25
IV.	April 16	——17	——11	——12	——13	——14	——15
V.	April 2	—— 3	—— 4	—— 5	—— 6	Mar. 31	April 1
VI.	April 23	——24	——25	——19	——20	——21	——22
VII.	April 9	——10	——11	——12	——13	——14	—— 8
VIII.	April 2	—— 3	Mar. 28	——29	——30	——31	April 1
IX.	April 16	——17	——18	——19	——20	——21	——22
X.	April 9	——10	——11	—— 5	—— 6	—— 7	—— 8
XI.	Mar. 26	——27	——28	——29	——30	——31	——25
XII.	April 16	——17	——18	——19	——13	——14	——15
XIII.	April 2	—— 3	—— 4	—— 5	—— 6	—— 7	—— 8
XIV.	Mar. 26	——27	——28	——22	——23	——24	——25
XV.	April 16	——10	——11	——12	——13	——14	——15
XVI.	April 2	—— 3	—— 4	—— 5	Mar. 30	——31	April 1
XVII.	April 23	——24	——18	——19	——20	——21	——22
XVIII.	April 9	——10	——11	——12	——13	—— 7	—— 8
XIX.	April 2	Mar. 27	——28	——29	——30	——31	April 1

TO make use of the preceding Table, find the Sunday Letter for the Year in the uppermost Line and the Gold en Number,or,Prime,in the Column of Golden Numbers, and against the Prime, in the same Line under the Sunday Letter, you have the day of the Month on which *Easter* falleth that Year. But Note, that the Name of the Month is set on the Left Hand, or just with the Figure, and followeth not, as in other Tables, by Descent, but Collateral.

A TABLE OF THE MOVEABLE FEASTS FOR SEVENTEEN YEARS. [1886

ACCORDING TO THE FOREGOING CALENDAR.

Year of our Lord.	Golden Number	The Epact.	Sunday Letter.	Sundays after Epiphany.	Septuagesima Sunday.	The First Day of Lent.	Easter Day.	Rogation Sunday.	Ascension Day.	Whit Sunday.	Sundays after Trinity.	Advent Sunday.
1878	17	26	F	Five	Feb. 17	Mar. 6	Apr. 21	May 26	May 30	June 9	23	Dec. 1
1879	18	7	E	Four	—— 9	Feb. 26	—— 13	—— 18	—— 22	—— 1	24	Nov. 30
1880	19	18	DC	Two	Jan. 25	—— 11	Mar. 28	—— 2	—— 6	May 16	26	—— 28
1881	1	0	B	Five	Feb. 13	Mar. 2	Apr. 17	—— 22	—— 26	June 5	23	—— 27
1882	2	11	A	Four	—— 5	Feb. 22	—— 9	—— 14	—— 18	May 28	25	Dec. 3
1883	3	22	G	Two	Jan. 21	—— 7	Mar 25	Apr. 29	—— 3	—— 13	27	—— 2
1884	4	3	FE	Four	Feb. 10	—— 27	Apr. 13	May 18	—— 22	June 1	24	Nov. 30
1885	5	14	D	Three	—— 1	—— 18	—— 5	—— 10	—— 14	May 24	25	—— 29
1886	6	25	C	Six	—— 21	Mar. 10	—— 25	—— 30	June 3	June 13	22	—— 28
1887	7	6	B	Four	—— 6	Feb. 23	—— 10	—— 15	May 19	May 29	24	—— 27
1888	8	17	AG	Three	Jan. 29	—— 15	—— 1	—— 6	—— 10	—— 20	26	Dec. 2
1889	9	28	F	Five	Feb. 17	Mar. 6	—— 21	—— 26	—— 30	June 9	23	—— 1
1890	10	9	E	Three	—— 2	Feb. 19	—— 6	—— 11	—— 15	May 25	25	Nov. 30
1891	11	20	D	Two	Jan. 25	—— 11	Mar. 29	—— 3	—— 7	—— 17	26	—— 29
1892	12	1	CB	Five	Feb. 14	Mar. 2	Apr. 17	—— 22	—— 26	June 5	23	—— 27
1893	13	12	A	Three	Jan. 29	Feb. 15	—— 2	—— 7	—— 11	May 21	26	Dec. 3
1894	14	23	G	Two	—— 21	—— 7	Mar. 25	Apr. 29	—— 3	—— 13	27	—— 2

A TABLE

OF THE MOVEABLE FEASTS,

ACCORDING TO THE SEVERAL DAYS THAT EASTER CAN POSSIBLY FALL UPON.

Easter Day.	Sundays after Epiphany.	Septuagesima Sunday.	The First Day of Lent.	Rogation Sunday.
March 22	One	Jan. 18	Feb. 4	April 26
—— 23	One	—— 19	—— 5	—— 27
—— 24	One	—— 20	—— 6	—— 28
—— 25	Two	—— 21	—— 7	—— 29
—— 26	Two	—— 22	—— 8	—— 30
—— 27	Two	—— 23	—— 9	May 1
—— 28	Two	—— 24	—— 10	—— 2
—— 29	Two	—— 25	—— 11	—— 3
—— 30	Two	—— 26	—— 12	—— 4
—— 31	Two	—— 27	—— 13	—— 5
April 1	Three	—— 28	—— 14	—— 6
—— 2	Three	—— 29	—— 15	—— 7
—— 3	Three	—— 30	—— 16	—— 8
—— 4	Three	—— 31	—— 17	—— 9
—— 5	Three	Feb. 1	—— 18	—— 10
—— 6	Three	—— 2	—— 19	—— 11
—— 7	Three	—— 3	—— 20	—— 12
—— 8	Four	—— 4	—— 21	—— 13
—— 9	Four	—— 5	—— 22	—— 14
—— 10	Four	—— 6	—— 23	—— 15
—— 11	Four	—— 7	—— 24	—— 16
—— 12	Four	—— 8	—— 25	—— 17
—— 13	Four	—— 9	—— 26	—— 18
—— 14	Four	—— 10	—— 27	—— 19
—— 15	Five	—— 11	—— 28	—— 20
—— 16	Five	—— 12	March 1	—— 21
—— 17	Five	—— 13	—— 2	—— 22
—— 18	Five	—— 14	—— 3	—— 23
—— 19	Five	—— 15	—— 4	—— 24
—— 20	Five	—— 16	—— 5	—— 25
—— 21	Five	—— 17	—— 6	—— 26
—— 22	Six	—— 18	—— 7	—— 27
—— 23	Six	—— 19	—— 8	—— 28
—— 24	Six	—— 20	—— 9	—— 29
—— 25	Six	—— 21	—— 10	—— 30

Note, that in a Bissextile or Leap Year, the Number of *Sundays* after Epiphany will be the same, as if *Easter Day* had fallen one day later than it really does. And for the same reason, One Day must, in every Leap-year, be added to the Day of the Month given by the Table for *Septuagesima* Sunday: And the like must be done for the First day of *Lent* (commonly called *Ash Wednesday*) unless the Table gives some Day in the Month of *March* for it; for in that case, the Day given by the Table is the right Day.

A TABLE

OF THE MOVEABLE FEASTS,

ACCORDING TO THE SEVERAL DAYS THAT EASTER CAN POSSIBLY FALL UPON.

Easter Day.	Ascension Day.	Whit Sunday.	Sundays after Trinity.	Advent Sunday.
March 22	April 30	May 10	27	Nov. 29
—— 23	May 1	—— 11	27	—— 30
—— 24	—— 2	—— 12	27	Dec. 1
—— 25	—— 3	—— 13	27	—— 2
—— 26	—— 4	—— 14	27	—— 3
—— 27	—— 5	—— 15	26	Nov. 27
—— 28	—— 6	—— 16	26	—— 28
—— 29	—— 7	—— 17	26	—— 29
—— 30	—— 8	—— 18	26	—— 30
—— 31	—— 9	—— 19	26	Dec. 1
April 1	—— 10	—— 20	26	—— 2
—— 2	—— 11	—— 21	26	—— 3
—— 3	—— 12	—— 22	25	Nov. 27
—— 4	—— 13	—— 23	25	—— 28
—— 5	—— 14	—— 24	25	—— 29
—— 6	—— 15	—— 25	25	—— 30
—— 7	—— 16	—— 26	25	Dec. 1
—— 8	—— 17	—— 27	25	—— 2
—— 9	—— 18	—— 28	25	—— 3
—— 10	—— 19	—— 29	24	Nov. 27
—— 11	—— 20	—— 30	24	—— 28
—— 12	—— 21	—— 31	24	—— 29
—— 13	—— 22	June 1	24	—— 30
—— 14	—— 23	—— 2	24	Dec. 1
—— 15	—— 24	—— 3	24	—— 2
—— 16	—— 25	—— 4	24	—— 3
—— 17	—— 26	—— 5	23	Nov. 27
—— 18	—— 27	—— 6	23	—— 28
—— 19	—— 28	—— 7	23	—— 29
—— 20	—— 29	—— 8	23	—— 30
—— 21	—— 30	—— 9	23	Dec. 1
—— 22	—— 31	—— 10	23	—— 2
—— 23	June 1	—— 11	23	—— 3
—— 24	—— 2	—— 12	22	Nov. 27
—— 25	—— 3	—— 13	22	—— 28

A TABLE TO FIND EASTER,

FROM

THE YEAR 1900, TO THE YEAR 2199 INCLUSIVE.

Golden Number.	Day of the Month.	Sunday Letter.
14	March 22	D
3	—— 23	E
	—— 24	F
11	—— 25	G
	—— 26	A
19	—— 27	B
8	—— 28	C
	—— 29	D
16	—— 30	E
5	—— 31	F
	April 1	G
13	—— 2	A
2	—— 3	B
	—— 4	C
10	—— 5	D
	—— 6	E
18	—— 7	F
7	—— 8	G
	—— 9	A
15	—— 10	B
4	—— 11	C
	—— 12	D
12	—— 13	E
1	—— 14	F
	—— 15	G
9	—— 16	A
17	—— 17	B
6	—— 18	C
	—— 19	D
	—— 20	E
	—— 21	F
	—— 22	G
	—— 23	A
	—— 24	B
	—— 25	C

THE Golden Numbers in the foregoing Calendar will point out the Days of the Paschal Full Moons, till the Year of our Lord 1900; at which Time, in order that the Ecclesiastical Full Moons may fall nearly on the same Days with the real Full Moons, the Golden Numbers must be removed to different Days of the Calendar, as is done in the annexed Table, which contains so much of the Calendar then to be used, as is necessary for finding the Paschal Full Moons, and the Feast of *Easter*, from the Year 1900, to the Year 2199 inclusive. This Table is to be made use of, in all respects, as the First Table before inserted, for finding *Easter* till the Year 1899.

GENERAL TABLES

FOR

FINDING THE DOMINICAL OR SUNDAY LETTER,

AND THE

PLACES OF THE GOLDEN NUMBERS IN THE CALENDAR.

TABLE I.

6	5	4	3	2	1	0
B	C	D.	E	F	G	A
				1600	1700	1800
1900 2000	2100	2200	2300 2400	2500	2600	2700 2800
2900	3000	3100 3200	3300	3400	3500 3600	3700
3800	3900 4000	4100	4200	4300 4400	4500	4600
4700 4800	4900	5000	5100 5200	5300	5400	5500 5600
5700	5800	5900 6000	6100	6200	6300 6400	6500
6600	6700 6800	6900	7000	7100 7200	7300	7400
7500 7600	7700	7800	7900 8000	8100	8200	8300 8400
8500	&c.					

TO find the Dominical or Sunday Letter for any given Year of our Lord, add to the Year its Fourth Part, omitting Fractions, and also the Number, which in Table I. standeth at the Top of the Column, wherein the number of Hundreds contained in that given Year is found: Divide the Sum by 7, and if there is no remainder, then A is the Sunday Letter; but if any Number remaineth, then the Letter which standeth under that Number at the Top of the Table, is the Sunday Letter.

TABLE II.

1	2	3	1	2	3
	Years of our Lord.			Years of our Lord.	
B	1600	0	B	5200	15
	1700	1		5300	16
	1800	1		5400	17
	1900	2		5500	17
B	2000	2	B	5600	17
	2100	2		5700	18
	2200	3		5800	18
	2300	4		5900	19
B	2400	3	B	6000	19
	2500	4		6100	19
	2600	5		6200	20
	2700	5		6300	21
B	2800	5	B	6400	20
	2900	6		6500	21
	3000	6		6600	22
	3100	7		6700	23
B	3200	7	B	6800	22
	3300	7		6900	23
	3400	8		7000	24
	3500	9		7100	24
B	3600	8	B	7200	24
	3700	9		7300	25
	3800	10		7400	25
	3900	10		7500	26
B	4000	10	B	7600	26
	4100	11		7700	26
	4200	12		7800	27
	4300	12		7900	28
B	4400	12	B	8000	27
	4500	13		8100	28
	4600	13		8200	29
	4700	14		8300	29
B	4800	14	B	8400	29
	4900	14		8500	0
	5000	15		&c.	
	5100	16			

TO find the Month and Days of the Month to which the Golden Numbers ought to be prefixed in the Calendar, in any given year of our Lord, consisting of entire Hundred Years, and in all the intermediate Years betwixt that and the next Hundredth Year following, look in the Second Column of Table II. for the given year, consisting of entire Hundreds, and Note the Number or Cypher which stands against it in the Third Column; then, in Table III. look for the same number in the Column under any given Golden Number, which when you have found, guide your Eye Side-ways to the Left Hand, and in the First Column you will find the Month and Day to which that Golden Number ought to be prefixed in the Calendar, during that Period of One Hundred Years.

The Letter B prefixed to certain Hundredth Years in Table II. denotes those Years which are still to be accounted Bissextile or Leap-Years in the New Calendar; whereas all the other Hundredth Years are to be accounted only Common Years.

TABLE III.

Sunday Letters.	THE GOLDEN NUMBERS.								
	1	2	3	4	5	6	7	8	9	10
C	8	19	0	11	22	3	14	25	6	17
D	9	20	1	12	23	4	15	26	7	18
E	10	21	2	13	24	5	16	27	8	19
F	11	22	3	14	25	6	17	28	9	20
G	12	23	4	15	26	7	18	29	10	21
A	13	24	5	16	27	8	19	0	11	22
B	14	25	6	17	28	9	20	1	12	23
C	15	26	7	18	29	10	21	2	13	24
D	16	27	8	19	0	11	22	3	14	25
E	17	28	9	20	1	12	23	4	15	26
F	18	29	10	21	2	13	24	5	16	27
G	19	0	11	22	3	14	25	6	17	28
A	20	1	12	23	4	15	26	7	18	29
B	21	2	13	24	5	16	27	8	19	0
C	22	3	14	25	6	17	28	9	20	1
D	23	4	15	26	7	18	29	10	21	2
E	24	5	16	27	8	19	0	11	22	3
F	25	6	17	28	9	20	1	12	23	4
G	26	7	18	29	10	21	2	13	24	5
A	27	8	19	0	11	22	3	14	25	6
B	28	9	20	1	12	23	4	15	26	7
C	29	10	21	2	13	24	5	16	27	8
D	0	11	22	3	14	25	6	17	28	9
E	1	12	23	4	15	26	7	18	29	10
F	2	13	24	5	16	27	8	19	0	11
G	3	14	25	6	17	28	9	20	1	12
A	4	15	26	7	18	29	10	21	2	13
B	5	16	27	8	19	0	11	22	3	14
B										
C	6	17	28	9	20	1	12	23	4	15
C	7	18	29	10	21	2	13	24	5	16

TABLE III. (CONTINUED.)

Paschal Full Moon.	Sunday Letters.	THE GOL NUMBE				
		11	12	13	14	15
March 21	C	28	9	20	1	12
March 22	D	29	10	21	2	13
March 23	E	0	11	22	3	14
March 24	F	1	12	23	4	15
March 25	G	2	13	24	5	16
March 26	A	3	14	25	6	17
March 27	B	4	15	26	7	18
March 28	C	5	16	27	8	19
March 29	D	6	17	28	9	20
Marcn 30	E	7	18	29	10	21
March 31	F	8	19	0	11	22
April 1	G	9	20	1	12	23
April 2	A	10	21	2	13	24
April 3	B	11	22	3	14	25
April 4	C	12	23	4	15	26
April 5	D	13	24	5	16	27
April 6	E	14	25	6	17	28
April 7	F	15	26	7	18	29
April 8	G	16	27	8	19	0
April 9	A	17	28	9	20	1
April 10	B	18	29	10	21	2
April 11	C	19	0	11	22	3
April 12	D	20	1	12	23	4
April 13	E	21	2	13	24	5
April 14	F	22	3	14	25	6
April 15	G	23	4	15	26	7
April 16	A	24	5	16	27	8
April 17	B	25	6	17	28	9
April 17	B		7	18	29	10
April 18	C	26				
April 18	C	27	8	19	0	11

CERTAIN NOTES FOR THE MORE PLAIN EXPLICATION AND DECENT MINISTRATION OF THINGS CONTAINED IN THIS BOOK. (b)

In the saying or singing of Matins and Evensong, Baptizing and Burying, the minister, in parish churches and chapels annexed to the same, shall use a Surplice. And in all Cathedral churches and Colleges, the Archdeacons, Deans, Provosts, Masters, Prebendaries, and Fellows, being graduates, may use in the quire, besides their Surplices, such hood as pertaineth to their several degrees, which they have taken in any university within this realm. But in all other places, every minister shall be at liberty to use any surplice or no. It is also seemly that graduates, when they do preach, shall use such hoods as pertaineth to their several degrees.

¶ *And whensoever the Bishop shall celebrate the holy communion in the church, or execute any other public ministration, he shall have upon him, besides his rochette, a Surplice or albe, and a cope or vestment, and also his pastoral staff in his hand, or else borne or holden by his chaplain.*

¶ *As touching kneeling, crossing, holding up of hands, knocking upon the breast, and other gestures, they may be used or left, as every man's devotion serveth, without blame.*

¶ *Also upon Christmas day, Easter day, the Ascension day, Whit-Sunday, and the feast of the Trinity, may be used any part of holy scripture hereafter to be certainly limited and appointed, in the stead of the Litany.*

¶ *If there be a sermon, or for other great cause, the Curate by his discretion may leave out the Litany, Gloria in Excelsis, the Creed, the Homily, and the Exhortation to the Communion.*

(b) In 1549 these NOTES appear at the end of the Book, and are followed by the word FINIS.

¶ THE ORDER FOR

MORNING AND EVENING PRAYER

Daily to be said and used throughout the Year.

THE Morning and Evening Prayer shall be used in the accustomed Place of the Church, Chapel, or Chancel; except it shall be otherwise determined by the Ordinary of the Place. And the Chancels shall remain as they have done in times past.

And here is to be noted, that such Ornaments of the Church, and of the Ministers thereof, at all Times of their Ministration, shall be retained, and be in use, as were in this Church of *England*, by the Authority of Parliament, in the Second Year of the reign of King *Edward* the Sixth.

AN ORDER

FOR MATINS, DAILY THROUGH THE YEAR.

The Priest being in the quire, shall begin with a loud voice the Lord's Prayer, called the Pater noster.

THE ORDER FOR

MORNING PRAYER,

DAILY THROUGHOUT THE YEAR.

¶ *At the beginning of Morning Prayer the Minister shall read with a loud voice some one or more of these Sentences of the Scriptures that follow. And then he shall say that which is written after the said Sentences.*

WHEN the wicked man turneth away from his wickedness that he hath committed, and doeth that which is lawful and right, he shall save his soul alive. *Ezek.* xviii. 27.

I acknowledge my transgressions, and my sin is ever before me. *Psalm* li. 3.

Hide Thy face from my sins, and blot out all mine iniquities. *Psalm.* li. 9.

The sacrifices of God are a broken spirit: a broken and a contrite heart, O God, thou wilt not despise. *Psalm* li. 17.

Rend your heart, and not your garments, and turn unto the Lord your God: for he is gracious and merciful, slow to anger, and of great kindness, and repenteth him of the evil. *Joel* ii. 13.

To the Lord our God belong mercies and forgivenesses, though we have rebelled against him: neither have we obeyed thé voice of the Lord our God, to walk in his laws which he set before us. *Dan.* ix. 9, 10.

O Lord, correct me, but with judgement; not in thine anger, lest thou bring me to nothing. *Jer.* x. 24. *Psalm* vi. 1.

Repent ye: for the Kingdom of Heaven is at hand. *St. Matt.* iii. 2.

I will arise, and go to my father, and will say unto him, Father, I have sinned against heaven, and before thee, and am no more worthy to be called thy son. *St. Luke* xv. 18, 19.

Enter not into judgement with thy servant, O Lord; for in thy sight shall no man living be justified. *Psalm* cxliii. 2.

If we say that we have no sin, we deceive ourselves, and the truth is not in us: but, if we confess our sins, he is faithful and just to forgive us our sins, and to cleanse us from all unrighteousness. 1 *St. John* i. 8, 9.

DEARLY beloved brethren, the Scripture moveth us in sundry places to acknowledge and confess our manifold sins and wickedness; and that we should not dissemble nor cloke them before the face of Almighty God our heavenly Father; but confess them with an humble, lowly, penitent, and obedient heart; to the end that we may obtain forgiveness of the same, by his infinite goodness and mercy. And although we ought at all times humbly to acknowledge our sins before God; yet ought we most chiefly so to do, when we assemble and meet together to render thanks for the great benefits that we have received at his hands, to set forth his most worthy praise, to hear his most holy Word, and to ask those things which are requisite and necessary, as well for the body as the soul. Wherefore I pray and beseech you, as many as are here present, to accompany me with a pure heart, and humble voice, unto the throne of the heavenly grace, saying after me;

¶ *A general Confession to be said of the whole Congregation after the Minister, all kneeling.*

ALMIGHTY and most merciful Father; We have erred, and strayed from thy ways like lost sheep. We have followed too much the devices and desires of our own hearts. We have offended against thy holy laws. We have left undone those things which we ought to have done; And we have done those things which we ought not to have done; And there is no health in us. But thou, O Lord, have mercy upon us, miserable offenders. Spare thou them, O God, which confess their faults. Restore thou them that are penitent; According to thy promises declared unto mankind in Christ Jesu our Lord. And grant, O most merciful Father, for his sake; That we may hereafter live a godly, righteous, and sober life, To the glory of thy holy Name. Amen.

¶ *The Absolution, or Remission of sins, to be pronounced by the Priest alone, standing; the people still kneeling.*

ALMIGHTY God, the Father of our Lord Jesus Christ, who desireth not the death of a sinner, but rather that he may turn from his wickedness, and live; and hath given power, and commandment, to his Ministers, to declare and pronounce to his people, being penitent, the Absolution and Remission of their sins: He pardoneth and absolveth all them that truly repent, and unfeignedly believe his holy Gospel. Wherefore let us beseech him to grant us true repentance, and his holy Spirit, that those things may please him, which we do at this present; and that the rest of our life hereafter may be pure, and holy; so that at the last we may come to his eternal joy; through Jesus Christ our Lord.

¶ *The people shall answer here, and at the end of all other prayers,* Amen.

¶ *Then the Minister shall kneel, and say the Lord's Prayer with an audible voice; the people also kneeling, and repeating it with him, both here, and wheresoever else it is used in Divine Service.*

Our Father, which art in heaven, hallowed be thy name. Thy kingdom come. Thy will be done in earth as it is in heaven. Give us this day our daily bread. And forgive us our trespasses, as we forgive them that trespass against us. And lead us not into temptation. But deliver us from evil. Amen.

Then likewise he shall say,

O Lord, open thou my lips.

Answer.

And my mouth shall shew forth thy praise.

Priest.

O God, make speed to save me.

Answer.

O Lord, make haste to help me.

Priest.

Glory be to the Father, and to the Son, and to the Holy Ghost.

As it was in the beginning, is now, and ever shall be world without end. Amen.

Praise ye the Lord.

And from Easter to Trinity Sunday.

Alleluia.

Then shall be said or sung without any Invitatory this Psalm. Venite exultemus, *&c. in English, as followeth :*

Psalm xcv.

O come let us sing unto the Lord : let us heartily rejoice in the strength of our salvation.

Let us come before his presence with thanksgiving : and shew ourself glad in him with Psalms.

For the Lord is a great God : and a great King, above all gods.

In his hand are all the corners of the earth : and the strength of the hills is his also.

OUR Father, which art in heaven, Hallowed be thy Name. Thy kingdom come. Thy will be done in earth, As it is in heaven. Give us this day our daily bread. And forgive us our trespasses, As we forgive them that trespass against us. And lead us not into temptation; But deliver us from evil: For thine is the kingdom, The power, and the glory, For ever and ever. Amen.

¶ *Then likewise he shall say,*

O Lord, open thou our lips.

Answer. And our mouth shall shew forth thy praise.

Priest. O God, make speed to save us.

Answer. O Lord, make haste to help us.

¶ *Here all standing up, the Priest shall say*

Glory be to the Father, and to, the Son : and to the Holy Ghost;

Answer. As it was in the beginning, is now, and ever shall be: world without end. Amen.

Priest. Praise ye the Lord.

Answer. The Lord's Name be praised.

¶ *Then shall be said or sung this Psalm following; except on* Easter-Day, *upon which another Anthem is appointed; and on the Nineteenth day of every Month it is not to be read here, but in the ordinary course of the Psalms.*

Venite, exultemus Domino.

Psalm xcv.

O COME, let us sing unto the Lord : let us heartily rejoice in the strength of our salvation.

Let us come before his presence with thanksgiving : and shew ourselves glad in him with Psalms.

For the Lord is a great God: and a great King above all gods.

In his hand are all the corners of the earth : and the strength of the hills is his also.

The sea is his, and he made it: and his hands prepared the dry land.

O come, let us worship and fall down: and kneel before the Lord our Maker.

For he is (the Lord) our God: and we are the people of his pasture, and the sheep of his hands.

To day if ye will hear his voice, harden not your hearts: as in the provocation, and as in the day of temptation in the wilderness.

When your fathers tempted me: proved me, and saw my works.

Forty year long was I grieved with this generation, and said: it is a people that do err in their hearts, for they have not known my ways.

Unto whom I sware in my wrath: that they should not enter into my rest.

Glory be to the Father, and to Son: and to the Holy Ghost. As it was in the beginning, is now, and ever shall be: world without end. Amen.

Then shall follow certain Psalms in order as they been appointed in a table made for that purpose, except there be proper Psalms appointed for that day. And at the end of every Psalm throughout the year, and likewise in the end of Benedictus, Benedicite, Magnificat, *aud* Nunc Dimittis, *shall be repeated.*

Glory be to the Father, and to the Son, &c.

Then shall be read two lessons distincly with a loud voice, that the people may hear. The first of the Old Testament, the second of the New; like as they be appointed by the Kalendar, except there be proper lessons assigned for that day: the minister that readeth the lesson, standing and turuing him so as he may best be heard of all such as be present. And before every lesson, the minister shall say thus. The first, second, third or fourth chapter of Genesis *or* Exodus, *Matthew, Mark, or other like as*

The sea is his, and he made it: and his hands prepared the dry land.

O come, let us worship, and fall down: and kneel before the Lord our Maker.

For he is the Lord our God: and we are the people of his pasture, and the sheep of his hand.

To day if ye will hear his voice, harden not your hearts: as in the provocation, and as in the day of temptation in the wilderness;

When your fathers tempted me: proved me, and saw my works.

Forty years long was I grieved with this generation, and said: It is a people that do err in their hearts, for they have not known my ways.

Unto whom I sware in my wrath: that they should not enter into my rest.

Glory be to the Father, and to the Son: and to the Holy Ghost;

As it was in the beginning, is now, and ever shall be: world without end. Amen.

¶ *Then shall follow the Psalms in order as they are appointed. And at the end of every Psalm throughout the year, and likewise at the end of* Benedicite, Benedictus, Magnificat *and* Nunc Dimittis *shall be repeated,*

Glory be to the Father, and to the Son: and to the Holy Ghost;

Answer. As it was in the beginning, is now, and ever shall be: world without end. Amen.

¶ *Then shall be read distinctly with an audible voice the First Lesson, taken out of the Old Testament, as is appointed in the Calendar, except there be proper Lessons assigned for that day: He that readeth so standing and turning himself, as he may best be heard of all such as are present. And after that, shall be said or sung, in* English, *the Hymn called* Te Deum Laudamus, *daily throughout the Year.*

is appointed in the Kalendar. And in the end of every Chapter, he shall say,

¶ Here endeth such a chapter of such a book.

And (to the end the people may the better hear) in such places where they do sing, there shall the lessons be sung in a plain tune after the manner of distinct reading: and likewise the Epistle and Gospel.

After the first lesson shall follow Te Deum laudamus, *in English daily throughout the year, except in Lent, all the which time in the place of* Te Deum *shall be used* Benedicite omnia Opera Domini Domino, *in English as followeth:*

Te Deum Laudamus.

We praise thee, O God, we acknowledge thee to be the Lord.

All the earth doth worship thee, the Father everlasting.

To thee all Angels cry aloud, the heavens and all the powers therein.

To thee Cherubim, and Seraphim continually do cry,

Holy, holy, holy, Lord God of Sabaoth.

Heaven and earth are replenished with the majesty of thy glory.

The glorious company of the Apostles, praise thee.

The goodly fellowship of the Prophets, praise thee.

The noble army of Martyrs, praise thee.

The holy church throughout all the world doth knowledge thee.

The Father of an infinite Majesty.

Thy honourable, true, and only Son.

Also the Holy Ghost the Comforter.

Thou art the King of Glory, O Christ.

Thou art the everlasting Son of the Father.

When thou tookest upon thee to deliver man, thou didst not abhor the virgin's womb.

When thou hadst overcome the sharpness of death, thou didst open

¶ *Note, That before every Lesson the Minister shall say,* Here beginneth such a Chapter *or* Verse of such a Chapter, of such a Book: *and after every Lesson,* Here endeth the First, *or* the Second Lesson.

Te Deum Laudamus.

WE praise thee, O God: we acknowledge thee to be the Lord.

All the earth doth worship thee: the Father everlasting.

To thee all angels cry aloud: the heavens, and all the powers therein.

To thee Cherubin, and Seraphin: continually do cry,

Holy, Holy, Holy: Lord God of Sabaoth.

Heaven and earth are full of the Majesty: of thy Glory.

The glorious company of the Apostles: praise thee.

The goodly fellowship of the Prophets: praise thee.

The noble army of Martyrs: praise thee.

The holy church throughout all the world: doth acknowledge thee;

The Father: of an infinite Majesty;

Thine honourable, true: and only Son;

Also the Holy Ghost: the Comforter.

Thou art the King of Glory: O Christ.

Thou art the everlasting Son: of the Father.

When thou tookest upon thee to deliver man: thou didst not abhor the Virgin's womb.

When thou hadst overcome the sharpness of death: thou didst

the kingdom of heaven to all believers.
Thou sittest on the right hand of God, in the Glory of the Father.
We believe that thou shalt come to be our judge.
We therefore pray thee, help thy servants, whom thou hast redeemed with thy precious blood.
Make them to be numbered with thy saints, in glory everlasting.
O Lord, save thy people: and bless thine heritage.
Govern them, and lift them up for ever.
Day by day we magnify thee.
And we worship thy name ever world without end.
Vouchsafe, O Lord, to keep us this day without sin.
O Lord, have mercy upon us: have mercy upon us.
O Lord, let thy mercy lighten upon us: as our trust is in thee.
O Lord, in thee have I trusted: let me never be confounded.

Benedicite omnia opera Domini Domino.

O ALL ye works of the Lord, speak good of the Lord: praise him, and set him up for ever.
O ye Angels of the Lord, speak good of the Lord: praise him, and set him up for ever.
O ye heavens, speak good of the Lord: praise him and set him up for ever.
O ye waters that be above the firmament, speak good of the Lord: praise him, and set him up for ever.
O all ye powers of the Lord, speak good of the Lord: praise him, and set him up for ever.
O ye Sun, and Moon, speak good of the Lord: praise him, and set him up for ever.
O ye stars of heaven, speak good of the Lord: praise him, and set him up for ever.
O ye showers, and dew, speak

open the Kingdom of Heaven to all believers.
Thou sittest at the right hand of God: in the Glory of the Father.
We believe that thou shalt come: to be our Judge.
We therefore pray thee, help thy servants: whom thou hast redeemed with thy precious blood.
Make them to be numbered with thy Saints: in glory everlasting.
O Lord, save thy people: and bless thine heritage.
Govern them: and lift them up for ever.
Day by day: we magnify thee;
And we worship thy Name: ever world without end.
Vouchsafe, O Lord: to keep us this day without sin.
O Lord, have mercy upon us: have mercy upon us.
O Lord, let thy mercy lighten upon us: as our trust is in thee.
O Lord, in thee have I trusted: let me never be confounded.

¶ *Or this Canticle,*
Benedicite, omnia Opera.

O ALL ye Works of the Lord, bless ye the Lord: praise him, and magnify him for ever.
O ye Angels of the Lord, bless ye the Lord: praise him, and magnify him for ever.
O ye Heavens, bless ye the Lord: praise him, and magnify him for ever.
O ye Waters that be above the Firmament, bless ye the Lord: praise him, and magnify him for ever.
O all ye Powers of the Lord, bless ye the Lord: praise him, and magnify him for ever.
O ye Sun, and Moon, bless ye the Lord: praise him, and magnify him for ever.
O ye Stars of Heaven, bless ye the Lord: praise him, and magnify him for ever.
O ye Showers, and Dew, bless

good of the Lord: praise him, and set him up for ever.

O ye winds of God, speak good of the Lord: praise him, and set him up for ever.

O ye fire and heat, praise ye the Lord: praise him, and set him up for ever.

O ye winter and summer, speak good of the Lord: praise him, and set him up for ever.

O ye dews and frosts, speak good of the Lord: praise him, and set him up for ever.

O ye frost and cold, speak good of the Lord: praise him and set him up for ever.

O ye ice and snow, speak good of the Lord: praise him, and set him up for ever.

O ye nights and days, speak good of the Lord: praise him and set him up for ever.

O ye light and darkness, speak good of the Lord: praise him, and set him up for ever.

O ye lightnings and clouds, speak good of the Lord: praise him, and set him up for ever.

O let the earth speak good of the Lord: yea, let it praise him, and set him up for ever.

O ye mountains and hills, speak good of the Lord: praise him, and set him up for ever.

O all ye green things upon the earth, speak good of the Lord: praise him, and set him up for ever.

O ye wells, speak good of the Lord: praise him, and set him up for ever.

O ye seas, and floods, speak good of the Lord: praise him, and set him up for ever.

O ye whales, and all that move in the waters, speak good of the Lord: praise him, and set him up for ever.

O all ye fowls of the air, speak good of the Lord: praise him, and set him up for ever.

O all ye beasts, and cattle, speak

ye the Lord: praise him, and magnify him for ever,

O ye Winds of God, bless ye the Lord: praise him, and magnify him for ever.

O ye Fire and Heat, bless ye the Lord: praise him, and magnify him for ever.

O ye Winter and Summer, bless ye the Lord: praise him, and magnify him for ever.

O ye Dews and Frosts, bless ye the Lord: praise him, and magnify him for ever.

O ye Frost and Cold, bless ye the Lord: praise him, and magnify him for ever.

O ye Ice and Snow, bless ye the Lord: praise him, and magnify him for ever.

O ye Nights, and Days, bless ye the Lord: praise him, and magnify him for ever.

O ye Light and Darkness, bless ye the Lord: praise him, and magnify him for ever.

O ye Lightnings, and Clouds, bless ye the Lord: praise him, and magnify him for ever.

O let the Earth bless the Lord: yea, let it praise him, and magnify him for ever.

O ye Mountains, and Hills, bless ye the Lord: praise him, and magnify him for ever.

O all ye Green Things upon the Earth, bless ye the Lord: praise him, and magnify him for ever.

O ye Wells, bless ye the Lord: praise him, and magnify him for ever.

O ye Seas, and Floods, bless ye the Lord: praise him, and magnify him for ever.

O ye Whales, and all that move in the Waters, bless ye the Lord: praise him, and magnify him for ever.

O all ye Fowls of the Air, bless ye the Lord: praise him, and magnify him for ever.

O all ye Beasts, and Cattle, bless

ye good of the Lord: praise him, and set him up for ever.

O ye children of men, speak good of the Lord: praise him, and set him up for ever.

O let Israel speak good of the Lord: praise him, and set him up for ever.

O ye priests of the Lord, speak good of the Lord: praise him, and set him up for ever.

O ye servants of the Lord, speak good of the Lord: praise him, and set him up for ever.

O ye spirits and souls of the righteous, speak good of the Lord: praise him, and set him up for ever.

O ye holy and humble men of heart, speak ye good of the Lord: praise ye him, and set him up for ever.

O Ananias, Azarias, and Misael, speak ye good of the Lord: praise ye him, and set him up for ever.

Glory be to the Father, and to the Son: and to the Holy Ghost.

As it was in the beginning, is now, &c.

And after the Second Lesson, throughout the whole year, shall be used Benedictus Dominus Deus Israel *&c. in English, as followeth:*

Benedictus. Luc. i.

Blessed be the Lord God of Israel: for he hath visited and redeemed his people;

And hath lifted up an horn of salvation to us: in the house of his servant David;

As he spake by the mouth of his holy Prophets: which hath been since the world began;

That we should be saved from our enemies: and from the hands of all that hate us;

To perform the mercy promised to our fathers: and to remember his holy covenant;

ye the Lord: praise him, and magnify him for ever.

O ye Children of Men, bless ye the Lord: praise him, and magnify him for ever.

O let Israel bless the Lord: praise him, and magnify him for ever.

O ye Priests of the Lord, bless ye the Lord: praise him, and magnify him for ever.

O ye Servants of the Lord, bless ye the Lord: praise him, and magnify him for ever.

O ye Spirits and Souls of the Righteous, bless ye the Lord: praise him, and magnify him for ever.

O ye holy and humble Men of heart, bless ye the Lord: praise him, and magnify him for ever.

O Ananias, Azarias, and Misael, bless ye the Lord: praise him, and magnify him for ever.

Glory be to the Father, and to the Son: and to the Holy Ghost;

As it was in the beginning, is now, and ever shall be: world without end. Amen.

¶ *Then shall be read in like manner the Second Lesson taken out of the New Testament. And after that, the Hymn following; except when that shall happen to be read in the Chapter for the Day, or for the Gospel on* Saint John Baptist's *Day.*

Benedictus. St. Luke i. 68.

BLESSED be the Lord God of Israel: for he hath visited, and redeemed his people;

And hath raised up a mighty salvation for us: in the house of his servant David;

As he spake by the mouth of his holy Prophets: which have been since the world began;

That we should be saved from our enemies: and from the hands of all that hate us;

To perform the mercy promised to our forefathers: and to remember his holy Covenant;

To perform the oath which he sware to our father Abraham: that he would give us;

That we being delivered out of the hands of our enemies: might serve him without fear;

In holiness and righteousness before him: all the days of our life.

And thou, Child, shalt be called the Prophet of the Highest: for thou shalt go before the face of the Lord, to prepare his ways;

To give knowledge of salvation unto his people: for the remission of their sins,

Through the tender mercy of our God: whereby the day-spring from on high hath visited us;

To give light to them that sit in darkness, and in the shadow of death: and to guide our feet into the way of peace.

Glory be to the Father, and to the Son, &c.

As it was in the beginning, is now, and ever, &c.

To perform the oath which he sware to our forefather Abraham: that he would give us;

That we being delivered out of the hand of our enemies: might serve him without fear;

In holiness and righteousness before him: all the days of our life.

And thou, Child, shalt be called the Prophet of the Highest: for thou shalt go before the face of the Lord to prepare his ways;

To give knowledge of salvation unto his people: for the remission of their sins,

Through the tender mercy of our God: whereby the day-spring from on high hath visited us;

To give light to them that sit in darkness, and in the shadow of death: and to guide our feet into the way of peace.

Glory be to the Father, and to the Son: and to the Holy Ghost;

As it was in the beginning, is now, and ever shall be: world without end. Amen.

¶ *Or this Psalm,*
Jubilate Deo. Psalm c.

O BE joyful in the Lord, all ye lands: serve the Lord with gladness, and come before his presence with a song.

Be ye sure that the Lord he is God: it is he that hath made us, and not we ourselves; we are his people, and the sheep of his pasture,

O go your way into his gates with thanksgiving, and into his courts with praise: be thankful unto him, and speak good of his Name.

For the Lord is gracious, his mercy is everlasting: and his truth endureth from generation to generation.

Glory be to the Father, and to the Son: and to the Holy Ghost;

As it was in the beginning, is now, and ever shall be: world without end. Amen.

Then shall be said daily through the year, the prayers following, as well at Evensong as at Matins, all devoutly kneeling.

Lord, have mercy upon us.
Christ, have mercy upon us.
Lord, have mercy upon us.

Then the Minister shall say the Creed *and the Lord's Prayer in English, with a loud voice, &c.*

Answer. But deliver us from evil. Amen.

Priest. O Lord, shew thy mercy upon us.

¶ *Then shall be sung or said the Apostles' Creed by the Minister and the people, standing: except only such days as the Creed of Saint* Athanasius *is appointed to be read.*

I BELIEVE in God the Father Almighty, Maker of heaven and earth:

And in Jesus Christ his only Son our Lord, Who was conceived by the Holy Ghost, Born of the Virgin Mary, Suffered under Pontius Pilate, Was crucified, dead, and buried, He descended into hell; The third day he rose again from the dead, He ascended into heaven, And sitteth on the right hand of God the Father Almighty; From thence he shall come to judge the quick and the dead.

I believe in the Holy Ghost; The holy Catholic Church; The Communion of Saints; The Forgiveness of sins; The Resurrection of the body, And the life everlasting. Amen.

¶ *And after that, these Prayers following, all devoutly kneeling; the Minister first pronouncing with a loud voice,*

The Lord be with you.
Answer. And with thy spirit.
Minister. Let us pray.
Lord, have mercy upon us.
Christ, have mercy upon us.
Lord, have mercy upon us.

¶ *Then the Minister, Clerks, and people, shall say the Lord's Prayer with a loud voice.*

OUR Father, which art in heaven, Hallowed be thy name. Thy kingdom come. Thy will be done in earth, As it is in heaven. Give us this day our daily bread. And forgive us our trespasses, As we forgive them that trespass against us, And lead us not into temptation; But deliver us from evil. Amen.

¶ *Then the Priest standing up shall say,*

O Lord, shew thy mercy upon us.

Answer. And grant us thy salvation.
Priest. O Lord save the king.
Answer. And mercifully hear us when we call upon thee.
Priest. Endue thy ministers with righteousness.
Answer. And make thy chosen people joyful.
Priest. O Lord save thy people.
Answer. And bless thine inheritance.
Priest. Give peace in our time, O Lord.
Answer. Because there is none other that fighteth for us, but only thou, O God.
Priest. O God, make clean our hearts within us.
Answer. And take not thine holy Spirit from us.
Priest. The Lord be with you
Answer. And with thy spirit.

Then shall daily follow three Collects. The first of the day, which shall be the same that is appointed at the Communion. The second for peace. The third for grace to live well. And the two last Collects shall never alter, but daily be said at Matins throughout all the year, as followeth: the Priest standing up and saying,

Let us pray.

Then the Collect of the day.

The Second Collect: for peace.

O God, which art author of peace, and lover of concord, in knowledge of whom standeth our eternal life, whose service is perfect freedom: defend us, thy humble servants, in all assaults of our enemies, that we, surely trusting in thy defence, may not fear the power of any adversaries: through the might of Jesu Christ our Lord. Amen.

The third Collect: for grace.

O Lord, our heavenly Father, almighty and everliving God, which hast safely brought us to the beginning of this day: defend us in

---

Answer. And grant us thy salvation.
Priest. O Lord, save the Queen.
Answer. And mercifully hear us when we call upon thee.
Priest. Endue thy Ministers with righteousness.
Answer. And make thy chosen people joyful.
Priest. O Lord, save thy people.
Answer. And bless thine inheritance.
Priest. Give peace in our time, O Lord.
Answer. Because there is none other that fighteth for us, but only thou, O God.
Priest. O God, make clean our hearts within us.
Answer. And take not thy holy Spirit from us.

¶ *Then shall follow three Collects: the first of the Day, which shall be the same that is appointed at the Communion; the second for Peace; the third for Grace to live well. And the two last Collects shall never alter, but daily be said at Morning Prayer throughout all the year, as followeth; all kneeling.*

The second Collect, for Peace.

O GOD, who art the author of peace and lover of concord, in knowledge of whom standeth our eternal life, whose service is perfect freedom; Defend us thy humble servants in all assaults of our enemies; that we, surely trusting in thy defence, may not fear the power of any adversaries, through the might of Jesus Christ our Lord. *Amen.*

The third Collect: for Grace.

O LORD, our heavenly Father, Almighty and everlasting God, who hast safely brought us to the beginning of this day; De-

the same with thy mighty power; and grant that this day we fall into no sin, neither run into any kind of danger, but that all our doings may be ordered by thy governance, to do always that is righteous in thy sight: through Jesus Christ our Lord. Amen.

fend us in the same with thy mighty power; and grant that this day we fall into no sin, neither run into any kind of danger; but that all our doings may be ordered by thy governance, to do always that is righteous in thy sight; through Jesus Christ our Lord. *Amen.*

¶ *In Quires and Places where they sing, here followeth the Anthem.*

¶ *Then these five Prayers following are to be read here, except when the Litany is read; and then only the two last are to be read, as they are there placed.*

A Prayer for the Queen's Majesty.

O LORD, our heavenly Father, high and mighty, King of kings, Lord of lords, the only Ruler of princes, who dost from thy throne behold all the dwellers upon earth; Most heartily we beseech thee with thy favour to behold our most gracious Sovereign Lady, Queen *VICTORIA;* and so replenish her with the grace of thy Holy Spirit, that she may alway incline to thy will, and walk in thy way: Endue her plenteously with heavenly gifts; grant her in health and wealth long to live; strengthen her that she may vanquish and overcome all her enemies; and finally, after this life, she may attain everlasting joy and felicity; through Jesus Christ our Lord. *Amen.*

A Prayer for the Royal Family.

ALMIGHTY God, the fountain of all goodness, we humbly beseech Thee to bless *Albert Edward* Prince of *Wales*, the Princess of *Wales*, and all the Royal Family: Endue them with thy holy Spirit; enrich them with thy heavenly grace; prosper them with all happiness; and bring them to thine everlasting kingdom; through Jesus Christ our Lord. *Amen.*

A Prayer for the Clergy and People.

ALMIGHTY and everlasting God, who alone workest great marvels; Send down upon our Bishops, and Curates, and all Congregations committed to their charge, the healthful Spirit of thy grace; and that they may truly please thee, pour upon them the continual dew of thy blessing. Grant this, O Lord, for the honour of our Advocate and Meditator, Jesus Christ. *Amen.*

A Prayer of St. Chrysostom.

ALMIGHTY God, who hast given us grace at this time with one accord to make our common supplications unto thee; and dost promise that when two or three are gathered together in thy Name thou wilt grant their requests: Fulfil now, O Lord, the desires and petitions of thy servants, as may be most expedient for them; granting us in this world knowledge of thy truth, and in the world to come life everlasting. *Amen.*

2 Cor. xiii.

THE grace of our Lord Jesus Christ, and the love of God, and the fellowship of the Holy Ghost, be with us all evermore. *Amen.*

Here endeth the Order of Morning Prayer throughout the Year.

AN ORDER

FOR EVENSONG

THROUGHOUT THE YEAR.

THE ORDER FOR

EVENING PRAYER,

DAILY THROUGHOUT THE YEAR.

¶ *At the beginning of Evening Prayer, the Minister shall read with a loud voice some one or more of these Sentences of the Scriptures that follow. And then he shall say that which is written after the said Sentences.*

WHEN the wicked man turneth away from his wickedness that he hath committed, and doeth that which is lawful and right, he shall save his soul alive. *Ezek.* xviii. 27.

I acknowledge my transgressions, and my sin is ever before me. *Psalm* li. 3.

Hide thy face from my sins, and blot out all mine iniquities. *Psalm* li. 9.

The sacrifices of God are a broken spirit: a broken and a contrite heart, O God, thou wilt not despise. *Psalm* li. 17.

Rend your heart, and not your garments, and turn unto the Lord your God: for he is gracious and merciful, slow to anger, and of great kindness, and repenteth him of the evil. *Joel.* ii. 13.

To the Lord our God belong mercies and forgivenesses, though we have rebelled against him: neither have we obeyed the voice of the Lord our God, to walk in his laws which he set before us. *Dan.* ix. 9, 10.

O Lord, correct me, but with judgement; not in thine anger, lest thou bring me to nothing. *Jer.* x. 24. *Psalm* vi. 1.

Repent ye; for the Kingdom of Heaven is at hand. *St. Matt.* iii. 2.

I will arise, and go to my father, and will say unto him, Father, I have sinned against heaven, and before thee, and am no more worthy to be called thy son. *St. Luke* xv. 18, 19.

Enter not into judgement with thy servant, O Lord; for in thy sight shall no man living be justified. *Psalm* cxliii. 2.

If we say that we have no sin, we deceive ourselves, and the truth is not in us: but, if we confess our sins, he is faithful and just to forgive our sins, and to cleanse us from all unrighteousness. 1 *St. John* i, 8, 9.

DEARLY beloved brethren, the Scripture moveth us in sundry places to acknowledge and confess our manifold sins and wickedness; and that we should not dissemble nor cloke them before the face of Almighty God our heavenly Father; but confess them with an humble, lowly, penitent, and obedient heart; to the end that we may obtain forgiveness of the same, by his infinite goodness and mercy. And although we ought at all times humbly to acknowledge our sins before God; yet ought we most chiefly so to do, when we assemble and meet together to render thanks for the great benefits that we have received at his hands, to set forth his most worthy praise, to hear his most holy Word, and to ask those things which are requisite and necessary, as well for the body as the soul. Wherefore I pray and beseech you, as many as are here present, to accompany me with a pure heart, and humble voice, unto the throne of the heavenly grace, saying after me;

¶ *A general Confession to be said of the whole Congregation after the Minister, all kneeling.*

ALMIGHTY and most merciful Father; we have erred, and strayed from thy ways like lost sheep. We have followed too much the devices and desires of our own hearts. We have offended against thy holy laws. We have left undone those things which we ought to have done; And we have done those things which we ought not to have done; And there is no health in us. But thou, O Lord, have mercy upon us, miserable offenders. Spare thou them, O God, which confess their faults. Restore thou them that are penitent; According to thy promises declared unto mankind in Christ Jesu our Lord. And grant, O most merciful Father, for his sake; That we may hereafter live a godly, righteous, and sober life, To the glory of thy holy Name. Amen.

¶ *The Absolution, or Remission of sins, to be pronounced by the Priest alone, standing; the people still kneeling.*

ALMIGHTY God, the Father of our Lord Jesus Christ, who desireth not the death of a sinner, but rather that he may turn from his wickedness, and live; and hath given power, and commandment, to his Ministers, to declare and pronounce to his people, being penitent, the Absolution and Remission of their sins: He pardoneth and absolveth all them that truly repent, and unfeignedly believe his holy Gospel. Wherefore let us beseech him to grant us true repentance, and his holy Spirit, that those things may please him, which we do at this present; and that the rest of our life hereafter may be pure, and holy; so that at the last we may come to his eternal joy; through Jesus Christ our Lord. *Amen.*

The Priest shall say.

Our Father, &c.

¶ *Then the Minister shall kneel, and say the Lord's Prayer; the people also kneeling, and repeating it with him.*

OUR Father, which art in heaven, Hallowed be thy Name. Thy kingdom come. Thy will be done in earth, as it is in heaven.

Give us this day our daily bread. And forgive us our trespasses, As we forgive them that trespass against us. And lead us not into temptation; But deliver us from evil: For thine is the kingdom, The power, and the glory, For ever and ever. Amen.

Then likewise he shall say.

O God, make speed to save me.

Answer.

O Lord, make haste to help me.

Priest.

Glory be to to the Father, and to the Son: and to the Holy Ghost; As it was in the beginning, is now, and ever shall be: world without end. Amen.

Praise ye the Lord.

And from Easter to Trinity Sunday.

Alleluia.

As before is appointed at Matins.

Then Psalms in order as they be appointed in the Table for Psalms, except there be proper Psalms appointed for that day. Then a Lesson of the Old Testament, as it is appointed likewise in the Calendar, except there be proper Lessons appointed for that day. After that (Magnificat anima mea Dominum) *in English, as followeth.*

Magnificat. Luc. i.

My soul doth magnify the Lord.

And my spirit hath rejoiced in God my Saviour.

For he hath regarded the lowliness of his hand-maiden.

For behold, from henceforth all generations shall call me blessed.

For he that is mighty hath magnified me: and holy is his name.

And his mercy is on them that fear him: throughout all generations.

He hath shewed strength with

¶ *Then likewise he shall say,*

O Lord, open thou our lips.

Answer. And our mouth shall shew forth thy praise.

Priest. O God, make speed to save us.

Answer. O Lord, make haste to help us.

¶ *Here all standing up, the Priest shall say,*

Glory be to the Father, and to the Son: and to the Holy Ghost;

Answer. As it was in the beginning, is now, and ever shall be: world without end. Amen.

Priest. Praise ye the Lord.

Answer. The Lord's name be praised.

¶ *Then shall be said or sung the Psalms in order as they are appointed. Then a Lesson of the Old Testament, as is appointed. And after that,* Magnificat *(or the Song of the Blessed Virgin* Mary) *in English, as followeth.*

Magnificat. St. Luke i.

MY soul doth magnify the Lord: and my spirit hath rejoiced in God my Saviour.

For he hath regarded: the lowliness of his hand-maiden.

For behold, from henceforth: all generations shall call me blessed.

For he that is mighty hath magnified me: and holy is his Name.

And his mercy is on them that fear him: throughout all generations.

He hath shewed strength with

his arm: he hath scattered the proud in the imagination of their hearts.

He hath put down the mighty from their seat; and hath exalted the humble and meek.

He hath filled the hungry with good things: and the rich he hath sent empty away.

He remembering his mercy, hath holpen his servant Israel: as he promised to our fathers, Abraham and his seed, for ever.

Glory be to the Father, and to the Son, &c.

As it was in the beginning, &c.

his arm: he hath scattered the proud in the imagination of their hearts.

He hath put down the mighty from their seat: and hath exalted the humble and meek.

He hath filled the hungry with good things: and the rich he hath sent empty away.

He remembering his mercy hath holpen his servant Israel: as he promised to our forefathers, Abraham and his seed, for ever.

Glory be to the Father, and to the Son: and to the Holy Ghost;

As it was in the beginning, is now, and ever shall be: world without end. Amen.

¶ *Or else this Psalm; except it be on the Nineteenth Day of the Month, when it is read in the ordinary Course of the Psalms.*

Cantate Domino. Psalm xcviii.

O SING unto the Lord a new song: for he hath done marvellous things.

With his own right hand, and with his holy arm: hath he gotten himself the victory.

The Lord declared his salvation: his righteousness hath he openly shewed in the sight of the heathen.

He hath remembered his mercy and truth toward the house of Israel: and all the ends of the world have seen the salvation of our God.

Shew yourselves joyful unto the Lord, all ye lands: sing, rejoice, and give thanks.

Praise the Lord upon the harp: sing to the harp with a psalm of thanksgiving.

With trumpets also and shawms: O shew yourselves joyful before the Lord the King.

Let the sea make a noise, and all that therein is: the round world, and they that dwell therein.

Let the floods clap their hands, and let the hills be joyful together before the Lord: for he cometh to judge the earth.

With righteousness shall he judge the world: and the people with equity.

Glory be to the Father, and to the Son: and to the Holy Ghost.

As it was in the beginning, is now, and ever shall be: world without end. Amen.

Then a Lesson of the New Testament. And after that (Nunc dimittis servum tuum) *in English as followeth.*

Nunc Dimittis. Luc. ii.

LORD, now lettest thou thy servant depart in peace: according to thy word.

For mine eyes have seen: thy salvation.

Which thou hast prepared: before the face of all people;

To be a light to lighten the Gentiles: and to be the glory of thy people Israel.

Glory be to the Father, and to the Son: and to the Holy Ghost.

As it was in the beginning, is now, and ever shall be: world without end. Amen.

¶ *Then a Lesson of the New Testament, as it is appointed. And after that,* Nunc Dimittis *(or the song of* Symeon*) in English, as followeth.*

Nunc dimittis. St. Luke ii. 29.

LORD, now lettest thou thy servant depart in peace: according to thy word.

For mine eyes have seen: thy salvation,

Which thou hast prepared: before the face of all people;

To be a light to lighten the Gentiles: and to be the glory of thy people Israel.

Glory be to the Father, and to the Son: and to the Holy Ghost;

As it was in the beginning, is now, and ever shall be: world without end. Amen.

¶ *Or else this Psalm; except it be on the Twelfth Day of the Month.*

Deus misereatur. Psalm lxvii.

GOD be merciful unto us, and bless us: and shew us the light of his countenance, and be merciful unto us:

That thy way may be known upon earth: thy saving health among all nations.

Let the people praise thee, O God: yea, let all the people praise thee.

O let the nations rejoice and be glad: for thou shalt judge the folk righteously, and govern the nations upon earth.

Let the people praise thee, O

God: yea, let all the people praise thee.

Then shall the earth bring forth her increase: and God, even our own God, shall give us his blessing.

God shall bless us: and all the ends of the world shall fear him.

Glory be to the Father, and to the Son: and to the Holy Ghost;

As it was in the beginning, is now, and ever shall be: world without end. Amen.

¶ *Then shall be said or sung the Apostles' Creed by the Minister and the people, standing.*

I BELIEVE in God the Father Almighty, Maker of heaven and earth;

And in Jesus Christ his only Son our Lord, Who was conceived by the Holy Ghost, Born of the Virgin Mary, Suffered under Pontius Pilate, Was crucified, dead, and buried, He descended into hell; The third day he rose again from the dead, He ascended into heaven, And sitteth on the right hand of God the Father Almighty; From thence he shall come to judge the quick and the dead.

I believe in the Holy Ghost; The holy Catholick Church; The Communion of Saints; The Forgiveness of Sins; The Resurrection of the body, And the life everlasting. Amen.

¶ *And after that, these Prayers following, all devoutly kneeling; the Minister first pronouncing with a loud voice,*

The Lord be with you.
Answer. And with thy spirit.
Minister. Let us pray.
Lord, have mercy upon us.
Christ, have mercy upon us.
Lord, have mercy upon us.

¶ *Then the Minister, Clerks, and people, shall say the Lord's Prayer with a loud voice.*

OUR Father, which art in heaven, Hallowed be thy Name,

Thy kingdom come. Thy will be done in earth, As it is in heaven. Give us this day our daily bread. And forgive us our trespasses, As we forgive them that trespass against us. And lead us not into temptation; But deliver us from evil. Amen.

¶ *Then the Priest standing up shall say,*

O Lord shew thy mercy upon us;

Answer. And grant us thy salvation.

Priest. O Lord, save the Queen.

Answer. And mercifully hear us when we call upon thee.

Priest. Endue thy Ministers with righteousness.

Answer. And make thy chosen people joyful.

Priest. O Lord, save thy people.

Answer. And bless thine inheritance.

Priest. Give peace in our time, O Lord.

Answer. Because there is none other that fighteth for us, but only thou, O God.

Priest. O God, make clean our hearts within us.

Answer. And take not thy holy Spirit from us.

Then the suffrages before assigned at Matins, the clerks kneeling likewise, with three Collects. First of the day: Second of peace: Third for aid against all perils, as here followeth. Which two last Collects shall be daily said at Evensong without alteration.

The second Collect at Evensong.

O God, from whom all holy desires, all good counsels, and all just works do proceed: Give unto thy servants that peace, which the world cannot give; that both our hearts may be set to obey thy commandments, and also that by thee we being defended from the fear of our enemies, may pass our time in rest and quietness: through the merits of Jesu Christ our Saviour. Amen.

¶ *Then shall follow three Collects; the first of the Day; the second for Peace; the third for Aid against all Perils, as hereafter followeth: which two last Collects shall be daily said at Evening Prayer without alteration.*

The second Collect at Evening Prayer.

O GOD, from whom all holy desires, all good counsels, and all just works do proceed; Give unto thy servants that peace which the world cannot give; that both our hearts may be set to obey thy commandments, and also that by thee we being defended from the fear of our enemies may pass our time in rest and quietness; through the merits of Jesus Christ our Saviour. *Amen.*

The third Collect for aid against all perils.

LIGHTEN our darkness, we beseech thee, O Lord, and by thy great mercy, defend us from all perils and dangers of this night, for the love of thy only Son, our Saviour Jesu Christ. Amen.

The third Collect, for Aid against all Perils.

LIGHTEN our darkness, we beseech thee, O Lord; and by thy great mercy defend us from all perils and dangers of this night; for the love of thy only Son, our Saviour, Jesus Christ. *Amen.*

¶ *In Quires and Places where they sing, here followeth the Anthem.*

A Prayer for the Queen's Majesty.

O LORD our heavenly Father, high and mighty, King of kings, Lord of lords, the only Ruler of princes, who dost from thy throne behold all the dwellers upon earth; Most heartily we beseech thee with thy favour to behold our most gracious Sovereign Lady, Queen *VICTORIA;* and so replenish her with the grace of thy Holy Spirit, that she may alway incline to thy will, and walk in thy way: Endue her plenteously with heavenly gifts; grant her in health and wealth long to live; strengthen her that she may vanquish and overcome all her enemies; and finally, after this life, she may attain everlasting joy and felicity; through Jesus Christ our Lord. *Amen.*

A Prayer for the Royal Family.

ALMIGHTY God, the fountain of all goodness, we humbly beseech thee to bless *Albert Edward* Prince of *Wales*, the Princess of *Wales*, and all the Royal Family: Endue them with thy holy Spirit: enrich them with thy heavenly grace; prosper them with all happiness; and bring them to thine everlasting kingdom; through Jesus Christ our Lord. *Amen.*

A Prayer for the Clergy and people.

ALMIGHTY and everlasting God, who alone workest great marvels; Send down upon our Bishops, and Curates, and all Congregations committed to their charge, the healthful Spirit of thy grace; and that they may truly please thee, pour upon them the continual dew of thy blessing. Grant this, O Lord, for the honour of our Advocate and Mediator, Jesus Christ. *Amen.*

A Prayer of St. Chrysostom.

ALMIGHTY God, who hast given us grace at this time with one accord to make our common supplications unto thee; and dost promise, that when two or three are gathered together in thy Name thou wilt grant their requests: Fulfil now, O Lord, the desires and petitions of thy servants as may be most expedient for them; granting us in this world knowledge of thy truth, and in the world to come life everlasting. *Amen.*

2 Cor. xiii.

THE grace of our Lord Jesus Christ, and the love of God, and the fellowship of the Holy Ghost, be with us all evermore. *Amen.*

Here endeth the Order of Evening Prayer throughout the Year.

AT MORNING PRAYER.

¶ *In the feasts of* Christmas, the Epiphany, Easter, the Ascension, Pentecost, *and upon* Trinity *Sunday, shall be sung or said immediately after* Benedictus *this Confession of our Christian Faith.*

Quicunque vult, &c.

WHOSOEVER will be saved: before all things it is necessary that he hold the Catholic faith.

Which faith except every one do keep holy and undefiled: without doubt he shall perish everlastingly.

And the Catholic faith is this: That we worship one God in Trinity, and Trinity in Unity;

Neither confounding the persons: nor dividing the substance.

For there is one person of the Father, another of the Son: and another of the Holy Ghost.

But the Godhead of the Father, of the Son, and of the Holy Ghost, is all one: the glory equal, the majesty co-eternal.

Such as the Father is, such is the Son: and such is the Holy Ghost.

The Father uncreate, the Son uncreate: and the Holy Ghost uncreate.

The Father incomprehensible, the Son incomprehensible; and the Holy Ghost incomprehensible.

The Father eternal, the Son eternal: and the Holy Ghost eternal.

And yet they are not three eternals: but one eternal.

As also there be not three incomprehensibles, nor three uncre-

¶ *Upon these Feasts;* Christmas-day, *the* Epiphany, *Saint* Matthias, Easter-day, Ascension-day, Whitsunday, *Saint* John Baptist, *Saint* James, *Saint* Bartholemew, *Saint* Matthew, *Saint* Simon *and Saint* Jude, *Saint* Andrew, *and upon* Trinity-Sunday, *shall be sung or said at Morning Prayer, instead of the Apostles' Creed, this Confession of our Christian Faith, commonly called the Creed of* Saint Athanasius, *by the Minister and people standing.*

Quicunque vult.

WHOSOEVER will be saved: before all things it is necessary that he hold the Catholic Faith.

Which Faith except every one do keep whole and undefiled: without doubt he shall perish everlastingly.

And the Catholick Faith is this: That we worship one God in Trinity, and Trinity in Unity;

Neither confounding the Persons: nor dividing the Substance.

For there is one Person of the Father, another of the Son: and another of the Holy Ghost.

But the Godhead of the Father, of the Son, and of the Holy Ghost, is all one: the Glory equal, the Majesty co-eternal.

Such as the Father is, such is the Son: and such is the Holy Ghost.

The Father uncreate, the Son uncreate: and the Holy Ghost uncreate.

The Father incomprehensible, the Son incomprehensible; and the Holy Ghost incomprehensible.

The Father eternal, the Son eternal: and the Holy Ghost eternal.

And yet they are not three eternals: but one eternal.

As also there are not three incomprehensibles, nor three uncreated: but one uncreated, and one incomprehensible.

So likewise the Father is almighty, the Son almighty: and the Holy Ghost almighty.

And yet are they not three almighties: but one almighty.

So the Father is God, the Son God: and the Holy Ghost God.

And yet are they not three Gods: but one God.

So likewise the Father is Lord, the Son Lord: and the Holy Ghost Lord.

And yet not three Lords: but one Lord.

For like as we be compelled by the Christian verity: to acknowledge every person by himself to be God and Lord:

So are we forbidden by the Catholic Religion: to say there be three Gods, or three Lords.

The Father is made of none: neither created nor begotten.

The Son is of the Father alone: not made nor created, but begotten.

The Holy Ghost is of the Father and of the Son: neither made nor created, nor begotten, but proceeding.

So there is one Father, not three Fathers; one Son, not three Sons: one Holy Ghost, not three Holy Ghosts.

And in this Trinity none is afore nor after other: none is greater nor less than other.

But the whole three persons: be co-eternal together and coequal.

So that in all things, as is aforesaid: the Unity in Trinity, and the Trinity in Unity is to be worshipped.

He therefore that will be saved: must thus think of the Trinity.

Furthermore, it is necessary to everlasting salvation: that he also believe rightly in the Incarnation of our Lord Jesu Christ.

ated: but one uncreated, and one incomprehensible.

So likewise the Father is Almighty, the Son Almighty: and the Holy Ghost Almighty.

And yet they are not three Almighties: but one Almighty.

So the Father is God, the Son is God: and the Holy Ghost is God.

And yet they are not three Gods: but one God.

So likewise the Father is Lord, the Son Lord: and the Holy Ghost Lord.

And yet not three Lords: but one Lord.

For like as we are compelled by the Christian verity: to acknowledge every Person by himself to be God and Lord:

So are we forbidden by the Catholic Religion: to say, There be three Gods, or three Lords.

The Father is made of none: neither created, nor begotten.

The Son is of the Father alone: not made, nor created, but begotten.

The Holy Ghost is of the Father and of the Son: neither made, nor created, nor begotten, but proceeding.

So there is one Father, not three Fathers; one Son, not three Sons: one Holy Ghost, not three Holy Ghosts.

And in this Trinity none is afore, or after other: none is greater, or less than another:

But the whole three Persons are co-eternal together: and coequal.

So that in all things, as is aforesaid: the Unity in Trinity, and the Trinity in Unity is to be worshipped.

He therefore that will be saved: must thus think of the Trinity.

Furthermore, it is necessary to everlasting salvation: that he also believe rightly the Incarnation of our Lord Jesus Christ.

For the right faith is that we believe and confess: that our Lord Jesus Christ, the Son of God, is God and man;

God of the Substance of the Father, begotten before the worlds: and man of the substance of his mother, born in the world.

Perfect God, and perfect man: of a reasonable soul, and human flesh subsisting.

Equal to the Father as touching his Godhead: and inferior to the Father touching his manhood.

Who although he be God and man: yet he is not two, but one Christ.

One, not by conversion of the Godhead into flesh: but by taking of the manhood into God;

One altogether, not by confusion of substance: but by unity of person.

For as the reasonable soul and flesh is one man: so God and man is one Christ.

Who suffered for our salvation: descended into hell, rose again the third day from the dead.

He ascended into heaven, he sitteth on the right hand of the Father God, Almighty: from whence he shall come to judge the quick and the dead.

At whose coming all men shall rise again with their bodies: and shall give account of their own works.

And they that have done good, shall go into life everlasting: and they that have done evil into everlasting fire.

This is the Catholic faith: which except a man believe faithfully, he cannot be saved.

Glory be to the Father, and to the Son: and to the Holy Ghost.

As it was in the beginning, is now, and ever shall be: world without end. Amen.

Thus endeth the Order of Matins and Evensong through the whole Year.

For the right Faith is, that we believe and confess: that our Lord Jesus Christ, the Son of God, is God and Man;

God, of the Substance of the Father, begotten before the worlds: and Man, of the Substance of his Mother, born in the world;

Perfect God, and perfect Man: of a reasonable soul and human flesh subsisting;

Equal to the Father, as touching his Godhead: and inferior to the Father, as touching his Manhood.

Who although he be God and Man: yet he is not two, but one Christ;

One; not by conversion of the Godhead into flesh: but by taking of the Manhood into God;

One altogether; not by confusion of Substance: but by unity of Person.

For as the reasonable soul and flesh is one man: so God and Man is one Christ;

Who suffered for our salvation: descended into hell, rose again the third day from the dead.

He ascended into heaven, he sitteth on the right hand of the Father, God Almighty: from whence he shall come to judge the quick and the dead.

At whose coming all men shall rise again with their bodies: and shall give account for their own works.

And they that have done good shall go into life everlasting: and they that have done evil into everlasting fire.

This is the Catholic Faith: which except a man believe faithfully he cannot be saved.

Glory be to the Father, and to the Son: and to the Holy Ghost;

As it was in the beginning, is now, and ever shall be: world without end. Amen.

THE
LITANY AND SUFFRAGES.
(d)

O God the Father of heaven: have mercy upon us, miserable sinners.

O God the Father of heaven: have mercy upon us miserable sinners.

O God the Son, Redeemer of world: have mercy upon us miserable sinners.

O God the Son, Redeemer of the world: have mercy upon us miserable sinners.

O God the Holy Ghost, proceeding from the Father and the Son: have mercy upon us miserable sinners.

O God the Holy Ghost, proceeding from the Father and the Son: have mercy upon us miserable sinners.

O holy, blessed, and glorious Trinity, three Persons and one God: have mercy upon us miserable sinners.

O holy, blessed, and glorious Trinity, three persons and one God: have mercy upon us miserable sinners.

Remember not, Lord, our offences, nor the offences of our forefathers, neither take thou vengeance of our sins: spare us, good Lord, spare thy people, whom thou hast redeemed with thy most precious blood, and be not angry with us for ever.

Spare us, good Lord.

From all evil and mischief, from sin, from the crafts and assaults

(d) In 1549, the Litany is placed after the Communion Office.

THE LITANY.

¶ *Here followeth the LITANY, or General Supplication, to be sung or said after Morning Prayer upon* Sundays, Wednesdays *and* Fridays, *and at other times when it shall be commanded by the Ordinary.*

O GOD the Father, of heaven: have mercy upon us miserable sinners.

O God the Father, of heaven: have mercy upon us miserable sinners.

O God the Son, Redeemer of the world: have mercy upon us miserable sinners.

O God the Son, Redeemer of the world: have mercy upon us miserable sinners.

O God the Holy Ghost, proceeding from the Father and the Son: have mercy upon us miserable sinners.

O God the Holy Ghost, proceeding from the Father and the Son: have mercy upon us miserable sinners.

O holy, blessed, and glorious Trinity, three Persons and one God: have mercy upon us miserable sinners.

O holy, blessed, and glorious Trinity, Three Persons and one God: have mercy upon us miserable sinners.

Remember not, Lord, our offences, nor the offences of our forefathers; neither take thou vengeance of our sins: spare us, good Lord, spare thy people, whom thou hast redeemed with thy most precious blood, and be not angry with us for ever.

Spare us, good Lord.

From all evil and mischief; from sin, from the crafts and assaults of the devil, from thy wrath, and from everlasting damnation :

Good Lord, deliver us.

From blindness of heart, from pride, vain-glory, and hypocrisy, from envy, hatred, and malice, and all uncharitableness :

Good Lord, deliver us.

From fornication, and all other deadly sin, and from all the deceits of the world, the flesh, and the devil :

Good Lord, deliver us.

From lightning and tempest, from plague, pestilence, and famine, from battle and murder, and from sudden death :

Good Lord, deliver us.

From all sedition, and privy conspiracy, from the tyranny of the Bishop of Rome and all his detestable enormities, from all false doctrine and heresy, from hardness of heart, and contempt of thy word and commandment :

Good Lord, deliver us.

By the mystery of thy holy incarnation, by thy holy nativity and Circumcision, by thy Baptism, fasting, and temptation.

Good Lord, deliver us.

By thine agony and bloody sweat, by thy cross and passion, by thy precious death and burial, by thy glorious resurrection and ascension, by the coming of the Holy Ghost :

Good Lord, deliver us.

In all time of our tribulation, in all time of our wealth, in the hour of death, in the day of judgement :

Good Lord, deliver us.

We sinners do beseech thee to hear us (O Lord God) and that it may please thee to rule and govern thy holy Church universal in the right way :

We beseech thee to hear us, good Lord.

That it may please thee to keep

of the devil ; from thy wrath, and from everlasting damnation,

Good Lord, deliver us.

From all blindness of heart ; from pride, vain-glory, and hypocrisy ; from envy, hatred, and malice, and all uncharitableness,

Good Lord, deliver us.

From fornication, and all other deadly sin ; and from all the deceits of the world, the flesh, and the devil,

Good Lord, deliver us.

From lightning and tempest ; from plague, pestilence, and famine ; from battle and murder, and from sudden death,

Good Lord, deliver us.

From all sedition, privy conspiracy, and rebellion ;

from all false doctrine, heresy, and schism ; from hardness of heart, and contempt of thy Word, and Commandment,

Good Lord, deliver us.

By the mystery of thy holy Incarnation ; by thy holy Nativity and Circumcision ; by thy Baptism, Fasting, and Temptation,

Good Lord, deliver us.

By thine Agony and bloody Sweat ; by thy Cross and Passion ; by thy precious Death and Burial ; by thy glorious Resurrection and Ascension ; and by the coming of the Holy Ghost,

Good Lord, deliver us.

In all time of our tribulation ; in all time of our wealth ; in the hour of death, and in the day of judgement,

Good Lord, deliver us.

We sinners do beseech thee to hear us, O Lord God ; and that it may please thee to rule and govern thy holy Church universal in the right way ;

We beseech thee to hear us, good Lord.

That it may please thee to keep and strengthen in the true wor-

	shipping of thee, in righteousness and holiness of life, thy Servant *VICTORIA*, our most gracious Queen and Governour;
Edward the vi., thy servant our king and governor:	
We beseech thee to hear us, good Lord.	*We beseech thee to hear us good Lord.*
That it may please thee to rule his heart in thy faith, fear, and love, that he may always have affiance in thee, and ever seek thy honour and glory:	That it may please thee to rule her heart, in thy faith, fear, and love, and that she may evermore have affiance in thee, and ever seek thy honour and glory;
We beseech thee to hear us, good Lord.	*We beseech thee to hear us, good Lord.*
That it may please thee to be his defender and keeper, giving him the victory over all his enemies:	That it may please thee to be her defender and keeper, giving her the victory over all her enemies;
We beseech thee to hear us good Lord.	*We beseech thee to hear us, good Lord.*
	That it may please thee to bless and preserve *Albert Edward* Prince of *Wales*, the Princess of *Wales*, and all the Royal family;
	We beseech thee to hear us, good Lord.
That it may please thee to illuminate all Bishops, pastors, and ministers of the Church, with true knowledge and understanding of thy word, and that both by their preaching and living they may set it forth, and shew it accordingly:	That it may please the to illuminate all Bishops, Priests, and Deacons, with true knowledge and understanding of thy Word; and that both by their preaching and living they may set it forth, and shew it accordingly;
We beseech thee to hear us, good Lord.	*We beseech thee to hear us good Lord.*
That it may please thee to endue the Lords of the council, and all the nobility, with grace, wisdom, and understanding:	That it may please thee to endue the Lords of the Council, and all the Nobility, with grace, wisdom, and understanding;
We beseech thee to hear us, good Lord.	*We beseech thee to hear us, good Lord.*
That it may please thee to bless and keep the magistrates, giving them grace to execute justice, and to maintain truth:	That it may please thee to bless and keep the Magistrates, giving them grace to execute justice, and to maintain truth;
We beseech thee to hear us, good Lord.	*We beseech thee to hear us, good Lord.*
That it may please thee to bless and keep all thy people:	That it may please thee to bless and keep all thy people;
We beseech thee to hear us, good Lord.	*We beseech thee to hear us, good Lord.*

That it may please thee to give to all nations unity, peace, and concord:

We beseech thee to hear us, good Lord.

That it may please thee to give us an heart to love and dread thee, and diligently to live after thy commandments:

We beseech thee to hear us, good Lord.

That it may please thee to give all thy people increase of grace, to hear meekly thy word, and to receive it with pure affection, and to bring forth the fruits of the Spirit:

We beseech thee to hear us, good Lord.

That it may please thee to bring into the way of truth all such as have erred and are deceived.

We beseech thee to hear us, good Lord.

That it may please thee to strengthen such as do stand, and to comfort and help the weak-hearted, and to raise up them that fall, and finally to beat down Satan under our feet:

We beseech thee to hear us, good Lord.

That it may please thee to succour, help, and comfort all that be in danger, necessity, and tribulation:

We beseech thee to hear us, good Lord.

That it may please thee to preserve all that travel by land or by water, all women labouring of child, all sick persons, and young children, and to shew thy pity upon all prisoners and captives:

We beseech thee to hear us, good Lord.

That it may please thee to defend and provide for the fatherless children and widows, and all that be desolate and oppressed:

We beseech thee to hear us, good Lord.

That it may please thee to give to all nations unity, peace, and concord;

We beseech thee to hear us, good Lord.

That it may please thee to give us an heart to love and dread thee, and diligently to live after thy commandments;

We beseech thee to hear us, good Lord.

That it may please thee to give to all thy people increase of grace to hear meekly thy Word, and to receive it with pure affection, and to bring forth the fruits of the Spirit;

We beseech thee to hear us, good Lord.

That it may please thee to bring into the way of truth all such as have erred, and are deceived;

We beseech thee to hear us good Lord.

That it may please thee to strengthen such as do stand; and to comfort and help the weak-hearted; and to raise up them that fall; and finally to beat down Satan under our feet;

We beseech thee to hear us, good Lord.

That it may please thee to succour, help, and comfort, all that are in danger, necessity, and tribulation;

We beseech thee to hear, us good Lord.

That it may please thee to preserve all that travel by land or by water, all women labouring of child, all sick persons, and young children; and to shew thy pity upon all prisoners and captives;

We beseech thee to hear us good Lord.

That it may please thee to defend, and provide for, the fatherless children, and widows, and all that are desolate and oppressed;

We beseech thee to hear us, good Lord.

That it may please thee to have mercy upon all men:
We beseech thee to hear us, good Lord.

That it may please thee to forgive our enemies, persecutors, and slanderers, and to turn their hearts:
We beseech thee to hear us, good Lord.

That it may please thee to give and preserve to our use the kindly fruits of the earth, so as in due time we may enjoy them:
We beseech thee to hear us, good Lord.

That it may please thee to give us true repentance; to forgive us all our sins, negligences, and ignorances, and to endue us with the grace of thy holy Spirit to amend our lives according to thy holy word:
We beseech thee to hear us, good Lord.

Son of God: we beseech thee to hear us.
Son of God: we beseech thee to hear us.

O Lamb of God, that takest away the sins of the world:
Grant us thy peace.

O Lamb of God, that takest away the sins of the world:
Have mercy upon us.

O Christ, hear us.
O Christ, hear us.

Lord, have mercy upon us.
Lord, have mercy upon us.

Christ, have mercy upon us.
Christ, have mercy upon us.

Lord, have mercy upon us.
Lord, have mercy us.

Our Father which art in heaven.
With the residue of the Paternoster.

And lead us not into temptation.
But deliver us from evil.

That it may please thee to have mercy upon all men.
We beseech thee to hear us, good Lord.

That it may please thee to forgive our enemies, persecutors, and slanderers, and to turn their hearts;
We beseech thee to hear us, good Lord.

That it may please thee to give and preserve to our use the kindly fruits of the earth, so as in due time we may enjoy them;
We beseech thee to hear us, good Lord.

That it may please thee to give us true repentance; to forgive us all our sins, negligences, and ignorances; and to endue us with the grace of thy Holy Spirit to amend our lives according to thy holy Word;
We beseech thee to hear us, good Lord.

Son of God: we beseech thee to hear us.
Son of God: we beseech thee to hear us.

O Lamb of God: that takest away the sins of the world;
Grant us thy peace.

O Lamb of God: that takest away the sins of the world;
Have mercy upon us.

O Christ, hear us.
O Christ hear us.

Lord, have mercy upon us.
Lord, have mercy upon us.

Christ, have mercy upon us.
Christ have mercy upon us.

Lord, have mercy upon us.
Lord, have mercy upon us.

¶ *Then shall the Priest, and the people with him, say the Lord's Prayer.*

OUR Father, which art in heaven, Hallowed be thy Name. Thy kingdom come. Thy will be done in earth, As it is in heaven. Give us this day our daily bread. And forgive us our trespasses, As we forgive them that trespass

The Versicle. O Lord, deal not with us after our sins.

The Answer. Neither reward us after our iniquities.

Let us pray.

O God merciful Father, that despisest not the sighing of a contrite heart, nor the desire of such as be sorrowful, mercifully assist our prayers, that we make before thee in all our troubles and adversities, whensoever they oppress us: And graciously hear us, that those evils, which the craft and subtilty of the devil or man worketh against us, be brought to nought, and by the providence of thy goodness they may be dispersed, that we thy servants, being hurt by no persecutions, may evermore give thanks unto thee, in thy holy Church: through Jesu Christ our Lord.

O Lord, arise, help us, and deliver us for thy name's sake.

O God, we have heard with our ears, and our fathers have declared unto us, the noble works that thou didst in their days, and in the old time before them.

O Lord, arise, help us, and deliver us, for thine honour.

Glory be to the Father, and to the Son, and to the Holy Ghost: as it was in the beginning, is now, and ever shall be world without end. Amen.

From our enemies defend us, O Christ.

Graciously look upon our afflictions.

Pitifully behold the sorrows of our heart.

Mercifully forgive the sins of thy people.

Favourably with mercy hear our prayers.

against us. And lead us not into temptation; But deliver us from evil. Amen.

Priest. O Lord, deal not with us after our sins.

Answer. Neither reward us after our iniquities.

Let us pray.

O God, merciful Father, that despisest not the sighing of a contrite heart, nor the desire of such as be sorrowful; Mercifully assist our prayers that we make before thee in all our troubles and adversities, whensoever they oppress us; and graciously hear us, that those evils, which the craft and subtility of the devil or man worketh against us, be brought to nought; and by the providence of thy goodness they may be dispersed; that we thy servants, being hurt by no persecutions, may evermore give thanks unto thee in thy holy Church; through Jesus Christ our Lord.

O Lord, arise, help us, and deliver us, for thy Name's sake.

O GOD, we have heard with our ears, and our fathers have declared unto us, the noble works that thou didst in their days, and in the old time before them.

O Lord, arise, help us, and deliver us, for thine honour.

Glory be to the Father, and to the Son: and to the Holy Ghost;

Answer. As it was in the beginning, is now, and ever shall be: world without end. Amen.

From our enemies defend us, O Christ.

Graciously look upon our afflictions.

Pitifully behold the sorrows of our hearts.

Mercifully forgive the sins of thy people.

Favourable with mercy hear our prayers.

O Son of David, have mercy upon us.

Both now and ever vouchsafe to hear us, Christ.

Graciously hear us, O Christ.

Graciously hear us, O Lord Christ.

The Versicle. O Lord, let thy mercy be shewed upon us.

The Answer. As we do put our trust in thee.

Let us pray.

We humbly beseech thee, O Father, mercifully to look upon our infirmities, and for the glory of thy name's sake, turn from us all those evils that we most righteously have deserved; and grant that in all our troubles we may put our whole trust and confidence in thy mercy, and evermore serve thee in pureness of living, to thy honour and glory: through our only mediator and advocate Jesus Christ our Lord. Amen.

Almighty God, which hast given us grace at this time with one accord to make our common suplications unto thee, and dost promise, that when two or three be gathered in thy name, thou wilt grant their requests: fulfil now O Lord, the desires and petitions of thy servants, as may be most expedient for them, granting us in this world knowledge of thy truth, and in the world to come, life everlasting. Amen.

O Son of David, have mercy upon us.

Both now and ever vouchsafe to hear us, O Christ.

Graciously hear us, O Christ: graciously hear us, O Lord Christ.

Priest. O Lord, let thy mercy be shewed upon us;

Answer. As we do put our trust in thee.

Let us pray.

WE humbly beseech thee, O Father, mercifully to look upon our infirmities; and for the glory of thy Name turn from us all those evils that we most righteously have deserved; and grant, that in all our troubles we may put our whole trust and confidence in thy mercy, and evermore serve thee in holiness and pureness of living, to thy honour and glory; through our only Mediator and Advocate, Jesus Christ our Lord. *Amen.*

A Prayer of St. Chrysostom.

ALMIGHTY God, who hast given us grace at this time with one accord to made our common supplications unto thee; and dost promise, that when two or three are gathered together in thy Name thou wilt grant their requests; Fulfil now, O Lord, the desires and petitions of thy servants, as may be most expedient for them; granting us in this world knowledge of thy truth, and in the world to come life everlasting. *Amen.*

2 Cor. xiii.

THE grace of our Lord Jesus Christ, and the love of God, and the fellowship of the Holy Ghost, be with us all evermore. *Amen.*

Here endeth the LITANY.

Prayers and Thanksgivings,

upon several occasions.

¶ *To be used before the two final Prayers of the Litany, or of Morning and Evening Prayer.*

PRAYERS.

For Rain. (e)

O GOD, heavenly Father, who by thy Son Jesus Christ hast promised to all them that seek thy kingdom, and the righteousness thereof, all things necessary to their bodily sustenance; Send us, we beseech thee, in this our necessity, such moderate rain and showers, that we may receive the fruits of the earth to our comfort, and to thy honour; through Jesus Christ our Lord.. *Amen.*

For fair Weather. (f)

O ALMIGHTY Lord God, who for the sin of man didst once drown all the world, except eight persons, and afterward of thy great mercy didst promise never to destroy it so again; We humbly beseech thee, that although we for our iniquities have worthily deserved a plague of rain and waters, yet upon our true repentance thou wilt send us such weather, as that we may receive the fruits of the earth in due season; and learn both by thy punishment to amend our lives, and for thy clemency to give thee praise and glory; through Jesus Christ our Lord. *Amen.*

In the time of Dearth and Famine.

O GOD, heavenly Father, whose gift it is that the rain doth fall, the earth is fruitful, beasts increase, and fishes do multiply;

(e) In 1549, the prayer for Rain is placed after the Collects, at end of Communion Office.

(f) In 1549, the prayer for fair Weather is placed after the Collects, at end of Communion Office.

Behold, we beseech thee, the afflictions of thy people; and grant that the scarcity and dearth, which we do now most justly suffer for our iniquity, may through thy goodness be mercifully turned into cheapness and plenty; for the love of Jesus Christ our Lord, to whom with thee and the Holy Ghost be all honour and glory, now and for ever. *Amen.*

Or this,

O GOD, merciful Father, who, in the time of Elisha the prophet, didst suddenly in Samaria turn great scarcity and dearth into plenty and cheapness; Have mercy upon us, that we, who are now for our sins punished with like adversity, may likewise find a seasonable relief: Increase the fruits of the earth by thy heavenly benediction; and grant that we, receiving thy bountiful liberality, may use the same to thy glory, the relief of those that are needy, and our own comfort; through Jesus Christ our Lord. *Amen.*

In the time of War and Tumults.

O ALMIGHTY God, King of all kings, and Governour of all things, whose power no creature is able to resist, to whom it belongeth justly to punish sinners, and to be merciful to them that truly repent; Save and deliver us, we humbly beseech thee, from the hands of our enemies; abate their pride, asswage their malice, and confound their devices; that we, being armed with thy defence, may be preserved evermore from all perils, to glorify thee, who art the only giver of all victory; through the merits of thy only Son, Jesus Christ our Lord. *Amen.*

In the time of any common Plague or Sickness.

O ALMIGHTY God, who in thy wrath didst send a plague upon thine own people in the wilderness, for their obstinate rebellion against Moses and Aaron; and also, in the time of king David, didst slay with the plague of Pestilence threescore and ten thousand, and yet remembering thy mercy didst save the rest; Have pity upon us miserable sinners, who now are visited with great sickness and mortality; that like as thou didst then accept of an atonement, and didst command the destroying Angel to cease from punishing, so it may now please thee to withdraw from us this plague and grievous sickness; through Jesus Christ our Lord. *Amen.*

¶ *In the Ember Weeks, to be said every day, for those that are to be admitted into Holy Orders.*

ALMIGHTY God, our heavenly Father, who hast purchased to thyself an universal Church by the precious blood of thy dear Son; Mercifully look upon the same, and at this time so guide and govern the minds of thy servants the Bishops and Pastors of thy flock, that they may lay hands suddenly on no man, but faithfully and wisely make choice of fit persons to serve in the sacred Ministry of thy Church. And to those which shall be ordained to any holy function give thy grace and heavenly benediction; that both by their life and doctrine they may set forth thy glory, and set forward the salvation of all men; through Jesus Christ our Lord. *Amen.*

Or this,

ALMIGHTY God, the giver of all good gifts, who of thy divine providence hast appointed divers orders in thy Church; Give thy grace, we humbly beseech thee, to all those who are to be called to any office and administration in the same; and so replenish them with the truth of thy doctrine, and endue them with innocency of life, that they may faithfully serve before thee, to the glory of thy great Name, and the benefit of thy holy Church; through Jesus Christ our Lord. *Amen.*

¶ *A Prayer that may be said after any of the former.*

O GOD, whose nature and property is ever to have mercy and to forgive, receive our humble petitions; and though we be tied and bound with the chain of our sins, yet let the pitifulness of thy great mercy loose us; for the honour of Jesus Christ, our Mediator and Advocate. *Amen.*

¶ *A Prayer for the High Court of Parliament, to be read during their Session.*

MOST gracious God, we humbly beseech thee, as for this Kingdom in general, so especially for the High Court of Parliament, under our most religious and gracious Queen at this time assembled: That thou wouldst be pleased to direct and prosper all their consultations to the advancement of thy glory, the good of thy Church, the safety, honour, and welfare of our Sovereign, and her Dominions; that all things may be so ordered and settled by their endeavours, upon the best and surest foundations, that peace and happiness, truth and justice, religion and piety, may be established among us for all generations. These and all other necessaries, for them, for us, and thy whole Church, we humbly beg in the Name and Mediation of Jesus Christ our most blessed Lord and Saviour. *Amen.*

¶ *A Collect or Prayer for all Conditions of men, to be used at such times when the Litany is not appointed to be said.*

O GOD, the Creator and Preserver of all mankind, we humbly beseech thee for all sorts and conditions of men; that thou wouldst be pleased to make thy ways known unto them, thy saving health unto all nations. More especially, we pray for the good estate of the Catholick Church; that it may be so guided and governed by thy good Spirit, that all who profess and call themselves Christians may be led into the way of truth, and hold the faith in unity of spirit, in the bond of peace, and in righteousness of life. Finally, we commend to thy fatherly goodness all those, who are any ways afflicted, or distressed, in mind, body, or estate; [**especially those for whom our prayers are desired*,] that it may please thee to comfort and relieve them, according to their several necessities, giving them patience under their sufferings, and a happy issue out of all their afflictions. And this we beg for Jesus Christ his sake. *Amen.*

* This to be said when any desire the Prayers of the Congregation.

¶ *A General Thanksgiving.*

ALMIGHTY God, Father of all mercies, we thine unworthy servants do give thee most humble and hearty thanks for all thy goodness and loving-kindness to us and to all men; [**particularly to those who desire now to offer up their praises and thanksgivings for thy late mercies vouchsafed unto them.*] We bless thee for our creation, preservation, and all the blessings of this life; but above all, for thine inestimable love in the redemption of the world by our Lord Jesus Christ; for the means of grace, and for the hope of glory. And, we beseech thee, give us that due sense of all thy mercies, that our hearts may be unfeignedly thankful, and that we shew forth thy praise, not only with our lips, but in our lives; by giving up ourselves to thy service, and by walking before thee in holiness and righteousness all our days; through Jesus Christ our Lord, to whom with thee and the Holy Ghost be all honour and glory, world without end. *Amen.*

* This to be said when any that have been prayed for desire to return praise.

For Rain.

O GOD our heavenly Father, who by thy gracious providence dost cause the former and the latter rain to descend upon the earth, that it may bring forth fruit for the use of man; We give thee humble thanks that it hath pleased thee, in our great necessity, to send us at the last a joyful rain upon thine inheritance, and to refresh it when it was dry, to the great comfort of us thy unworthy servants, and to the glory of thy holy Name; through thy mercies in Jesus Christ our Lord. *Amen.*

For fair Weather.

O LORD God, who hast justly humbled us by thy late plague of immoderate rain and waters, and in thy mercy hast relieved and comforted our souls by this seasonable and blessed change of weather; We praise and glorify thy holy Name for this thy mercy, and will always declare thy loving-kindness from generation to generation; through Jesus Christ our Lord. *Amen.*

For Plenty.

O MOST merciful Father, who of thy gracious goodness hast heard the devout prayers of thy Church, and turned our dearth and scarcity into cheapness and plenty; We give thee humble thanks for this thy special bounty; beseeching thee to continue thy loving-kindness unto us, that our land may yield us her fruits of increase, to thy glory and our comfort; through Jesus Christ our Lord. *Amen.*

¶ *For Peace and Deliverance from our Enemies.*

O ALMIGHTY God, who art a strong tower of defence unto thy servants against the face of their enemies; We yield thee praise and thanksgiving for our deliverance from those great and apparent dangers wherewith we were compassed: We acknowledge it thy goodness that we were not delivered over as a prey unto them; beseeching thee still to continue such thy mercies towards us, that all the world may know that thou art our Saviour and mighty Deliverer; through Jesus Christ our Lord. *Ameu.*

For restoring Publick Peace at Home.

O ETERNAL God, our heavenly Father, who alone makest men to be of one mind in a house, and stillest the outrage of a violent and unruly people; We bless thy holy Name, that it hath pleased thee to appease the seditious tumults which have been lately raised up amongst us; most humbly beseeching thee to grant to all of us grace, that we may henceforth obediently walk in thy holy commandments; and, leading a quiet and peaceable life in all godliness and honesty, may continually offer unto thee our sacrifice of praise and thanksgiving for these thy mercies towards us; through Jesus Christ our Lord. *Amen.*

For Deliverance from the Plague, or other common Sickness.

O LORD God, who hast wounded us for our sins, and consumed us for our transgressions, by thy late heavy and dreadful visitation; and now, in the midst of judgement remembering mercy, hast redeemed our souls from the jaws of death; We offer unto thy fatherly goodness ourselves, our souls and bodies which thou hast delivered, to be a living sacrifice unto thee, always praising and magnifying thy mercies in the midst of thy Church; through Jesus our Lord. *Amen.*

Or this,

WE humbly acknowledge before thee, O most merciful Father, that all the punishments which are threatened in thy law might justly have fallen upon us, by reason of our manifold transgressions and hardness of heart: Yet seeing it hath pleased thee of thy tender mercy, upon our weak and unworthy humiliation, to asswage the contagious sickness wherewith we lately have been sore afflicted, and to restore the voice of joy and health into our dwellings; We offer unto thy Divine Majesty the sacrifice of praise and thanksgiving, lauding and magnifying thy glorious Name for such thy preservation and providence over us; through Jesus Christ our Lord. *Amen.*

THE INTROITS, COLLECTS, EPISTLES AND GOSPELS. (*g*)

TO BE USED AT THE CELEBRATION OF THE LORD'S SUPPER AND HOLY COMMUNION, THROUGH THE YEAR: WITH PROPER PSALMS AND LESSONS FOR DIVERS FEASTS AND DAYS.

¶ *The first Sunday in Advent.*

Beatus vir. Psalm i.

BLESSED is that man that hath not walked......

Glory be to the Father, and to the Son, and to the Holy Ghost;

As it was in the beginning, and is now, and ever shall be: world without end. Amen.

And so must every Introit be ended.

Let us pray.

The Collect.

ALMIGHTY God, give us grace that we may cast away the works of darkness, and put upon us the armour of light, now in the time of this mortal life, (in the which thy Son Jesus Christ came to visit us in great humility:) that in the last day, when he shall come again in his glorious majesty, to judge both the quick and the dead, we may rise to the life immortal, through him, who liveth and reigneth with thee and the Holy Ghost, now and ever. Amen.

(*g*) The Introits, Epistles, and Gospels are printed entire, from the Great Bible (1539), in the Prayer Book of 1549, but the Editor has not thought it here needful to give more than the opening words.

THE COLLECTS, EPISTLES, AND GOSPELS (*h*)

TO BE USED THROUGHOUT THE YEAR.

¶ *Note, that the Collect appointed for every Sunday, or for any Holy-day that hath a Vigil or Eve, shall be said at the Evening Service next before.*

THE FIRST SUNDAY IN ADVENT.

The Collect.

ALMIGHTY God, give us grace that we may cast away the works of darkness, and put upon us the armour of light, now in the time of this mortal life, in which thy Son Jesus Christ came to visit us in great humility; that in the last day, when he shall come again in his glorious Majesty to judge both the quick and dead, we may rise to the life immortal, through him who liveth and reigneth with thee and the Holy Ghost, now and ever. *Amen.*

¶ *This Collect is to be repeated every day, with the other Collects in Advent, until Christmas Eve.*

(*h*) The Epistles and Gospels are printed entire, from the Authorized Version (1604), in the Book of Common Prayer (1886) but it has not been thought needful to give here more than the opening words.

The Epistle. Rom. xiii. Owe nothing to any man but this......

The Gospel. Matt. xxi. And when they drew nigh, to Jerusalem..

The second Sunday.

Ad Dominum cum tribularer. Psalm cxx,

WHEN I was in trouble I called upon the Lord,......

The Collect.

BLESSED Lord, who hast caused all holy scriptures to be written for our learning: grant us that we may in such wise hear them, read, mark, learn, and inwardly digest them, that by patience and comfort of thy holy word, we may embrace and ever hold fast the blessed hope of everlasting life, which thou hast given us in our Saviour Jesus Christ.

The Epistle. Roma. xv. Whatsoever things are written......

The Gospel. Luc. xxi. There shall be signs in the sun and in moon......

The third Sunday.

Cum invocarem. Psalm iv.

HEAR me when I call, O God...

The Collect.

LORD, we beseech thee, give ear to our prayers, and by thy gracious visitation lighten the darkness of our heart, by our Lord Jesus Christ.

The Epistle. Rom. xiii. 8.

OWE no man any thing, but to love one another: for......

The Gospel. St. Matt. xxi. 1.

WHEN they drew nigh unto Jerusalem, and were come to Bethphage, unto the mount......

THE SECOND SUNDAY IN ADVENT.

The Collect.

BLESSED Lord, who hast caused all holy Scriptures to be written for our learning: Grant that we may in such wise hear them, read, mark, learn, and inwardly digest them, that by patience and comfort of thy holy Word, we may embrace, and ever hold fast the blessed hope of everlasting life, which thou hast given us in our Saviour Jesus Christ. *Amen.*

The Epistle. Rom. xv. 4.

WHATSOEVER things were written aforetime, were written for our learning; that......

The Gospel. St. Luke, xxi. 25.

AND there shall be signs in the sun, and in the moon, and in the stars; and upon......

THE THIRD SUNDAY IN ADVENT.

The Collect.

O LORD Jesu Christ, who at thy first coming didst send thy messenger to prepare thy way before thee; Grant that the min-

The Epistle. 1 Cori. iv. Let a man this wise esteem......

The Gospel. Math. xi. When John being in prison heard the works......

¶ *The fourth Sunday.*

Verba mea auribus. Psalm v.

PONDER my words, O Lord: consider......

The Collect.

LORD, raise up (we pray thee) thy power, and come among us, and with great might succour us, that whereas through our sins and wickedness we be sore let and hindered, thy bountiful grace and mercy, through the satisfaction of thy Son our Lord, may speedily deliver us; to whom with thee and the Holy Ghost be honour and glory world without end.

The Epistle. Philip. iv. Rejoice in the Lord alway, and again. ......

The Gospel. John i. This is the record of John, when the Jews...

isters and stewards of thy mysteries may likewise so prepare and make ready thy way, by turning the hearts of the disobedient to the wisdom of the just, that at thy second coming to judge the world we may be found an acceptable people in thy sight, who livest and reignest with the Father and the Holy Spirit, ever one God, world without end. *Amen,*

The Epistle. 1 Cor. iv. 1.

LET a man so account of us, as of the ministers of Christ, and stewards of the mysteries ......

The Gospel. St. Matt. xi. 2.

NOW when John had heard in the prison the works of Christ, he sent two of his......

THE FOURTH SUNDAY IN ADVENT.

The Collect.

O LORD, raise up (we pray thee) thy power, and come among us, and with great might succour us, that whereas, through our sins and wickedness, we are sore let and hindered in running the race that is set before us, thy bountiful grace and mercy may speedily help and deliver us; through the satisfaction of thy Son our Lord, to whom with thee and the Holy Ghost be honour and glory, world without end. *Amen.*

The Epistle. Phil. iv. 4.

REJOICE in the Lord alway, and again I say, Rejoice......

The Gospel. St. John i. 19.

THIS is the record of John, when the Jews sent Priests...

Proper Psalms and Lessons on Christmas Day.

¶ *At Matins.*

Psalms xix. xlv. lxxxv.

The first lesson, Esai. ix. *unto the end.*
The second lesson, Math. i. *unto the end.*

¶ *At the first Communion.*

Cantate Domino. Psalm xcviii.

O SING unto the Lord a new song: for he......

The Collect.

GOD, which makest us glad with the yearly remembrance of the birth of thy only Son Jesus Christ; grant that as we joyfully receive him for our Redeemer, so we may with sure confidence behold him, when he shall come to be our Judge, who liveth and reigneth, &c.

The Epistle. Tit. ii. The grace of God that bringeth......

The Gospel. Luc. ii. And it chanced in those days that there went......

¶ *At the Second Communion.*

Domine Dominus noster. Psalm viii.

O LORD our governour, how excellent......

The Collect.

ALMIGHTY God, which hast given us thy only-begotten Son to take our nature upon him, and this day to be born of a pure virgin; Grant that we being regenerate, and made thy children by adoption and grace, may daily be renewed by thy Holy Spirit, through the same our Lord Jesus Christ, who liveth and reigneth, &c.

THE NATIVITY OF OUR LORD, OR THE BIRTH-DAY OF CHRIST,

COMMONLY CALLED

CHRISTMAS-DAY.

The Collect.

ALMIGHTY God, who hast given us thy only-begotten Son to take our nature upon him, and as at this time to be born of a pure Virgin; grant that we being regenerate, and made thy children by adoption and grace, may daily be renewed by thy Holy Spirit; through the same our Lord Jesus Christ, who liveth and reigneth with thee and the same Spirit, ever one God, world without end. *Amen.*

The Epistle. Hebre. i. God in times past diversely......

The Gospel. John i. In the beginning was the word......

Proper Psalms and Lessons at Evensong. Psalms lxxxix. cx. cxxxii.

The first lesson, Esai. vii. "God spake once again to Achas," &c....*unto the end.*

The second lesson, Tit. iii. "The kindness and love of our Saviour," &c. *unto* "foolish questions."

¶ *St. Stephin's Day.*

¶ *At Matins.*

The second lesson, Acts vi. vii. "Stephin full of faith and power," *unto*, "And when forty years."

At the Communion. Quid gloriaris in malicia? Psalm lii.

Why boastest thou thyself, thou tyrant......

The Collect.

GRANT us, O Lord, to learn to love our enemies by the example of thy martyr Saint Stephin, who prayed to thee for his persecutors; which livest and reignest, &c.

Then shall follow a Collect of the Nativity.

The Epistle. Heb. i. 1.

GOD, who at sundry times, and in divers manners spake in time past unto the fathers by......

The Gospel. St. John i. 1.

IN the beginning was the Word, and the Word was with God. and the Word was God......

ST. STEPHEN'S DAY.

The Collect.

GRANT, O Lord, that, in all our sufferings here upon earth for the testimony of thy truth, we may steadfastly look up to heaven, and by faith behold the glory that shall be revealed; and, being filled with the holy Ghost, may learn to love and bless our persecutors by the example of thy first Martyr Saint Stephen, who prayed for his murderers to thee, O blessed Jesus, who standest at the right hand of God to succour all those that suffer for thee, our only Mediator and Advocate. *Amen.*

¶ *Then shall follow the Collect of the Nativity which shall be said continually unto New-year's Eve.*

The Epistle. Acts vii. And Stephen being full of the Holy Ghost ......

The Gospel. Math. xxiii. Behold, I send unto you prophets and wise men......

The second Lesson at Evensong.

Acts vii. ¶ "And when forty years were expired, there appeared unto Moses," *unto* "Stephin full of the Holy Ghost," &c.

¶ *Saint John Evangelist's Day.*

At Matins.

¶ The second lesson, Apoca. i. *unto the end.*

At the Communion.

In Domino confido. Psalm xi.

In the Lord put I my trust: how......

The Collect.

MERCIFUL Lord, we beseech thee to cast thy bright beams of light upon thy Church: that it being lightened by the doctrine of thy blessed Apostle and Evangelist John may attain to thy everlasting gifts: through Jesus Christ our Lord.

The Epistle. 1 John i. That which was from the beginning......

The Gospel. John xxi. Jesus said unto Peter......

For the Epistle. Acts vii. 55.

STEPHEN, being full of the holy Ghost, looked up stedfastly into heaven, and saw the......

The Gospel. St. Matt. xxiii. 34.

BEHOLD, I send unto you prophets, and wise men, and scribes; and some of them ye......

SAINT JOHN THE EVANGELIST'S DAY.

The Collect.

MERCIFUL Lord, we beseech thee to cast thy bright beams of light upon thy Church, that it being enlightened by the doctrine of thy blessed Apostle and Evangelist Saint John may so walk in the light of thy truth, that it may at length attain to the light of everlasting life; through Jesus Christ our Lord. *Amen.*

The Epistle. 1 St. John i. 1.

THAT which was from the beginning, which we have heard, which we have seen......

The Gospel. St. John xxi. 19.

JESUS said unto Peter, Follow me. Then Peter......

¶ *At Evensong.*

¶ The second lesson, Apoca. xxii. *unto the end.*

¶ *The Innocents' Day.*

¶ *At Matins.*

¶ The first lesson, Hiere, xxxi. *unto*, "Moreover I heard Ephraim."

Deus, venerunt gentes. Psalm lxxix.

O God, the heathen are come into thine inheritance......

The Collect.

Almighty God, whose praise this day the young innocents thy witnesses hath confessed, and shewed forth, not in speaking, but in dying: mortify and kill all vices in us, that in our conversation, our life may express thy faith, which with our tongues we do confess: through Jesus Christ our Lord.

The Epistle. Apoca. xiv. I looked, and lo a lamb stood on the......

The Gospel. Matt. ii. The angel of the Lord appeared......

¶ *The Sunday after Christmas Day.*

Levavi oculos. Psalm cxxi.

I will lift up mine eyes unto the hills......

The Collect.

Almighty God, which hast given us, &c. *as upon Christmas Day.*

The Innocents' Day.

The Collect.

O ALMIGHTY God, who out of the mouths of babes and sucklings hast ordained strength, and madest infants to glorify thee by their deaths; Mortify and kill all vices in us, and so strengthen us by thy grace, that by the innocency of our lives, and constancy of our faith even unto death, we may glorify thy holy Name; through Jesus Christ our Lord. *Amen.*

For the Epistle. Rev. xiv. 1.

I LOOKED, and lo, a Lamb stood on the mount Sion...

The Gospel. St. Matt. ii. 13.

THE Angel of the Lord appeareth to Joseph in a dream, saying, Arise, and take the......

The Sunday after Christmas-Day.

The Collect.

ALMIGHTY God, who hast given us thy only-begotten Son to take our nature upon him,

The Epistle. Gala. iv. And I say, that the heir as long as......

The Gospel. Math. i. This is the book of the generation......

¶ *The Circumcision of Christ.*

At Matins.

The first lesson, Gene. xvii. *unto the end.*
The second lesson, Rom. ii. *unto the end.*

At the Communion.

Lætatus sum. Psalm cxxii.

I WAS glad when they said unto me......

The Collect.

ALMIGHTY God, which madest thy blessed Son to be circumcised and obedient to the law for man: grant us the true circumcision of thy Spirit: that our hearts, and all our members, being mortified from all worldly and carnal lusts, may in all things obey thy blessed will, through the same thy Son Jesus Christ our Lord.

The Epistle. Rom. iv. Blessed is that man to whom the......

and as at this time to be born of a pure Virgin; Grant that we being regenerate, and made thy children by adoption and grace, may daily be renewed by thy Holy Spirit; through the same our Lord Jesus Christ, who liveth and reigneth with thee and the same Spirit: ever one God, world without end. *Amen.*

The Epistle. Gal. iv. 1.

NOW I say, that the heir, as long as he is a child,......

The Gospel. St. Matt. i. 18.

THE birth of Jesus Christ was on this wise: When as......

THE CIRCUMCISION OF CHRIST.

The Collect.

ALMIGHTY God, who madest thy blessed Son to be circumcised, and obedient to the law for man; Grant us the true circumcision of the Spirit; that, our hearts, and all our members, being mortified from all worldly and carnal lusts, we may in all things obey thy blessed will; through the same thy Son Jesus Christ our Lord, *Amen.*

The Epistle. Rom. iv. 8.

BLESSED is the man to whom the Lord will not impute sin. Cometh this blessedness then......

The Gospel. Luc. ii. And it fortuned, as soon as the angels were gone......

¶ *At Evensong.*

The first lesson, Deute. x. "And now Israel," *unto the end.*

The second lesson, Coloss. ii. *unto the end.*

The Epiphany.

At Matins.

The first lesson, Esai. lx. *unto the end.*

The second lesson, Luke iii. "And it fortuned," *unto the end.*

[*At the Communion.*]

[*Cantate Domino.*] Psalm xcvi.

O SING unto the Lord a new song ......

The Collect.

[O] GOD, which by the leading of a star didst manifest thy only-begotten Son to the Gentiles; Mercifully grant, that we, which know thee now by faith, may after this life have the fruition of thy glorious Godhead; through Christ our Lord.

The Epistle. Ephe. iii. For this cause I Paul,......

The Gospel. Matt. ii. When Jesus was born,......

At Evensong.

The first lesson, Esai. xlix. *unto the end.*

The second lesson, John ii. "After this he went down to Capernaum," *unto the end.*

The Gospel. St. Luke ii. 15.

AND it came to pass as the angels were gone away from them into heaven, the ....

¶ *The same Collect, Epistle, and Gospel shall serve for every day after unto the Epiphany.*

THE EPIPHANY,

OR THE MANIFESTATION OF CHRIST TO THE GENTILES.

The Collect.

O GOD, who by the leading of a star didst manifest thy only-begotten Son to the Gentiles; Mercifully grant, that we, which know thee now by faith, may after this life have the fruition of thy glorious Godhead; through Jesus Christ our Lord. *Amen.*

The Epistle. Ephes. iii. 1.

FOR this cause, I Paul, the prisoner of Jesus Christ for you Gentiles; if ye have heard......

The Gospel. St. Matt. ii. 1.

WHEN Jesus was born in Bethlehem of Judæa, in the days of Herod the king,............

The first Sunday after the Epiphany

Usquequo Domine? Psalm xiii.

How long wilt thou forget me, O Lord......

The Collect.

LORD, we beseech thee, mercifully to receive the prayers of thy people which call upon thee: and grant that they may both perceive and know what things they ought to do, and also have grace and power faithfully to fulfil the same.

The Epistle. Roma. xii. I beseech you therefore brethren......

The Gospel. Luc. ii. The father and mother of Jesus went......

¶ *The second Sunday.*

Dixit insipiens. Psalm xiiii.

The fool hath said in his heart ......

The Collect.

ALMIGHTY and everlasting God, which dost govern all things in heaven and earth: mercifully hear the supplications of thy people, and grant us thy peace all the days of our life.

The Epistle. Rom. xii. Seeing that we have divers gifts......

THE FIRST SUNDAY AFTER THE EPIPHANY.

The Collect.

O Lord, we beseech thee mercifully to receive the prayers of thy people which call upon thee; and grant that they may both perceive and know what things they ought to do, and also may have grace and power faithfully to fulfil the same; through Jesus Christ our Lord. *Amen.*

The Epistle. Rom. xii. 1.

I BESEECH you therefore, brethren, by the mercies of ......

The Gospel. St. Luke ii. 41.

NOW his parents went to Jerusalem every year at the feast of the passover. And.........

THE SECOND SUNDAY AFTER THE EPIPHANY.

The Collect.

ALMIGHTY and everlasting God, who dost govern all things in heaven and earth; Mercifully hear the supplications of thy people, and grant us thy peace all the days of our life; through Jesus Christ our Lord. *Amen.*

The Epistle. Rom. xii. 6.

HAVING then gifts differing according to the grace that is given to us, whether prophecy, let us prophesy according to......

The Gospel. John ii. And the third day was there a marriage in Cana......

¶ *The third Sunday.*

Domine, quis habitabit? Psalm xv.

Lord, who shall dwell in thy tabernacle......

The Collect.

ALMIGHTY and everlasting God, mercifully look upon our infirmities, and in all our dangers and necessities, stretch forth thy right hand to help and defend us, through Christ our Lord.

The Epistle. Rom. xii. Be not wise in your own opinions......

The Gospel. Math viii. When he was come down from the mountain......

¶ *The fourth Sunday.*

Quare fremuerunt gentes? Psalm ii.

WHY do the heathen so furiously rage together,......

The Collect.

GOD, which knowest us to be set in the midst of so many and great dangers, that for man's frailness we cannot always stand uprightly: Grant to us the health of body and soul, that all those things which we suffer for sin, by thy help we may well pass and overcome, through Christ our Lord.

The Gospel. St. John ii. 1.

AND the third day there was a marriage in Cana of Galilee, and the mother of Jesus was .....

THE THIRD SUNDAY AFTER THE EPIPHANY.

The Collect.

ALMIGHTY and everlasting God, mercifully look upon our infirmities, and in all our dangers and necessities stretch forth thy right hand to help and defend us; through Jesus Christ our Lord. *Amen.*

The Epistle. Rom. xii. 16

BE not wise in your own conceits. Recompense to no man evil for evil. Provide things...

The Gospel. St. Matt. viii. 1.

WHEN HE was come down from the mountain, great multitudes followed him......

THE FOURTH SUNDAY AFTER THE EPIPHANY.

The Collect.

O GOD, who knowest us to be set in the midst of so many and great dangers, that by reason of the frailty of our nature we cannot always stand upright; Grant to us such strength and protection, as may support us in all dangers, and carry us through all temptations; through Jesus Christ our Lord. *Amen.*

The Epistle. Rom. xiii. Let every soul submit himself......

The Gospel. Math. viii. And when he entered into a ship......

¶ *The fifth Sunday.*

Exaudiat te Dominus. Psalm xx.

THE Lord hear thee in the day of trouble......

The Collect.

LORD, we beseech thee tc keep thy church and household continually in thy true religion: that they which do lean only upon hope of thy heavenly grace, may evermore be defended by thy mighty power; through Christ our Lord.

The Epistle. Coloss. iii. Put upon you as the elect of God......

The Gospel. Math. xiii. The kingdom of heaven is like unto ......

The sixth Sunday (if there be so many) shall have the same Psalm, Collect, Epistle, and Gospel, that was upon the fifth.

The Epistle. Rom. xiii. 1.

LET every soul be subject unto the higher powers; for there is no power but of God: the......

The Gospel. St. Matt. viii. 23.

AND when he was entered into a ship, his disciples followed him. And behold, there arose......

THE FIFTH SUNDAY AFTER THE EPIPHANY.

The Collect.

O LORD, we beseech thee to keep thy church and household continually in thy true religion; that they who do lean only upon the hope of thy heavenly grace may evermore be defended by thy mighty power; through Jesus Christ our Lord. *Amen.*

The Epistle. Col. iii. 12.

PUT on therefore, as the elect of God, holy and beloved, bowels of mercies, kindness......

The Gospel. St. Matt. xiii. 24.

THE kingdom of heaven is likened unto a man which sowed good seed in his field. But while men slept, his enemy......

THE SIXTH SUNDAY AFTER THE EPIPHANY.

The Collect.

O GOD, whose blessed Son was manifested that he might destroy the works of the devil, and make us the sons of God, and heirs of eternal life; Grant us, we beseech thee, that, having this hope, we may purify ourselves, even as he is pure; that, when he shall appear again with power and great glory, we may be made like unto him in his eternal and glorious kingdom; where with thee, O Father, and thee, O Holy Ghost, he liveth and reigneth, ever one God, world without end. *Amen.*

The Epistle. 1 St. John iii. 1.

BEHOLD, what manner of love the Father hath bestowed upon us, that we should be called the sons of God: therefore the......

The Gospel. St. Matt. xxiv. 23.

THEN if any man shall say unto you, Lo, here is Christ, or there; believe it not. For......

¶ *The Sunday called Septuagesima.*

Dominus regit. Psalm xxiii.

THE Lord is my shepherd: therefore......

The Collect.

O LORD, we beseech thee favourably to hear the prayers of thy people; that we, which are justly punished for our offences, may be mercifully delivered by thy goodness, for the glory of thy name; through Jesu Christ our Saviour, who liveth and reigneth, &c.

The Epistle. 1 Cor. ix. Perceive ye not, how that they......

The Gospel. Math xx. The kingdom of heaven is like unto a man......

THE SUNDAY CALLED SEPTUAGESIMA.

OR THE THIRD SUNDAY BEFORE LENT.

The Collect.

O LORD, we beseech thee favourably to hear the prayers of thy people; that we, who are justly punished for our offences, may be mercifully delivered by thy goodness, for the glory of thy Name; through Jesus Christ our Saviour, who liveth and reigneth with thee and the Holy Ghost, ever one God, world without end. *Amen.*

The Epistle. 1 Cor. ix. 24.

KNOW ye not, that they which run in a race run all, but......

The Gospel. St. Matt. xx. 1.

THE kingdom of heaven is like unto a man that is an householder, which went out early......

1549	1886
¶ *The Sunday called Sexagesima.*	THE SUNDAY CALLED SEXAGESIMA, OR THE SECOND SUNDAY BEFORE LENT.
¶ [*At the Communion.*] *Domini est terra.* Psalm xxiiii. THE earth is the Lord's, and all that therein is, the compass......	
The Collect.	*The Collect.*
LORD God, which seest that we put not our trust in any thing that we do: mercifully grant that by thy power we may be defended against all adversity, through Jesus Christ our Lord.	O LORD God, who seest that we put not our trust in anything that we do; Mercifully grant that by thy power we may be defended against all adversity; through Jesus Christ our Lord. *Amen.*
The Epistle. 2 Cor. xi. Ye suffer fools gladly......	*The Epistle.* 2 Cor. xi. 19. YE suffer fools gladly, seeing ye yourselves are wise. For ye suffer if a man bring you into bondage, if a man devour you......
The Gospel. Luc. viii. When much people were gathered......	*The Gospel.* St. Luke viii. 4. WHEN much people were gathered together, and were come to him out of every city......
¶ *The Sunday called Quinquagesima.*	THE SUNDAY CALLED QUINQUAGESIMA, OR THE NEXT SUNDAY BEFORE LENT.
Judica me Domine. Psalm xxvi. BE thou my judge, O Lord, for I have walked......	
The Collect.	*The Collect.*
O LORD, which dost teach us that all our doings without charity are nothing worth: send thy Holy Ghost, and pour into our hearts that most excellent gift of charity, the very bond of peace and all virtues, without the which, whosoever liveth is counted dead before thee: Grant this, for thy only son Jesus Christ's sake.	O LORD, who hast taught us that all our doings without charity are nothing worth: Send thy Holy Ghost, and pour into our hearts that most excellent gift of charity, the very bond of peace and of all virtues, without which whosoever liveth is counted dead before thee: Grant this for thine only Son Jesus Christ's sake. *Amen.*
The Epistle. 1 Cor. xiii. Though I speak with the tongues......	*The Epistle.* 1 Cor. xiii. 1. THOUGH I speak with the tongues of men and of angels, and have not charity, I am become as sounding brass......

The Gospel. Luc. xviii. Jesus took unto him the twelve......

The Gospel. St. Luke xiii. 31.

THEN Jesus took unto him the twelve, and said unto them, Behold, we go up to Jerusalem, and all things that......

¶ *The first day of Lent, commonly called Ashwednesday.*

Domine ne. Psalm vi.

O LORD, rebuke me not in thine indignation......

THE FIRST DAY OF LENT

COMMONLY CALLED

ASH-WEDNESDAY.

The Collect.

ALMIGHTY and everlasting God, which hatest nothing that thou hast made, and dost forgive the sins of all them that be penitent: Create and make in us new and contrite hearts, that we worthily lamenting our sins, and knowledging our wretchedness, may obtain of thee the God of all mercy, perfect remission and forgiveness, through Jesus Christ.

The Collect.

ALMIGHTY and everlasting God, who hatest nothing that thou hast made, and dost forgive the sins of all them that are penitent; Create and make in us new and contrite hearts, that we worthily lamenting our sins, and acknowledging our wretchedness, may obtain of thee, the God of all mercy, perfect remission and forgiveness; through Jesus Christ our Lord. *Amen.*

¶ *This Collect is to be read every day in Lent after the Collect appointed for the Day.*

The Epistle. Joel ii. Turn you unto me with all your hearts......

For the Epistle. Joel ii. 12.

TURN ye even to me, saith the Lord, with all your heart, and with fasting, and with......

The Gospel. Math. vi. When ye fast be not sad as the hypocrites are......

The Gospel. St. Matt. vi. 16

WHEN ye fast, be not as the hypocrites, of a sad countenance: for they disfigure......

¶ *The first Sunday in Lent.*

Beati quorum. Psalm xxxii.

BLESSED is he whose unrighteousness is forgiven; and whose ......

THE FIRST SUNDAY IN LENT.

The Collect.

O LORD, which for our sake didst fast forty days and forty

The Collect.

O LORD, who for our sake didst fast forty days and forty

nights: Give us grace to use such abstinence, that, our flesh being subdued to the Spirit, we may ever obey thy godly motions, in righteousness and true holiness, to thy honour and glory, which livest and reignest, &c.

The Epistle. 2 Cor. vi. We as helpers exhort you that ye receive not......

The Gospel. Math. iv. Then was Jesus led away of the Spirit ......

¶ *The second Sunday.*

De profundis. Psalm cxxx.

Out of the deep have I called unto thee, O Lord: Lord hear......

The Collect.

Almighty God, which dost see that we have no power of ourselves to help ourselves: keep thou us both outwardly in our bodies, and inwardly in our souls, that we may be defended from all adversities which may happen to the body, and from all evil thoughts which may assault and hurt the soul; through Jesus Christ, &c. Amen.

The Epistle. 1 Thess. iv. We beseech you brethren and exhort ......

The Gospel. Math. xv. Jesus went thence......

nights; Give us
abstinence, that,
subdued to the s
obey thy godly n
ousness, and true
honour and glor
reignest with th
Holy Ghost, one
out end. Amen

The Epistle.

WE then, as
with hin
that ye receive r

The Gospel.

THEN was Je
Spirit, int
be tempted of th

The Second S

The

ALMIGHTY
that we ha
selves to help o
both outwardly
inwardly in our s
be defended fr
which may happ
from all evil th
assault and hurt
Jesus Christ our

The Epistle.

WE beseech
exhort
Jesus, that as y

The Gospel.

JESUS went
parted int
and Sidon. An
of Canaan came

¶ *The third Sunday.*

Judica me Deus. Psalm xliii.

GIVE sentence with me, (O God,) and defend......

The Collect.

WE beseech thee, almighty God, look upon the hearty desire[s] of thy humble servants: and stretch forth the right hand of thy majesty, to be our defence against all our enemies: through Jesus Christ our Lord.

The Epistle. Ephe. v. Be you the followers of God......

The Gospel. Luc. xi. Jesus was casting out a devil that was dumb ......

¶ *The fourth Sunday.*

Deus noster refugium. Psalm xlvi.

GOD is our hope and strength: a very......

The Collect.

GRANT, we beseech thee, almighty God, that we, which for our evil deeds are worthily punished: by the comfort of thy grace may mercifully be relieved, through our Lord Jesus Christ.

The Epistle. Gala. iv. Tell me, ye that desire......

The Gospel. John vi. Jesus departed over the sea of Galilee......

THE THIRD SUNDAY IN LENT.

The Collect.

WE beseech thee, Almighty God, look upon the hearty desires of thy humble servants, and stretch forth the right hand of thy Majesty, to be our defence against all our enemies; through Jesus Christ our Lord. *Amen.*

The Epistle. Ephes. v. 1.

BE ye therefore followers of God, as dear children; and walk in love, as Christ also......

The Gospel. St. Luke xi. 14.

JESUS was casting out a devil, and it was dumb. And it came to pass, when the devil was gone out, the dumb spake; and the people wondered. But some......

THE FOURTH SUNDAY IN LENT.

The Collect.

GRANT, we beseech thee, Almighty God, that we, who for our evil deeds do worthily deserve to be punished, by the comfort of thy grace may mercifully be relieved; through our Lord and Saviour Jesus Christ. *Amen.*

The Epistle. Gal. iv. 21

TELL me, ye that desire to be under the law, do ye not......

The Gospel. St. John vi. 1.

JESUS went over the sea of Galilee, which is the sea of Tiberias. And a great multitude......

¶ *The fifth Sunday.*

Deus, in nomine tuo. Psalm liv.

SAVE me, (O God,) for thy Name's sake......

The Collect.

WE beseech thee, almighty God, mercifully to look upon thy people: that by thy great goodness, they may be governed and preserved evermore, both in body and soul: through Jesus Christ our Lord.

The Epistle. Hebrues ix. Christ being an high priest......

The Gospel. John viii. Which of you can rebuke me of sin......

The Sunday next before Easter.

Exaudi deus deprecationem. Psalm lxi.

HEAR my crying, O God......

The Collect.

ALMIGHTY and everlasting God, which of thy tender love toward man, has sent our Saviour Jesus Christ to take upon him our flesh, and to suffer death upon the cross, that all mankind should follow the example of his great humility: mercifully grant, that we both follow the example of his patience, and be made partakers of his resurrection: through the same Jesus Christ our Lord.

The Epistle. Philip ii. Let the same mind be in you......

THE FIFTH SUNDAY IN LENT.

The Collect.

WE beseech thee, Almighty God, mercifully to look upon thy people; that by thy great goodness they may be governed and preserved evermore, both in body and soul; through Jesus Christ our Lord. *Amen.*

The Epistle. Heb. ix. 11.

CHRIST being come an High Priest of good things to come, by a greater and more perfect......

The Gospel. St. John viii. 46.

JESUS said, Which of you convinceth me of sin? and if I say the truth, why do ye not......

THE SUNDAY NEXT BEFORE EASTER.

The Collect.

ALMIGHTY and everlasting God, who, of thy tender love towards mankind, hast sent thy Son, our Saviour Jesus Christ, to take upon him our flesh, and to suffer death upon the cross, that all mankind should follow the example of his great humility; mercifully grant, that we may both follow the example of his patience, and also be made partakers of his resurrection; through the same Jesus Christ our Lord. *Amen.*

The Epistle. Phil. ii. 5.

LET this mind be in you, which was also in Christ Jesus: who, being in the form of God, thought it not robbery to be......

The Gospel. Math. xxvi. and xxvii. And it came to pass......

The Gospel. St. Matt. xxvii. 1.

WHEN the morning was come, all the chief priests and elders of the people took counsel against Jesus, to put him to......

Monday before Easter.

The Epistle. Esai. lxiii. What is he this that cometh......

The Gospel. Mar. xiv. After two days was Easter and the days ......

MONDAY BEFORE EASTER.

For the Epistle. Isai. lxiii. 1.

WHO is this that cometh from Edom, with dyed garments from Bozrah? this that is......

The Gospel. St. Mark xiv. 1.

AFTER two days was the feast of the Passover, and of unleavened bread: and the chief priests and the scribes sought......

¶ *Tuesday before Easter.*

The Epistle. Esai. l. The Lord God hath opened mine ear......

The Gospel. Mar. xv. And anon in the dawning the high priests......

TUESDAY BEFORE EASTER.

For the Epistle. Isai. l. 5.

THE Lord God hath opened mine ear, and I was not rebellious, neither turned away back. I gave my back to the smiters......

The Gospel. St. Mark xv. 1.

AND straightway in the morning the chief priests held......

¶ *Wednesday before Easter.*

¶ *At the Communion.*

The Epistle. Hebr. ix. Whereas is a testament there must also......

The Gospel. Luc. xxii. The feast of sweet bread which is called Easter......

¶ *At Evensong.*

The first lesson, Lamenta. i. *unto the end.*

WEDNESDAY BEFORE EASTER.

The Epistle. Heb. ix. 16.

WHERE a testament is, there must also of necessity be the death of the testator: for......

The Gospel. St. Luke xxii. 1.

NOW the feast of unleavened bread drew nigh, which......

¶ *Thursday before Easter.*

¶ *At Matins.*

The first lesson, Lamenta. ii. *unto the end.*

The Epistle. 1 Cor. xi. This I warn you of and commend not that......

The Gospel. Luc. xxiii. The whole multitude of them......

At Evensong.

The first lesson, Lamenta. iii. *unto the eud.*

On Good Friday.

At Matins.

The first lesson, Gen. xxii. *unto the end.*

The Collect.

ALMIGHTY God, we beseech thee graciously to behold this thy family: for the which our Lord Jesus Christ was contented to be betrayed, and given up into the hands of wicked men, and to suffer death upon the cross: who liveth and reigneth, &c.

At the Communion.

Deus, deus meus. Psalm xxii.

MY God, my God, (look upon me)......

¶ *After the two Collects at the Communion, shall be said these two Collects following.*

The Collect.

ALMIGHTY and everlasting God, by whose Spirit the whole body of the Church is governed and sanctified: receive our supplications and prayers, which we offer before thee for all estates of men in thy holy congregation, that every member of the same, in his vocation and ministry, may truly and godly serve thee: through our Lord Jesus Christ.

THURSDAY BEFORE EASTER.

The Epistle. 1 Cor. xi. 17.

IN this that I declare unto you, I praise you not; that ye come together not for the better......

The Gospel. St. Luke xxiii. 1.

THE whole multitude of them arose, and led him into Pilate. And they began to......

GOOD FRIDAY.

The Collects.

ALMIGHTY God, we beseech thee graciously to behold this thy family, for which our Lord Jesus Christ was contented to be betrayed, and given up into the hands of wicked men, and to suffer death upon the cross, who now liveth and reigneth with thee and the Holy Ghost, ever one God, world without end. *Amen.*

ALMIGHTY and everlasting God, by whose Spirit the whole body of the Church is governed and sanctified; Receive our supplications and prayers, which we offer before thee for all estates of men in thy holy Church, that every member of the same, in his vocation and ministry, may truly and godly serve thee; through our Lord and Saviour Jesus Christ. *Amen.*

MERCIFUL God, who hast made all men, and hatest nothing that thou hast made, nor wouldest the death of a sinner, but rather that he should be converted and live: Have mercy upon all Jews, Turks, Infidels, and Heretics, and take from them all ignorance, hardness of heart, and contempt of thy word: and so fetch them home, blessed Lord, to thy flock, that they may be saved among the remnant of the true Israelites, and be made one fold under one shepherd, Jesus Christ our Lord: who liveth and reigneth, &c.

The Epistle. Heb. x. The law which hath but a shadow......

The Gospel. John xviii. When Jesus had spoken these words......

At Evensong.

¶ The first lesson, Esai. liii. *unto the end*

Easter Even.

At Matins.

¶ The first lesson, Lamenta. iv. v. *unto the end.*

At the Communion.

Domine deus salutis, Psal. lxxxviii.

O LORD God of my salvation...

O MERCIFUL God, who hast made all men, and hatest nothing that thou hast made, nor wouldest the death of a sinner, but rather that he should be converted and live; Have mercy upon all Jews, Turks, Infidels, and Hereticks, and take from them all ignorance, hardness of heart, and contempt of thy Word: and so fetch them home, blessed Lord, to thy flock, that they may be saved among the remnant of the true Israelites, and be made one fold under one shepherd, Jesus Christ our Lord, who liveth and reigneth with thee and the Holy Spirit, one God, world without end. *Amen.*

The Epistle. Heb. x. 1.

THE law having a shadow of good things to come, and not the very image of the things......

The Gospel. St. John xix. 1.

PILATE therefore took Jesus, and scourged him. And the soldiers platted a crown of thorns, and put it on his head, and......

EASTER-EVEN.

GRANT, O Lord, that as we are baptized into the death of thy blessed Son our Saviour Jesus Christ, so by continual mortifying our corrupt affections we may be buried with him; and that through the grave, and gate of death, we may pass to our joyful resurrection; for his merits, who died, and was buried, and rose again for us, thy Son Jesus Christ our Lord. *Amen.*

The Epistle. 1 Pet. iii. It is better......

The Epistle. 1 St. Pet. iii. 17

IT is better, if the will of God be so, that ye suffer for......

The Gospel Matt. xxvii. When the even......

The Gospel. St. Matt. xxvii. 57.

WHEN the even was come, there came a rich man of Arimathæa, named Joseph......

¶ *Easter day.*

In the morning afore Matins, the people being assembled in the church: these Anthems shall be first solemnly sung or said.

EASTER-DAY.

¶ *At Morning Prayer, instead of the Psalm,* O come let us sing, *&c. these Anthems shall be sung or said.*

CHRIST our passover is sacrificed for us: therefore let us keep the feast;

Not with the old leaven, nor with the leaven of malice and wickedness: but with the unleavened bread of sincerity and truth. 1 *Cor.* v. 7.

CHRIST rising again from the dead, now dieth not. Death from henceforth hath no power upon him. For in that he died, he died but once to put away sin: but in that he liveth, he liveth unto God. And so likewise, count yourselves dead unto sin, but living unto God in Christ Jesus our Lord. Alleluia, Alleluia.

CHRIST being raised from the dead dieth no more; death hath no more dominion over him.

For in that he died, he died unto sin once: but in that he liveth, he liveth unto God.

Likewise reckon ye also yourselves to be dead indeed unto sin: but alive unto God through Jesus Christ our Lord. *Rom.* vi. 9.

CHRIST is risen again, the firstfruits of them that sleep: for seeing that by man came death, by man also cometh the resurrection of the dead. For as by Adam all men do die, so by Christ all men shall be restored to life. Alleluia.

CHRIST is risen from the dead: and became the first-fruits of them that slept.

For since by man came death: by man came also the resurrection of the dead.

For as in Adam all die: even so in Christ shall all be made alive. 1 *Cor.* xv. 20.

The Priest.

¶ Shew forth to all nations the glory of God.

The Answer.

¶ And among all people his wonderful works.

Let us pray.

O God, who for our redemption didst give thine only begotten Son to the death of the cross: and by his glorious resurrection hast delivered us from the power of our enemy: Grant us so to die daily from sin, that we may evermore live with him in the joy of his resurrection: through the same Christ our Lord. Amen.

¶ *Proper Psalms and Lessons.*

At Matins.

Psalms ii., lvii., cxi.

The first lesson, Exo. xii. *unto the end.*

The second lesson, Roma. vi. *unto the end.*

At the first Communion.

Conserva me domine. Psalm xvi.

Preserve me O God; for in thee......

The Collect.

Almighty God, which through thy only begotten Son Jesus Christ, hast overcome death, and opened unto us the gate of everlasting life: we humbly beseech thee, that as by thy special grace, preventing us, thou dost put in our minds good desires; so by thy continual help, we may bring the same to good effect, through Jesus Christ our Lord: who liveth and reigneth, &c. Amen.

Glory be to the Father, and to the Son: and to the Holy Ghost;

As it was in the beginning, is now, and ever shall be: world without end. Amen.

The Collect.

ALMIGHTY God, who through thine only-begotten Son Jesus Christ hast overcome death, and opened unto us the gate of everlasting life; We humbly beseech thee, that, as by thy special grace preventing us thou dost put into our minds good desires, so by thy continual help we may bring the same to good effect; through Jesus Christ our Lord, who liveth and reigneth with thee and the Holy Ghost, ever one God, world without end. *Amen.*

The Epistle. Coloss. iii. If ye be risen again with Christ......

The Gospel. John xx. The first day of the Sabbaths......

At the second Communion.

Domine quid multiplicati? Psalm iii.

Lord, how are they increased that trouble me......

The Collect.

ALMIGHTY Father, which hast given thy only Son to die for our sins, and to rise again for our justification: Grant us so to put away the leaven of malice and wickedness, that we may alway serve thee in pureness of living and truth, through Jesus Christ our Lord.

The Epistle. 1 Cor. v. Know ye not that a little leaven......

The Gospel. Mar. xvi. When the Sabbath was past......

At Evensong.

¶ *Proper Psalms and Lessons.*

Psalms cxiii. cxiv. cxviii.

The second lesson, Act. ii. *unto the end.*

¶ *Monday in Easter Week.*

At Matins.

The second lesson, Mat. xxviii. *unto the end.*

At the Communion.

Nonne deo [*subjecta?*] Psalm lxii.

MY soul truly waiteth still upon God......

The Epistle. Col. iii. 1.

IF ye then be risen with Christ, seek those things which are above, where Christ sitteth on......

The Gospel. St. John xx. 1.

THE first day of the week cometh Mary Magdalene......

MONDAY IN EASTER-WEEK.

The Collect.

Almighty God, which through thy only begotten Son Jesus Christ, hast overcome death, and opened unto us the gate of everlasting life: we humbly beseech thee, that as by thy especial grace, preventing us, thou dost put in our minds good desires; so by thy continual help, we may bring the same to good effect, through Jesus Christ our Lord: who liveth and reigneth, &c.

The Epistle. Acts x. Peter opened his mouth and said......

The Gospel. Luc. xxiv. Behold two of the disciples went......

At Evensong.

¶ The second lesson, Acts iii. *unto the end.*

¶ *Tuesday in Easter-Week.*

At Matins.

The second lesson, Luke xxiv. *unto* " And behold two [of them]."

At the Communion.

Laudate pueri. Psalm cxiii.

Praise the Lord, (ye servants)...

The Collect.

Almighty Father, which hast given thy only Son to die for our sins and to rise again for our justification: Grant us so to put away the leaven of malice and wickedness, that we may alway serve thee in pureness of living and truth, through Jesus Christ our Lord.

The Collect

ALMIGHTY God, who through thy only-begotten Son Jesus Christ hast overcome death, and opened unto us the gate of everlasting life; We humbly beseech thee, that, as by thy special grace preventing us thou dost put into our minds good desires, so by thy continual help we may bring the same to good effect; through Jesus Christ our Lord, who liveth and reigneth with thee and the Holy Ghost, ever one God, world without end. *Amen.*

For the Epistle. Acts x. 34.

PETER opened his mouth, and said, Of a truth I perceive that God is no respecter of......

The Gospel. St. Luke xxiv. 13.

BEHOLD, two of his disciples went that same day to a village called Emmaus, which......

Tuesday in Easter-Week.

The Collect.

ALMIGHTY God, who through thy only-begotten Son Jesus Christ hast overcome death, and opened unto us the gate of everlasting life; We humbly beseech thee, that, as by thy special grace preventing us thou dost put into our minds good desires, so by thy continual help we may bring the same to good effect; through Jesus Christ our Lord, who liveth and reigneth with thee and the Holy Ghost, ever one God, world without end. *Amen.*

The Epistle. Acts. xiii. Ye men and brethren......

For the Epistle. Acts xiii, 26.

MEN and brethren, children of the stock of Abraham, and whosoever among you feareth......

The Gospel. Luc. xxiv. Jesus stood in the midst of his disciples ......

The Gospel. St. Luke xxiv. 36.

JESUS himself stood in the midst of them, and saith unto them, Peace be unto you.......

At Evensong.

The second lesson, 1 Cor. xv. *unto the end.*

¶ *The first Sunday after Easter.*

THE FIRST SUNDAY AFTER EASTER.

Beatus vir. Psalm cxii.

BLESSED is the man that feareth the Lord......

The Collect.

ALMIGHTY Father, &c. *As at the second Communion on Easter Day.*

The Collect.

ALMIGHTY Father, who hast given thine only Son to die for our sins, and to rise again for our justification; Grant us so to put away the leaven of malice and wickedness, that we may alway serve thee in pureness of living and truth; through the merits of the same thy Son Jesus Christ our Lord. *Amen.*

The Epistle. 1 John v. All that is born of God......

The Epistle. 1 St. John v. 4.

WHATSOEVER is born of God overcometh the......

The Gospel. John xx. The same day at night.......

The Gospel. St. John xx. 19.

THE same day at evening, being the first day of the week, when the doors were......

¶ *The second Sunday after Easter.*

Deus in adjutorium. Psalm lxx.

HASTE thee, O God, to deliver me......

The Collect.

ALMIGHTY God, which hast given thy holy Son to be unto us, both a sacrifice for sin, and also an example of Godly life: Give us the grace that we may always most thankfully receive that his inestimable benefit, and also daily endeavour ourselves to follow the blessed steps of his most holy life.

The Epistle. I Peter ii. This is thankworthy......

The Gospel. John x. Christ said to his disciple I am the good shepherd......

¶ *The third Sunday.*

Confitebimur. Psalm lxxv.

UNTO thee, (O God) do we give thanks......

The Collect.

ALMIGHTY God, which shewest to all men that be in error the light of thy truth, to the intent that they may return into the way of righteousness: Grant unto all them that be admitted into the fellowship of Christ's religion, that they may eschew those things that be contrary to their profession, and follow all such things as be agree- to the same: through our Lord Jesus Christ.

THE SECOND SUNDAY AFTER EASTER.

The Collect.

ALMIGHTY God, who hast given thine only son to be unto us both a sacrifice for sin, and also an ensample of godly life; Give us grace that we may always most thankfully receive that his inestimable benefit, and also daily endeavour ourselves to follow the blessed steps of his most holy life; through the same Jesus Christ our Lord. *Amen.*

The Epistle. 1 St. Pet. ii. 19.

THIS is thank-worthy, if a man for conscience toward God endure grief, suffering wrong-......

The Gospel. St. John x. 11.

JESUS said, I am the good shepherd: the good shepherd giveth his life for the sheep.......

THE THIRD SUNDAY AFTER EASTER.

The Collect.

ALMIGHTY God, who shewest to them that be in error the light of thy truth, to the intent that they may return into the way of righteousness; Grant unto all them that are admitted into the fellowship of Christ's Religion, that they may eschew those things that are contrary to their profession, and follow all such things as are agreeable to the same; through our Lord Jesus Christ. *Amen.*

The Epistle. I Peter ii. Dearly beloved, I beseech you......

The Gospel. John xvi. Jesus said to his disciples After a......

¶ *The fourth Sunday.*

Deus stetit in synagoga. Psalm lxxxiii.

God standeth in the congregation of princes......

The Collect.

Almighty God, which dost make the minds of all faithful men to be of one will: grant unto thy people, that they may love the thing, which thou commandest, and desire that which thou dost promise, that among the sundry and manifold changes of the world, our hearts may surely there be fixed, where as true joys are to be found: through Christ our Lord.

The Epistle. James i. Every good gift......

The Gospel. John xvi. Jesus said unto his disciples.

¶ *The fifth Sunday.*

Quam dilecta tabernacula Psalm lxxxiv.

O how amiable are thy dwellings......

The Epistle. I St. Pet. ii. 11.

DEARLY beloved, I beseech you as strangers and pilgrims, abstain from fleshly......

The Gospel. St. John xvi. 16.

JESUS said to his disciples, A little while and ye shall not see me; and again, a little......

THE FOURTH SUNDAY AFTER EASTER.

The Collect.

O ALMIGHTY God, who alone canst order the unruly wills and affections of sinful men; Grant unto thy people, that they may love the thing which thou commandest, and desire that which thou dost promise; that so, among the sundry and manifold changes of the world, our hearts may surely there be fixed, where true joys are to be found; through Jesus Christ our Lord. *Amen.*

The Epistle. St. James i. 17.

EVERY good gift, and every perfect gift is from above, and cometh down from the......

The Gospel. St. John xvi. 5.

JESUS said unto his disciples, Now I go my way to him that sent me, and none of you......

THE FIFTH SUNDAY AFTER EASTER

The Collect.

LORD, from whom all good things do come; grant us thy humble servants, that by thy holy inspiration we may think those things that be good, and by thy merciful guiding may perform the same; through our Lord Jesus Christ.

The Epistle. James i. See that ye be doers of the word......

The Gospel. John xvi. Verily, verily I say unto you......

¶ *The Ascension Day.*

¶ *Proper Psalms and Lessons.*

At Matins.

Psalms viii. xv. xxi.

The second Lesson, John xiv. *unto the end.*

¶ *At the Communion.*

Omnes gentes plaudite. Psalm xlvii.

O CLAP your hands together, (all ye people)......

The Collect.

GRANT, we beseech thee, almighty God, that like as we do believe thy only begotten Son our Lord to have ascended into the heavens: so we may also in heart and mind thither ascend, and with him continually dwell.

The Epistle. Acts i. In the former treatise......

The Collect.

O LORD, from whom all good things do come; Grant to us thy humble servants, that by thy holy inspiration we may think those things that be good, and by thy merciful guiding may perform the same; through our Lord Jesus Christ. *Amen.*

The Epistle. St. James i. 22.

BE ye doers of the Word, and not hearers only,......

The Gospel. St. John xvi. 23.

VERILY, verily I say unto you, Whatsoever ye shall ask the Father in my Name,......

THE ASCENSION-DAY.

The Collect.

GRANT, we beseech thee, Almighty God, that like as we do believe thy only-begotten Son our Lord Jesus Christ to have ascended into the heavens; so we may also in heart and mind thither ascend, and with him continually dwell, who liveth and reigneth with thee and the Holy Ghost, one God, world without end. *Amen.*

For the Epistle. Acts. i. 1.

THE former treatise have I made, O Theophilus, of all that Jesus began both to do......

The Gospel. Mar. xvi. Jesus appeared unto the eleven......

¶ *Proper Psalms and Lessons at Evensong.*
Psalms xxiv. lxviii. cxlviii.
The second lesson, Ephe. iv. *unto the end.*

The Gospel. St. Mark xvi. 14.

JESUS appeared unto the eleven as they sat at meat, and upbraided them with their......

¶ *The Sunday after the Ascension.*

SUNDAY AFTER ASCENSION-DAY.

Dominus regnavit. Psalm xciii.

THE lord is king, and hath put on glorious apparel......

The Collect.

O GOD, the King of glory, which hast exalted thine only Son Jesus Christ, with great triumph unto thy kingdom in heaven: we beseech thee leave us not comfortless, but send to us thine Holy Ghost to comfort us, and exalt us unto the same place, whither our Saviour Christ is gone before; who liveth and reigneth, &c.

The Collect.

O GOD the King of glory, who hast exalted thine only Son Jesus Christ with great triumph unto thy kingdom in heaven; We beseech thee, leave us not comfortless; but send to us thine Holy Ghost to comfort us, and exalt us unto the same place whither our Saviour Christ is gone before, who liveth and reigneth with thee and the Holy Ghost, one God, world without end. *Amen.*

The Epistle. 1 Peter iv. The end of all things is at hand......

The Epistle. 1 St. Pet. iv. 7.

THE end of all things is at hand; be ye therefore sober, and watch unto prayer. And......

The Gospel. John xv., John xvi. When the Comforter is come......

The Gospel. St. John xv. 26, *and part of* Chap. xvi.

WHEN the Comforter is come, whom I will send unto you from the Father, even the......

¶ *Whit-Sunday.*

WHIT-SUNDAY.

¶ *Proper Psalms and Lessons at Matins.*
Psalms xlviii. lxvii. cxlv.
The second lesson, Act. x. "Then Peter opened his mouth," *unto the end.*

¶ *At the Communion.*

Exultate justi in Domino. Psalm xxxiii.

REJOICE in the Lord, O ye......

The Collect.

God, which as upon this day hast taught the hearts of thy faithful people, by the sending to them the light of thy Holy Spirit: Grant us by the same Spirit to have a right judgement in all things, and evermore to rejoice in his holy comfort, through the merits of Christ Jesus our Saviour, who liveth and reigneth with thee in the unity of the same Spirit one God, world without end. Amen.

The Epistle. Acts ii. When the fifty days were come......

The Gospel. John xiv. Jesus said unto his disciples......

¶ *Proper Psalms and Lessons at Evensong.* Psalm civ., cxlv.

The second lesson, Acts xix. "It fortuned when Apollo went to Corinthum," *unto* "After these things."

¶ *Monday in Whitsun-week.*

Jubilate Deo. Psalm c.

O be joyful in the Lord, (all ye lands)......

The Collect.

¶ God, which, &c., *as upon Whit-Sunday.*

The Collect.

GOD, who as at this time didst teach the hearts of thy faithful people, by the sending to them the light of thy Holy Spirit; Grant us by the same Spirit to have a right judgement in all things, and evermore to rejoice in his holy comfort; through the merits of Christ Jesus our Saviour, who liveth and reigneth with thee, in the unity of the same Spirit, one God, world without end. *Amen.*

For the Epistle. Acts ii. 1.

WHEN the day of Pentecost was fully come, they were all with one accord in one place......

The Gospel. St. John xiv. 15.

JESUS said unto his disciples, If ye love me, keep my commandment. And I will pray......

Monday in Whitsun-Week.

The Collect.

GOD, who as at this time didst teach the hearts of thy faithful people, by the sending to them the light of thy Holy Spirit; Grant us by the same Spirit to have a right judgement in all things, and evermore to rejoice in his holy comfort; through the merits of Christ Jesus our Saviour, who liveth and reigneth with thee, in the unity of the same Spirit, one God, world without end. *Amen.*

The Epistle. Act x. Then Peter opened his mouth and said......

For the Epistle. Acts x. 34.

THEN Peter opened his mouth, and said, Of a truth I......

The Gospel. John iii. So God loved the world......

The Gospel. St. John iii. 16.

GOD so loved the world, that he gave his only begotten Son, that whosoever believeth....

¶ *Tuesday.*

¶ [*At the Communion.*]

Misericordiam. Psalm ci.

MY song shall be of mercy and judgment......

The Collect.

GOD, which, &c., *as upon Whit-Sunday.*

TUESDAY IN WHITSUN-WEEK.

The Collect.

GOD, who as at this time didst teach the hearts of thy faithful people, by the sending to them the light of thy Holy Spirit; Grant us by the same Spirit to have a right judgement in all things, and evermore to rejoice in his holy comfort; through the merits of Christ Jesus our Saviour, who liveth and reigneth with thee, in the unity of the same Spirit, one God, world without end. *Amen.*

The Epistle. Acts viii. When the Apostles which were at......

For the Epistle. Acts viii. 14.

WHEN the Apostles, which were at Jerusalem, heard that Samaria had received the......

The Gospel. John x. Verily, verily I say unto you......

The Gospel. St. John x. 1.

VERILY, verily I say unto you, He that entereth not by the door into the sheep-fold,......

¶ *Trinity Sunday.*

¶ *At Matins.*

The first lesson, Gene. xviii. *unto the end.*
The second lesson, Math. iii. *unto the end.*

TRINITY-SUNDAY.

¶ *At the Communion.*

Deus misereatur. Psalm lxvii.

God be merciful unto us, and bless us......

The Collect.

Almighty and everlasting God, which hast given unto us thy servants grace by the confession of a true faith to acknowledge the glory of the eternal Trinity, and in the power of the divine majesty to worship the Unity: We beseech thee that through the steadfastness of this faith, we may evermore be defended from all adversity: which livest and reignest, one God, world without end. Amen.

The Epistle. Apoca. iv, After this I looked, and behold......

The Gospel. John iii. There was a man of the Pharisees... ..

¶ *The first Sunday after Trinity Sunday.*

Beati immaculati. Ps. cxix. [v. 1—8.]

Blessed are those that be undefiled in the way,......

The Collect.

God, the strength of all them that trust in thee, mercifully accept our prayers; and because the weakness of our mortal nature can do no good thing without thee, grant us the help of thy grace, that in keeping of thy commandments, we may please thee both in will and deed; through Jesus Christ our Lord.

The Collect.

ALMIGHTY and everlasting God, who hast given unto us thy servants grace by the confession of a true faith to acknowledge the glory of the eternal Trinity, and in the power of the Divine Majesty to worship the Unity; We beseech thee, that thou wouldest keep us steadfast in this faith, and evermore defend us from all adversities, who livest and reignest, one God, world without end. *Amen.*

For the Epistle. Rev. iv. 1.

AFTER this I looked, and behold, a door was opened in heaven: and the first voice......

The Gospel. St. John iii. 1.

THERE was a man of the Pharisees, named Nicodemus, a ruler of the Jews: the same......

The First Sunday after Trinity.

The Collect.

O GOD, the strength of all them that put their trust in thee, mercifully accept our prayers; and because through the weakness of our mortal nature we can do no good thing without thee, grant us the help of thy grace, that in keeping of thy commandments we may please thee, both in will and deed; through Jesus Christ our Lord. *Amen.*

The Epistle. 1 John iv. Dearly beloved, let us love one another...

The Gospel. Luc. xvi. There was a certain rich man......

¶ *The Second Sunday.*

In quo corriget. Psalm cxix. [v. 9—16.]

WHEREWITHAL shall a young man cleanse his way......

The Collect.

LORD, make us to have a perpetual fear and love of thy holy name: for thou never failest to help and govern them whom thou dost bring up in thy steadfast love. Grant this, &c.

The Epistle. 1 John iii. Marvel not, my brethren though......

The Gospel, Luke xiv. A certain man ordained a great......

¶ *The third Sunday.*

Retribue servo tuo. Psalm cxix. [v. 17—24.]

O DO well unto thy servant: that I may live......

The Collect.

LORD, we beseech thee mercifully to hear us, and unto whom thou

The Epistle. 1 St. John iv. 7.

BELOVED, let us love one another: for love is of God, and every one that loveth is......

The Gospel. St. Luke xvi. 19.

THERE was a certain rich man, which was clothed in purple, and fine linen, and......

THE SECOND SUNDAY AFTER TRINITY.

The Collect.

O LORD, who never failest to help and govern them whom thou dost bring up in thy steadfast fear and love; Keep us, we beseech thee, under the protection of thy good providence, and make us to have a perpetual fear and love of thy holy Name; through Jesus Christ our Lord. *Amen.*

The Epistle. 1 St. John iii. 13.

MARVEL not, my brethren, if the world hate you. We know that we have passed......

The Gospel. St. Luke xiv. 16.

A CERTAIN man made a great supper, and bade many; and sent his servant at. ....

THE THIRD SUNDAY AFTER TRINITY.

The Collect.

O LORD, we beseech thee mercifully to hear us; and grant

hast given an hearty desire to pray, grant that by thy mighty aid we may be defended: through Jesu[s] Christ our Lord.

The Epistle. 1 Peter v. Submit yourselves every man......

The Gospel. Luc. xv. Then resorted unto him......

¶ *The fourth Sunday.*

¶ *At the Communion.*

Adhesit pavimento anima. Psalm cxix. [v. 25—32.]

My soul cleaveth to the dust: O quicken thou me......

The Collect.

God, the Protector of all that trust in thee, without whom nothing is strong, nothing is holy: increase and multiply upon us thy mercy, that thou being our ruler and guide, we may so pass through things temporal, that we finally lose not the things eternal: Grant this, heavenly Father, for Jesus Christ's sake our Lord.

The Epistle. Roma. viii. I suppose that the afflictions......

The Gospel. Luc. vi. Be ye merciful, as your Father......

that we, to whom thou hast given an hearty desire to pray, may by thy mighty aid be defended and comforted in all dangers and adversities; through Jesus Christ our Lord. *Amen.*

The Epistle. 1 St. Pet. v. 5.

ALL of you be subject one to another, and be clothed in humility: for God resisteth......

The Gospel. St. Luke xv. 1.

THEN drew near unto him all the Publicans and......

THE FOURTH SUNDAY AFTER TRINITY.

The Collect.

O God, the protector of all that trust in thee, without whom nothing is strong, nothing is holy; Increase and multiply upon us thy mercy; that, thou being our ruler and guide, we may so pass through things temporal, that we finally lose not the things eternal. Grant this, O heavenly Father: for Jesus Christ's sake our Lord, *Amen.*

The Epistle. Rom. viii. 18.

I RECKON that the sufferings of this present time are not worthy to be compared with......

The Gospel. St. Luke vi. 36.

BE ye therefore merciful, as your Father also is merciful. Judge not, and ye shall not be......

¶ *The fifth Sunday.*	THE FIFTH SUNDAY AFTER TRINITY
Legem pone. Psalm cxix. [v. 33—40.]	
TEACH me, O Lord, the way of thy statutes......	
The Collect.	*The Collect.*
GRANT Lord, we beseech thee, that the course of this world may be so peaceably ordered by thy governance: that thy congregation may joyfully serve thee in all godly quietness: through Jesus Christ our Lord.	GRANT, O Lord, we beseech thee, that the course of this world may be so peaceably ordered by thy governance, that thy Church may joyfully serve thee in all godly quietness; through Jesus Christ our Lord. *Amen.*
	The Epistle. 1 St. Pet. iii. 8.
The Epistle. 1 Peter iii. Be you all of one mind and of......	BE ye all of one mind, having compassion one of another, love as brethren, be pitiful,......
	The Gospel. St. Luke v. 1.
The Gospel. Luc. v. It came to pass that......	IT came to pass, that as the people pressed upon him to hear the Word of God, he......
¶ *The sixth Sunday.*	THE SIXTH SUNDAY AFTER TRINITY
Et veniat super me. Psalm cxix. [v. 41-48.]	
LET thy loving mercy come also unto me......	
The Collect.	*The Collect.*
GOD, which hast prepared to them that love thee, such good things as pass all man's understanding: Pour into our hearts such love toward thee, that we loving thee in all things, may obtain thy promises, which exceed all that we can desire; Through Jesus Christ our Lord.	O GOD, who hast prepared for them that love thee such good things as pass man's understanding; Pour into our hearts such love toward thee, that we, loving thee above all things, may obtain thy promises, which exceed all that we can desire; through Jesus Christ our Lord. *Amen.*
	The Epistle. Rom. vi. 3.
The Epistle. Roma. vi. Know ye not, that all we which are......	KNOW ye not, that so many of us as were baptized into Jesus Christ were baptized......

The Gospel. Mat. v. Jesus said unto his disciples, Except your....

The Gospel. St. Matt. v. 20.

JESUS said unto his disciples, Except your righteousness shall exceed the righteousness......

¶ *The seventh Sunday.*

Memor esto. Psalm cxix. [v. 49—56.]

O THINK upon thy servant, as concerning thy word......

The Collect.

LORD of all power and might, which art the author and giver of all good things; graff in our hearts the love of thy name, increase in us true religion, nourish us with all goodness, and of thy great mercy keep us in the same: Through Jesus Christ our Lord.

The Epistle. Roma. vi. I speak grossly, because of the infirmity...

The Gospel. Mar. viii. In those days, when there was......

THE SEVENTH SUNDAY AFTER TRINITY.

The Collect.

LORD of all power and might, who art the author and giver of all good things; Graft in our hearts the love of thy Name, increase in us true religion, nourish us with all goodness, and of thy great mercy keep us in the same; through Jesus Christ our Lord. *Amen.*

The Epistle. Rom. vi. 19.

I SPEAK after the manner of men, because of the infirmity of your flesh: for as ye have......

The Gospel. St. Mark, viii. 1.

IN those days the multitude being very great, and having nothing to eat, Jesus called......

¶ *The eighth Sunday.*

¶ *At the Communion.*

Portio mea Domine. Psalm cxix. [v. 57—64.]

THOU art my portion, O Lord...

The Collect.

GOD, whose providence is never deceived, we humbly beseech thee, that thou wilt put away from us all hurtful things, and give those things which be profitable for us: through Jesus Christ our Lord.

THE EIGHTH SUNDAY AFTER TRINITY.

The Collect.

O GOD, whose never-failing providence ordereth all things both in heaven and earth; We humbly beseech thee to put away from us all hurtful things, and to give us those things which be profitable for us; through Jesus Christ our Lord. *Amen.*

The Epistle. Roma. viii. Brethren, we are debtors not to the......

The Gospel. Mat. vii. Beware of false prophets which come......

¶ *The ninth Sunday.*

Bonitatem. Psalm cxix. [v. 65—72]

O Lord, thou hast dealt graciously with thy servant......

The Collect.

Grant to us, Lord, we beseech thee, the spirit to think and do always such things as be rightful: that we, which cannot be without thee, may by thee be able to live according to thy will: Through Jesus Christ our Lord.

The Epistle. 1 Cor. x. Brethren, I would not that......

The Gospel. Luc. xvi. Jesus said unto his disciples......

The tenth Sunday.

Manus tuæ. Psalm cxix. [v. 73—80.]

Thy hands have made me and fashioned me......

The Collect.

Let thy merciful ears, O Lord, be open to the prayers of thy humble servants: and that they may obtain their petitions, make them to ask such things as shall please thee: Through Jesus Christ our Lord.

The Epistle. Rom. viii. 12.

BRETHREN, we are debtors, not to the flesh, to live......

The Gospel. St. Matt. vii. 15.

BEWARE of false prophets, which come to you in......

THE NINTH SUNDAY AFTER TRINITY.

The Collect.

GRANT to us, Lord, we beseech thee, the spirit to think and do always such things as be rightful; that we, who cannot do any thing that is good without thee, may by thee be enabled to live according to thy will; through Jesus Christ our Lord. *Amen.*

The Epistle. 1 Cor. x. 1.

BRETHREN, I would not that ye should be ignorant, how that all our fathers were......

The Gospel, St. Luke xvi. 1.

JESUS said unto his disciples, There was a certain rich man which had a steward; and......

THE TENTH SUNDAY AFTER TRINITY.

The Collect.

LET thy merciful ears, O Lord, be open to the prayers of thy humble servants; and that they may obtain their petitions make them to ask such things as shall please thee; through Jesus Christ our Lord. *Amen.*

The Epistle. 1 Cor. xii. Concerning spiritual things......

The Gospel. Luc. xix. And when he was come near......

The eleventh Sunday.

Defecit. Psalm cxix. [v. 81—88.]

My soul hath longed for thy salvation......

The Collect.

God, which declarest thy almighty power, most chiefly in shewing mercy and pity: Give unto us abundantly thy grace, that we running to thy promises, may be made partakers of thy heavenly treasure: through Jesus Christ our Lord.

The Epistle. 1 Cor. xv. Brethren, as pertaining to the Gospel...

The Gospel. Luc. xviii. Christ told this parable......

The twelfth Sunday.

In eternum Domine. Psalm cxix. [v. 89-96.]

O Lord, thy word: endureth for ever......

The Collect.

Almighty and everlasting God, which art always more ready to

The Epistle. 1 Cor. xii. 1.

CONCERNING spiritual gifts, brethren, I would not have you ignorant. Ye know that......

The Gospel. St. Luke xix. 41.

AND when he was come near, he beheld the city, and wept over it, saying, If thou......

THE ELEVENTH SUNDAY AFTER TRINITY.

The Collect.

O GOD, who declarest thy almighty power most chiefly in shewing mercy and pity; Mercifully grant unto us such a measure of thy grace, that we, running the way of thy commandments, may obtain thy gracious promises, and be made partakers of thy heavenly treasure; through Jesus Christ our Lord. *Amen.*

The Epistle. 1 Cor. xv. 1.

BRETHREN, I declare unto you the Gospel which I preached unto you, which......

The Gospel. St. Luke xviii. 9.

JESUS spake this parable unto certain which trusted in themselves that they were righteous......

THE TWELFTH SUNDAY AFTER TRINITY.

The Collect.

ALMIGHTY and everlasting God, who art always more

hear than we to pray; and art wont to give more than either we desire or deserve: Pour down upon us the abundance of thy mercy, forgiving us those things whereof our conscience is afraid, and giving unto us that that our prayer dare not presume to ask; through Jesus Christ our Lord.

ready to hear than we to pray, and art wont to give more than either we desire, or deserve; Pour down upon us the abundance of thy mercy; forgiving us those things whereof our conscience is afraid, and giving us those good things which we are not worthy to ask, but through the merits and mediation of Jesus Christ, thy Son our Lord. *Amen.*

The Epistle. 2 Cor. iii. Such trust have we through Christ......

The Epistle. 2 Cor. iii. 4.

SUCH trust have we through Christ to God-ward: not that we are sufficient of ourselves......

The Gospel. Mar. vii. Jesus departed from the coasts......

The Gospel. St. Mark vii. 31.

JESUS departing from the coasts of Tyre and Sidon, came unto the sea of Galilee......

The thirteenth Sunday.

THE THIRTEENTH SUNDAY AFTER TRINITY.

Quomodo dilexi. Psalm cxix. [v. 97–104.]

LORD, what love have I unto thy law......

The Collect.

ALMIGHTY and merciful God, of whose only gift it cometh, that thy faithful people do unto thee true and laudable service: grant, we beseech thee, that we may so run to thy heavenly promises, that we fail not finally to attain the same: through Jesus Christ our Lord.

The Collect.

ALMIGHTY and merciful God, of whose only gift it cometh that thy faithful people do unto thee true and laudable service; Grant, we beseech thee, that we may so faithfully serve thee in this life, that we fail not finally to attain thy heavenly promises; through the merits of Jesus Christ our Lord. *Amen.*

The Epistle. Gala. iii. To Abraham and his seed......

The Epistle. Gal. iii. 16.

TO Abraham and his seed were the promises made. He saith not, And to seeds, as of......

The Gospel. Luc. x. Happy are the eyes which see......

The Gospel. St. Luke 23.

BLESSED are the eyes which see the things that ye see. For I tell you that many......

The fourteenth Sunday.

Lucerna pedibus meis. Psalm cxix. [v. 105—112.]

THY word is a lantern unto my feet......

The Collect.

ALMIGHTY and everlasting God, give unto us the increase of faith, hope, and charity: and, that we may obtain that which thou dost promise, make us to love that which thou dost command, through Jesus Christ our Lord.

The Epistle. Gala. v. I say walk in the Spirit......

The Gospel. Luc. xvii. And it chanced as Jesus went to......

The fifteenth Sunday.

Iniquos odio habui. Psalm cxix. [v. 113—120.]

I HATE them that imagine evil things......

The Collect.

KEEP, we beseech thee, O Lord, thy church with thy perpetual mercy, and, because the frailty of man without thee cannot but fall, keep us ever by thy help, and lead us to all things profitable to our salvation: through Jesus our Lord.

The Epistle. Gala. vi. Ye see how large a letter......

THE FOURTEENTH SUNDAY AFTER TRINITY.

The Collect.

ALMIGHTY and everlasting God, give unto us the increase of faith, hope, and charity: and, that we may obtain that which thou dost promise, make us to love that which thou dost command; through Jesus Christ our Lord. *Amen.*

The Epistle. Gal. v. 16.

I SAY then, Walk in the Spirit, and ye shall not fulfil the lust of the flesh. For the flesh......

The Gospel. St. Luke xvii. 11.

AND it came to pass, as Jesus went to Jerusalem, that he passed through the midst of......

THE FIFTEENTH SUNDAY AFTER TRINITY.

The Collect.

KEEP, we beseech thee, O Lord, thy church with thy perpetual mercy; and, because the frailty of man without thee cannot but fall, keep us ever by thy help from all things hurtful, and lead us to all things profitable to our salvation; through Jesus Christ our Lord. *Amen.*

The Epistle. Gal. vi. 11.

YE see how large a letter I have written unto you with mine own hand. As many as......

The Gospel. Matt. vi. No man can serve two masters......

The Gospel. St. Matt. vi. 24.

NO man can serve two masters: for either he will hate the one, and love the other: or......

The sixteenth Sunday.

THE SIXTEENTH SUNDAY AFTER TRINITY.

Feci judicium. Psalm cxix. [v. 121—128.]

I DEAL with the thing that is lawful and right......

The Collect.

LORD we beseech thee, let thy continual pity cleanse and defend thy congregation: and because it cannot continue in safety without thy succour, preserve it evermore by thy help and goodness; through Jesus Christ our Lord.

The Collect.

O LORD, we beseech thee, let thy continual pity cleanse and defend thy Church: and, because it cannot continue in safety without thy succour, preserve it evermore by thy help and goodness; through Jesus Christ our Lord. *Amen.*

The Epistle. Ephes. iii. I desire that you faint not......

The Epistle. Ephes. iii. 13.

I DESIRE that ye faint not at my tribulations for you, which is your glory. For this cause......

The Gospel. Luc. vii. And it fortuned that Jesus......

The Gospel. St. Luke vii. 11.

AND it came to pass the day after, that Jesus went into a city called Naim; and many......

¶ *The seventeenth Sunday.*

THE SEVENTEENTH SUNDAY AFTER TRINITY.

Mirabilia. Psalm cxix. [v. 129—136.]

THY testimonies are wonderful: therefore......

The Collect.

LORD, we pray thee that thy grace may always prevent and follow us, and make us continually to be given to all good works; through Jesus Christ our Lord.

The Collect.

LORD, we pray thee that thy grace may always prevent and follow us, and make us continually to be given to all good works; through Jesus Christ our Lord. *Amen.*

The Epistle. Ephes. iv. I (which am a prisoner of the Lord's)......

The Epistle. Ephes. iv. 1.

I THEREFORE the prisoner of the Lord beseech you......

The Gospel. Luc. xiv. It chanced that Jesus went......

¶ *The eighteenth Sunday.*

Justus es domine. Psalm cxix. [v. 137—144]

RIGHTEOUS art thou, O Lord: and true......

The Collect.

LORD, we beseech thee, grant thy people grace to avoid the infections of the devil, and with pure heart and mind to follow thee, the only God: Through Jesus Christ our Lord.

The Epistle. 1 Cor. i. I thank my God always......

The Gospel. Math. xxii. When the Pharisees had heard......

¶ *The nineteenth Sunday.*

Clamavi. Psalm cxix. [v. 145—152]

I CALL with my whole heart: hear me......

The Collect.

O GOD, forasmuch as without thee we are not able to please thee: Grant that the working of thy mercy may in all things direct and rule our hearts; Through Jesus Christ our Lord.

The Epistle. Ephe. iv. This I say and testify through the......

The Gospel. St. Luke xiv. 1.

IT came to pass, as Jesus went into the house of one of the chief Pharisees to eat bread on......

THE EIGHTEENTH SUNDAY AFTER TRINITY.

The Collect.

LORD, we beseech thee, grant thy people grace to withstand the tempations of the world, the flesh, and the devil, and with pure hearts and minds to follow thee the only God; through Jesus Christ our Lord. *Amen.*

The Epistle. 1 Cor. i. 4.

I THANK my God always on your behalf, for the grace of God which is given you by......

The Gospel. St. Matt. xxii. 34.

WHEN the Phariseeshad heard that Jesus had put the Sadducees to silence, they......

THE NINETEENTH SUNDAY AFTER TRINITY.

The Collect.

O GOD, forasmuch as without thee we are not able to please thee; Mercifully grant, that thy Holy Spirit may in all things direct and rule our hearts; through Jesus Christ our Lord. *Amen.*

The Epistle. Ephes. iv. 17.

THIS I say therefore, and testify in the Lord, that ye henceforth walk not as other......

The Gospel. Mat. ix. Jesus entered into a ship......

The Gospel.

JESUS enter
passed ove

The twentieth Sunday.

THE TWENTIET
TI

Vide humilitatem meam. Psalm cxix. [v. 153—160]

O CONSIDER mine adversity, and deliver me......

The Collect.

Th

ALMIGHTY and merciful God, of thy bountiful goodness, keep us from all things that may hurt us: that we being ready both in body and soul, may with free hearts accomplish those things, that thou wouldest have done; through Jesus Christ our Lord.

O ALMIGH
ciful God
goodness keep
from all things
that we, being
and soul, may
lish those things
have done; thr
our Lord. *Am*

The Epistle. Ephe v. Take heed therefore how ye walk......

The Epistle.

SEE then tha
spectly, nc

The Gospel. Matt. xxii. Jesus said to his disciples, the kingdom of heaven......

The Gospel.

JESUS said,
heaven is
king, who made

¶ *The twenty-first Sunday.*

THE TWENTY-F
TI

Principes persecuti. Psalm cxix. [v. 161—168.]

PRINCES have persecuted me without cause......

The Collect.

Th

GRANT, we beseech thee, merciful Lord, to thy faithful people, pardon and peace; that they may be cleansed from all their sins, and serve thee with a quiet mind: Through Jesus Christ our Lord.

GRANT,
merciful
ful people pard
they may be
their sins, and
quiet mind; th
our Lord. *Am*

The Epistle. Ephe. vi. My brethren, be strong......

The Gospel. John iv. There was a certain ruler.

¶ *The twenty-second Sunday.*

Appropinquet deprecatio. Psalm cxix. [v. 169—176.]

LET my complaint come before thee, O Lord......

The Collect.

LORD, we beseech thee to keep thy household the church in continual godliness: that through thy protection, it may be free from all adversities, and devoutly given to serve thee in good works, to the glory of thy name: Through Jesus Christ our Lord.

The Epistle. Phil. i. I thank my God with all remembrance......

The Gospel. Math. xviii. Peter said unto Jesus......

¶ *The twenty-third Sunday.*

Nisi quia dominus. Psalm cxxiv.

IF the Lord himself had not been on our side......

The Collect.

GOD our refuge and strength, which art the author of all godliness, be ready to hear the devout prayers of thy church: and grant

---

The Epistle. Ephes vi. 10.

MY brethren, be strong in the Lord, and in the power of his might. Put on the whole......

The Gospel. St. John iv. 46.

THERE was a certain nobleman, whose son was sick at Capernaum. When he......

THE TWENTY-SECOND SUNDAY AFTER TRINITY.

The Collect.

LORD, we beseech thee to keep thy household the Church in continual godliness; that through thy protection it may be free from all adversities, and devoutly given to serve thee in good works, to the glory of thy name; through Jesus Christ our Lord. *Amen.*

The Epistle. Phil. i. 3.

I THANK my God upon every remembrance of you......

The Gospel. St. Matt. xviii. 21.

PETER said unto Jesus, Lord, how oft shall my brother sin against me, and I forgive him......

THE TWENTY-THIRD SUNDAY AFTER TRINITY.

The Collect.

O GOD, our refuge and strength, who art the author of all godliness; Be ready, we beseech thee, to hear the devout prayers

that those things which we ask faithfully, we may obtain effectually: through Jesu Christ our Lord.

The Epistle. Phil. iii. Brethren, be followers together......

The Gospel. Math. xxii. Then the Pharisees went out and......

¶ *The twenty-fourth Sunday.*

Qui confidunt. Psalm cxxv.

THEY that put their trust in the Lord......

The Collect.

LORD, we beseech thee, assoil thy people from their offences: that through thy bountiful goodness, we may be delivered from the bands of all those sins, which by our frailty we have committed: Grant this, &c.

The Epistle. Coloss. i. We give thanks to God......

The Gospel. Math. ix. While Jesus spake unto the people......

¶ *The twenty-fifth Sunday.*

Nisi dominus. Psalm cxxvii.

EXCEPT the Lord build the house: their labour......

of thy Church: and grant that those things which we ask faithfully we may obtain effectually; through Jesus Christ our Lord. *Amen.*

The Epistle. Phil. iii. 17.

BRETHREN, be followers together of me, and mark......

The Gospel. St. Matt. xxii. 15.

THEN went the Pharisees and took counsel how they might entangle him in his talk......

THE TWENTY-FOURTH SUNDAY AFTER TRINITY.

The Collect.

O LORD, we beseech thee, absolve thy people from their offences; that through thy bountiful goodness we may all be delivered from the bands of those sins, which by our frailty we have committed: Grant this, O heavenly Father, for Jesus Christ's sake, our blessed Lord and Saviour. *Amen.*

The Epistle. Col. i. 3.

WE give thanks to God and the Father of our Lord Jesus Christ, praying always for.....

The Gospel. St. Matt. ix. 18.

WHILE Jesus spake these things unto John's disciples, behold there came a......

THE TWENTY-FIFTH SUNDAY AFTER TRINITY.

The Collect.

STIR up, we beseech thee, O Lord, the wills of thy faithful people, that they plenteously bringing forth the fruit of good works, may of thee be plenteously rewarded: through Jesus Christ our Lord.

The Epistle. Jere. xxiii. Behold, the time cometh......

The Gospel. John vi. When Jesus lift up his eyes......

The Collect.

STIR up, we beseech thee, O Lord, the wills of thy faithful people; that they, plenteously bringing forth the fruit of good works, may of thee be plenteously rewarded: through Jesus Christ our Lord. *Amen.*

For the Epistle. Jer. xxiii. 5.

BEHOLD, the days come, saith the Lord, that I will......

The Gospel. St. John vi. 5.

WHEN Jesus then lift up his eyes, and saw a great company come unto him, he saith......

¶ *If there be any more Sundays before Advent-Snnday, the Service of some of those Sundays that were omitted after the Epiphany shall be taken in to supply so many as are here wanting. And if there be fewer, the overplus may be omitted: Provided that this last Collect, Epistle, and Gospel shall always be used upon the Sunday next before Advent.*

Saint Andrew's Day.

At the Communion.

Sepe expugnaverunt. Psalm cxxix.

MANY a time have they fought against me......

The Collect.

ALMIGHTY God, which hast given such grace to thy Apostle saint Andrewe, that he counted the sharp and painful death of the cross to be an high honour, and a great glory: Grant us to take and esteem all troubles and adversities which shall come unto us for thy sake, as things profitable for us toward the obtaining of everlasting life: through Jesus Christ our Lord.

SAINT ANDREW'S DAY.

The Collect.

ALMIGHTY God, who didst give such grace unto thy holy Apostle Saint Andrew, that he readily obeyed the calling of thy Son Jesus Christ, and followed him without delay; Grant unto us all, that we, being called by thy holy Word, may forthwith give up ourselves obediently to fulfil thy holy commandments; through the same Jesus Christ our Lord. *Amen.*

The Epistle. Roma. x. If thou knowledge with thy mouth......

The Gospel. Math. iv. As Jesus walked by the sea of Galilee...

Saint Thomas the Apostle.

At the Communion.

Beati omnes. Psalm cxxviii.

BLESSED are all they that fear the Lord......

The Collect.

ALMIGHTY everliving God, which for the more confirmation of the faith, didst suffer thy holy apostle Thomas to be doubtful in thy Son's resurrection: Grant us so perfectly, and without all doubt, to believe in thy Son Jesus Christ, that our faith in thy sight never be reproved: hear us, O Lord, through the same Jesus Christ; to whom with thee and the Holy Ghost be all honour, &c.

The Epistle. Ephes. ii. Now ye are not strangers......

The Gospel. John xx. Thomas one of the twelve which......

¶ *The Conversion of St. Paul.*

At Matins.

The second lesson, Acts xxii. *unto* "They heard him."

Confitebor tibi. Psalm cxxxviii.

I WILL give thanks unto thee, O Lord......

The Epistle. Rom. x. 9.

IF thou shalt confess with thy mouth the Lord Jesus, and shalt believe in thine heart......

The Gospel. St. Matt. iv. 18.

JESUS, walking by the sea of Galilee, saw two brethren, Simon called Peter, and Andrew......

SAINT THOMAS THE APOSTLE.

The Collect.

ALMIGHTY and everliving God, who for the more confirmation of the faith, didst suffer thy holy Apostle Thomas to be doubtful in thy Son's resurrection; Grant us so perfectly, and without all doubt, to believe in thy Son Jesus Christ, that our faith in thy sight may never be reproved. Hear us, O Lord, through the same Jesus Christ, to whom, with thee and the Holy Ghost, be all honour and glory, now and for evermore. *Amen.*

The Epistle. Ephes. ii. 19.

NOW therefore ye are no more strangers and foreigners....

The Gospel. St. John xx. 24.

THOMAS, one of the twelve, called Didymus, was......

THE CONVERSION OF ST. PAUL.

The Collect.

God, which hast taught all the world, through the preaching of thy blessed Apostle Saint Paul: grant we beseech thee, that we which have his wonderful conversion in remembrance, may follow and fulfil the holy doctrine that he taught: through Jesus Christ our Lord.

The Epistle. Acts ix. And Saul yet breathing out......

The Gospel. Math. xix. Peter answered and said

¶ *At Evensong.*

¶The second lesson, Acts xxvi. *unto the end.*

¶ *The Purification of Saint Mary the virgin.*

Ecce nunc benedicite. Psalm cxxxiv.

Behold (now), praise the Lord...

The Collect.

Almighty and everlasting God, we humbly beseech thy Majesty, that as thy only begotten Son was this day presented in the Temple, in the substance of our flesh: so grant that we may be presented unto thee with pure and clear minds: By Jesus Christ our Lord.

The Epistle.

The same that is appointed for the Sunday.

The Collect.

O GOD, who through the preaching of the blessed Apostle Saint Paul, hast caused the light of the Gospel to shine throughout the world; Grant, we beseech thee, that we, having his wonderful conversion in remembrance, may shew forth our thankfulness unto thee for the same, by following the holy doctrine which he taught; through Jesus Christ our Lord. *Amen.*

For the Epistle. Acts ix. 1.

AND Saul, yet breathing out threatenings and slaughter against the disciples of the......

The Gospel. St. Matt. xix. 27.

PETER answered and said unto Jesus, Behold, we have forsaken all, and followed......

The Presentation of Christ in the Temple,

commonly called

The Purification of St. Mary the Virgin.

The Collect.

ALMIGHTY and everliving God, we humbly beseech thy Majesty, that, as thy only-begotten Son was this day presented in the temple in substance of our flesh, so we may be presented unto thee with pure and clean hearts, by the same thy Son Jesus Christ our Lord. *Amen.*

For the Epistle. Mal. iii. 1.

BEHOLD, I will send my messenger, and he shall prepare the way before me: and the......

The Gospel. Luc. ii. When the time of their purification......

The Gospel. St. Luke ii. 22.

AND when the days of her purification, according to the Law of Moses, were......

¶ *Saint Mathies day.*

SAINT MATTHIAS'S DAY.

Eripe me. Psalm cxl.

DELIVER me, O Lord, from the evil man...

The Collect.

ALMIGHTY God, which in the place of the traitor Judas, didst choose thy faithful servant Mathie to be of the number of thy twelve Apostles: Grant that thy church being alway preserved from false Apostles, may be ordered and guided by faithful and true pastors: Through Jesus Christ our Lord.

The Collect.

O ALMIGHTY God, who into the place of the traitor Judas didst choose thy faithful servant Matthias to be of the number of the twelve Apostles; Grant that thy Church, being alway preserved from false Apostles, may be ordered and guided by faithful and true pastors; through Jesus Christ our Lord. *Amen.*

The Epistle. Acts i. In those days Peter stood up.

For the Epistle. Acts. i. 15.

IN those days Peter stood up in the midst of the disciples .....

The Gospel. Math xi. In that time Jesus answered......

The Gospel. St. Matt. xi. 25.

AT that time Jesus answered and said, I thank thee......

The Annunciation of the virgin Mary.

THE ANNUNCIATION OF THE BLESSED VIRGIN MARY.

Domine, non est exal. Psalm cxxxi.

LORD, I am not high-minded...

The Collect.

WE beseech thee, Lord, pour thy grace into our hearts, that as we have known Christ thy Son's incarnation, by the message of an Angel; so by his cross and passion, we may be brought unto the glory of his resurrection: Through the same Christ our Lord.

The Collect.

WE beseech thee, O Lord, pour thy grace into our hearts; that, as we have known the incarnation of thy Son Jesus Christ by the message of an Angel, so by his cross and passion we may be brought unto the glory of his resurrection; through the same Jesus Christ our Lord. *Amen.*

The Epistle. Esai. vii. God spake once again unto Ahaz......

The Gospel. Luc. i. And in the sixth month the angel......

¶ *Saint Mark's Day.*

Domine clamavi. Psalm cxli.

LORD, I call upon thee, haste thee unto me......

The Collect.

ALMIGHTY God, which hast instructed thy holy Church with the heavenly doctrine of thy Evangelist Saint Mark: give us grace so to be established by thy holy gospel, that we be not, like children, carried away with every blast of vain doctrine: Through Jesus Christ our Lord.

The Epistle. Ephes. iv. Unto every one of us is given grace......

The Gospel. John xv. I am the true vine......

¶ *Saint Philip and James.*

¶ *At Matins.*

The second lesson, Acts viii. *unto* "When the apostles."

¶ *At the Communion.*

Ecce quam bonum. Psalm. cxxxiii.

BEHOLD, how good and joyful a thing it is......

For the Epistle. Isai. vii. 10.

MOREOVER, the Lord spake again unto Ahaz, saying, Ask thee a sign of the Lord......

The Gospel. St. Luke i. 26.

AND in the sixth month the angel Gabriel was sent from God unto a city of Galilee......

SAINT MARK'S DAY.

The Collect.

O ALMIGHTY God, who hast instructed thy holy Church with the heavenly doctrine of thy Evangelist Saint Mark; Give us grace, that, being not like children carried away with every blast of vain doctrine, we may be established in the truth of thy holy Gospel; through Jesus Christ our Lord. *Amen.*

The Epistle. Ephes. iv. 7.

UNTO every one of us is given grace, according to the......

The Gospel. St. John xv. 1.

I AM the true vine, and my Father is the husbandman. Every branch in me that......

SAINT PHILIP AND SAINT JAMES'S DAY.

The Collect.

Almighty God, whom truly to know is everlasting life: Grant us perfectly to know thy Son Jesus Christ, to be the way, the truth, and the life, as thou hast taught Saint Philip, and other the Apostles: Through Jesus Christ our Lord.

The Epistle. James i. James the servant of God......

The Gospel. John xiv. And Jesus said unto his disciples......

Saint Barnabe Apostle.

At Matins.

¶ The second lesson, Acts xiv. *unto the end.*

¶ *At the Communion.*

Voce mea ad Dominum. Psalm cxlii.

I cried unto the Lord with my voice......

The Collect.

Lord Almighty, which hast endued thy holy Apostle Barnabas with singular gifts of thy holy Ghost: let us not be destitute of thy manifold gifts, nor yet of grace to use them alway to thy honour and glory: Through Jesus Christ our Lord.

The Epistle. Act. xi. Tidings of these things came unto......

The Collect.

O ALMIGHTY God, whom truly to know is everlasting life; Grant us perfectly to know thy Son Jesus Christ to be the way, the truth, and the life; that, following the steps of thy holy Apostles, Saint Philip and Saint James, we may stedfastly walk in the way that leadeth to eternal life; through the same thy Son Jesus Christ our Lord. *Amen.*

The Epistle. St. James i. 1.

JAMES, a servant of God and of the Lord Jesus Christ, to the twelve tribes which are......

The Gospel. St. John xiv. 1.

AND Jesus said unto his disciples, Let not your heart be troubled; ye believe in......

Saint Barnabas the Apostle.

The Collect.

O LORD God Almighty, who didst endue thy holy Apostle Barnabas with singular gifts of the Holy Ghost; leave us not, we beseech thee, destitute of thy manifold gifts, nor yet of grace to use them always to thy honour and glory; through Jesus Christ our Lord. *Amen.*

For the Epistle. Acts xi. 22.

TIDINGS of these things came unto the ears of the church which was in Jerusalem......

The Gospel, John xv. This is my commandment that ye love...

¶ *At Evensong.*

¶ The second lesson, Acts xv. *unto*, "After certain days."

¶ *Saint John Baptist.*

¶ *Proper Lessons at Matins.*

The first lesson, Malach. iii. *unto the end.*

The second lesson, Mat. iii. *unto the end.*

At the Communion.

Domine exaudi. Psalm cxliii.

HEAR my prayer, O Lord, and consider my desire......

The Collect.

ALMIGHTY God, by whose providence thy servant John Baptist was wonderfully born, and sent to prepare the way of thy Son our Saviour by preaching of penance: make us so to follow his doctrine and holy life, that we may truly repent according to his preaching, and after his example constantly speak the truth, boldly rebuke vice, and patiently suffer for the truth's sake: through Jesus Christ our Lord.

The Epistle. Esai. xl. Be of good cheer my people......

The Gospel. Luc. i. Elizabeth's time came......

Proper Lessons at Evensong.

The first lesson, Malach. iv. *unto the end.*

The second lesson, Mat. xiv. *unto* "When Jesus heard."

The Gospel. St. John xv. 12.

THIS is my commandment, That ye love one......

SAINT JOHN BAPTIST'S DAY.

The Collect.

ALMIGHTY God, by whose providence thy servant John Baptist was wonderfully born, and sent to prepare the way of thy Son our Saviour, by preaching of repentance; Make us so to follow his doctrine and holy life, that we may truly repent according to his preaching; and after his example constantly speak the truth, boldly rebuke vice, and patiently suffer for the truth's sake; through Jesus Christ our Lord. *Amen.*

For the Epistle. Isai. xl. 1.

COMFORT ye, comfort ye my people, saith your......

The Gospel. St. Luke i. 57.

ELISABETH'S full time came that she should be delivered; and she brought forth a son......

¶ *Saint Peter's Day.*

At Matins.

The second lesson, Acts iii. *unto the end.*

At the Communion.

Benedictus dominus. Psalm cxliv.

BLESSED be the Lord my strength ......

The Collect.

ALMIGHTY God, which by thy Son Jesus Christ hast given to thy Apostle Saint Peter many excellent gifts, and commandedst him earnestly to feed thy flock; make, we beseech thee, all bishops and pastors diligently to preach thy holy word, and the people obediently to follow the same, that they may receive the crown of everlasting Glory, through Jesus Christ our Lord.

The Epistle. Acts xii. At the same time, Herod the King .....

The Gospel. Mat. xvi. When Jesus came into the coasts......

At Evensong.

The second Lesson, Acts iv. *unto the end.*

¶ *Saint Mary Magdalene.*

Lauda anima mea. Psalm cxlvi.

PRAISE the Lord, O my soul...

The Collect.

MERCIFUL Father, give us grace, that we never presume to sin through the example of any creature, but if it shall chance us at any time to offend thy divine majesty, that then we may truly repent, and

SAINT PETER'S DAY.

The Collect.

O ALMIGHTY God, who by thy Son Jesus Christ didst give to thy Apostle Saint Peter many excellent gifts, and commandedst him earnestly to feed thy flock; Make, we beseech thee, all Bishops and Pastors diligently to preach thy holy Word, and the people obediently to follow the same, that they may receive the crown of everlasting glory; through Jesus Christ our Lord. *Amen.*

For the Epistle. Acts xii. 1.

ABOUT that time Herod the king stretched forth his hands to vex certain of the......

The Gospel. St. Matt. xvi. 13.

WHEN Jesus came into the coasts of Cæsarea Philippi, he asked his disciples, saying......

lament the same, after the example of Mary Magdalene, and by lively faith obtain remission of all our sins: through the only merits of thy Son our Saviour Christ.

The Epistle. Prov. xxxi. Whosoever findeth an honest......

The Gospel. Luc. vii. And one of the Pharisees desired Jesus......

¶ *Saint James the Apostle.*

Laudate Dominum de celis. Psalm cxlviii.

O PRAISE the Lord of Heaven...

The Collect.

GRANT, O merciful God, that as thine holy Apostle James leaving his father and all that he had, without delay, was obedient unto the calling of thy Son Jesus Christ, and followed him: So we forsaking all worldly and carnal affections, may be evermore ready to follow thy commandments: through Jesus Christ our Lord.

The Epistle. Act. xi. Acts xii. In those days came prophets......

The Gospel. Math. xx. Then came to him the mother of......

Saint Bartholomewe.

Non nobis domine. Psalm cxv.

NOT unto us, (O Lord,) not unto us......

The Collect

O ALMIGHTY and everlasting God, which hast given grace to thy

SAINT JAMES THE APOSTLE.

The Collect.

GRANT, O merciful God, that as thine holy Apostle Saint James, leaving his father and all that he had, without delay was obedient unto the calling of thy Son Jesus Christ, and followed him; so we, forsaking all worldly and carnal affections, may be evermore ready to follow thy holy commandments; through Jesus Christ our Lord. *Amen.*

For the Epistle. Acts xi. 27, *and part of* Chap. 12.

IN those days came prophets from Jerusalem unto......

The Gospel. St. Matt. xx. 20.

THEN came to him the mother of Zebedee's......

SAINT BARTHOLOMEW THE APOSTLE.

The Collect.

O ALMIGHTY and everlasting God, who didst give to thine

apostle Bartholomewe truly to believe and to preach thy word: grant, we beseech thee, unto thy church, both to love that he believed, and to preach that he taught: through Christ our Lord.	Apostle Bartholomew grace truly to believe and to preach thy Word; Grant, we beseech thee, unto thy Church, to love that Word which he believed, and both to preach and receive the same; through Jesus Christ our Lord. *Amen.*
	For the Epistle. Acts v. 12.
The Epistle. Acts v. By the hands of the Apostles......	BY the hands of the Apostles were many signs and wonders wrought among the......
	The Gospel. St. Luke xxii. 24.
The Gospel. Luc. xxii. And there was a strife among them......	AND there was also a strife among them, which of them should be accounted the......
¶ *Saint Mathewe.*	SAINT MATTHEW THE APOSTLE.
Laudate Dominum omnes gentes. Psalm cxvii.	
O PRAISE the Lord, all ye......	
The Collect.	*The Collect.*
ALMIGHTY God, which by thy blessed Son didst call Mathewe from the receipt of custom to be an Apostle and Evangelist: Grant us grace to forsake all covetous desires and inordinate love of riches, and to follow thy said Son Jesus Christ: who liveth and reigneth, &c.	ALMIGHTY God, who by thy blessed Son didst call Matthew from the receipt of custom to be an Apostle and Evangelist; Grant us grace to forsake all covetous desires, and inordinate love of riches, and to follow the same thy Son Jesus Christ, who liveth and reigneth with thee and the Holy Ghost, one God, world without end. *Amen.*
	The Epistle. 2 Cor. iv. 1.
The Epistle. 2 Cor. iv. Seeing that we have such an office......	THEREFORE seeing we have this ministry, as we have received mercy, we faint not......
	The Gospel. St. Matt. ix. 9.
The Gospel. Math ix. And as Jesus passed forth......	AND as Jesus passed forth from thence, he saw a man......

¶ *Saint Michael and all Angels.*

¶ *At the Communion.*

Laudate pueri. Psal. cxiii.

PRAISE the Lord, (ye servants)...

The Collect.

EVERLASTING God, which hast ordained and constituted the services of all Angels and men in a wonderful order: mercifully grant, that they which alway do thee service in heaven, may by thy appointment succour and defend us in earth: through Jesus Christ our Lord, &c.

The Epistle. Apoca. xii. There was a great battle in heaven......

The Gospel. Math. xviii. At the same time came the......

¶ *Saint Luke Evangelist.*

Super flumina. Psalm cxxxvii.

BY the waters of Babylon we sat down and wept......

The Collect.

ALMIGHTY God, which calledst Luke the physician, whose praise is in the gospel, to be a physician of the soul: it may please thee by the wholesome medicines of his doctrine, to heal all the diseases of our souls: through thy Son Jesus Christ our Lord.

The Epistle. 2 Tim. iv. Watch thou in all things......

SAINT MICHAEL AND ALL ANGELS

The Collect.

O EVERLASTING God, who hast ordained and constituted the services of Angels and men in a wonderful order; Mercifully grant, that as thy holy Angels alway do thee service in heaven, so by thy appointment they may succour and defend us on earth; through Jesus Christ our Lord. *Amen.*

For the Epistle. Rev. xii. 7.

THERE was war in heaven: Michael and his angels......

The Gospel. St. Matt. xviii. 1.

AT the same time came the disciples unto Jesus, saying, Who is the greatest in the......

SAINT LUKE THE EVANGELIST.

The Collect.

ALMIGHTY God, who calledst Luke the Physician, whose praise is in the Gospel, to be an Evangelist, and Physician of the soul; May it please thee, that, by the wholesome medicines of the doctrine delivered by him, all the diseases of our souls may be healed; through the merits of thy Son Jesus Christ our Lord. *Amen.*

The Epistle. 2 Tim. iv. 5.

WATCH thou in all things, endure afflictions, do the work of an Evangelist, make......

The Gospel. Luc. x. The Lord appointed other seventy......

¶ *Symon and Jude Apostles.*

Laudate Dominum. Psalm cl.

O PRAISE God in his holiness...

The Collect.

ALMIGHTY God, which hast builded the congregation upon the foundation of the Apostles and prophets, Jesu Christ himself being the head corner-stone: grant us so to be joined together in unity of spirit by their doctrine, that we may be made an holy temple acceptable to thee: through Jesu Christ our Lord.

The Epistle. Jude I. Judas the servant of Jesus Christ......

The Gospel. John xv. This command I you......

¶ *All Saints.*

Proper Lessons at Matins.

The first lesson, Sapi. iii. *unto* "Blessed is rather the Barren."

The second lesson, Hebre. xi. xii. "Saints by faith subdued," *unto*, "If ye endure chastising."

At the Communion.

Cantate Domino. Psalm cxlix.

O SING unto the Lord a new...

The Collect.

ALMIGHTY God, which hast knit together thy elect in one communion and fellowship in the mystical body of thy Son Christ our Lord;

The Gospel. St. Luke x. 1.

THE Lord appointed other seventy also, and sent......

SAINT SIMON AND SAINT JUDE, APOSTLES.

The Collect.

O ALMIGHTY God who hast built thy Church upon the foundation of the Apostles and Prophets, Jesus Christ himself being the head corner-stone; Grant us so to be joined together in unity of spirit by their doctrine, that we may be made an holy temple acceptable unto thee; through Jesus Christ our Lord. *Amen.*

The Epistle. St. Jude 1.

JUDE, the servant of Jesus Christ, and brother of......

The Gospel. St. John xv. 17.

THESE things I command you, that ye love......

ALL SAINTS' DAY.

The Collect.

O ALMIGHTY God, who hast knit together thine elect in one communion and fellowship, in the mystical body of thy Son grant us grace so to follow thy holy Saints in all virtues, and godly living, that we may come to those unspeakable joys, which thou hast prepared for all them that unfeignedly love thee; through Jesus Christ.

The Epistle. Apoca. vii. Behold, I John saw another angel......

The Gospel. Math. v. Jesus seeing the people......

¶ *Proper Lessons at Evensong.*

The first lesson, Sapi. v. *unto*, "His jealousy also."

The second lesson, Apoc. xix. *unto* "And I saw an angel stand."

Christ our Lord; Grant us grace so to follow thy blessed Saints in all virtuous and godly living, that we may come to those unspeakable joys, which thou hast prepared for them that unfeignedly love thee; through Jesus Christ our Lord. *Amen.*

For the Epistle. Rev. vii. 2.

AND I saw another angel ascending from the east......

The Gospel. St. Matt. v. 1.

JESUS, seeing the multitudes, went up into a mountain...

THE

SUPPER OF THE LORD,

AND

THE HOLY COMMUNION,

COMMONLY CALLED THE MASS.

¶ *SO many as intend to be partakers of the holy Communion, shall signify their names to the Curate over night, or else in the morning, afore the beginning of Matins, or immediately after.*

¶ *And if any of those be an open and notorious evil liver, so that the congregation by him is offended, or have done any wrong to his neighbours by word or deed: The Curate shall call him, and advertise him, in any wise not to presume to the Lord's table, until he have openly declared himself to have truly repented, and amended his former naughty life: that the congregation may thereby be satisfied, which afore were offended: and that he have recompensed the parties, whom he hath done wrong unto, or at the least be in full purpose so to do, as soon as he conveniently may.*

¶ *The same order shall the Curate use, with those betwixt whom he perceiveth malice and hatred to reign, not suffering them to be partakers of the Lord's table, until he know them to be reconciled. And if one of the parties so at varience be content to forgive from the bottom of his heart all that the other hath trespassed against him, and to make amends for that he himself hath offended: and the other party will not be persuaded to a godly unity: but remain still in his frowardness and malice: the Minister in that case ought to admit the penitent person to the holy Communion, and not him that is obstinate.*

¶ *Upon the day, and at the time appointed for the ministration of the holy Communion, the Priest that shall execute the holy ministry, shall put upon him the vesture appointed for that ministration, that is to say: a white*

THE ORDER OF THE

ADMINISTRATION OF THE LORD'S SUPPER,

OR

HOLY COMMUNION.

¶ *SO many as intend to be partakers of the holy Communion shall signify their names to the Curate, at least some time the day before.*

¶ *And if any of those be an open and notorious evil liver, or have done any wrong to his neighbours by word or deed, so that the congregation be thereby offended; the Curate, having knowledge thereof, shall call him and advertise him, that in any wise he presume not to come to the Lord's Table, until he hath openly declared himself to have truly repented and amended his former naughty life, that the Congregation may thereby be satisfied, which before were offended; and that he hath recompensed the parties, to whom he hath done wrong; or at least declare himself to be in full purpose so to do, as soon as he conveniently may.*

¶ *The same order shall the Curate use with those betwixt whom he perceiveth malice and hatred to reign; not suffering them to be partakers of the Lord's Table, until he know them to be reconciled. And if one of the parties so at variance be content to forgive from the bottom of his heart all that the other hath trespassed against him, and to make amends for that he himself hath offended; and the other party will not be persuaded to a godly unity, but remain still in his frowardness and malice: the Minister in that case ought to admit the penitent person to the holy Communion, and not him that is obstinate. Provided that every Minister so repelling any, as is specified in this, or the next precedent Paragraph of this Rubrick, shall be obliged to give an account of the same to the Ordinary within fourteen days after at the farthest. And the Ordinary shall proceed against the offending person according to the Canon.*

Albe plain, with a vestment or Cope. And where there be many Priests or Deacons, there so many shall be ready to help the Priest, in the ministration, as shall be requisite: And shall have upon them likewise the vestures appointed for their ministry, that is to say, Albes with tunicles. Then shall the Clerks sing in English for the office, or Introit, (as they call it,) a Psalm appointed for that day.

The priest standing humbly afore the midst of the Altar, shall say the Lord's prayer, with this Collect.

ALMIGHTY God, unto whom all hearts be open, and all desires known, and from whom no secrets are hid: cleanse the thoughts of our hearts, by the inspiration of thy Holy Spirit: that we may perfectly love thee, and worthily magnify thy holy name: through Christ our Lord. Amen.

Then shall he say a Psalm appointed for the introit: which Psalm ended, the Priest shall say, or else the Clerks shall sing,

iii. Lord have mercy upon us.
iii. Christ have mercy upon us.
iii. Lord have mercy upon us.

Then the Priest standing at God's board shall begin,

Glory be to God on high.

The Clerks. And in earth peace, good will towards men.

¶ *The Table, at the Communion-time having a fair white linen cloth upon it, shall stand in the Body of the Church, or in the Chancel, where Morning and Evening Prayer are appointed to be said. And the Priest standing at the North-side of the Table shall say the Lord's Prayer, with the Collect following, the people kneeling.*

OUR Father which art in heaven, Hallowed be thy Name. Thy kingdom come. Thy will be done in earth, As it is in heaven. Give us this day our daily bread. And forgive us our trespasses, As we forgive them that trespass against us. And lead us not into temptation; But deliver us from evil. Amen.

The Collect.

ALMIGHTY God unto whom all hearts be open, all desires known, and from whom no secrets are hid; Cleanse the thoughts of our hearts by the inspiration of thy Holy Spirit, that we may perfectly love thee, and worthily magnify thy holy Name; through Christ our Lord. *Amen.*

We praise thee, we bless thee, we worship thee, we glorify thee, we give thanks to thee for thy great glory, O Lord GOD, heavenly King, God the Father Almighty.

O Lord the only begotten Son Jesu Christ, O Lord GOD, Lamb of GOD, Son of the Father, that takest away the sins of the world, have mercy upon us: thou that takest away the sins of the world, receive our prayer.

Thou that sittest at the right hand of God the Father, have mercy upon us: For thou only art holy, thou only art the Lord. Thou only, O Christ, with the Holy Ghost, are most high in the glory of God the Father. Amen.

Then the priest shall turn him to the people and say.

The Lord be with you.

The Answer. And with thy spirit.

The Priest. Let us pray.

¶ *Then shall the Priest, turning to the people, rehearse distinctly all the TEN COMMANDMENTS; and the people still kneeling shall, after every Commandment, ask God mercy for their transgression thereof for the time past, and grace to keep the same for the time to come, as followeth.*

Minister.

GOD spake these words, and said; I am the Lord thy God: Thou shalt have none other gods but me.

People. Lord, have mercy upon us, and incline our hearts to keep this law.

Minister. Thou shalt not make to thyself any graven image, nor the likeness of anything that is in heaven above, or in the earth beneath, or in the water under the earth. Thou shalt not bow down to them, nor worship them: for I the Lord thy God am a jealous God, and visit the sins of the fathers upon the children, unto the third and fourth generation of them that hate me, and shew mercy unto thousands in them that love me, and keep my commandments.

People. Lord, have mercy upon us, and incline our hearts to keep this law.

Minister. Thou shalt not take the Name of the Lord thy God in vain: for the Lord will not hold him guiltless, that taketh his Name in vain.

People. Lord have mercy upon us, and incline our hearts to keep this law.

Minister. Remember that thou keep holy the Sabbath-day. Six days shalt thou labour, and do all that thou hast to do; but the seventh day is the Sabbath of the Lord thy God. In it thou shalt do no manner of work, thou, and thy son, and thy daughter, thy man-servant, and thy maid-servant, thy cattle, and the stranger that is within thy gates. For in six days the Lord made heaven and earth, the sea, and all that in them is, and rested the seventh day: wherefore the Lord blessed the seventh day, and hallowed it.

People. Lord, have mercy upon us, and incline our hearts to keep this law.

Minister. Honour thy father and thy mother; that thy days may be long in the land, which the Lord thy God giveth thee.

People. Lord, have mercy upon us, and incline our hearts to keep this law.

Minister. Thou shalt do no murder.

People. Lord, have mercy upon us, and incline our hearts to keep this law.

Minister. Thou shalt not commit adultery.

People. Lord, have mercy upon us, and incline our hearts to keep this law.

Minister. Thou shalt not steal.

People. Lord, have mercy upon us, and incline our hearts to keep this law.

Minister. Thou shalt not bear false witness against thy neighbour.

People. Lord, have mercy upon us, and incline our hearts to keep this law.

Minister. Thou shalt not covet thy neighbour's house, thou shalt not covet thy neighbour's wife, nor his servant, nor his maid, nor his ox, nor his ass, nor any thing that is his.

People. Lord, have mercy upon us, and write all these thy laws in our hearts, we beseech thee.

Then shall follow the Collect of the day, with one of these two Collects following for the King.

Priest. Let us pray.

ALMIGHTY God, whose kingdom is everlasting, and power infinite, have mercy upon the whole congregation, and so rule the heart of thy chosen servant Edward the sixth, our king and governor, that he (knowing whose minister he is) may above all things, seek thy honour and glory, and that we his subjects (duly considering whose authority he hath) may faithfully serve, honour, and humbly obey him, in thee, and for thee, according to thy blessed word and ordinance: through Jesus Christ our Lord, who with thee, and the Holy Ghost, liveth and reigneth, ever one God, world without end. Amen

ALMIGHTY and everlasting GOD, we be taught by thy holy word, that the hearts of Kings are in thy rule and governance, and that thou dost dispose, and turn them as it seemeth best to thy godly wisdom: We humbly beseech thee so to

¶ *Then shall follow one of these two Collects for the Queen, the Priest standing as before, and saying,*

Let us pray.

ALMIGHTY God, whose kingdom is everlasting, and power infinite; Have mercy upon the whole Church; and so rule the heart of thy chosen Servant *VICTORIA*, our Queen and Governour, that she (knowing whose minister she is) may above all things seek thy honour and glory: and that we all her subjects (duly considering whose authority she hath) may faithfully serve, honour, and humbly obey her, in thee, and for thee, according to thy blessed Word and ordinance; through Jesus Christ our Lord, who with thee and the Holy Ghost liveth and reigneth, ever one God, world without end. *Amen.*

Or,

ALMIGHTY and everlasting God, we are taught by thy holy Word, that the hearts of Kings are in thy rule and governance, and that thou dost dispose and turn them as it seemeth best to thy godly wisdom: We humbly

dispose and govern the heart of Edward the sixth, thy servant, our King and governor, that in all his thoughts, words, and works, he may ever seek thy honour and glory, and study to preserve thy people committed to his charge, in wealth, peace, and godliness: Grant this, O merciful Father, for thy dear Son's sake, Jesus Christ our Lord. Amen.

The Collects ended, the priest, or he that is appointed, shall read the Epistle, in a place assigned for the purpose, saying,

The Epistle of Saint Paul, written in the Chapter of to the

The Minister then shall read the Epistle. Immediately after the Epistle ended, the priest, or one appointed to read the Gospel, shall say,

The holy Gospel, written in the Chapter of

The Clerks and people shall answer.

Glory be to thee, O Lord.

The Priest or Deacon then shall read the Gospel: After the Gospel ended, the Priest shall begin,

I BELIEVE in one God.

The Clerks shall sing the rest.

The Father almighty, maker of heaven and earth, and of all things visible and invisible: And in one Lord Jesu Christ, the only begotten Son of God, begotten of his Father before all worlds, God of GOD, light of light, very God of very God, begotten, not made, being of one substance with the Father, by whom all things were made, who for us men, and for our salvation, came down from heaven, and was incarnate by the Holy Ghost of the Virgin Mary, and was made man, and was crucified also for us under Pontius Pilate, he suffered and was

beseech thee so to dispose and govern the heart of *VICTORIA* thy Servant, our Queen and Governour, that, in all her thoughts, words, and works, she may ever seek thy honour and glory, and study to preserve thy people committed to her charge, in wealth, peace, and godliness; Grant this, O merciful Father, for thy dear Son's sake, Jesus Christ our Lord. *Amen.*

¶ *Then shall be said the Collect of the Day.*

And immediately after the Collect the Priest shall read the Epistle, saying, The Epistle [*or,* The portion of Scripture appointed for the Epistle] is written in the —— Chapter of —— beginning at the —— Verse.

And the Epistle ended, he shall say, Here endeth the Epistle.

Then shall he read the Gospel (the people all standing up) saying, The holy Gospel is written in the —— Chapter of —— beginning at the —— Verse.

And the Gospel ended, shall be sung or said the Creed following, the people still standing, as before.

I BELIEVE in one God the Father Almighty, Maker of heaven and earth, And of all things visible and invisible:

And in one Lord Jesus Christ, the only-begotten Son of God, Begotten of his Father before all worlds, God of God, Light of Light, Very God of very God, Begotten, not made, Being of one substance with the Father; By whom all things were made, Who for us men, and for our salvation, came down from heaven, And was incarnate by the Holy Ghost of the Virgin Mary, And was made man, And was crucified also for us under Pontius Pilate. He suffered and was buried, And the third day he

buried, and the third day he arose again according to the scriptures, and ascended into heaven, and sitteth at the right hand of the Father: and he shall come again with glory, to judge both the quick and the dead.

And I believe in the Holy Ghost, the Lord and giver of life, who proceedeth from the Father and the Son, who with the Father and the Son together, is worshipped and glorified, who spake by the prophets. And I believe one Catholic and Apostolic Church. I acknowledge one Baptism, for the remission of sins. And I look for the resurrection of the dead: and the life of the world to come. Amen.

¶ *After the Creed ended, shall follow the Sermon or Homily, or some portion of one of the Homilies, as they shall be hereafter divided: wherein if the people be not exhorted to the worthy receiving of the holy Sacrament of the body and blood of our Saviour Christ, then shall the Curate give this exhortation, to those that be minded to receive the same.*

DEARLY beloved in the Lord, ye that mind to come to the holy Communion of the body and blood of our Saviour Christ, must consider what St. Paul writeth to the Corinthians, how he exhorteth all persons diligently to try and examine themselves, before they presume to eat of that bread and drink of that cup: for as the benefit is great, if with a truly penitent heart, and lively faith, we receive that holy Sacrament; (for then we spiritually eat the flesh of Christ, and drink his blood, then we dwell in Christ and Christ in us, we be made one with Christ and Christ with us;) so is the danger great, if we receive the same unworthily; for then we become guilty of the body and blood of Christ our Saviour, we eat and drink our own damnation, not considering the Lord's body. We kindle God's wrath over us, we provoke

rose again according to the Scriptures, And ascended into heaven, And sitteth on the right hand of the Father. And he shall come again with glory to judge both the quick and the dead: Whose kingdom shall have no end.

And I believe in the Holy Ghost, The Lord and Giver of life, Who proceedeth from the Father and the Son, Who with the Father and the Son together is worshipped and glorified, Who spake by the Prophets. And I believe one Catholick and Apostolick Church. I acknowledge one Baptism for the Remission of sins, And I look for the Resurrection of the dead, And the life of the world to come. Amen.

him to plague us with divers diseases and sundry kinds of death.

Therefore if any here be a blasphemer, advouterer, or be in malice, or envy, or in any other grievous crime (except he be truly sorry therefore, and earnestly minded to leave the same vices, and do trust himself to be reconciled to Almighty God, and in charity with all the world), let him bewail his sins, and not come to that holy table; lest after the taking of that most blessed bread, the devil enter into him, as he did into Judas, to fill him full of all iniquity, and bring him to destruction, both of body and soul.

Judge therefore yourselves (brethren) that ye be not judged of the Lord. Let your minds be without desire to sin, repent you truly for your sins past, have an earnest and lively faith in Christ our Saviour, be in perfect charity with all men; so shall ye be meet partakers of those holy mysteries. And above all things: ye must give most humble and hearty thanks to God the Father, the Son, and the Holy Ghost, for the redemption of the world by the death and passion of our Saviour Christ, both God and man, who did humble himself even to the death upon the cross, for us miserable sinners, which lay in darkness and shadow of death, that he might make us the children of God, and exalt us to everlasting life. And to the end that we should alway remember the exceeding love of our Master, and only Saviour Jesu Christ, thus dying for us, and the innumerable benefits, which (by his precious blood-shedding) he hath obtained to us, he hath left in those holy mysteries, as a pledge of his love, and a continual remembrance of the same, his own blessed body, and precious blood, for us to feed upon spiritually, to our endless comfort and consolation. To him therefore, with the Father and the

Holy Ghost, let us give (as we are most bounden) continual thanks, submitting ourselves wholly to his holy will and pleasure, and studying to serve him in true holiness and righteousness, all the days of our life. Amen.

¶ *In Cathedral churches or other places, where there is daily Communion, it shall be sufficient to read this exhortation above written, once in a month. And in parish churches, upon the week days it may be left unsaid.*

¶ *And if upon the Sunday or holyday, the people be negligent to come to the Communion: Then shall the Priest earnestly exhort his parishioners, to dispose themselves to the receiving of the holy communion more diligently, saying these or like words unto them.*

DEAR friends, and you especially upon whose souls I have cure and charge, on next, I do intend by God's grace, to offer to all such as shall be godly disposed, the most comfortable Sacrament of the body and blood of Christ, to be taken of them in the remembrance of his most fruitful and glorious Passion: by the which passion we have obtained remission of our sins, and be made partakers of the kingdom of heaven, whereof we be assured and ascertained, if we come to the said Sacrament with hearty repentance for our offences, steadfast faith in God's mercy, and earnest mind to obey God's will, and to offend no more. Wherefore our duty is to come to these holy mysteries, with most hearty thanks to be given to Almighty GOD for his infinite mercy and benefits given and bestowed upon us his unworthy servants, for whom he hath not only given his body to death, and shed his blood, but also doth vouchsafe in a Sacrament and mystery to give us his said body and blood to feed upon spiritually. The which Sacrament being so divine and holy a thing, and so comfortable to them which receive it worthily, and so dangerous to them that will presume to take the same unworthily: My duty is to exhort you in the mean season, to consider the greatness of the thing, and to search and examine your own consciences, and that not lightly nor after the manner of dissimulers with GOD: but as they which should come to a most Godly and heavenly banquet, not to come but in the marriage garment required of God in scripture; that you may (so much as lieth in you) be found worthy to come to such a table. The ways and means thereto is,

First, that you be truly repentant of your former evil life, and that you confess with an unfeigned heart to Almighty God your sins and unkindness towards his Majesty committed, either by will, word, or deed, infirmity or ignorance: and that with inward sorrow and tears you bewail your offences, and require of Almighty God mercy and pardon, promising to him (from the bottom of your hearts) the amendment of your former life. And amongst all others, I am commanded of God, especially to move and exhort you to reconcile yourselves to your neighbours, whom you have offended, or who hath offended you, putting out of your hearts all hatred and malice against them, and to be in love and charity with all the world, and to forgive other as you would that God should forgive you. And if any man have done wrong to any other, let him make satisfaction, and due restitution of all lands and goods, wrongfully taken away or withholden, before he come to God's board, or at the least be in full mind and purpose so to do, as soon as he is able; or else let him not come to this holy table, thinking to deceive God, who seeth all men's hearts. For neither the absolution of the priest can any thing avail them, nor the receiving of this holy sacrament doth anything but increase their damnation. And if there be any of you, whose conscience is troubled and grieved in any thing, lacking comfort or counsel, let him come to me, or to some other discreet and learned priest, taught in the law of God, and confess and open his sin and grief secretly, that he may receive such ghostly counsel, advice, and comfort, that his conscience may be relieved, and that of us (as of the ministers of GOD and of the church) he may receive comfort and absolution, to the satisfaction of his mind, and avoiding of all scruple and doubtfulness: requiring such as shall be satisfied with a general confession, not to be offended with them that do use, to their further satisfying, the auricular and secret confession to the priest; nor those also which think needful or convenient, for the quietness of their own consciences, particularly to open their sins to the priest, to be offended with them that are satisfied with their humble confession to GOD, and the general confession to the church. But in all things to follow and keep the rule of charity, and every man to be satisfied with his own conscience, not judging other men's minds or consciences; where as he hath no warrant of God's word to the same.

¶ *Then the Curate shall declare unto the people what Holy-days, or Fasting-days are in the Week following to be observed. And then also (if occasion be) shall notice be given of the Communion; and Briefs, Citations, and Excommunications read. And nothing shall be proclaimed or published in the Church, during the time of Divine Service, but by the Minister; nor by him any thing, but what is prescribed in the Rules of this Book, or enjoined by the Queen, or by the Ordinary of the place.*

¶ *Then shall follow the Sermon, or one of the Homilies already set forth, or hereafter to be set forth, by authority.*

¶ *Then shall follow for the Offertory one or more of these Sentences of holy scripture, to be sung whiles the people do offer, or else one of them to be said by the minister, immediately afore the offering.*

Let your light so shine before men, that they may see your good works, and glorify your Father which is in heaven. *Math.* v.

Lay not up for yourselves treasure upon the earth, where the rust and moth doth corrupt, and where thieves break through and steal: But lay up for yourselves treasure in heaven, where neither rust nor moth doth corrupt, and where thieves do not break through nor steal. *Math.* vi.

Whatsoever you would that men should do unto you, even so do you unto them: for this is the law and the Prophets. *Math.* vii.

Not every one that saith unto me, Lord, Lord, shall enter into the kingdom of heaven, but he that doeth the will of my Father which is in heaven. *Math.* vii.

Zachee stood forth, and said unto the Lord, Behold, Lord, the half of my goods I give to the poor, and if I have done any wrong to any man, I restore fourfold. *Luc.* xix.

Who goeth a warfare at any time at his own cost? Who planteth a vineyard, and eateth not of the fruit thereof? Or who feedeth a flock, and eateth not of the milk of the flock? 1 *Cor.* ix.

If we have sown unto you spiritual things, is it a great matter if we shall reap your wordly things? 1 *Cor.* ix.

Do ye not know, that they which minister about holy things, live of the sacrifice? They which wait of the altar are partakers with the altar? Even so hath the Lord also ordained: that they which preach the Gospel, should live of the Gospel. 1 *Cor.* ix.

He which soweth little, shall reap

¶ *Then shall the Priest return to the Lord's Table, and begin the Offertory, saying one or more of these Sentences following, as he thinketh most convenient in his discretion.*

LET your light so shine before men, that they may see your good works, and glorify your Father which is in heaven. *St. Matt.* v.

Lay not up for yourselves treasure upon the earth; where the rust and moth doth corrupt, and where thieves break through and steal: but lay up for yourselves treasures in heaven, where neither rust nor moth doth corrupt, and where thieves do not break through and steal. *St. Matt.* vi.

Whatsoever ye would that men should do unto you, even so do unto them; for this is the Law and the Prophets. *St. Matt.* vii.

Not every one that saith unto me, Lord, Lord, shall enter into the Kingdom of heaven; but he that doeth the will of my Father which is in heaven. *St. Matt.* vii.

Zacchæus stood forth, and said unto the Lord, Behold, Lord, the half of my goods I give to the poor; and if I have done any wrong to any man, I restore fourfold. *St. Luke* xix.

Who goeth a warfare at any time of his own cost? Who planteth a vineyard, and eateth not of the fruit thereof? Or who feedeth a flock, and eateth not of the milk of the flock? 1 *Cor.* ix.

If we have sown unto you spiritual things, is it a great matter if we shall reap your worldly things? 1 *Cor.* ix.

Do ye not know, that they who minister about holy things live of the sacrifice; and they who wait at the altar are partakers with the altar? Even so hath the Lord also ordained, that they who preach the Gospel should live of the Gospel. 1 *Cor.* ix.

He that soweth little shall reap

little, and he that soweth plenteously, shall reap plenteously. Let every man do according as he is disposed in his heart; not grudgingly, or of necessity; for God loveth a cheerful giver. 2 *Cor.* ix.

Let him that is taught in the word, minister unto him that teacheth, in all good things. Be not deceived; GOD is not mocked. For whatsoever a man soweth, that shall he reap. *Gala.* vi.

While we have time, let us do good unto all men, and specially unto them, which are of the household of faith. *Gala.* vi.

Godliness is great riches, if a man be contented with that he hath: For we brought nothing into the world, neither may we carry any thing out. 1 *Timo.* vi.

Charge them which are rich in this world, that they be ready to give, and glad to distribute, laying up in store for themselves a good foundation, against the time to come, that they may attain eternal life. 1 *Timo.* vi.

GOD is not unrighteous, that he will forget your works and labour, that proceedeth of love, which love ye have shewed for his name's sake, which have ministered unto the saints, and yet do minister. *Hebre.* vi.

To do good, and to distribute, forget not, for with such sacrifices God is pleased. *Hebre* xiii.

Whoso hath this world's good, and seeth his brother have need, and shutteth up his compassion from him, how dwelleth the love of God in him? 1 *John* iii.

Give alms of thy goods, and turn never thy face from any poor man, and then the face of the Lord shall not be turned away from thee. *Toby* iv.

Be merciful after thy power: if thou hast much, give plenteously; if thou hast little, do thy diligence gladly to give of that little: for so

little; and he that soweth plenteously shall reap plenteously. Let every man do according as he is disposed in his heart, not grudgingly, or of necessity; for God loveth a cheerful giver. 2 *Cor.* ix.

Let him that is taught in the Word, minister unto him that teacheth, in all good things. Be not deceived, God is not mocked: for whatsoever a man soweth that shall he reap. *Gal.* vi.

While we have time, let us do good unto all men, and specially unto them that are of the houshold of faith. *Gal.* vi.

Godliness is great riches, if a man be content with that he hath: for we brought nothing into the world, neither may we carry any thing out. 1 *Tim.* vi.

Charge them who are rich in this world, that they be ready to give, and glad to distribute; laying up in store for themselves a good foundation against the time to come, that they may attain eternal life. 1 *Tim.* vi.

God is not unrighteous, that he will forget your works, and labour that proceedeth of love; which love ye have shewed for his Name's sake, who have ministered unto the saints, and yet do minister. *Heb.* vi

To do good, and to distribute, forget not; for with such sacrifices God is well pleased. *Heb.* xiii.

Whoso hath this world's good, and seeth his brother have need, and shutteth up his compassion from him, how dwelleth the love of God in him? 1 *St. John* iii.

Give alms of thy goods, and never turn thy face from any poor man; and then the face of the Lord shall not be turned away from thee. *Tobit* iv.

Be merciful after thy power. If thou hast much, give plenteously: if thou hast little, do thy diligence gladly to give of that little; for so gatherest thou thyself a good reward in the day of necessity. *Toby* iv.

He that hath pity upon the poor lendeth unto the Lord; and look, what he layeth out, it shall be paid him again. *Prov.* xix.

Blessed be the man that provideth for the sick and needy; the Lord shall deliver him in the time of trouble. *Psalm* xli.

Where there be Clerks, they shall sing one, or many of the sentences above written, according to the length and shortness of the time, that the people be offering.

In the mean time whiles the Clerks do sing the Offertory, so many as are disposed, shall shall offer unto the poor men's box every one according to his ability and charitable mind. And at the offering days appointed, every man and woman shall pay to the Curate the due and accustomed offerings.

Then so many as shall be partakers of the holy Communion, shall tarry still in the quire, or in some convenient place nigh the quire, the men on the one side, and the women on the other side. All other (that mind not to receive the said holy Communion) shall depart out of the Quire, except the ministers and Clerks.

Then shall the minister take so much Bread and Wine, as shall suffice for the persons appointed to receive the holy Communion, laying the bread upon the corporas, or else in the paten, or in some other comely thing prepared for that purpose: And putting the wine into the Chalice, or else in some fair or convenient cup (if the Chalice will not serve), putting thereto a little pure and clean water: And setting both the bread and wine upon the Altar: then the Priest shall say,

gatherest thou thyself a good reward in the day of necessity. *Tobit* iv.

He that hath pity upon the poor lendeth unto the Lord; and look, what he layeth out, it shall be paid him again. *Prov.* xix.

Blessed be the man that provideth for the sick and needy: the Lord shall deliver him in the time of trouble. *Psalm* xli.

¶ *Whilst these Sentences are in reading, the Deacons, Churchwardens, or other fit person appointed for that purpose, shall receive the Alms for the Poor, and other devotions of the people, in a decent bason to be provided by the Parish for that purpose; and reverently bring it to the Priest, who shall humbly present and place it upon the holy Table.*

¶ *And when there is a Communion, the Priest shall then place upon the Table so much Bread and Wine, as he shall think sufficient.*

After which done, the Priest shall say,

Let us pray for the whole state of Christ's Church militant here in earth.

ALMIGHTY and everliving God, who by thy holy Apostle hast taught us to make prayers, and supplications, and to give thanks, for all men; We humbly beseech thee most mercifully [* *to accept our alms and oblations, and*] to receive these our prayers, which we offer unto thy Divine Majesty; beseeching thee to inspire continually the universal Church with the spirit of truth, unity, and concord: And grant, that all they that do confess thy holy Name may agree in the truth of thy holy Word, and live in unity, and godly love. We beseech thee also to save and defend all Christian Kings, Princes, and Governours; and specially thy servant *VICTORIA* our Queen; that under her we may be godly and quietly governed: And grant unto her whole Council, and to all that are put in authority under her, that they may truly and indifferently minister justice, to the punishment of wickedness and vice, and to the maintenance of thy true religion, and virtue. Give grace, O heavenly Father, to all Bishops, and Curates, that they may both by their life and doctrine set forth thy true and lively Word, and rightly and duly administer thy holy Sacraments: And to all thy people give thy heavenly grace; and especially to this congregation here present; that, with meek heart and due reverence, they may hear, and receive thy holy Word; truly serving thee in holiness and righteousness all the days of their life. And we most humbly beseech thee of thy goodness, O Lord, to comfort and succour all them, who in this transitory life are in trouble, sorrow, need, sickness, or any other adversity. And we also bless thy holy Name for all thy servants departed this life in thy faith and fear; beseeching thee to give us grace so to follow their good examples, that with them we may be partakers of thy heavenly king-

* *If there be no alms or oblations, then shall the words* [of accepting our alms and oblations] *be left out unsaid.*

dom: Grant this, O Father, for Jesus Christ's sake, our only Mediator and Advocate. *Amen.*

¶ *When the Minister giveth warning for the celebration of the holy Communion, (which he shall always do upon the Sunday, or some Holy-day, immediately preceding,) after the Sermon or Homily ended, he shall read this Exhortation following.*

DEARLY beloved, on —— day next I purpose, through God's assistance, to administer to all such as shall be religiously and devoutly disposed the most comfortable Sacrament of the Body and blood of Christ; to be by them received in remembrance of his meritorious Cross and Passion; whereby alone we obtain remission of our sins, and are made partakers of the Kingdom of heaven. Wherefore it is our duty to render most humble and hearty thanks to Almighty God our heavenly Father, for that he hath given his Son our Saviour Jesus Christ, not only to die for us, but also to be our spiritual food and sustenance in that holy Sacrament. Which being so divine and comfortable a thing to them who receive it worthily, and so dangerous to them that will presume to receive it unworthily; my duty is to exhort you in the mean season to consider the dignity of that holy mystery, and the great peril of the unworthy receiving thereof; and so to search and examine your own consciences, (and that not lightly, and after the manner of dissemblers with God; but so) that ye may come holy and clean to such a heavenly Feast, in the marriage-garment required by God in holy Scripture, and be received as worthy partakers of that holy Table.

The way and means thereto is; First, to examine your lives and conversations by the rule of God's commandments; and whereinsoever ye shall perceive yourselves to have offended, either by will, word, or deed, there to bewail your own sinfulness, and to confess yourselves to Almighty God, with full purpose of amendment of life. And if ye shall perceive your offences to be such as are not only against God, but also against your neighbours; then ye shall reconcile yourselves unto them; being ready to make restitution and satisfaction, according to the uttermost of your powers, for all injuries and wrongs done by you to any other; and being likewise ready to forgive others that have offended you, as ye would have forgiveness of your offences at God's hand: for otherwise the receiving of the holy Communion doth nothing else but increase your damnation. Therefore if any of you be a blasphemer of God, an hinderer or slanderer of his Word, an adulterer, or be in malice, or envy, or in any other grievous crime, repent you of your sins, or else come not to that holy Table: lest, after the taking of that holy Sacrament, the devil enter into you, as he entered into Judas, and fill you full of all iniquities, and bring you to destruction both of body and soul.

And because it is requisite, that no man should come to the holy Communion, but with a full trust in God's mercy, and with a quiet conscience; therefore if there be any of you, who by this means cannot quiet his own conscience herein, but requireth further comfort or counsel, let him come to me, or to some other discreet and learned Minister of God's Word, and open his grief; that by the ministry of God's holy Word he may receive the benefit of absolution, together with ghostly counsel and advice, to the quieting of his conscience, and avoiding of all scruple and doubtfulness.

¶ *Or, in case he shall see the people negligent to come to the holy Communion, instead of the former, he shall use this Exhortation.*

DEARLY beloved brethren, on——I intend, by God's grace, to celebrate the Lord's supper: unto which, in God's behalf, I bid you all that are here present; and beseech you, for the Lord Jesus Christ's sake, that ye will not refuse to come thereto, being so lovingly called and bidden by God himself. Ye know how grievous and unkind a thing it is, when a man hath prepared a rich feast, decked his table with all kind of provision, so that there lacketh nothing but the guests to sit down; and yet they who are called (without any cause) most unthankfully refuse to come. Which of you in such a case would not be moved? Who would not think a great injury and wrong done unto him? Wherefore, most dearly beloved in Christ, take ye good heed, lest ye, withdrawing yourselves from this holy Supper, provoke God's indignation against you. It is an easy matter for a man to say, I will not communicate, because I am otherwise hindered with worldly business. But such excuses are not so easily accepted and allowed before God. If any man say I am a grievous sinner, and therefore am afraid to come: wherefore then do ye not repent and amend? When God calleth you, are ye not ashamed to say ye will not come? When ye should return to God, will ye excuse yourselves, and say ye are not ready? Consider earnestly with yourselves how little such feigned excuses will avail before God. They that refused the feast in the Gospel, because they had bought a farm, or would try their yokes of oxen, or because they were married, were not so excused, but counted unworthy of the heavenly feast. I, for my part, shall be ready; and according to mine Office, I bid you in the Name of God, I call you in Christ's behalf, I exhort you, as ye love your own salvation, that ye will be partakers of this holy Communion. And as the Son of God did vouchsafe to yield up his soul by death upon the Cross for your salvation; so it is your duty to receive the Communion in remembrance of the sacrifice of his death, as he himself hath commanded: which if ye shall neglect to do, consider with yourselves how great injury ye do unto God, and how sore punishment hangeth over your heads for the same; when ye wilfully abstain from the Lord's Table, and separate from your brethren, who come to feed on the banquet of that most heavenly food. These things if ye earnestly consider, ye will by God's grace return to a better mind: for the obtaining whereof we shall not cease to make our humble petitions unto Almighty God our heavenly Father.

¶ *At the time of the celebration of the Communion, the Communicants being conveniently placed for the receiving of the holy Sacrament, the Priest shall say this Exhortation.*

DEARLY beloved in the Lord, ye that mind to come to the holy Communion of the Body and Blood of our Saviour Christ, must consider how Saint Paul exhorteth all persons diligently to try and examine themselves, before they presume to eat of that Bread, and drink of that Cup. For as the benefit is great, if with a true penitent heart and lively faith we receive that holy Sacrament; (for then we spiritually eat the flesh of Christ, and drink his blood; then we dwell in Christ, and Christ in us; we are one with Christ, and

Christ with us;) so is the danger great, if we receive the same unworthily. For then we are guilty of the Body and Blood of Christ our Saviour; we eat and drink our own damnation, not considering the Lord's Body; we kindle God's wrath against us; we provoke him to plague us with divers diseases, and sundry kinds of death. Judge therefore yourselves, brethren, that ye be not judged of the Lord; repent you truly for your sins past; have a lively and steadfast faith in Christ our Saviour; amend your lives, and be in perfect charity with all men; so shall ye be meet partakers of those holy mysteries. And above all things ye must give most humble and hearty thanks to God, the Father, the Son, and the Holy Ghost, for the redemption of the world by the death and passion of our Saviour Christ, both God and man; who did humble himself, even to the death upon the Cross, for us, miserable sinners, who lay in darkness and the shadow of death; that he might make us the children of God, and exalt us to everlasting life. And to the end that we should alway remember the exceeding great love of our Master, and only Saviour, Jesus Christ, thus dying for us, and the innumerable benefits which by his precious blood-shedding he hath obtained to us; he hath instituted and ordained holy mysteries, as pledges of his love, and for a continual remembrance of his death, to our great and endless comfort. To him therefore, with the Father and the Holy Ghost, let us give (as we are most bounden) continual thanks; submitting ourselves wholly to his holy will and pleasure, and studying to serve him in true holiness and righteousness all the days of our life. *Amen.*

¶ *Then shall the Priest say to them that come to receive the holy Communion,*

YE that do truly and earnestly repent you of your sins, and are in love and charity with your neighbours, and intend to lead a new life, following the commandments of God, and walking from henceforth in his holy ways; Draw near with faith, and take this holy Sacrament to your comfort; and make your humble confession to Almighty God, meekly kneeling upon your knees.

¶ *Then shall this general Confession be made, in the name of all those that are minded to receive the holy Communion, by one of the Ministers; both he and all the people kneeling humbly upon their knees, and saying,*

ALMIGHTY God, Father of our Lord Jesus Christ, Maker of all things, Judge of all men; We acknowledge and bewail our manifold sins and wickedness, Which we, from time to time, most grievously have committed, By thought, word, and deed, Against thy Divine Majesty, Provoking most justly thy wrath and indignation against us. We do earnestly repent, And are heartily sorry for these our misdoings; The remembrance of them is grievous unto us; The burden of them is intolerable. Have mercy upon us, Have mercy upon us, most merciful Father; For thy Son our Lord Jesus Christ's sake, Forgive us all that is past; And grant that we may ever hereafter Serve and please thee In newness of life, To the honour and glory of thy Name; Through Jesus Christ our Lord. Amen.

¶ *Then shall the Priest (or the Bishop, being present,) stand up, and turning himself to the people, pronounce this Absolution.*

ALMIGHTY God, our heavenly Father, who of his great mercy hath promised forgiveness of sins to all them that with hearty

th you.
with thy spirit.
your hearts.
ift them up unto

give thanks to

neet and right so

ery meet, right,
duty, that we
, and in all places,
ee, O Lord, holy
everlasting God.

repentance and true faith turn unto him; Have mercy upon you; pardon and deliver you from all your sins; confirm and strengthen you in all goodness; and bring you to everlasting life; through Jesus Christ our Lord. *Amen.*

¶ *Then shall the Priest say.*

Hear what comfortable words our Saviour Christ saith unto all that truly turn to him.

COME unto me all that travail and are heavy laden, and I will refresh you. *St. Matt.* xi. 28.

So God loved the world, that he gave his only-begotten Son, to the end that all that believe in him should not perish, but have everlasting life. *St. John* iii. 16.

Hear also what Saint Paul saith.

This is a true saying, and worthy of all men to be received, That Christ Jesus came into the world to save sinners. 1 *Tim.* i. 15.

Hear also what Saint John saith.

If any man sin, we have an Advocate with the Father, Jesus Christ the righteous; and he is the propitiation for our sins. 1 *St. John* ii. 1.

¶ *After which the Priest shall proceed, saying,*

Lift up your hearts.

Answer. We lift them up unto the Lord.

Priest. Let us give thanks unto our Lord God.

Answer. It is meet and right so to do.

¶ *Then shall the Priest turn to the Lord's Table, and say.*

IT is very meet, right, and our bounden duty that we should at all times, and in all places, give thanks unto thee, O Lord, *Holy Father, Almighty, Everlasting God.

* *These words* [Holy Father] *must be omitted on* Trinity-Sunday.

¶ *Here shall follow the proper preface according to the time (if there be any specially appointed,) or else immediately shall follow,*

Therefore with angels, &c.

PROPER PREFACES.

¶ *Upon Christmas Day.*

BECAUSE thou didst give Jesus Christ, thine only Son, to be born as this day for us, who by the operation of the Holy Ghost was made very man, of the substance of the Virgin Mary his mother, and that without spot of sin, to make us clean from all sin. Therefore &c.

¶ *Upon Easter Day.*

BUT chiefly are we bound to praise thee, for the glorious resurrection of thy Son Jesus Christ, our Lord; for he is the very Paschal Lamb, which was offered for us, and hath taken away the sin of the world, who by his death hath destroyed death, and by his rising to life again hath restored to us everlasting life. Therefore &c.

¶ *Upon the Ascension Day.*

THROUGH thy most dear beloved Son, Jesus Christ our Lord, who after his most glorious resurrection manifestly appeared to all his disciples, and in their sight ascended up into heaven, to prepare a place for us, that where he is, thither might

¶ *Here shall follow the Proper Preface, according to the time, if there be any specially appointed: or else immediately shall follow.*

THEREFORE with Angels and Archangels, and with all the company of heaven, we laud and magnify thy glorious Name; evermore praising thee, and saying, Holy, holy, holy, Lord God of hosts, heaven and earth are full of thy glory: Glory be to thee, O Lord most High. *Amen.*

PROPER PREFACES.

Upon Christmas-day, *and seven days after.*

BECAUSE thou didst give Jesus Christ thine only Son to be born as at this time for us; who, by the operation of the Holy Ghost, was made very man of the substance of the Virgin Mary his mother; and that without spot of sin, to make us clean from all sin. Therefore with Angels, *&c.*

Upon Easter-day, *and seven days after.*

BUT chiefly are we bound to praise thee for the glorious Resurrection of thy Son Jesus Christ our Lord: for he is the very Paschal Lamb, which was offered for us, and hath taken away the sin of the world; who by his death hath destroyed death, and by his rising to life again hath restored to us everlasting life. Therefore with Angels, *&c.*

Upon Ascension-day, *and seven days after.*

THROUGH thy most dearly beloved Son Jesus Christ our Lord; who after his most glorious Resurrection manifestly appeared to all his Apostles, and in their sight ascended up into heaven to prepare a place for us; that where

we also ascend, and reign with him in glory. Therefore &c,

¶ *Upon Whitsunday.*

THROUGH Jesus Christ our Lord, according to whose most true promise, the Holy Ghost came down this day from heaven, with a sudden great sound, as it had been a mighty wind, in the likeness of fiery tongues, lighting upon the Apostles, to teach them, and to lead them to all truth, giving them both the gift of divers languages, and also boldness with fervent zeal, constantly to preach the Gospel unto all nations, whereby we are brought out of darkness and error, into the clear light and true knowledge of thee, and of thy Son Jesus Christ. Therefore &c.

¶ *Upon the feast of the Trinity.*

IT is very meet, right, and our bounden duty, that we should at all times, and in all places, give thanks to thee, O Lord almighty, everlasting God, which art one God, one Lord, not one only person, but three persons in one substance: For that which we believe of the glory of the Father, the same we believe of the Son, and of the Holy Ghost, without any difference, or inequality: whom the angels &c.

After which preface shall follow immediately,

Therefore with Angels and Archangels, and with all the holy company of heaven, we laud and magnify thy glorious name, evermore praising thee, and saying,

¶ Holy, holy, holy, Lord God of Hosts: heaven and earth are full

he is, thither we might also ascend, and reign with him in glory. Therefore with Angels, *&c.*

Upon Whit-sunday, *and six days after.*

THROUGH Jesus Christ our Lord; according to whose most true promise, the Holy Ghost came down as at this time from heaven with a sudden great sound, as it had been a mighty wind, in the likeness of fiery tongues, lighting upon the Apostles, to teach them, and to lead them to all truth; giving them both the gift of divers languages, and also boldness with fervent zeal constantly to preach the Gospel unto all nations; whereby we have been brought out of darkness and error into the clear light and true knowledge of thee, and of thy Son Jesus Christ. Therefore with Angels, *&c.*

Upon the feast of Trinity *only.*

WHO art one God, one Lord not one only Person, but Three Persons in one Substance. For that which we believe of the glory of the Father, the same we believe of the Son, and of the Holy Ghost, without any difference or inequality. Therefore with Angels, *&c.*

¶ *After each of which Prefaces shall immediately be sung or said.*

THEREFORE with Angels and Archangels, and with all the company of heaven, we laud and magnify thy glorious Name; evermore praising thee, and saying, Holy, holy, holy, Lord God of hosts, heaven and earth are full of thy glory: Osannah in the highest. Blessed is he that cometh in the name of the Lord: Glory to thee, O Lord, in the highest.

This the Clerks shall also sing.

¶ *When the Clerks have done singing, then shall the Priest, or Deacon, turn him to the people, and say,*

Let us pray for the whole state of Christ's church.

¶ *Then the Priest, turning him to the Altar, shall say or sing, plainly and distinctly, this prayer following:*

ALMIGHTY and everliving God, which by thy holy Apostle hast taught us to make prayers and supplications, and to give thanks for all men: We humbly beseech thee most mercifully to receive these our prayers, which we offer unto thy divine Majesty, beseeching thee to inspire continually the universal church with the spirit of truth, unity, and concord: And grant that all they that do confess thy holy name, may agree in the truth of thy holy word, and live in unity and godly love. Specially we beseech thee to save and defend thy servant Edward our King, that under him we may be Godly and quietly governed. And grant unto his whole council, and to all that be put in authority under him, that they may truly and indifferently minister justice, to the punishment of wickedness and vice, and to the maintenance of God's true religion and virtue. Give grace (O heavenly Father) to all Bishops, Pastors, and Curates, that they may both by their life and doctrine set forth thy true and lively word, and rightly and duly administer thy holy Sacraments: and to all thy people give thy heavenly grace, that with meek heart and due reverence they may hear and receive thy holy word, truly serving thee in holiness

of thy glory: Glory be to thee, O Lord most High. *Amen.*

and righteousness all the days of their life. And we most humbly beseech thee of thy goodness (O Lord) to comfort and succour all them, which in this transitory life be in trouble, sorrow, need, sickness, or any other adversity. And especially we commend unto thy merciful goodness this congregation which is here assembled in thy name, to celebrate the commemoration of the most glorious death of thy Son: And here we do give unto thee most high praise, and hearty thanks, for the wonderful grace and virtue, declared in all thy saints, from the beginning of the world: And chiefly in the glorious and most blessed virgin Mary, mother of thy Son Jesu Christ our Lord and God, and in the holy Patriarchs, Prophets, Apostles and Martyrs, whose examples (O Lord) and stedfastness in thy faith, and keeping thy holy commandments, grant us to follow. We commend unto thy mercy (O Lord) all other thy servants, which are departed hence from us, with the sign of faith, and now do rest in the sleep of peace: Grant unto them, we beseech thee, thy mercy, and everlasting peace, and that, at the day of the general resurrection, we and all they which be of the mystical body of thy Son, may altogether be set on his right hand, and hear that his most joyful voice: Come unto me, O ye that be blessed of my Father, and possess the kingdom, which is prepared for you from the beginning of the world: grant this, O Father, for Jesus Christ's sake, our only Mediator and Advocate.

O God heavenly Father, which of thy tender mercy didst give thine only Son Jesu Christ, to suffer death upon the cross for our redemption, who made there (by his one oblation, once offered) a full, perfect, and sufficient sacrifice, oblation, and satisfaction, for the sins of the whole world, and did institute, and in his holy Gospel command us to celebrate, a perpetual memory of that his precious death, until his coming again; Hear us (O merciful Father) we beseech thee; and with thy holy Spirit and word vouchsafe to bl✠ess and sanc✠tify these thy gifts, and creatures of bread and wine, that they may be unto us the body and blood of thy most dearly beloved Son Jesus Christ.

Here the Priest must take the bread into his hands.

Who, in the same night that he was betrayed, took bread, and when he had blessed, and given thanks, he brake it, and gave it to his disciples, saying: Take, eat, this is my body which is given for you: do this in remembrance of me.

Likewise after supper he took the cup, and when he had given thanks, he gave it to them, saying: Drink ye all of this, for this is my blood of the new Testament, which is shed for you and for many, for remission of sins: Do this as oft as you shall drink it, in remembrance of me.

Here the Priest shall take the cup into his hands.

These words before rehearsed are to be said, turning still to the Altar, without any elevation, or shewing the Sacrament to the people.

WHEREFORE, O Lord and heavenly Father, according to the Institution of thy dearly beloved Son, our Saviour Jesu Christ, we thy humble servants do celebrate, and make here before thy divine Majesty, with these thy holy gifts, the memorial which thy Son hath willed us to make: having in remembrance his blessed passion, mighty resurrection, and glorious ascension, rendering unto thee most hearty thanks, for the innumerable benefits procured unto us by the same, entirely desiring thy fatherly goodness, mercifully to accept this our Sacrifice of praise and thanksgiving: most humbly beseeching thee to grant, that by the merits and death of thy Son Jesus Christ, and through faith in his blood, we and all thy whole church may obtain remission of our sins, and all other benefits of his passion. And here we offer and present unto thee (O Lord) ourself, our souls, and bodies, to be a reasonable, holy, and lively sacrifice unto thee: humbly beseeching thee, that whosoever shall be partakers of this holy Communion, may worthily receive the most precious body and blood of thy Son Jesus Christ, and be fulfilled with thy grace and heavenly benediction, and made one body with thy Son Jesus Christ, that he may dwell in them, and they in him. And although we be unworthy (through our manifold sins) to offer unto thee any Sacrifice: Yet we beseech thee to accept this our bounden duty and service, and command these our prayers and supplications, by the ministry of thy holy Angels, to be brought up into thy holy Tabernacle before the sight of thy divine Majesty; not weighing our merits, but pardoning our offences, through Christ our Lord; by whom, and with whom, in the unity of the holy Ghost, all honour and glory be unto thee, O Father Almighty, world without end. Amen.

¶ *Then shall the Priest kneeling down at the Lord's Table, say in the name of all them that shall receive the Communion this Prayer following.*

WE do not presume to ccme to this thy Table, O merciful Lord, trusting in our own righteousness, but in thy manifold and great mercies. We are not worthy so much as to gather up the crumbs under thy Table. But thou art the same Lord, whose property is always to have mercy: Grant us therefore, gracious Lord, so to eat the flesh of thy dear Son Jesus Christ, and to drink his blood, that our sinful bodies may be made clean by his body, and our souls washed through his most precious blood, and that we may evermore dwell in him, and he in us. *Amen.*

¶ *When the Priest, standing before the Table, hath so ordered the Bread and Wine, that he may with the more readiness and decency break the Bread before the people, and take the Cup into his hands, he shall say the Prayer of Consecration, as followeth.*

ALMIGHTY God, our heavenly Father, who of thy tender mercy didst give thine only Son Jesus Christ to suffer death upon the cross for our redemption; who made there (by his one oblation of himself once offered) a full, perfect, and sufficient sacrifice, oblation, and satisfaction, for the sins of the whole world; and did institute, and in his holy Gospel command us to continue, a perpetual memory of that his precious death, until his coming again; Hear us, O merciful Father, we most humbly beseech thee; and grant that we receiving these thy creatures of bread and wine, according to thy Son our Saviour Jesus Christ's holy institution, in remembrance of his death and passion, may be partakers of his most blessed Body and Blood: who in the same night that he was betrayed [a] took Bread; and, when he had given thanks, [b] he brake it, and gave it to his disciples, saying, Take, eat, [c] this is my Body which is given for you: Do this in remembrance of me. Likewise after supper he [d] took the Cup; and, when he had given thanks, he gave it to them, saying, Drink

[a] *Here the Priest is to take the Paten into his hands:*

[b] *And here to break the Bread.*

[c] *And here to lay his hand upon all the Bread.*

[d] *Here he is to take the Cup into his hand:*

Let us pray.

As our Saviour Christ hath commanded and taught us, we are bold to say. Our Father, which art in heaven, hallowed be thy name. Thy kingdom come. Thy will be done in earth, as it is in heaven. Give us this day our daily bread. And forgive us our trespasses, as we forgive them that trespass against us. And lead us not into temptation.

The Answer. But deliver us from evil. Amen.

Then shall the Priest say.

The peace of the Lord be alway with you.

The Clerks. And with thy spirit.

The Priest. Christ our paschal Lamb is offered up for us, once for all, when he bare our sins on his body upon the cross; for he is the very Lamb of God, that taketh away the sins of the world: wherefore let us keep a joyful and holy feast with the Lord.

Here the Priest shall turn him toward those that come to the holy Communion, and shall say,

You that do truly and earnestly repent you of your sins to Almighty God, and be in love and charity with your neighbours, and intend to lead a new life, following the commandments of God, and walking from henceforth in his holy ways: draw near and take this holy Sacrament to your com-

e And here to lay his hand upon every vessel (be it Chalice or Flagon) in which there is any Wine to be consecrated.

ye all of this; for this e is my Blood of the New Testament, which is shed for you and for many for the remission of sins: Do this, as oft as ye shall drink it, in remembrance of me. *Amen.*

fort, make your humble confession to Almighty God, and to his holy church here gathered together in his name, meekly kneeling upon your knees.

Then shall this general Confession be made, in the name of all those that are minded to receive the holy Communion, either by one of them, or else by one of the ministers, or by the Priest himself, all kneeling humbly upon their knees.

ALMIGHTY GOD, Father of our Lord Jesus Christ, maker of all things, judge of all men, we knowledge and bewail our manifold sins and wickedness, which we from time to time, most grievously have committed, by thought, word and deed, against thy divine majesty, provoking most justly thy wrath and indignation against us: we do earnestly repent, and be heartily sorry for these our misdoings: the remembrance of them is grievous unto us, the burden of them is intolerable: have mercy upon us, have mercy upon us, most merciful Father, for thy Son our Lord Jesus Christ's sake, forgive us all that is past, and grant that we may ever hereafter serve and please thee in newness of life, to the honour and glory of thy name: Through Jesus Christ our Lord.

Then shall the Priest stand up, and turning himself to the people, say thus,

ALMIGHTY GOD, our heavenly Father, who of his great mercy, hath promised forgiveness of sins to all them, which with hearty repentance and true faith turn unto him: have mercy upon you, pardon and deliver you from all your sins, confirm and strengthen you in all goodness, and bring you to everlasting life: through Jesus Christ our Lord. Amen.

Then shall the Priest also say.

Hear what comfortable words

our Saviour Christ saith, to all that truly turn to him.

Come unto me all that travail, and be heavy laden, and I shall refresh you. So God loved the world that he gave his only begotten Son, to the end that all that believe in him should not perish, but have life everlasting.

Hear also what Saint Paul sayeth.

This is a true saying, and worthy of all men to be received, that Jesus Christ came into this world to save sinners.

Hear also what Saint John sayeth.

If any man sin, we have an advocate with the Father, Jesus Christ the righteous, and he is the propitiation for our sins.

Then shall the Priest, turning him to God's board, kneel down, and say in the name of all them, that shall receive the Communion, this prayer following.

WE do not presume to come to this thy table (O merciful Lord) trusting in our own righteousness, but in thy manifold and great mercies: we be not worthy so much as to gather up the crumbs under thy table: but thou art the same Lord whose property is always to have mercy: Grant us therefore (gracious Lord) so to eat the flesh of thy dear Son Jesus Christ, and to drink his blood in these holy Mysteries, that we may continually dwell in him, and he in us, that our sinful bodies may be made clean by his body, and our souls washed through his most precious blood. Amen.

¶ *Then shall the Priest first receive the Communion in both kinds himself, and next deliver it to other Ministers, if any be there present, (that they may be ready to help the chief Minister,) and after to the people.*

¶ *And when he delivereth the Sacrament of the body of Christ, he shall say to every one these words:*

The body of our Lord Jesus Christ which was given for thee,

¶ *Then shall the Minister first receive the Communion in both kinds himself, and then proceed to deliver the same to the Bishops, Priests, and Deacons, in like manner (if any be present,) and after that to the people also in order, into their hands, all meekly kneeling. And when he delivereth the Bread to any one, he shall say,*

THE Body of our Lord Jesus Christ, which was given for

preserve thy body and soul unto everlasting life.

And the Minister delivering the Sacrament of the Blood, and giving every one to drink once and no more, shall say,

The blood of our Lord Jesus Christ which was shed for thee, preserve thy body and soul unto everlasting life.

If there be a Deacon or other Priest, then shall he follow with the Chalice: and as the Priest ministereth the Sacrament of the body, so shall he (for more expedition) minister the Sacrament of the blood, in form before written.

In the communion time the Clerks shall sing,

ii. O Lamb of God, that takest away the sins of the world: have mercy upon us.

O Lamb of God, that takest away the sins of the world: grant us thy peace.

Beginning so soon as the Priest doth receive the holy Communion, and when the Communion is ended, then shall the Clerks sing the post-Communion.

¶ *Sentences of holy Scripture, to be said or sung every day one, after the holy Communion, called the post-Communion.*

If any man will follow me, let him forsake himself, and take up

thee, preserve thy body and soul unto everlasting life. Take and eat this in remembrance that Christ died for thee, and feed on him in thy heart by faith with thanksgiving.

¶ *And the Minister that delivereth the Cup to any one shall say,*

THE Blood of our Lord Jesus Christ, which was shed for thee, preserve thy body and soul unto everlasting life. Drink this in remembrance that Christ's Blood was shed for thee, and be thankful.

¶ *If the consecrated Bread or Wine be all spent before all have communicated, the Priest is to consecrate more according to the Form before prescribed; beginning at* [Our Saviour Christ in the same night, &c.] *for the blessing of the Bread; and at* [Likewise after Supper, &c.] *for the blessing of the Cup.*

¶ *When all have communicated, the Minister shall return to the Lord's Table, and reverently place upon it what remaineth of the consecrated Elements, covering the same with a fair linen cloth.*

his cross, and follow me. *Math.* xvi.

Whosoever shall endure to the end, he shall be saved. *Mar.* xiii.

Praised be the Lord God of Israel, for he hath visited and redeemed his people: therefore let us serve him all the days of our life, in holiness and righteousness accepted before him. *Luc.* i.

Happy are those servants whom, the Lord (when he cometh) shall find waking. *Luc.* xii.

Be ye ready, for the Son of man will come at an hour when ye think not. *Luc.* xii.

The servant that knoweth his master's will, and hath not prepared himself, neither hath done according to his will, shall be beaten with many stripes. *Luc.* xii.

The hour cometh, and now it is, when true worshippers shall worship the Father in spirit and truth. *John* iv.

Behold, thou art made whole, sin no more, lest any worse thing happen unto thee. *John* v.

If ye shall continue in my word, then are ye my very disciples, and ye shall know the truth, and the truth shall make you free. *John* viii.

While ye have light, believe on the light, that ye may be the children of light. *John* xii.

He that hath my commandments, and keepeth them, the same is he that loveth me. *John* xiv.

If any man love me, he will keep my word, and my Father will love him, and we will come unto him, and dwell with him. *John* xiv.

If ye shall bide in me, and my word shall abide in you, ye shall ask what ye will, and it shall be done to you. *John* xv.

Herein is my Father glorified, that ye bear much fruit, and become my disciples. *John* xv.

This is my commandment, that you love together, as I have loved you. *John* xv.

If God be on our side, who can be against us? which did not spare his own Son, but gave him for us all. *Roma.* viii.

Who shall lay any thing to the charge of God's chosen? it is GOD that justifieth; who is [he] that can condemn? *Roma.* viii.

The night is past, and the day is at hand; let us therefore cast away the deeds of darkness, and put on the armour of light. *Rom.* xiii.

Christ Jesus is made of GOD, unto us, wisdom and righteousness, and sanctifying, and redemption, that (according as it is written) He which rejoiceth should rejoice in the Lord. 1 *Corin.* i.

Know ye not that ye are the temple of GOD, and that the Spirit of GOD dwelleth in you? If any man defile the temple of GOD, him shall God destroy. 1 *Corin.* iii.

Ye are dearly bought; therefore glorify God in your bodies, and in your spirits, for they belong to God. 1 *Cor.* vi.

Be you followers of God as dear children, and walk in love, even as Christ loved us, and gave himself for us an offering and a Sacrifice of a sweet savour to God. *Ephes.* v.

¶ *Then shall the Priest say the Lord's Prayer, the People repeating after him every Petition.*

OUR Father, which art in heaven, Hallowed be thy Name. Thy kingdom come. Thy will be done in earth, As it is in heaven. Give us this day our daily bread. And forgive us our trespasses, As we forgive them that trespass against us. And lead us not into temptation; But deliver us from evil; For thine is the kingdom, The power, and the glory, For ever and ever. Amen.

¶ *After shall be said as followeth.*

O LORD and heavenly Father, we thy humble servants entirely desire thy fatherly goodness mercifully to accept this our sacrifice of praise and thanksgiving; most humbly beseeching thee to grant, that by the merits and death of thy Son Jesus Christ, and through faith in his blood, we and all thy whole church may obtain remission of our sins, and all other benefits of his passion. And here we offer and present unto thee, O Lord, ourselves, our souls and bodies, to be a reasonable, holy, and lively sacrifice unto thee; humbly beseeching thee, that all we, who are partakers of this holy Communion, may be fulfilled with thy grace and heavenly benediction. And although we be unworthy, through our manifold sins, to offer unto thee any sacrifice, yet we beseech thee to accept this our bounden duty and service; not weighing our merits, but pardoning our offences, through Jesus Christ our Lord; by whom, and with whom, in the unity of the Holy Ghost, all honour and glory be unto thee, O Father Almighty, world without end. *Amen.*

Then the Priest shall give thanks to God, in the name of all them that have communicated, turning him first to the people, and saying,

The Lord be with you.

The Answer. And with thy spirit.

The Priest. Let us pray,

ALMIGHTY and everliving GOD, we most heartily thank thee, for that thou hast vouchsafed to feed us in these holy Mysteries, with the spiritual food of the most precious body and blood of thy Son our Saviour Jesus Christ, and hast assured us (duly receiving the same) of thy favour and goodness toward us, and that we be very members incorporate in thy mystical body, which is the blessed company of

Or this,

ALMIGHTY and everliving God, we most heartily thank thee, for that thou dost vouchsafe to feed us, who have duly received these holy mysteries, with the spiritual food of the most precious Body and Blood of thy Son our Saviour Jesus Christ; and dost assure us thereby of thy favour and goodness towards us; and that we are very members incorporate in the mystical body of thy

all faithful people, and heirs through hope of thy everlasting kingdom, by the merits of the most precious death and passion of thy dear Son. We therefore most humbly beseech thee, O heavenly Father, so to assist us with thy grace, that we may continue in that holy fellowship, and do all such good works, as thou hast prepared for us to walk in: through Jesus Christ our Lord, to whom, with thee and the holy Ghost, be all honour and glory, world without end.

Then the Priest turning him to the people, shall let them depart with this blessing:

The peace of GOD (which passeth all understanding) keep your hearts and minds in the knowledge and love of GOD, and of his Son Jesus Christ our Lord: And the blessing of God Almighty, the

Son, which is the blessed company of all faithful people; and are also heirs through hope of thy everlasting kingdom, by the merits of the most precious death and passion of thy dear Son. And we most humbly beseech thee, O heavenly Father, so to assist us with thy grace, that we may continue in that holy fellowship, and do all such good works as thou hast prepared for us to walk in; through Jesus Christ our Lord, to whom, with thee and the Holy Ghost, be all honour and glory, world without end. *Amen.*

¶ *Then shall be said or sung.*

GLORY be to God on high, and in earth peace, good will towards men. We praise thee, we bless thee, we worship thee, we glorify thee, we give thanks to thee for thy great glory, O Lord God, heavenly King, God the Father Almighty.

O Lord, the only-begotten Son Jesu Christ; O Lord God, Lamb of God, Son of the Father, that takest away the sins of the world, have mercy upon us. Thou that takest away the sins of the world, have mercy upon us. Thou that takest away the sins of the world, receive our prayer. Thou that sittest at the right hand of God the Father, have mercy upon us.

For thou only art holy; thou only art the Lord; thou only, O Christ, with the Holy Ghost, art most high in the glory of God the Father. *Amen.*

¶ *Then the Priest (or Bishop if he be present) shall let them depart with this Blessing.*

THE peace of God, which passeth all understanding, keep your hearts and minds in the knowledge and love of God, and of his Son Jesus Christ our Lord: and the blessing of God Almighty,

Father, the Son, and the Holy Ghost, be amongst you and remain with you alway.

Then the people shall answer,

Amen.

Where there are no clerks, there the Priest shall say all things appointed here for them to sing.

When the holy Communion is celebrate on the workday, or in private houses: Then may be omitted, the Gloria in excelsis, the Creed, the Homily, and the exhortation, beginning,

DEARLY beloved, &c.

¶ *Collects to be said after the Offertory, when there is no Communion, every such day one.*

ASSIST us mercifully, O Lord, in these our supplications and prayers, and dispose the way of thy servants toward the attainment of everlasting salvation: that among all the changes and chances of this mortal life, they may ever be defended by thy most gracious and ready help; through Christ our Lord. Amen.

O ALMIGHTY Lord and everliving GOD, vouchsafe, we beseech thee, to direct, sanctify, and govern, both our hearts and bodies, in the ways of thy laws, and in the works of thy commandments: that through thy most mighty protection, both here and ever, we may be preserved in body and soul: Through our Lord and Saviour Jesus Christ. Amen.

GRANT, we beseech thee, Almighty God, that the words which we have heard this day with our outward ears, may through thy grace be so grafted inwardly in our hearts, that they may bring forth in us the fruit of good living,

the Father, the Son, and the Holy Ghost, be amongst you and remain with you always. *Amen.*

¶ *Collects to be said after the Offertory, when there is no Communion, every such day one or more; and the same may be said also, as often as occasion shall serve, after the Collects either of Morning or Evening Prayer, Communion, or Litany, by the discretion of the Minister.*

ASSIST us mercifully, O Lord, in these our supplications and prayers, and dispose the way of thy servants towards the attainment of everlasting salvation; that, among all the changes and chances of this mortal life, they may ever be defended by thy most gracious and ready help; through Jesus Christ our Lord. *Amen.*

O ALMIGHTY Lord, and everlasting God, vouchsafe, we beseech thee, to direct, sanctify, and govern, both our hearts and bodies, in the ways of thy laws, and in the works of thy commandments; that through thy most mighty protection, both here and ever, we may be preserved in body and soul; through our Lord and Saviour Jesus Christ. *Amen.*

GRANT, we beseech thee, Almighty God, that the words, which we have heard this day with our outward ears, may through thy grace be so grafted inwardly in our hearts, that they may bring forth in us the fruit of good liv-

to the honour and praise of thy name: through Jesus Christ our Lord. Amen.

PREVENT us, O Lord, in all our doings, with thy most gracious favour, and further us with thy continual help, that in all our works begun, continued, and ended in thee, we may glorify thy holy name, and finally by thy mercy obtain everlasting life: Through Jesus Christ our Lord. Amen.

ALMIGHTY God, the fountain of all wisdom, which knowest our necessities before we ask, and our ignorance in asking: we beseech thee to have compassion upon our infirmities, and those things, which for our unworthiness we dare not, and for our blindness we cannot ask, vouchsafe to give us for the worthiness of thy Son Jesu Christ our Lord. Amen.

ALMIGHTY God, which hast promised to hear the petitions of them that ask in thy Son's name, we beseech thee mercifully to incline thine ears to us that have made now our prayers and supplications unto thee: and grant that those things which we have faithfully asked according to thy will, may effectually be obtained to the relief of our necessity, and to the setting forth of thy glory: Through Jesus Christ our Lord.

¶ *For rain.* (*i*)

O GOD heavenly Father, which by thy Son Jesu Christ hast promised to all them that seek thy kingdom, and the righteousness thereof, all things necessary to the bodily sustenance: send us, we beseech thee, in this our necessity,

(*i*) In the Book of Common Prayer (1886) the prayers for rain and for fair weather stand among Prayers upon Several Occasions.

ing, to the honour and praise of thy Name; through Jesus Christ our Lord. *Amen.*

PREVENT us, O Lord, in all our doings with thy most gracious favour, and further us with thy continual help: that in all our works begun, continued, and ended in thee, we may glorify thy holy Name, and finally by thy mercy obtain everlasting life; through Jesus Christ our Lord. *Amen.*

ALMIGHTY God, the fountain of all wisdom, who knowest our necessities before we ask, and our ignorance in asking; We beseech thee to have compassion upon our infirmities; and those things, which for our unworthiness we dare not, and for our blindness we cannot ask, vouchsafe to give us, for the worthiness of thy Son Jesus Christ our Lord. *Amen.*

ALMIGHTY God, who hast promised to hear the petitions of them that ask in thy Son's Name; We beseech thee mercifully to incline thine ears to us that have made now our prayers and supplications unto thee; and grant, that those things, which we have faithfully asked according to thy will, may effectually be obtained, to the relief of our necessity, and to the setting forth of thy glory; through Jesus Christ our Lord. *Amen.*

such moderate rain and showers, that we may receive the fruits of the earth, to our comfort and to thy honour; through Jesus Christ our Lord.

For fair weather.

O Lord God, which for the sin of man, didst once drown all the world, except eight persons, and afterwards of thy great mercy, didst promise never to destroy it so again: We humbly beseech thee, that although we for our iniquities have worthily deserved this plague of rain and waters, yet, upon our true repentance, thou wilt send us such weather whereby we may receive the fruits of the earth in due season, and learn both by thy punishment to amend our lives, and by the granting of our petition to give thee praise and glory: Through Jesu Christ our Lord.

¶ *Upon Wednesdays and Fridays, the English Litany shall be said or sung in all places, after such form as is appointed by the king's majesty's Injunctions: Or as is or shall be otherwise appointed by his highness. And though there be none to communicate with the Priest, yet these days (after the Litany ended) the Priest shall put upon him a plain Albe or surplice, with a cope, and say all things at the Altar (appointed to be said at the celebration of the Lord's supper,) until after the offertory. And then shall add one or two of the Collects aforewritten, as occasion shall serve, by his discretion. And then turning him to the people shall let them depart with the accustomed blessing. And the same order shall be used all other days, whensoever the people be customably assembled to pray in the church, and none disposed to communicate with the Priest. Likewise in Chapels annexed, and all other places, there shall be no celebration of the Lord's supper, except there be some to communicate with the Priest.*

And in such Chapels annexed where the people hath not been accustomed to pay any holy bread, there they must either make some charitable provision for the bearing of the charges of the Communion, or else (for receiving of the same) resort to their parish church.

¶ *Upon the Sundays and other Holy-days (if there be no Communion) shall be said all that is appointed at the Communion, until the end of the general Prayer* [For the whole state of Christ's Church militant here in earth] *together with one or more of these Collects last before rehearsed, concluding with the Blessing.*

¶ *And there shall be no celebration of the Lord's Supper, except there be a convenient number to communicate with the Priest, according to his discretion.*

¶ *And if there be not above twenty persons in the Parish of discretion to receive the Communion; yet there shall be no Communion, except four (or three at the least) communicate with the Priest.*

¶ *And in Cathedral and Collegiate Churches, and Colleges, where there are many Priests and Deacons, they shall all receive the Communion with the Priest every Sunday at the least, except they have a reasonable cause to the contrary.*

For avoiding of all matters and occasion of dissension, it is meet that the bread prepared for the Communion be made, through all this realm, after one sort and fashion: that is to say, unleavened, and round, as it was afore, but without all manner of print, and something more larger and thicker than it was, so that it may be aptly divided in divers pieces: and every one shall be divided in two pieces, at the least, or more, by the discretion of the minister, and so distributed. And men must not think less to be received in part than in the whole, but in each of them the whole body of our Saviour Jesu Christ.

¶ *And to take away all occasion of dissention, and superstition, which any person hath or might have concerning the Bread and Wine, it shall suffice that the Bread be such as is usual to be eaten; but the best and purest Wheat Bread that conveniently may be gotten.*

¶ *And if any of the Bread and Wine remain unconsecrated, the Curate shall have it to his own use: but if any remain of that which was consecrated, it shall not be carried out of the Church, but the Priest and such other of the Communicants as he shall then call unto him, shall, immediately after the Blessing, reverently eat and drink the same.*

And forsomuch as the Pastors and Curates within this realm shall continually find at their costs and charges in their cures sufficient bread and wine for the holy Communion (as oft as their Parishioners shall be disposed for their spiritual comfort to receive the same) it is therefore ordered, that in recompence of such costs and charges, the Parishioners of every Parish shall offer every Sunday, at the time of the Offertory, the just valour and price of the holy loaf (with all such money and other things as were wont to be offered with the same) to the use of their Pastors and Curates, and that in such order and course, as they were wont to find and pay the said holy loaf.

¶ *The Bread and Wine for the Communion shall be provided by the Curate and the Church-wardens at the charges of the Parish.*

Also that the receiving of the Sacrament of the blessed body and blood of Christ, may be most agreeable to the institution thereof, and to the usage of the primitive Church: In all Cathedrals and Collegiate churches, there shall always some communicate with the Priest that ministereth. And that the same may be also observed every where abroad in the country: Some one at the least of that house in every parish, to whom by course, after the ordinance herein made, it appertaineth to offer for the charges of the Communion, or some other whom they shall provide to offer for them, shall receive the holy Communion with the Priest: the which may be the better done, for that they know before, when their course cometh, and may therefore dispose themselves to the worthy receiving of the Sacrament. And with him or them who doth so offer the charges of the Communion, all other, who be then Godly disposed thereunto, shall likewise receive the Communion. And by this means the Minister having always some to communicate with him, may accordingly solemnise so high and holy mysteries, with all the suffrages and due order appointed for the same. And the Priest on the week day shall forbear to celebrate the Communion, except he shall have some that will communicate with him.

Furthermore, every man and woman to be bound to hear and be at the divine service, in the Parish church where they be resident, and there with devout prayer, or Godly silence and meditation, to occupy themselves. There to pay their duties, to communicate once in the year at the least, and there to receive and take all other Sacraments and rites, in this book appointed. And whosoever willingly, upon no just cause, doth absent themselves, or doth ungodly in the Parish church occupy themselves: upon proof thereof, by the Ecclesiastical laws of the Realm, to be excommunicate, or suffer other punishment, as shall to the Ecclesiastical judge (according to his discretion) seem convenient.

And although it be read in ancient writers, that the people, many years past, received at the Priest's hands the Sacrament of the body of Christ in their own hands, and no commandment of Christ to the contrary: Yet forasmuch as they many times conveyed the same secretly away, kept it with them, and diversely abused it to superstition and wickedness: lest any such thing hereafter should be attempted, and that an uniformity might be used throughout the whole realm, it is thought convenient the people commonly receive the Sacrament of Christ's body in their mouths, at the Priest's hand.

¶ *And note, that every Parishoner shall communicate at least three times in the year, of which Easter to be one. And yearly at Easter every Parishioner shall reckon with the Parson, Vicar or Curate, or his or their Deputy or Deputies; and pay to them or him all Ecclesiastical Duties, accustomably due, then and at that time to be paid.*

¶ *After the Divine Service ended, the money given at the offertory shall be disposed of to such pious and charitable uses, as the Minister and Church-wardens shall think fit. Wherein if they disagree, it shall be disposed of as the Ordinary shall appoint.*

"WHEREAS it is ordained in "this Office for the Ad-"ministration of the Lord's Supper, "that the Communicants should "receive the same kneeling; (which "order is well meant, for a signi-"fication of our humble and grate-"ful acknowledgement of the be-"nefits of Christ therein given to "all worthy Receivers, and for the "avoiding of such profanation and "disorder in the holy Communion, "as might otherwise ensue;) yet, "lest the same kneeling should by "any persons, either out of ignor-"ance and infirmity, or out of mal-"ice and obstinacy, be miscon-"strued and depraved; It is here-"by declared, That thereby no "adoration is intended, or ought "to be done, either unto the Sacra-"mental Bread or Wine there "bodily received, or unto any Cor-"poral presence of Christ's natural "Flesh and Blood. For the Sacra-"mental Bread and Wine remain "still in their very natural sub-"stances, and therefore may not "be adored; (for that were Idolatry, "to be abhorred of all faithful "Christians;) and the natural Body "and Blood of our Saviour Christ "are in Heaven, and not here; it "being against the truth of Christ's "natural Body to be at one time in "more places than one."

Note *(j)*.

In 1549 'The Litany' followed immediately after the Communion Office; but in this volume it has been thought well to print it after the Athanasian Creed, as in 1552, and in all editions afterwards.

OF THE

ADMINISTRATION OF PUBLIC BAPTISM

TO BE USED IN THE CHURCH.

It appeareth by ancient writers, that the Sacrament of Baptism in the old time was not commonly ministered but at two times in the year, at Easter and Whitsuntide, at which times it was openly ministered in the presence of all the congregation: Which custom (now being grown out of use) although it cannot for many considerations be well restored again, yet it is thought good to follow the same as near as conveniently may be: Wherefore the people are to be admonished, that it is most convenient that Baptism should not be ministered but upon Sundays and other holy days, when the most number of people may come together. As well for that the congregation there present may testify the receiving of them, that be newly baptized, into the number of Christ's Church, as also because in the Baptism of Infants, every man present may be put in remembrance of his own profession made to God in his Baptism. For which cause also, it is expedient that Baptism be ministered in the English tongue. Nevertheless (if necessity so require) children ought at all times to be baptized, either at the church or else at home.

PUBLIC BAPTISM.

When there are children to be baptized upon the Sunday or holy day, the parents shall give knowledge over night or in the morning, afore the beginning of Matins, to the curate. And then the Godfathers, Godmothers, and people, with the children, must be ready at the church door, either immediately afore the last Canticle at Matins, or else immediately afore the last Canticle at Evensong, as the Curate by his discretion shall appoint. And then, standing there, the Priest shall ask whether the children be baptized or no.

If they answer, No, then shall the Priest say thus.

THE

MINISTRATION OF PUBLICK BAPTISM OF INFANTS,

TO BE USED IN THE CHURCH.

¶ *The people are to be admonished, that it is most convenient that Baptism should not be administered but upon Sundays, and other Holy-days, when the most number of people come together; as well for that the Congregation there present may testify the receiving of them that be newly baptized into the number of Christ's Church; as also because in the Baptism of Infants every Man present may be put in remembrance of his own profession made to God in his Baptism. For which cause also it is expedient that Baptism be ministered in the vulgar tongue. Nevertheless, (if necessity so require,) Children may be baptized upon any other day.*

¶ *And note, that there shall be for every Male-child to be baptized two Godfathers and one Godmother; and for every Female, one Godfather and two Godmothers.*

¶ *When there are Children to be baptized, the Parents shall give knowledge thereof over night, or in the morning before the beginning of Morning Prayer, to the Curate. And then the Godfathers and Godmothers, and the people with the Children, must be ready at the Font, either immediately after the last Lesson at Morning Prayer, or else immediately after the last Lesson at Evening Prayer, as the Curate by his discretion shall appoint. And the Priest coming to the Font, (which is then to be filled with pure Water,) and standing there, shall say,*

HATH this Child been already baptized, or no?

¶ *If they answer,* No: *Then shall the Priest proceed as followeth.*

DEAR beloved, forasmuch as all men be conceived and born in sin, and that no man born in sin can enter into the kingdom of God (except he be regenerate and born anew of water and the Holy Ghost;) I beseech you to call upon God the Father through our Lord Jesus Christ, that of his bounteous mercy he will grant to these children that thing which by nature they cannot have, that is to say, they may be baptized with the Holy Ghost, and received into Christ's holy church, and be made lively members of the same.

Then the Priest shall say,

Let us pray.

ALMIGHTY and everlasting God, which of thy justice didst destroy by floods of water the whole world for sin, except eight persons, whom of thy mercy (the same time) thou didst save in the Ark: And when thou didst drown in the Red Sea wicked King Pharao, with all his army, yet (at the same time) thou didst lead thy people the children of Israel safely through the midst thereof: whereby thou didst figure the washing of thy holy baptism: and by the baptism of thy wellbeloved Son Jesus Christ, thou didst sanctify the flood Jordan, and all other waters to this mystical washing away of sin: we beseech thee (for thy infinite mercies) that thou wilt mercifully look upon these children, and sanctify them with thy Holy Ghost, that by this wholesome laver of regeneration, whatsoever sin is in them, may be washed clean away; that they, being delivered from thy wrath, may be received into the ark of Christ's Church, and so saved from perishing: and being fervent in spirit, steadfast in faith, joyful through hope, rooted in charity, may ever

DEARLY beloved, forasmuch as all men are conceived and born in sin; and that our Saviour Christ saith, None can enter into the kingdom of God, except he be regenerate and born anew of Water and of the holy Ghost; I beseech you to call upon God the Father, through our Lord Jesus Christ, that of his bounteous mercy he will grant to *this Child* that thing which by nature *he* cannot have: that *he* may be baptized with Water and the holy Ghost, and received into Christ's holy Church, and be made *a lively member* of the same.

¶ *Then shall the Priest say,*

Let us pray.

ALMIGHTY and everlasting God, who of thy great mercy didst save Noah and his family in the ark from perishing by water; and also didst safely lead the children of Israel thy people through the Red Sea, figuring thereby thy holy Baptism; and by the Baptism of thy well-beloved Son Jesus Christ, in the river Jordan, didst sanctify Water to the mystical washing away of sin; We beseech thee, for thine infinite mercies, that thou wilt mercifully look upon *this Child;* wash *him* and sanctify *him* with the Holy Ghost; that *he*, being delivered from thy wrath, may be received into the ark of Christ's Church; and being steadfast in faith, joyful through hope, and rooted in charity, may so pass the waves of this troublesome world, that finally *he* may come to the land of everlasting life, there to reign with thee world without end; through Jesus Christ our Lord. *Amen.*

serve thee: And finally attain to everlasting life, with all thy holy and chosen people. This grant us, we beseech thee, for Jesus Christ's sake our Lord. Amen.

¶ *Here shall the Priest ask what shall be the name of the child, and when the Godfathers and Godmothers have told the name, then he shall make a cross upon the child's forehead and breast, saying,*

¶ *N.* Receive the sign of the holy Cross, both in thy forehead, and in thy breast, in token that thou shalt not be ashamed to confess thy faith in Christ crucified, and manfully to fight under his banner against sin, the world, and the devil, and to continue his faithful soldier and servant unto thy life's end. Amen.

And this he shall do and say to as many children as be present to be baptized, one after another.

Let us pray.

Almighty and immortal God, the aid of all that need, the helper of all that flee to thee for succour, the life of them that believe, and the resurrection of the dead: we call upon thee for these infants, that they coming to thy holy baptism, may receive remission of their sins, by spiritual regeneration. Receive them (O Lord) as thou hast promised by thy well beloved Son, saying: Ask, and you shall have: seek, and you shall find: knock, and it shall be opened unto you. So give now unto us that ask: let us that seek find: open thy gate upon us that knock: that these infants may enjoy the everlasting benediction of thy heavenly washing, and may come to the eternal kingdom which thou hast promised by Christ our Lord. Amen.

ALMIGHTY and immortal God, the aid of all that need, the helper of all that flee to thee for succour, the life of them that believe, and the resurrection of the dead; We call upon thee for *this Infant*, that *he*, coming to thy holy Baptism, may receive remission of *his* sins by spiritual regeneration. Receive *him*, O Lord, as thou hast promised by thy well-beloved Son, saying, Ask, and ye shall have; seek, and ye shall find; knock, and it shall be opened unto you: So give now unto us that ask; let us that seek find; open the gate unto us that knock; that *this Infant* may enjoy the everlasting benediction of thy heavenly washing, and may come to the eternal kingdom which thou hast promised by Christ our Lord. *Amen.*

Then let the Priest looking upon the children, say,

I COMMAND thee, unclean spirit, in the name of the Father, of the Son, and of the Holy Ghost, that thou come out, and depart from these infants, whom our Lord Jesus Christ hath vouchsafed to call to his holy Baptism, to be made members of his body, and of his holy congregation. Therefore, thou cursed spirit, remember thy sentence, remember thy judgment, remember the day to be at hand wherein thou shalt burn in fire everlasting, prepared for thee and thy Angels. And presume not hereafter to exercise any tyranny toward these infants, whom Christ hath bought with his precious blood, and by this his holy Baptism calleth to be of his flock.

Then shall the Priest say,

The Lord be with you.

The People. And with thy spirit.

The Minister. ¶ Hear now the Gospel written by St. Mark.

At a certain time they brought children to Christ that he should touch them, and his disciples rebuked those that brought them. But when Jesus saw it, he was displeased, and said unto them: Suffer little children to come unto me, and forbid them not; (for to such belongeth the kingdom of God). Verily I say unto you: whosoever doth not receive the kingdom of God, as a little child, he shall not enter therein. And when he had taken them up in his arms, he put his hands upon them, and blessed them.

Mark x.

After the Gospel is read, the Minister shall make this brief exhortation upon the words of the Gospel.

FRIENDS, you hear in this Gospel the words of our Saviour Christ,

¶ *Then shall the people stand up, and the Priest shall say,*

Hear the words of the Gospel, written by St. *Mark*, in the tenth Chapter, at the thirteenth Verse.

THEY brought young children to Christ that he should touch them; and his disciples rebuked those that brought them. But when Jesus saw it, he was much displeased, and said unto them, Suffer the little children to come unto me, and forbid them not; for of such is the kingdom of God. Verily I say unto you, Whosoever shall not receive the kingdom of God as a little child, he shall not enter therein. And he took them up in his arms, put his hands upon them, and blessed them.

¶ *After the Gospel is read, the Minister shall make this brief Exhortation upon the words of the Gospel.*

BELOVED, ye hear in this Gospel the words of our Sa-

that he commanded the children to be brought unto him: how he blamed those that would have kept them from him: how he exhorteth all men to follow their innocency. Ye perceive how by his outward gesture and deed he declared his good will toward them. For he embraced them in his arms, he laid his hands upon them, and blessed them. Doubt ye not therefore, but earnestly believe, that he will likewise favourably receive these present infants, that he will embrace them with the arms of his mercy, that he will give unto them the blessing of eternal life, and make them partakers of his everlasting kingdom. Wherefore we being thus persuaded of the good will of our heavenly Father toward these infants, declared by his Son Jesus Christ; and nothing doubting but that he favourably alloweth this charitable work of ours, in bringing these children to his holy baptism: let us faithfully and devoutly give thanks unto him; and say the prayer which the Lord himself taught. And in declaration of our faith, let us also recite the articles contained in our Creed.

Here the Minister, with the Godfathers, Godmothers, and people present, shall say,

¶ Our Father, which art in heaven, hallowed be thy name, &c.

And then shall say openly.

I believe in God the Father Almighty, &c.

The Priest shall add also this prayer,

ALMIGHTY and everlasting God, heavenly Father, we give thee humble thanks, that thou hast vouchsafed to call us to knowledge of thy grace, and faith in thee: increase and confirm this faith in us evermore: Give thy Holy Spirit to these infants, that they may be

viour Christ, that he commanded the children to be brought unto him; how he blamed those that would have kept them from him; how he exhorteth all men to follow their innocency. Ye perceive how by his outward gesture and deed he declared his good will toward them; for he embraced them in his arms, he laid his hands upon them, and blessed them. Doubt ye not therefore, but earnestly believe, that he will likewise favourably receive *this* present *Infant;* that he will embrace *him* with the arms of his mercy; that he will give unto *him* the blessing of eternal life, and make *him partaker* of his everlasting kingdom. Wherefore we being thus persuaded of the good will of our heavenly Father towards *this Infant*, declared by his Son Jesus Christ; and nothing doubting but that he favourably alloweth this charitable work of our's in bringing *this Infant* to his holy Baptism; let us faithfully and devoutly give thanks unto him, and say,

ALMIGHTY and everlasting God, heavenly Father, we give thee humble thanks, for that thou hast vouchsafed to call us to the knowledge of thy grace, and faith in thee: Increase this knowledge, and confirm this faith in us evermore. Give thy holy

born again, and be made heirs of everlasting salvation, through our Lord Jesus Christ: who liveth and reigneth with thee and the Holy Spirit, now and for ever. Amen.

Then let the Priest take one of the children by the right hand, the other being brought after him. And coming into the Church toward the font, say,

THE Lord vouchsafe to receive you into his holy household, and to keep and govern you alway in the same, that you may have everlasting life. Amen.

Then standing at the font the Priest shall speak to the Godfathers and Godmothers on this wise.

Wellbeloved friends, ye have brought these children here to be baptized; ye have prayed that our Lord Jesus Christ would vouchsafe to receive them, to lay his hands upon them, to bless them, to release them of their sins, to give them the kingdom of heaven, and everlasting life. Ye have heard also that our Lord Jesus Christ hath promised in his gospel, to grant all these things that ye have prayed for: which promise he for his part will most surely keep and perform. Wherefore, after this promise made by Christ, these infants must also faithfully for their part promise by you that be their sureties, that they will forsake the devil and all his works, and constantly believe God's holy word, and obediently keep his commandments.

Then shall the Priest demand of the child (which shall be first baptized) these questions following: first naming the child, and saying,

N. Dost thou forsake the devil and all his works?

Answer. I forsake them.

Spirit to *this Infant*, that *he* may be born again, and be made *an heir* of everlasting salvation; through our Lord Jesus Christ, who liveth and reigneth with thee and the Holy Spirit, now and for ever. *Amen.*

¶ *Then shall the Priest speak unto the Godfathers and Godmothers on this wise.*

DEARLY beloved, ye have brought *this Child* here to be baptized, ye have prayed that our Lord Jesus Christ would vouchsafe to receive *him*, to release *him* of *his* sins, to sanctify *him* with the holy Ghost, to give *him* the kingdom of heaven, and everlasting life. Ye have heard also that our Lord Jesus Christ hath promised in his Gospel to grant all these things that ye have prayed for: which promise he, for his part, will most surely keep and perform. Wherefore, after this promise made by Christ, *this Infant* must also faithfully, for *his* part, promise by you that are *his* sureties, (until *he* come of age to take it upon *himself*,) that *he* will renounce the devil and all his works, and constantly believe God's holy Word, and obediently keep his commandments.

I demand therefore,

DOST thou, in the name of this Child, renounce the devil and all his works, the vain pomp

Minister. Dost thou forsake the vain pomp and glory of the world, with all the covetous desires of the same?

Answer. I forsake them.

Minister. Dost thou forsake the carnal desires of the flesh, so that thou wilt not follow nor be led by them?

Answer. I forsake them.

Minister. Dost thou believe in God the Father Almighty, Maker of heaven and earth?

Answer. I believe.

Minister. Dost thou believe in Jesus Christ his only begotten Son our Lord, and that he was conceived by the Holy Ghost, born of the virgin Mary, that he suffered under Poncius Pilate, was crucified, dead, and buried; that he went down into hell, and also did rise again the third day; that he ascended into heaven, and sitteth on the right hand of God the Father Almighty: And from thence shall come again at the end of the world, to judge the quick and the dead: Dost thou believe this?

Answer. I believe.

Minister. Dost thou believe in the Holy Ghost, the holy Catholic Church, the Communion of Saints, Remission of Sins, Resurrection of the flesh and everlasting life after death?

Answer. I believe.

Minister. What dost thou desire?

Answer. Baptism.

Minister. Wilt thou be baptized?

Answer. I will.

and glory of the world, with all covetous desires of the same, and the carnal desires of the flesh, so that thou wilt not follow, nor be led by them?

Answer. I renounce them all.

Minister.

DOST thou believe in God the Father Almighty, Maker of heaven and earth?

And in Jesus Christ his only-begotten Son our Lord? And that he was conceived by the Holy Ghost; born of the Virgin Mary; that he suffered under Pontius Pilate, was crucified, dead, and buried; that he went down into hell, and also did rise again the third day; that he ascended into heaven, and sitteth at the right hand of God the Father Almighty; and from thence shall come again at the end of the world, to judge the quick and the dead?

And dost thou believe in the Holy Ghost; the holy Catholick Church; the Communion of Saints; the Remission of sins; the Resurrection of the flesh; and everlasting life after death?

Answer. All this I stedfastly believe.

Minister.

WILT thou be baptized in this faith?

Answer. That is my desire.

Minister.

WILT thou then obediently keep God's holy will and commandments, and walk in the same all the days of thy life?

Answer. I will.

¶ *Then shall the Priest say,*

O MERCIFUL God, grant that the old Adam in *this Child* may be so buried, that the new man may be raised up in *him. Amen.*

Grant that all carnal affections may die in *him*, and that all things belonging to the Spirit may live and grow in *him. Amen.*

Grant that *he* may have power and strength to have victory, and to triumph, against the devil, the world, and the flesh. *Amen.*

Grant that whosoever is here dedicated to thee by our office and ministry may also be endued with heavenly virtues, and everlastingly rewarded, through thy mercy, O blessed Lord God, who dost live, and govern all things, world without end. *Amen.*

ALMIGHTY, everliving God, whose most dearly beloved Son Jesus Christ, for the forgiveness of our sins, did shed out of his most precious side both water and blood; and gave commandment to his disciples, that they should go teach all nations, and baptize them In the Name of the Father, the Son, and the Holy Ghost; Regard, we beseech thee, the supplications of thy congregation; sanctify this Water to the mystical washing away of sin; and grant that *this Child*, now to be baptized therein, may receive the fulness of thy grace, and ever remain in the number of thy faithful and elect children; through Jesus Christ our Lord. *Amen.*

¶ *Then the Priest shall take the child in his hands, and ask the name.*

¶ *Then the Priest shall take the Child into his hands, and shall say to the Godfathers and Godmothers,*

Name this Child.

And naming the child, shall dip it in the water thrice. First dipping the right side: Second, the left side: The third time dipping the face toward the font: so it be discreetly and warily done, saying,

¶ *And then naming it after them (if they shall certify him that the Child may well endure it) he shall dip it in the Water discreetly and warily, saying,*

¶ *N.* I baptize thee in the name of the Father, and of the Son, and of the Holy Ghost. Amen.

¶ *And if the child be weak, it shall suffice to pour water upon it, saying the foresaid words. N. I baptize thee, &c.*

N. I baptize thee In the Name of the Father, and of the Son, and of the Holy Ghost. Amen.

¶ *But if they certify that the Child is weak, it shall suffice to pour water upon it, saying the foresaid words,*

N. I baptize thee in the Name of the Father, and of the Son, and of the Holy Ghost. Amen.

¶ *Then the Priest shall say,*

WE receive this Child into the congregation of Christ's flock, * and do sign *him* with the sign of the Cross, in token that hereafter *he* shall not be ashamed to confess the faith of Christ crucified, and manfully to fight under his banner, against sin, the world, and the devil; and to continue Christ's faithful soldier and servant unto *his* life's end. Amen.

* *Here the Priest shall make a Cross upon the Child's forehead.*

¶ *Then shall the Priest say,*

SEEING now, dearly beloved brethren, that *this Child is* regenerate, and grafted into the body of Christ's Church, let us give thanks unto Almighty God for these benefits; and with one accord make our prayers unto him, that *this Child* may lead the rest of *his* life according to this beginning.

¶ *Then shall be said, all kneeling;*

OUR Father, which art in heaven, Hallowed be thy Name. Thy kingdom come. Thy will be done in earth, As it is in heaven. Give us this day our daily bread. And forgive us our trespasses, As we forgive them that trespass against us. And lead us not into temptation; But deliver us from evil. Amen.

Then the Godfathers and Godmothers shall take and lay their hands upon the child, and the minister shall put upon him his white vesture, commonly called the Chrisom; and say,

Take this white vesture for a token of the innocency, which by God's grace in this holy sacrament of baptism is given unto thee; and for a sign whereby thou art admonished, so long as thou livest, to give thyself to innocency of living, that, after this transitory life, thou mayest be partaker of the life everlasting. Amen.

Then the Priest shall anoint the infant upon the head, saying,

ALMIGHTY God, the Father of our Lord Jesus Christ, who hath regenerate thee by water and the Holy Ghost, and hath given unto thee remission of all thy sins: he vouchsafe to anoint thee with the unction of his Holy Spirit, and bring thee to the inheritance of everlasting life. Amen.

¶ *Then shall the Priest say,*

WE yield thee hearty thanks, most merciful Father, that it hath pleased thee to regenerate *this Infant* with thy holy Spirit, to receive *him* for thine own *Child* by adoption, and to incorporate *him* into thy holy Church. And humbly we beseech thee to grant, that *he*, being dead unto sin, and living unto righteousness, and being buried with Christ in his death, may crucify the old man, and utterly abolish the whole body of sin; and that, as *he* is made *partaker* of the death of thy Son, *he* may also be *partaker* of his resurrection; so that finally, with the residue of thy holy Church, *he* may be *an inheritor* of thine everlasting kingdom; through Christ our Lord. *Amen.*

When there are many to be baptized, this order of demanding, baptizing, putting on the Chrisom, and anointing, shall be used severally with every child: those that be first baptized departing from the font, and remaining in some convenient place within the Church until all be baptized. At the last end, the Priest, calling the Godfathers and Godmothers together, shall say this short exhortation following:

FORASMUCH as these children have promised by you to forsake the devil and all his works, to believe in God, and to serve him; you must remember, that it is your parts and duty to see that these infants be taught, so soon as they shall be able to learn, what a solemn vow, promise, and profession they have made by you. And that they may know these things the better, ye shall call upon them to hear sermons; and chiefly you shall provide that they may learn the Creed, the Lord's Prayer, and the Ten Commandments, in the English tongue, and all other things which a Christian man ought to know and believe to his soul's health: and that these children may be virtuously brought up to lead a godly and Christian life; remembering always that baptism doth represent unto us our profession, which is, to follow the example of our Saviour Christ, and to be made like unto him; that as he died and rose again for us, so should we (which are baptized) die from sin, and rise again unto righteousness, continually mortifying all our evil and corrupt affections, and daily proceeding in all virtue and godliness of living.

¶ *The Minister shall command that the Chrisoms be brought to the church, and delivered to the Priests after the accustomed manner, at the purification of the mother of every child; And that the children be brought to the Bishop to be confirmed of him, so soon as they can say in their vulgar tongue the Articles of the Faith, the Lord's Prayer, and the Ten Commandments, and be further instructed in the Catechism, set forth for that purpose, accordingly as it is there expressed.*

¶ *Then, all standing up, the Priest shall say to the Godfathers and Godmothers this Exhortation following.*

FORASMUCH as *this Child hath* promised by you *his* sureties to renounce the devil and all his works, to believe in God, and to serve him; ye must remember, that it is your parts and duties to see that *this Infant* be taught, so soon as *he* shall be able to learn, what a solemn vow, promise, and profession, *he hath* here made by you. And that *he* may know these things the better, ye shall call upon *him* to hear Sermons; and chiefly ye shall provide, that *he* may learn the Creed, the Lord's Prayer, and the Ten Commandments, in the vulgar tongue, and all other things which a Christian ought to know and believe to his soul's health; and that *this Child* may be virtuously brought up to lead a godly and a christian life; remembering always, that Baptism doth represent unto us our profession; which is, to follow the example of our Saviour Christ, and to be made like unto him; that, as he died, and rose again for us, so should we, who are baptized, die from sin, and rise again unto righteousness; continually mortifying all our evil and corrupt affections, and daily proceeding in all virtue and godliness of living.

¶ *Then shall he add and say,*

YE are to take care that *this Child* be brought to the Bishop to be confirmed by him, so soon as *he* can say the Creed, the Lord's Prayer, and the Ten

And so let the congregation depart in the name of the Lord.

¶ *Note, that if the number of children to be baptized, and multitude of people present, be so great that they cannot conveniently stand at the church door, then let them stand within the church, in some convenient place, nigh unto the church door; and there all things be said and done, appointed to be said and done at the church door.*

Commandments, in the vulgar tongue, and be further instructed in the Church-Catechism set forth for that purpose.

IT is certain by God's Word, that Children which are baptized, dying before they commit actual sin, are undoubtedly saved.

To take away all scruple concerning the use of the sign of the cross in Baptism; the true explication thereof, and the just reasons for the retaining of it, may be seen in the xxxth Canon, first published in the Year MDCIV.

OF THEM THAT BE

BAPTIZED IN PRIVATE HOUSES

IN TIME OF NECESSITY.

¶ *The Pastors and Curates shall oft admonish the people, that they defer not the baptism of infants any longer than the Sunday, or other holy day next after the child be born, unless upon a great and reasonable cause declared to the Curate and by him approved.*

And also they shall warn them, that without great cause, and necessity they baptize not children at home in their houses. And when great need shall compel them so to do, that then they minister it on this fashion.

¶ *First let them that be present call upon God for his grace, and say the Lord's prayer, if the time will suffer. And then one of them shall name the child, and dip him in the water, or pour water upon him, saying these words :*

¶ *N.* I baptize thee in the name of the Father, and of the Son, and of the Holy Ghost. Amen.

THE MINISTRATION OF

PRIVATE BAPTISM OF CHILDREN

IN HOUSES.

¶ *The Curates of every Parish shall often admonish the people, that they defer not the Baptism of their children longer than the first or second Sunday next after their birth, or other holy-day falling between, unless upon a great and reasonable cause, to be approved by the Curate.*

¶ *And also they shall warn them, that without like great cause and necessity they procure not their Children to be baptized at home in their houses. But when need shall compel them so to do, then Baptism shall be administered on this fashion :*

¶ *First, let the Minister of the Parish (or, in his absence, any other lawful Minister that can be procured) with them that are present call upon God, and say the Lord's Prayer, and so many of the Collects appointed to be said before in the Form of Publick Baptism, as the time and present exigence will suffer. And then, the Child being named by some one that is present, the Minister shall pour Water upon it, saying these words ;*

N. I baptize thee In the Name of the Father, and of the Son, and of the Holy Ghost. Amen.

¶ *Then, all kneeling down, the Minister shall give thanks unto God, and say,*

WE yield thee hearty thanks, most merciful Father, that it hath pleased thee to regenerate *this Infant*, with thy holy Spirit, to receive *him* for thine own *Child* by adoption, and to incorporate *him* into thy holy Church. And we humbly beseech thee to grant, that as *he* is now made *partaker* of the death of thy Son, so *he* may be also of his resurrection; and that finally, with the residue of thy Saints, *he* may inherit thine everlasting kingdom; through the same thy Son Jesus Christ our Lord. *Amen.*

And let them not doubt, but that the child so baptized is lawfully and sufficiently baptized, and ought not to be baptized again in the Church. But yet nevertheless, if the child which is after this sort baptized do afterward live, it is expedient that he be brought into the Church, to the intent the Priest may examine and try whether the child be lawfully baptized or no.

And if those that bring any child to the church do answer that he is already baptized: Then shall the Priest examine them further.

¶ By whom the child was baptized?

Who was present when the child was baptized?

Whether they called upon God for grace and succour in that necessity?

With what thing, or what matter, they did baptize the child?

With what words the child was baptized?

Whether they think the child to be lawfully and perfectly baptized?

And if the minister shall prove by the answers of such as brought the child, that all things were done, as they ought to be: Then shall not he christen the child again, but shall receive him, as one of the flock of the true christian people, saying thus.

I CERTIFY you, that in this case ye have done well, and according unto due order concerning the baptizing of this child, which being born in original sin, and in the wrath of God, is now by the laver of regeneration in Baptism

¶ *And let them not doubt, but that the Child so baptized is lawfully and sufficiently baptized, and ought not to be baptized again. Yet nevertheless, if the Child, which is after this sort baptized, do afterward live, it is expedient that it be brought into the Church, to the intent that, if the Minister of the same Parish did himself baptize that Child, the Congregation may be certified of the true Form of Baptism, by him privately before used: In which case he shall say thus,*

I CERTIFY you, that according to the due and prescribed Order of the Church, *at such a time*, and *at such a place*, before divers witnesses I baptized this Child.

¶ *But if the Child were baptized by any other lawful Minister, then the Minister of the Parish, where the Child was born or christened, shall examine and try whether the Child be lawfully baptized, or no. In which case, if those that bring any Child to the Church do answer that the same Child is already baptized, then shall the Minister examine them further, saying,*

BY whom was this Child baptized?

Who was present when this Child was baptized?

Because some things essential to this Sacrament may happen to be omitted through fear or haste, in such times of extremity; therefore I demand further of you,

With what matter was this Child baptized?

With what words was this Child baptized?

¶ *And if the Minister shall find by the answers of such as bring the Child, that all things were done as they ought to be; then shall not he christen the Child again, but shall receive him as one of the flock of true christian people, saying thus.*

I CERTIFY you, that in this case all is well done, and according unto due order, concerning the baptizing of this Child; who being born in original sin, and in the wrath of God, is now, by the laver of Regeneration in made the child of God, and heir of everlasting life: for our Lord Jesus Christ doth not deny his grace and mercy unto such infants, but most lovingly doth call them unto him: as the holy gospel doth witness to our comfort on this wise.

At a certain time they brought children unto Christ that he should touch them, and his disciples rebuked those that brought them. But when Jesus saw it, he was displeased, and said unto them: Suffer little children to come unto me, and forbid them not, for to such belongeth the kingdom of God. Verily I say unto you, whosoever doth not receive the kingdom of God as a little child, he shall not enter therein. And when he had taken them up in his arms, he put his hands upon them and blessed them. Mark x.

After the Gospel is read: the minister shall make this exhortation upon the words of the gospel.

Friends, ye hear in this gospel the words of our Saviour Christ, that he commanded the children to be brought unto him, how he blamed those that would have kept them from him, how he exhorted all men to follow their innocency: ye perceive how by his outward gesture and deed he declared his good will toward them; for he embraced them in his arms, he laid his hands upon them, and blessed them. Doubt you not therefore, but earnestly believe, that he hath likewise favourably received this present infant, that he hath embraced him with the arms of his mercy, that he hath given unto him the blessing of eternal life, and made him partaker of his everlasting kingdom.

Baptism, received into the number of the children of God, and heirs of everlasting life: for our Lord Jesus Christ doth not deny his grace and mercy unto such Infants, but most lovingly doth call them unto him, as the holy Gospel doth witness to our comfort on this wise.

St. *Mark* x. 13.

THEY brought young children to Christ, that he should touch them; and his disciples rebuked those that brought them. But when Jesus saw it, he was much displeased and said unto them, Suffer the little children to come unto me, and forbid them not; for of such is the kingdom of God. Verily I say unto you, Whosoever shall not receive the kingdom of God as a little child, he shall not enter therein. And he took them up in his arms, put his hands upon them, and blessed them.

¶ *After the Gospel is read, the Minister shall make this brief Exhortation upon the words of the Gospel.*

BELOVED, ye hear in this Gospel the words of our Saviour Christ, that he commanded the children to be brought unto him; how he blamed those that would have kept them from him; how he exhorted all men to follow their innocency. Ye perceive how by his outward gesture and deed he declared his good will toward them; for he embraced them in his arms, he laid his hands upon them, and blessed them. Doubt ye not therefore, but earnestly believe, that he hath likewise favourably received *this* present *Infant;* that he hath embraced *him* with the arms of his mercy; and (as he hath promised in his holy Word) will give unto *him* the blessing of eternal

Wherefore we being thus persuaded of the good will of our heavenly Father, declared by his Son Jesus Christ towards this infant: Let us faithfully and devoutly give thanks unto him, and say the prayer which the Lord himself taught; and in declaration of our Faith, let us also recite the articles contained in our Creed.

Here the minister with the Godfathers and Godmothers shall say.

Our Father which art in heaven, hallowed be thy name: let Thy kingdom come, &c.

Then shall they say the Creed, and then the Priest shall demand the name of the child, which being by the Godfathers and Godmothers pronounced, the minister shall say,

¶ *N.* Dost thou forsake the devil and all his works?

Answer. I forsake them.

Minister. Dost thou forsake the vain pomp and glory of the world, with all the covetous desires of the same?

Answer. I forsake them.

Minister. Dost thou forsake the carnal desires of the flesh, so that thou wilt not follow and be led by them?

Answer. I forsake them.

Minister. Dost thou believe in God the Father almighty, maker of heaven and earth?

Answer. I believe.

Minister. Dost thou believe in Jesus Christ his only-begotten Son our Lord, and that he was conceived by the Holy Ghost, born of the virgin Mary, that he suffered under Pontius Pilate, was crucified, dead and buried, that he went

life, and make *him partaker* of his everlasting kingdom. Wherefore, we being thus persuaded of the good will of our heavenly Father, declared by his Son Jesus Christ, towards *this Infant*, let us faithfully and devoutly give thanks unto him, and say the Prayer which the Lord himself taught us:

OUR Father, which art in heaven, Hallowed be thy Name. Thy kingdom come. Thy will be done in earth, As it is in heaven. Give us this day our daily bread. And forgive us our trespasses, As we forgive them that trespass against us. And lead us not into temptation; But deliver us from evil. Amen.

down into hell, and also did arise again the third day, that he ascended into heaven, and sitteth on the right hand of God the Father almighty, and from thence shall come again at the end of the world to judge the quick and the dead: dost thou believe thus?

Answer. I believe.

Minister. Dost thou believe in the Holy Ghost, the holy catholic Church, the Communion of Saints, Remission of Sins, Resurrection of the flesh, and everlasting life after death?

Answer. I believe.

Then the Minister shall put the white vesture, commonly called the Chrisom, upon the child, saying,

TAKE this white vesture for a token of the innocency, which by God's grace in the holy sacrament of Baptism is given unto thee, and for a sign whereby thou art admonished so long as thou shalt live, to give thyself to innocency of living, that after this transitory life thou mayest be partaker of the life everlasting. Amen.

¶ Let us pray.

ALMIGHTY and everlasting God, heavenly Father, we give thee humble thanks that thou hast vouchsafed to call us to the knowledge of thy grace, and faith in thee: Increase and confirm this faith in us evermore: Give thy Holy Spirit to this infant, that he being born again, and being made heir of everlasting salvation through our Lord Jesus Christ, may continue thy servant, and attain thy promises, through the same our Lord Jesus Christ thy Son: who liveth and reigneth with thee in unity of the same Holy Spirit everlastingly. Amen.

ALMIGHTY and everlasting God, heavenly Father, we give thee humble thanks, that thou hast vouchsafed to call us to the knowledge of thy grace, and faith in thee; Increase this knowledge, and confirm this faith in us evermore. Give thy holy Spirit to *this Infant*, that *he*, being born again, and being made *an heir* of everlasting salvation, through our Lord Jesus Christ, may continue thy *servant*, and attain thy promise; through the same our Lord Jesus Christ thy Son, who liveth and reigneth with thee and the Holy Spirit, now and for ever. *Amen.*

¶ *Then shall the Priest demand the Name of the Child; which being by the Godfathers and Godmothers pronounced, the Minister shall say,*

DOST thou in the name of this Child, renounce the devil and all his works, the vain pomp and glory of this world, with all covetous desires of the same, and the carnal desires of the flesh, so that thou wilt not follow, nor be led by them?

Answer. I renounce them all.

Minister.

DOST thou believe in God the Father Almighty, Maker of heaven and earth?

And in Jesus Christ his only-begotten Son our Lord? And that he was conceived by the Holy Ghost; born of the Virgin Mary; that he suffered under Pontius Pilate, was crucified, dead, and buried; that he went down into hell, and also did rise again the third day; that he ascended into heaven, and sitteth at the right hand of God the Father Almighty; and from thence shall come again at the end of the world, to judge the quick and the dead?

And dost thou believe in the Holy Ghost; the holy Catholick Church; the Communion of Saints; the Remission of Sins; the Resurrection of the flesh; and everlasting life after death;

Answer. All this I stedfastly believe.

Minister.

WILT thou then obediently keep God's holy will and commandments, and walk in the same all the days of thy life?

Answer. I will.

¶ *Then the Priest shall say,*

WE receive this Child into the congregation of Christ's

**Here the Priest shall make a Cross upon the Child's forehead.*

flock, * and do sign *him* with the sign of the Cross, in token that hereafter *he* shall not be ashamed to confess the faith of Christ crucified, and manfully to fight under his banner, against sin, the world, and the devil; and to continue Christ's faithful soldier and servant unto *his* life's end. Amen.

¶ *Then shall the Priest say,*

SEEING now, dearly beloved brethren, that *this Child is* by Baptism regenerate, and grafted into the body of Christ's Church, let us give thanks unto Almighty God for these benefits; and with one accord make our prayers unto him, that *he* may lead the rest of *his* life according to this beginning.

¶ *Then shall the Priest say,*

WE yield thee most hearty thanks, most merciful Father, that it hath pleased thee to regenerate *this Infant* with thy Holy Spirit, to receive *him* for thine own *Child* by adoption, and to incorporate *him* into thy holy Church. And humbly we beseech thee to grant, that *he* being dead unto sin, and living unto righteousness, and being buried with Christ in his death, may crucify the old man, and utterly abolish the whole body of sin; and that, as *he is* made *partaker* of the death of thy Son, *he* may also be *partaker* of his resurrection; so that finally, with the residue of thy holy Church, *he* may be *an inheritor* of thine everlasting kingdom; through Jesus Christ our Lord. *Amen.*

Then shall the minister make this exhortation to the Godfathers and Godmothers.

FORASMUCH as this child hath promised by you to forsake the devil and all his works, to believe

¶ *Then, all standing up, the Minister shall make this Exhortation to the Godfathers and Godmothers.*

FORASMUCH as *this Child hath* promised by you *his* sureties to renounce the devil

in God, and to serve him, you must remember that it is your parts and duty to see that this infant be taught, so soon as he shall be able to learn, what a solemn vow, promise, and profession he hath made by you: and that he may know these things the better, ye shall call upon him to hear sermons: and chiefly ye shall provide that he may learn the Creed, the Lord's prayer, and the ten commandments in the English tongue, and all other things which a christian man ought to know and believe to his soul's health, and that this child may be virtuously brought up to lead a godly and a christian life: remembering alway that Baptism doth represent unto us our profession, which is to follow the example of our Saviour Christ, and to be made like unto him, that as he died and rose again for us, so should we, which are baptized, die from sin, and rise again unto righteousness, continually mortifying all our evil and corrupt affections, and daily proceeding in all virtue and godliness of living.

&c. as in Public Baptism.

¶ *But if they which bring the infants to the church, do make an uncertain answer to the priest's questions, and say that they cannot tell what they thought, did, or said, in that great fear and trouble of mind (as oftentimes it chanceth): Then let the Priest baptize him in form above written, concerning public baptism, saving that at the dipping of the child in the font he shall use this form of words.*

If thou be not baptized already, *N.* I baptize thee in the name of the Father, and of the Son, and of the Holy Ghost. Amen.

The Water in the Font shall be changed every month once at the least, and afore any child be baptized in the water so changed, the Priest shall say at the font these prayers following.

O most merciful God our Saviour

and all his works, to believe in God, and to serve him; ye must remember, that it is your parts and duties to see that *this Infant* be taught, so soon as *he* shall be able to learn, what a solemn vow, promise, and profession *he hath* made by you. And that *he* may know these things the better, ye shall call upon *him* to hear Sermons; and chiefly ye shall provide, that *he* may learn the Creed, the Lord's Prayer, and the Ten Commandments, in the vulgar tongue, and all other things which a christian ought to know and believe to his soul's health; and that *this Child* may be virtuously brought up to lead a godly and a christian life; remembering alway, that Baptism doth represent unto us our profession; which is, to follow the example of our Saviour Christ, and to be made like unto him; that, as he died, and rose again for us, so should we, who are baptized, die from sin, and rise again unto righteousness; continually mortifying all our evil and corrupt affections, and daily proceeding in all virtue and godliness of living.

¶ *But if they which bring the Infant to the Church do make such uncertain answers to the Priest's questions, as that it cannot appear that the Child was baptized with* Water, In the Name of the Father, and of the Son, and of the Holy Ghost, *(which are essential parts of Baptism,) then let the Priest baptize it in the form before appointed for Public Baptism of Infants; saving that at the dipping of the child in the Font, he shall use this form of words.*

IF thou art not already baptized, *N.* I baptize thee In the Name of the Father, and of the Son, and of the Holy Ghost. Amen.

Jesu Christ, who hast ordained the element of water for the regeneration of thy faithful people, upon whom, being baptized in the river of Jordan, the Holy Ghost came down in likeness of a dove: Send down, we beseech thee, the same thy Holy Spirit to assist us, and to be present at this our invocation of thy holy name: Sanctify ✠ this fountain of baptism, thou that art the sanctifier of all things, that by the power of thy word all those that shall be baptized therein may be spiritually regenerated, and made the children of everlasting adoption. Amen.

O MERCIFUL God, grant that the old Adam, in them that shall be baptized in this fountain, may be so buried, that the new man may be raised up again. Amen.

GRANT that all carnal affections may die in them; and that all things belonging to the Spirit, may live and grow in them. Amen.

GRANT to all them which at this fountain forsake the devil and all his works: that they may have power and strength to have victory and to triumph against him, the world, and the flesh. Amen.

WHOSOEVER shall confess thee, O Lord: recognise him also in thy kingdom. Amen.

GRANT that all sin and vice here may be so extinct: that they never have power to reign in thy servants. Amen.

GRANT that whosoever here shall begin to be of thy flock: may evermore continue in the same. Amen.

GRANT that all they which for thy sake in this life do deny and forsake themselves: may win and purchase thee, O Lord, which art everlasting treasure. Amen.

GRANT that whosoever is here dedicated to thee by our office and ministry: may also be endued with heavenly virtues, and everlastingly rewarded through thy mercy, O blessed Lord God, who dost live and govern all things world without end. Amen.

The Lord be with you.

Answer. And with thy spirit.

ALMIGHTY everliving God, whose most dearly beloved Son JesusChrist for the forgiveness of our sins did shed out of his most precious side both water and blood, and gave commandment to his disciples that they should go teach all nations, and baptize them in the name of the Father, the Son, and the Holy Ghost: Regard, we beseech thee, the supplications of thy congregation, and grant that all thy servants which shall be baptized in this water, prepared for the ministration of thy holy sacrament, may receive the fulness of thy grace, and ever remain in the number of thy faithful and elect children, through Jesus Christ our Lord.

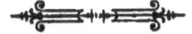

THE MINISTRATION OF

BAPTISM TO SUCH AS ARE OF RIPER YEARS,

AND ABLE TO ANSWER FOR THEMSELVES.

¶ *When any such persons, as are of riper years, are to be baptized, timely notice shall be given to the Bishop, or whom he shall appoint for that purpose, a week before at the least, by the Parents, or some other discreet persons; that so due care may be taken for their Examination, whether they be sufficiently instructed in the Principles of the Christian Religion; and that they may be exhorted to prepare themselves with Prayers and Fasting for the receiving of this holy Sacrament.*

¶ *And if they shall be found fit, then the Godfathers and Godmothers (the people being assembled upon the Sunday or Holy-day appointed) shall be ready to present them at the Font immediately after the second Lesson, either at Morning or Evening Prayer, as the Curate in his discretion shall think fit.*

¶ *And standing there, the Priest shall ask, whether any of the persons here presented be baptized, or no: If they shall answer,* No; *then shall the Priest say thus,*

DEARLY beloved, forasmuch as all men are conceived and born in sin, (and that which is born of the flesh is flesh,) and they that are in the flesh cannot please God, but live in sin, committing many actual transgressions; and that our Saviour Christ saith, None can enter into the kingdom of God, except he be regenerate and born anew of Water and of the Holy Ghost: I beseech you to call upon God the Father, through our Lord Jesus Christ, that of his bounteous goodness he will grant to *these persons* that which by nature *they* cannot have: that *they* may be baptized with Water and the holy Ghost, and received into Christ's holy Church, and be made lively *members* of the same.

¶ *Then shall the Priest say.*

Let us pray.

(¶ *And here all the Congregation shall kneel.*)

ALMIGHTY and everlasting God, who of thy great mercy didst save Noah and his family in the ark from perishing by water; and also didst safely lead the children of Israel thy people through the Red Sea, figuring thereby thy holy Baptism; and by the baptism of thy well-beloved Son Jesus Christ, in the river Jordan, didst sanctify the element of Water to the mystical washing away of sin; We beseech thee, for thine infinite mercies, that thou wilt mercifully look upon *these* thy *servants*; wash *them* and sanctify *them* with the holy Ghost, that *they*, being delivered from thy wrath, may be received into the ark of Christ's Church; and being steadfast in faith, joyful through hope, and rooted in charity, may so pass the waves of this troublesome world, that finally *they* may come to the land of everlasting life, there to reign with thee world without end; through Jesus Christ our Lord. *Amen.*

ALMIGHTY and immortal God, the aid of all that need, the helper of all that flee to thee for succour, the life of them that believe, and the resurrection of the dead; We call upon thee for *these persons*, that *they*, coming to thy holy Baptism, may receive remission of *their* sins by spiritual regeneration. Receive *them*, O Lord, as thou hast promised by thy well-beloved Son, saying, Ask, and ye shall receive; seek, and ye shall find; knock, and it shall be opened unto you: So give now unto us that ask; let us that seek find; open the gate unto us that knock; that *these persons* may enjoy the everlasting benediction of thy heavenly washing, and may come to the eternal kingdom which thou hast promised by Christ our Lord. *Amen.*

¶ *Then shall the people stand up, aud the Priest shall say,*

Hear the words of the Gospel, written by Saint *John*, in the third Chapter, beginning at the first Verse.

THERE was a man of the Pharisees, named Nicodemus, a ruler of the Jews. The same came to Jesus by night, and said unto him, Rabbi, we know that thou art a teacher come from God; for no man can do these miracles that thou doest, except God be with him. Jesus answered and said unto him, Verily, verily I say unto thee, Except a man be born again, he cannot see the kingdom of God. Nicodemus saith unto him, How can a man be born when he is old? Can he enter the second time into his mother's womb, and be born? Jesus answered, Verily, verily I say unto thee, Except a man be born of water and of the Spirit, he cannot enter into the kingdom of God. That which is born of the flesh is flesh; and that which is born of the Spirit is spirit. Marvel not that I said unto thee, Ye must be born again. The wind bloweth where it listeth, and thou hearest the sound thereof; but canst not tell whence it cometh, and whither it goeth: so is every one that is born of the Spirit.

¶ *After which he shall say this Exhortation following.*

BELOVED, ye hear in this Gospel the express words of our Saviour Christ, that except a man be born of water and of the Spirit, he cannot enter into the kingdom of God. Whereby ye may perceive the great necessity of this Sacrament, where it may be had. Likewise, immediately before his ascension into heaven, (as we read in the last Chapter of Saint Mark's Gospel,) he gave command to his disciples, saying, Go ye into all the world, and preach the Gospel to every creature. He that believeth and is baptized shall be saved; but he that believeth not shall be damned. Which also sheweth unto us the great benefit we reap thereby. For which cause Saint Peter the Apostle, when upon his first preaching of the Gospel many were pricked at the heart, and said to him and the rest of the Apostles, Men and brethren, what shall we do? replied and said unto them, Repent, and be baptized every one of you for the remission of sins, and ye shall receive the gift of the Holy Ghost. For the promise is to you and your children, and to all that are afar off, even as many as the Lord our God shall call. And with many other words exhorted he them, saying, Save yourselves from this untoward generation. For (as the same Apostle testifieth in another place) even Baptism doth also now save us, (not the putting away of the filth of the flesh, but the answer of a good conscience towards God,) by the resurrection of Jesus Christ. Doubt ye not therefore, but earnestly believe, that he will favourably receive *these* present *persons*, truly repenting, and coming unto him by faith; that he will grant *them* remission of *their* sins, and bestow upon *them* the holy Ghost; that he will give them the blessing of eternal life, and make *them partakers* of his everlasting kingdom.

Wherefore we being thus persuaded of the good will of our heavenly Father towards *these persons*, declared by his Son Jesus Christ; let us faithfully and devoutly give thanks to him, and say,

ALMIGHTY and everlasting God, heavenly Father, we give thee humble thanks, for that thou hast vouchsafed to call us to the knowledge of thy grace, and faith in thee: Increase this knowledge, and confirm this faith in us evermore. Give thy holy Spirit to *these persons*, that *they* may be born again and be made *heirs* of everlasting salvation; through our Lord Jesus Christ, who liveth and reigneth with thee and the Holy Spirit, now and for ever. *Amen.*

¶ *Then the Priest shall speak to the* persons *to be baptized on this wise:*

WELL-BELOVED, who are come hither desiring to receive holy Baptism, *ye* have heard how the congregation hath prayed, that our Lord Jesus Christ would vouchsafe to receive you and bless you, to release you of your sins, to give you the kingdom of heaven, and everlasting life. *Ye* have heard also, that our Lord Jesus Christ hath promised in his holy Word to grant all those things that we have prayed for; which promise he, for his part, will most surely keep and perform.

Wherefore, after this promise made by Christ, *ye* must also faithfully, for your part, promise in the presence of these your Witnesses, and this whole congregation, that *ye* will renounce the devil and all his works, and constantly believe God's holy Word, and obediently keep his commandments.

¶ *Then shall the Priest demand of each of the persons to be baptized, severally, these Questions following:*

Question.

DOST thou renounce the devil and all his works, the vain pomp and glory of the world, with all covetous desires of the same, and the carnal desires of the flesh, so that thou wilt not follow, nor be led by them?

Answer. I renounce them all.

Question.

DOST thou believe in God the Father Almighty, Maker of heaven and earth?

And in Jesus Christ his only begotten Son our Lord? And that he was conceived by the Holy Ghost; born of the Virgin Mary; that he suffered under Pontius Pilate, was crucified, dead, and buried; that he went down into hell, and also did rise again the third day; that he ascended into heaven, and sitteth at the right hand of God the Father Almighty; and from thence shall come again at the end of the world, to judge the quick and the dead?

And dost thou believe in the Holy Ghost; the holy Catholick Church; the Communion of Saints; the Remission of sins; the Resurrection of the flesh; and everlasting life after death?

Answer. All this I stedfastly believe.

Question.

WILT thou be baptized in this faith?

Answer. That is my desire.

Question.

WILT thou then obediently keep God's holy will and commandments, and walk in the same all the days of thy life?

Answer. I will endeavour so to do, God being my helper.

¶ *Then shall the Priest say,*

O MERCIFUL GOD, grant that the old Adam in *these persons* may be so buried, that the new man may be raised up in *them*. *Amen.*

Grant that all carnal affections may die in *them*, and that all things belonging to the Spirit may live and grow in *them*. *Amen.*

Grant that *thev* may have power and strength to have victory, and to triumph, against the devil, the world, and the flesh. *Amen.*

Grant that *they*, being here dedicated to thee by our office and ministry, may also be endued with heavenly virtues, and everlastingly rewarded, through thy mercy, O blessed Lord God, who dost live, and govern all things, world without end. *Amen.*

ALMIGHTY, everliving God, whose most dearly beloved Son Jesus Christ, for the forgiveness of our sins, did shed out of his most precious side both water and blood, and gave commandment to his disciples, that they should go teach all nations, and baptize them In the Name of the Father, the Son, and the Holy Ghost; Regard, we beseech thee, the supplications of this congregation; sanctify this Water to the mystical washing away of sin; and grant that the *persons* now to be baptized therein may receive the fulness of thy grace, and ever remain in the number of thy faithful and elect children, through Jesus Christ our Lord. *Amen.*

¶ *Then shall the Priest take each person to be baptized by the right hand, and placing him conveniently by the Font, according to his discretion, shall ask the Godfathers and Godmothers the Name; and then shall dip him in the water, or pour water upon him, saying,*

N. I baptize thee In the Name of the Father, and of the Son, and of the Holy Ghost. Amen.

¶ *Then shall the Priest say,*

WE receive this person into the congregation of Christ's

flock; *and do sign *him* with the sign of the Cross, in token that hereafter *he* shall not be ashamed to confess the faith of Christ crucified, and manfully to fight under his banner, against sin, the world, and the devil; and to continue Christ's faithful soldier and servant unto *his* life's end. Amen.

** Here the Priest shall make a Cross upon the person's forehead.*

¶ *Then shall the Priest say,*

SEEING now, dearly beloved brethren, that *these persons are* regenerate, and grafted into the body of Christ's Church, let us give thanks unto Almighty God, for these benefits, and with one accord make our prayers unto him, that *they* may lead the rest of *their* life according to this beginning.

¶ *Then shall be said the Lord's Prayer, all kneeling.*

OUR Father, which art in heaven, Hallowed be thy Name. Thy kingdom come. Thy will be done in earth, As it is in heaven. Give us this day our daily bread. And forgive us our trespasses, As we forgive them that trespass against us. And lead us not into temptation; But deliver us from evil. Amen.

WE yield thee humble thanks, O heavenly Father, that thou hast vouchsafed to call us to the knowledge of thy grace, and faith in thee; Increase this knowledge, and confirm this faith in us evermore. Give thy holy Spirit to *these persons;* that, being now born again, and made *heirs* of everlasting salvation, through our Lord Jesus Christ, *they* may continue thy *servants*, and attain thy promises; through the same Lord Jesus Christ, thy Son, who liveth and reigneth with thee, in the unity of the same Holy Spirit, everlastingly. *Amen.*

¶ *Then, all standing up, the Priest shall use this Exhortation following: speaking to the Godfathers and Godmothers first.*

FORASMUCH as *these persons have* promised in your presence to renounce the devil and all his works, to believe in God, and to serve him; ye must remember, that it is your part and duty to put *them* in mind, what a solemn vow, promise, and profession *they have* now made before this congregation, and especially before you *their* chosen witnesses. And ye are also to call upon *them* to use all diligence to be rightly instructed in God's holy Word; that so *they* may grow in grace, and in the knowledge of our Lord Jesus Christ, and live godly, righteously, and soberly in this present world.

(¶ *And then, speaking to the new baptized* persons, *he shall proceed, and say,)*

AND as for you, who have now by Baptism put on Christ, it is your part and duty also, being made the *children* of God and of the light, by faith in Jesus Christ, to walk answerably to your Christian calling, and as becometh the children of light; remembering always that Baptism representeth unto us our profession; which is, to follow the example of our Saviour Christ, and to be made like unto him; that as he died, and rose again for us; so should we, who are baptized, die from sin, and rise again unto righteousness; continually mortifying all our evil and corrupt affections, and daily proceeding in all virtue and godliness of living.

¶ *It is expedient that every person, thus baptized, should be confirmed by the Bishop so soon after his Baptism as conveniently may be; that so he may be admitted to the holy Communion.*

¶ *If any persons not baptized in their infancy shall be brought to be baptized before they come to years of discretion to answer for themselves; it may suffice to use the Office for Public Baptism of Infants, or (in case of extreme danger) the Office for Private Baptism; only changing the word* [Infant] *for* [Child *or* Person] *as occasion requireth.*

CONFIRMATION,

WHEREIN IS CONTAINED A CATECHISM FOR CHILDREN.

To the end that confirmation may be ministered to the more edifying of such as shall receive it (according to St. Paul's doctrine, who teacheth that all things should be done in the church to the edification of the same) it is thought good that none hereafter shall be confirmed, but such as can say in their mother tongue the articles of the faith, the Lord's prayer, and the ten commandments; and can also answer to such questions of this short Catechism, as the Bishop (or such as he shall appoint) shall by his discretion appose them in. And this order is most convenient to be observed for divers considerations.

¶ *First, because that when children come to the years of discretion, and have learned what their Godfathers and Godmothers promised for them in Baptism, they may then themselves with their own mouth, and with their own consent, openly before the church, ratify and confess the same, and also promise that by the grace of God they will evermore endeavour themselves faithfully to observe and keep such things, as they by their own mouth and confession have assented unto. (k)*

¶ *Secondly, forasmuch as confirmation is ministered to them that be baptized, that by imposition of hands and prayer they may receive strength and defence against all temptations to sin, and the assault of the world, and the devil: it is most meet to be ministered, when children come to that age, that partly by the frailty of their own flesh, partly by the assaults of the world and the devil, they begin to be in danger to fall into sin.*

¶ *Thirdly, for that it is agreeable with the usage of the church in times past, whereby it was ordained, that Confirmation should be ministered to them that were of perfect age, that they being instructed in Christ's religion, should openly profess their own faith, and promise to be obedient unto the will of God.*

¶ *And that no man shall think that any detriment shall come to children by deferring of their confirmation: he shall know for truth, that it is certain by God's word, that children being baptized (if they depart out of this life in their infancy) are undoubtedly saved. (l)*

(*k*) These first two rubrics (1549) are embodied in the Exhortation in the Confirmation Office (1886).

(*l*) This rubric is embodied in the Note at the end of Publick Baptism of Infants (1886).

A CATECHISM,

THAT IS TO SAY

AN INSTRUCTION TO BE LEARNED OF EVERY CHILD, BEFORE HE BE BROUGHT TO BE CONFIRMED OF THE BISHOP.

Question. WHAT is your name?

Answer. *N.* or *M.*

Question. Who gave you this name?

Answer. My Godfathers and Godmothers in my Baptism, wherein I was made a member of Christ, the child of God, and an inheritor of the kingdom of heaven.

Question. What did your Godfathers and Godmothers then for you?

Answer. They did promise and vow three things in my name. First, that I should forsake the devil and all his works and pomps, the vanities of the wicked world, and all the sinful lusts of the flesh. Secondly, that I should believe all the articles of the Christian faith. And thirdly, that I should keep God's holy will and commandments, and walk in the same all the days of my life.

Question. Dost thou not think that thou art bound to believe, and to do as they have promised for thee?

Answer. Yes verily. And by God's help so I will. And I heartily thank our heavenly Father, that he hath called me to this state of salvation, through Jesus Christ our Saviour. And I pray God to give me his grace, that I may continue in the same unto my life's end.

A CATECHISM,

THAT IS TO SAY

AN INSTRUCTION TO BE LEARNED OF EVERY PERSON, BEFORE HE BE BROUGHT TO BE CONFIRMED BY THE BISHOP.

Question.

WHAT is your Name?

Answer. *N.* or *M.*

Question. Who gave you this Name?

Answer. My Godfathers and Godmothers in my Baptism; wherein I was made a member of Christ, the child of God, and an inheritor of the kingdom of heaven.

Question. What did your Godfathers and Godmothers then for you?

Answer. They did promise and vow three things in my name. First, that I should renounce the devil and all his works, the pomps and vanity of this wicked world, and all the sinful lusts of the flesh. Secondly, that I should believe all the Articles of the Christian Faith. And thirdly, that I should keep God's holy will and commandments, and walk in the same all the days of my life?

Question. Dost thou not think that thou art bound to believe, and to do, as they have promised for thee?

Answer. Yes verily; and by God's help so I will. And I heartily thank our heavenly Father, that he hath called me to this state of salvation, through Jesus Christ our Saviour. And I pray unto God to give me his grace, that I may continue in the same unto my life's end.

Question. Rehearse the articles of thy belief.

Answer. I believe in God the Father Almighty, maker of heaven and earth. And in Jesus Christ his only Son our Lord. Which was conceived by the Holy Ghost, born of the virgin Mary. Suffered under Ponce Pilate, was crucified, dead, and buried, he descended into hell. The third day he rose again from the dead. He ascended into heaven, and sitteth on the right hand of God the Father almighty. From thence shall he come to judge the quick and the dead. I believe in the Holy Ghost. The holy catholic church. The communion of saints. The forgiveness of sins. The resurrection of the body. And the life everlasting. Amen.

Question. What dost thou chiefly learn in these articles of thy belief?

Answer. First, I learn to believe in God the Father, who hath made me and all the world.

Secondly, in God the Son, who hath redeemed me and all mankind.

Thirdly, in God the Holy Ghost, who sanctifieth me and all the elect people of God.

Question. You said that your Godfathers and Godmothers did promise for you that ye should keep God's commandments. Tell me how many there be?

Answer. Ten.

Question. Which be they?

Catechist.

Rehearse the Articles of thy Belief.

Answer.

I BELIEVE in God the Father, Almighty, Maker of heaven and earth:

And in Jesus Christ his only Son our Lord, Who was conceived by the Holy Ghost, Born of the Virgin Mary, Suffered under Pontius Pilate, Was crucified, dead, and buried, He descended into hell; The third day he rose again from the dead, He ascended into heaven, And sitteth at the right hand of God the Father Almighty; From thence he shall come to judge the quick and the dead.

I believe in the Holy Ghost; The holy Catholick Church; The Communion of Saints; The Forgiveness of sins; The Resurrection of the Body: And the Life everlasting. Amen.

Question. What dost thou chiefly learn in these Articles of thy Belief?

Answer. First, I learn to believe in God the Father, who hath made me, and all the world.

Secondly, in God the Son, who hath redeemed me, and all mankind.

Thirdly, in God the Holy Ghost, who sanctifieth me, and all the elect people of God.

Question.

You said, that your Godfathers and Godmothers did promise for you, that you should keep God's Commandments. Tell me how many there be?

Answer. Ten.

Question. Which be they?

Answer.

THE same which God spake in the twentieth Chapter of Exodus, saying, I am the Lord thy God, who brought thee out of the land of Egypt, out of the house of bondage.

Answer. Thou shalt have none other Gods but me.

II. Thou shalt not make to thyself any graven image, nor the likeness of anything that is in heaven above, or in the earth beneath, nor in the water under the earth: thou shalt not bow down to them, nor worship them.

III. Thou shalt not take the name of the Lord thy God in vain.

IV. Remember that thou keep holy the Sabbath day.

V. Honour thy father and thy mother.

VI. Thou shalt do no murder.

VII. Thou shalt not commit adultery.

VIII. Thou shalt not steal.

IX. Thou shalt not bear false witness against thy neighbour.

X. Thou shalt not covet thy neighbour's wife, nor his servant, nor his maid, nor his ox, nor his

I. Thou shalt have none other gods but me.

II. Thou shalt not make to thyself any graven image, nor the likeness of anything that is in heaven above, or in the earth beneath, or in the water under the earth. Thou shalt not bow down to them, nor worship them: for I the Lord thy God am a jealous God, and visit the sins of the fathers upon the children, unto the third and fourth generation of them that hate me, and shew mercy unto thousands in them that love me, and keep my commandments.

III. Thou shalt not take the Name of the Lord thy God in vain: for the Lord will not hold him guiltless that taketh his Name in vain.

IV. Remember that thou keep holy the Sabbath-day. Six days shalt thou labour, and do all that thou hast to do; but the seventh day is the Sabbath of the Lord thy God. In it thou shalt do no manner of work, thou, and thy son, and thy daughter, thy man-servant, and thy maid-servant, thy cattle, and the stranger that is within thy gates. For in six days the Lord made heaven and earth, the sea, and all that in them is, and rested the seventh day; wherefore the Lord blessed the seventh day, and hallowed it.

V. Honour thy father and thy mother, that thy days may be long in the land which the Lord thy God giveth thee.

VI. Thou shalt do no murder.

VII. Thou shalt not commit adultery.

VIII. Thou shalt not steal.

IX. Thou shalt not bear false witness against thy neighbour.

X. Thou shalt not covet thy neighbour's house, thou shalt not covet thy neighbour's wife, nor his servant, nor his maid, nor his ass, nor any thing that is his.

Question. What dost thou chiefly learn by these commandments?

Answer. I learn two things: my duty towards God, and my duty towards my neighbour.

Question. What is thy duty towards God?

Answer. My duty towards God is, to believe in him. To fear him. And to love him with all my heart, with all my mind, with all my soul, and with all my strength. To worship him. To give him thanks. To put my whole trust in him. To call upon him. To honour his holy name and his word, and to serve him truly all the days of my life.

Question. What is thy duty towards thy neighbour?

Answer. My duty towards my neighbour is, to love him as myself. And to do to all men as I would they should do to me. To love, honour, and succour my father and mother. To honour and obey the king and his ministers. To submit myself to all my governors, teachers, spiritual pastors, and masters. To order myself lowly and reverently to all my betters. To hurt no body by word nor deed. To be true and just in all my dealing. To bear no malice nor hatred in my heart. To keep my hands from picking and stealing, and my tongue from evil speaking, lying, and slandering. To keep my body in temperance, soberness, and chastity. Not to covet nor desire other men's goods. But learn and labour truly to get my own living, and to do my duty in that state of life, unto which it shall please God to call me.

Question. My good son, know

ox, nor his ass, nor any thing that is his.

Question.

What dost thou chiefly learn by these Commandments?

Answer. I learn two things: my duty towards God, and my duty towards my Neighbour.

Question. What is thy duty towards God?

Answer. My duty towards God, is to believe in him, to fear him, and to love him with all my heart, with all my mind, with all my soul, and with all my strength; to worship him, to give him thanks, to put my whole trust in him, to call upon him, to honour his holy Name and his Word, and to serve him truly all the days of my life.

Question. What is thy duty towards thy Neighbour?

Answer. My duty towards my Neighbour, is to love him as myself, and to do to all men, as I would they should do unto me: To love, honour, and succour my father and mother: To honour and obey the Queen, and all that are put in authority under her: To submit myself to all my governours, teachers, spiritual pastors and masters: To order myself lowly and reverently to all my betters: To hurt no body by word nor deed: To be true and just in all my dealing: To bear no malice nor hatred in my heart: To keep my hands from picking and stealing, and my tongue from evil-speaking, lying, and slandering: To keep my body in temperance, soberness, and chastity: Not to covet nor desire other men's goods; but to learn and labour truly to get mine own living, and to do my duty in that state of life, unto which it shall please God to call me.

Catechist.

My good Child, know this, that

this, that thou art not able to do these things of thyself, nor to walk in the commandments of God and to serve him, without his special grace, which thou must learn at all times to call for by diligent prayer. Let me hear therefore if thou canst say the Lord's prayer.

Answer. Our Father which art in heaven, hallowed be thy name. Thy kingdom come. Thy will be done in earth as it is in heaven. Give us this day our daily bread. And forgive us our trespasses, as we forgive them that trespass against us. And lead us not into temptation, but deliver us from evil. Amen.

Question. What desirest thou of God in this prayer?

Answer. I desire my Lord God our heavenly Father, who is the giver of all goodness, to send his grace unto me, and to all people, that we may worship him, serve him, and obey him, as we ought to do. And I pray unto God, that he will send us all things that be needful both for our souls and bodies: And that he will be merciful unto us, and forgive us our sins; And that it will please him to save and defend us in all dangers ghostly and bodily: And that he will keep us from all sin and wickedness, and from our ghostly enemy, and from everlasting death. And this I trust he will do of his mercy and goodness, through our Lord Jesu Christ. And therefore I say, Amen, So be it.

thou art not able to do these things of thyself, nor to walk in the Commandments of God, and to serve him, without his special grace; which thou must learn at all times to call for by diligent prayer. Let me hear therefore, if thou canst say the Lord's Prayer.

Answer.

OUR Father, which art in heaven, Hallowed be thy Name. Thy kingdom come. Thy will be done in earth, As it is in heaven. Give us this day our daily bread. And forgive us our trespasses, As we forgive them that trespass against us. And lead us not into temptation; But deliver us from evil. Amen.

Question. What desirest thou of God in this Prayer?

Answer. I desire my Lord God our heavenly Father, who is the giver of all goodness, to send his grace unto me, and to all people; that we may worship him, serve him, and obey him, as we ought to do. And I pray unto God, that he will send us all things that be needful both for our souls and bodies; and that he will be merciful unto us, and forgive us our sins; and that it will please him to save and defend us in all dangers ghostly and bodily; and that he will keep us from all sin and wickedness, and from our ghostly enemy, and from everlasting death. And this I trust he will do of his mercy and goodness, through our Lord Jesus Christ. And therefore I say, Amen, So be it.

Question.

HOW many Sacraments hath Christ ordained in his Church?

Answer. Two only, as generally necessary to salvation, that is to say, Baptism, and the Supper of the Lord.

Question. What meanest thou by this word *Sacrament?*

Answer. I mean an outward and visible sign of an inward and spiritual grace given unto us, ordained by Christ himself, as a means whereby we receive the same, and a pledge to assure us thereof.

Question. How many parts are there in a Sacrament?

Answer. Two; the outward visible sign, and the inward spiritual grace.

Question. What is the outward visible sign or form in Baptism?

Answer. Water; wherein the person is baptized *In the Name of the Father, and of the Son, and of the Holy Ghost.*

Question. What is the inward and spiritual grace?

Answer. A death unto sin, and a new birth unto righteousness: for being by nature born in sin, and the children of wrath, we are hereby made the children of grace.

Question. What is required of persons to be baptized?

Answer. Repentance, whereby they forsake sin; and Faith, whereby they stedfastly believe the promises of God made to them in that Sacrament.

Question. Why then are Infants baptized, when by reason of their tender age they cannot perform them?

Answer. Because they promise them both by their Sureties; which promise, when they come to age, themselves are bound to perform.

Question. Why was the Sacrament of the Lord's Supper ordained?

Answer. For the continual remembrance of the sacrifice of the death of Christ, and of the benefits which we receive thereby.

Question. What is the outward part or sign of the Lord's Supper?

Answer. Bread and Wine, which the Lord hath commanded to be received.

Question. What is the inward part, or thing signified?

Answer. The Body and Blood of Christ, which are verily and indeed taken and received by the faithful in the Lord's Supper.

Question. What are the benefits whereof we are partakers thereby?

Answer. The strengthening and refreshing of our souls by the Body and Blood of Christ, as our bodies are by the Bread and Wine.

Question. What is required of them who come to the Lord's Supper?

Answer. To examine themselves, whether they repent them truly of their former sins, stedfastly purposing to lead a new life; have a lively faith in God's mercy through Christ, with a thankful remembrance of his death; and be in charity with all men.

¶ *The Curate of every Parish shall diligently upon Sundays and Holy-days, after the second Lesson at Evening Prayer, openly in the Church instruct and examine so many Children of his Parish sent unto him, as he shall think convenient, in some part of this Catechism.*

¶ *And all Fathers, Mothers, Masters, and Dames, shall cause their Children, Servants, and Apprentices, (which have not learned their Catechism,) to come to the Church at the time appointed, and obediently to hear, and be ordered by the Curate, until such time as they have learned all that is here appointed for them to learn.*

[1549] ¶ *So soon as the children can say in their mother tongue the articles of the faith, the Lord's prayer, the ten commandments, and also can answer to such questions of this short Catechism as the Bishop (or such as he shall appoint) shall by his discretion appose them in: then shall they be brought to the Bishop by one that shall be his Godfather or Godmother, that every child may have a witness of his Confirmation.*

[1886] ¶ *So soon as Children are come to a competent age, and can say, in their Mother Tongue, the Creed, the Lord's Prayer, and the Ten Commandments, and also can answer to the other Questions of this short Catechism; they shall be brought to the Bishop. And every one shall have a Godfather, or a Godmother, as a Witness of their Confirmation.*

¶ *And the Bishop shall confirm them on this wise.*

¶ *And whensoever the Bishop shall give knowledge for Children to be brought unto him for their Confirmation the Curate of every Parish shall either bring, or send in writing, with his hand subscribed thereunto, the names of all such persons within his Parish, as he shall think fit to be presented to the Bishop to be confirmed. And, if the Bishop approve of them, he shall confirm them in manner following.*

¶ CONFIRMATION.

THE ORDER OF

CONFIRMATION,

OR LAYING ON OF HANDS UPON THOSE THAT ARE BAPTIZED AND COME TO YEARS OF DISCRETION.

¶ *Upon the day appointed, all that are to be then confirmed, being placed, and standing in order, before the Bishop; he (or some other Minister appointed by him) shall read this Preface following.*

TO the end that Confirmation may be ministered to the more edifying of such as shall receive it, the Church hath thought good to order, That none hereafter shall be Confirmed, but such as can say the Creed, the Lord's Prayer, and the Ten Commandments: and can also answer to such other Questions, as in the short Catechism are contained: which order is very convenient to be observed; to the end, that children, being now come to the years of discretion, and having learned what their Godfathers and Godmothers promised for them in Baptism, they may themselves, with their own mouth and consent, openly before the Church, ratify and confirm the same; and also promise, that by the grace of God they will evermore endeavour themselves faithfully to observe such things, as they, by their own confession, have assented unto. *(m)*

¶ *Then shall the Bishop say.*

DO ye here, in the presence of God, and of this congregation, renew the solemn promise and vow that was made in your name at your Baptism; ratifying and confirming the same in your

(*m*) This Exhortation embodies the rubrics at head of Confirmation Service (1549).

Our help is in the name of the Lord.

Answer. Which hath made both heaven and earth.

Minister. Blessed is the name of the Lord.

Answer. Henceforth world without end.

Minister. The Lord be with you.

Answer. And with thy spirit.

Let us pray.

ALMIGHTY and everliving God, who hast vouchsafed to regenerate these thy servants of water and the Holy Ghost: And hast given unto them forgiveness of all their sins: Send down from heaven, we beseech thee, O Lord, upon them thy Holy Ghost the Comforter, with the manifold gifts of grace, the spirit of wisdom and understanding; the spirit of counsel and ghostly strength; the spirit of knowledge and true godliness, and fulfil them, O Lord, with the spirit of thy holy fear.

Answer. Amen.

Minister. Sign them, O Lord, and mark them to be thine for ever, by the virtue of thy holy cross and passion. Confirm and strength them with the inward unction of thy Holy Ghost, mercifully unto everlasting life. Amen.

Then the Bishop shall cross them in the forehead, and lay his hand upon their head, saying,

N. I sign thee with the sign of the cross, and lay my hand upon

---

own persons, and acknowledging yourselves bound to believe, and to do, all those things, which your Godfathers and Godmothers then undertook for you?

¶ *And every one shall audibly answer,*

I do.

The Bishop.

OUR help is in the Name of the Lord;

Answer. Who hath made heaven and earth.

Bishop. Blessed be the Name of the Lord;

Answer. Henceforth, world without end.

Bishop. Lord, hear our prayers.

Answer. And let our cry come unto thee.

The Bishop. Let us pray.

ALMIGHTY and everliving God, who hast vouchsafed to regenerate these thy servants by Water, and the Holy Ghost, and hast given unto them forgiveness of all their sins; Strengthen them, we beseech thee, O Lord, with the Holy Ghost the Comforter, and daily increase in them thy manifold gifts of grace; the spirit of wisdom and understanding; the spirit of counsel and ghostly strength; the spirit of knowledge and true godliness; and fill them, O Lord, with the spirit of thy holy fear, now and for ever. *Amen.*

thee: In the name of the Father, and of the Son, and of the Holy Ghost. Amen.

And thus shall he do to every child one after another.

And when he hath laid his hand upon every child, then shall he say.

The peace of the Lord abide with you.

Answer. And with thy spirit.

Then shall the Bishop say.

¶ Let us pray.

ALMIGHTY everliving God, which makest us both to will and to do those things that be good and acceptable unto thy majesty: we make our humble supplications unto thee for these children, upon whom (after the example of thy holy apostles) we have laid our hands, to certify them (by this sign) of thy favour and gracious goodness toward them: let thy fatherly hand (we beseech thee) ever be over them, let thy Holy Spirit ever be with them, and

¶ *Then all of them in order kneeling before the Bishop, he shall lay his hand upon the head of every one severally, saying,*

DEFEND, O Lord, this thy Child [or *this thy Servant*] with thy heavenly grace, that *he* may continue thine for ever; and daily increase in thy holy Spirit more and more, until *he* come unto thy everlasting kingdom. Amen.

¶ *Then shall the Bishop say,*

The Lord be with you.

Answer. And with thy spirit.

¶ *And (all kneeling down) the Bishop shall add,*

Let us pray.

OUR Father, which art in heaven, Hallowed be thy Name. Thy kingdom come. Thy will be done in earth, As it is in heaven. Give us this day our daily bread. And forgive us our trespasses, As we forgive them that trespass against us. And lead us not into temptation; But deliver us from evil. Amen.

And this Collect.

ALMIGHTY and everliving God, who makest us both to will and to do those things that be good and acceptable unto thy divine Majesty; We make our humble supplications unto thee for these thy servants, upon whom (after the example of thy holy Apostles) we have now laid our hands, to certify them (by this sign) of thy favour and gracious goodness towards them. Let thy fatherly hand we beseech thee, ever be over them; let thy Holy

so lead them in the knowledge and obedience of thy word, that in the end they may obtain the life everlasting, through our Lord Jesus Christ, who with thee and the Holy Ghost liveth and reigneth one God world without end. Amen.

Then shall the Bishop bless the children, thus saying.

The blessing of God Almighty, the Father, the Son, and the Holy Ghost, be upon you, and remain with you for ever. Amen.

The Curate of every parish once in six weeks at the least, upon warning by him given, shall upon some Sunday or holy day, half an hour before evensong, openly in the church instruct and examine so many children of his parish sent unto him, as the time will serve, and as he shall think convenient, in some part of this Catechism. And all fathers, mothers, masters, and dames, shall cause their children, servants, and prentices (which are not yet confirmed), to come to the church at the day appointed, and obediently hear and be ordered by the Curate, until such time as they have learned all that is here appointed for them to learn.

¶ *And whensoever the Bishop shall give knowledge for children to be brought afore him to any convenient place, for their confirmation: Then shall the Curate of every parish either bring, or send in writing, the names of all those children of his parish which can say the articles of their faith, the Lord's prayer, and the ten commandments. And also how many of them can answer to the other questions contained in this Catechism.*

¶ *And there shall none be admitted to the holy communion, until such time as he be confirmed.*

Spirit ever be with them; and so lead them in the knowledge and obedience of thy Word, that in the end they may obtain everlasting life; through our Lord Jesus Christ, who with thee and the Holy Ghost liveth and reigneth, ever one God, world without end. *Amen.*

O ALMIGHTY Lord, and everlasting God, vouchsafe, we beseech thee, to direct, sanctify, and govern, both our hearts and bodies, in the ways of thy laws, and in the works of thy commandments; that, through thy most mighty protection both here and ever, we may be preserved in body and soul; through our Lord and Saviour Jesus Christ. *Amen.*

¶ *Then the Bishop shall bless them, saying thus,*

THE Blessing of God Almighty, the Father, the Son, and the Holy Ghost, be upon you, and remain with you for ever. *Amen.*

¶ *And there shall none be admitted to the holy Communion, until such time as he be confirmed, or be ready and desirous to be confirmed.*

THE FORM OF

SOLEMNIZATION OF MATRIMONY.

¶ *First the banns must be asked three several Sundays or holy days, in the service time, the people being present, after the accustomed manner.*

And if the persons that would be married dwell in divers parishes, the banns must be asked in both parishes, and the Curate of the one parish shall not solemnize matrimony betwixt them, without a certificate of the banns being thrice asked, from the Curate of the other parish.

At the day appointed for the solemnization of Matrimony, the persons to be married shall come into the body of the Church, with their friends and neighbours. And there the priest shall thus say.

DEARLY beloved friends, we are gathered together here in the sight of God, and in the face of his congregation, to join together this man and this woman in holy matrimony, which is an honourable estate, instituted of God in paradise, in the time of man's innocency, signifying unto us the mysical union that is betwixt Christ and his church: which holy estate Christ adorned and beautified with his presence, and first miracle that he wrought, in Cana of Galilee, and is commended of St. Paul to

THE FORM OF

SOLEMNIZATION OF MATRIMONY.

¶ *First the Banns of all that are to be married together must be published in the Church three several Sundays, during the time of Morning Service, or of Evening Service, (if there be no Morning Service,) immediately after the second Lesson; the Curate saying after the accustomed manner,*

I PUBLISH the Banns of Marriage between *M.* of——and *N.* of——. If any of you know cause, or just impediment, why these two persons should not be joined together in holy Matrimony, ye are to declare it. This is the first [*second* or *third*] time of asking.

¶ *And if the persons that are to be married dwell in divers Parishes, the Banns must be asked in both Parishes; and the Curate of the one Parish shall not solemnize Matrimony betwixt them, without a Certificate of the Banns being thrice asked, from the Curate of the other Parish.*

¶ *At the day and time appointed for solemnization of Matrimony, the persons to be married shall come into the body of the Church with their friends and neighbours: and there standing together, the Man on the right hand, and the Woman on the left, the Priest shall say,*

DEARLY beloved, we are gathered together here in the sight of God, and in the face of this congregation, to join together this Man and this Woman in holy Matrimony; which is an honourable estate, instituted of God in the time of man's innocency, signifying unto us the mystical union that is betwixt Christ and his Church; which holy estate Christ adorned and beautified with his presence, and first miracle that he wrought, in Cana of Galilee; and is commended of St. Paul to be honour-

be honourable among all men; and therefore is not to be enterprised, nor taken in hand unadvisedly, lightly or wantonly, to satisfy men's carnal lusts and appetites, like brute beasts that have no understanding: but reverently, discreetly, advisedly, soberly, and in the fear of God: duly considering the causes for the which matrimony was ordained.

One cause was the procreation of children, to be brought up in the fear and nurture of the Lord, and praise of God.

Secondly it was ordained for a remedy against sin, and to avoid fornication, that such persons as be married, might live chastely in matrimony, and keep themselves undefiled members of Christ's body. Thirdly for the mutual society, help, and comfort, that the one ought to have of the other, both in prosperity and adversity. Into the which holy estate these two persons present come now to be joined. Therefore if any man can shew any just cause why they may not lawfully be joined so together: Let him now speak, or else hereafter for ever hold his peace.

And also speaking to the persons that shall be married, he shall say.

I REQUIRE and charge you (as you will answer at the dreadful day of judgment, when the secrets of all hearts shall be disclosed) that if either of you do know any impediment, why ye may not be lawfully joined together in matrimony, that ye confess it. For be ye well assured, that so many as be coupled together otherwise than God's word doth allow, are not joined of God, neither is their matrimony lawful.

At which day of marriage if any man do allege any impediment why they may not be

able among all men: and therefore is not by any to be enterprised, nor taken in hand, unadvisedly, lightly, or wantonly, to satisfy men's carnal lusts and appetites, like brute beasts that have no understanding; but reverently, discreetly, advisedly, soberly, and in the fear of God; duly considering the causes for which Matrimony was ordained.

First, It was ordained for the procreation of children, to be brought up in the fear and nurture of the Lord, and to the praise of his holy Name.

Secondly, It was ordained for a remedy against sin, and to avoid fornication; that such persons as have not the gift of continency might marry, and keep themselves undefiled members of Christ's body.

Thirdly, It was ordained for the mutual society, help, and comfort, that the one ought to have of the other, both in prosperity and adversity. Into which holy estate these two persons present come now to be joined. Therefore if any man can shew any just cause, why they may not lawfully be joined together, let him now speak, or else hereafter for ever hold his peace.

¶ *And also, speaking unto the persons that shall be married, he shall say,*

I REQUIRE and charge you both, as ye will answer at the dreadful day of judgement when the secrets of all hearts shall be disclosed, that if either of you know any impediment, why ye may not be lawfully joined together in Matrimony, ye do now confess it. For be ye well assured, that so many as are coupled together otherwise than God's Word doth allow are not joined together by God; neither is their Matrimony lawful.

¶ *At which day of Marriage, if any man do alledge and declare any impediment, why*

coupled together in matrimony; and will be bound, and sureties with him, to the parties, or else put in a caution to the full value of such charges as the persons to be married do sustain, to prove his allegation: then the Solemnization must be deferred, unto such time as the truth be tried.

If no impediment be alleged, then shal the Curate say unto the mdn.

N. Wilt thou have this woman to thy wedded wife, to live together after God's ordinance in the holy estate of matrimony? Wilt thou love her, comfort her, honour, and keep her in sickness and in health? and forsaking all other keep thee only to her, so long as you both shall live?

The man shall answer,

I will.

Then shall the Priest say to the woman.

N. Wilt thou have this man to thy wedded husband, to live together after God's ordinance, in the holy estate of matrimony? Wilt thou obey him, and serve him, love, honour, and keep him in sickness and in health? and forsaking all other keep thee only to him, so long as you both shall live?

The woman shall answer,

I will.

Then shall the Minister say,

Who giveth this woman to be married to this man?

And the minister receiving the woman at her father or friend's hands, shall cause the man to take the woman by the right hand, and so either to give their troth to other: The man first saying,

I *N.* take thee *N.* to my wedded wife, to have and to hold from this

they may not be coupled together in Matrimony, by God's Law, or the Laws of this Realm; and will be bound, and sufficient snreties with him, to the parties; or else put in a Caution (to the full value of such charges as the persons to be married do thereby sustain) to prove his allegation: then the solemnization must be deferred, until such time as the truth be tried.

¶ *If no impediment be alledged, then shall the Curate say unto the Man,*

M. WILT thou have this Woman to thy wedded wife, to live together after God's ordinance in the holy estate of Matrimony? Wilt thou love her, comfort her, honour, and keep her in sickness and in health; and, forsaking all other, keep thee only unto her, so long as ye both shall live?

¶ *The Man shall answer,*

I will.

¶ *Then shall the Priest say unto the Woman.*

N. WILT thou have this Man to thy wedded husband, to live together after God's ordinance in the holy estate of Matrimony? Wilt thou obey him, and serve him, love, honour, and keep him in sickness and in health; and, forsaking all other, keep thee only unto him, so long as ye both shall live?

¶ *The Woman shall answer.*

I will.

¶ *Then shall the Minister say,*

Who giveth this Woman to be married to this Man?

¶ *Then shall they give their troth to each other in this manner.*

The Minister receiving the Woman at her father's or friend's hands, shall cause the Man with his right hand to take the Woman by her right hand, and to say after him as followeth.

I *M.* take thee *N.* to my wedded wife, to have and to hold

day forward, for better, for worse, for richer, for poorer, in sickness, and in health, to love, and to cherish, till death us depart: according to God's holy ordinance: And thereto I plight thee my troth.

Then shall they loose their hands, and the woman taking again the man by the right hand shalt say,

I *N.* take thee *N.* to my wedded husband, to have and to hold from this day forward, for better, for worse, for richer, for poorer, in sickness, and in health, to love, cherish, and to obey, till death us depart: according to God's holy ordinance: And thereto I give thee my troth.

¶ *Then shall they again loose their hands, and the man shall give unto the woman a ring, and other tokens of spousage, as gold or silver, laying the same upon the book. And the Priest taking the ring shall deliver it unto the man, to put it upon the fourth finger of the woman's left hand. And the man taught by the priest, shall say,*

¶ With this ring I thee wed: This gold and silver I thee give: with my body I thee worship: and with all my wordly goods I thee endow: In the name of the Father, and of the Son, and of the Holy Ghost. Amen.

Then the man leaving the ring upon the fourth finger of the woman's left hand, the minister shall say,

¶ Let us pray.

O ETERNAL God, creator and preserver of all mankind, giver of all spiritual grace, the author of everlasting life: send thy blessing upon these thy servants, this man and this woman, whom we bless in thy name, that as Isaac and Rebecca (after bracelets and jewels of gold given of the one to the other for

from this day forward, for better for worse, for richer for poorer, in sickness and in health, to love and to cherish, till death us do part, according to God's holy ordinance; and thereto I plight thee my troth.

¶ *Then shall they loose their hands; and the Woman with her right hand taking the Man by his right hand, shall likewise say after the Minister,*

I *N.* take thee *M.* to my wedded husband, to have and to hold from this day forward, for better for worse, for richer for poorer, in sickness and in health, to love, cherish, and to obey, till death us do part, according to God's holy ordinance; and thereto I give thee my troth.

¶ *Then shall they again loose their hands; and the Man shall give unto the Woman a Ring, laying the same upon the book with the accustomed duty to the Priest and Clerk. And the Priest, taking the Ring, shall deliver it unto the Man, to put it upon the fourth finger of the Woman's left hand. And the Man holding the Ring there, and taught by the Priest, shall say,*

WITH this Ring I thee wed, with my body I thee worship, and with all my worldly goods I thee endow: In the Name of the Father, and of the Son, and of the Holy Ghost. Amen.

¶ *Then the Man leaving the Ring upon the fourth finger of the Woman's left hand, they shall both kneel down; and the Minister shall say,*

Let us pray.

O ETERNAL God, Creator and preserver of all mankind, Giver of all spiritual grace, the Author of everlasting life; Send thy blessing upon these thy servants, this man and this woman, whom we bless in thy Name; that, as Isaac and Rebecca

tokens of their matrimony) lived faithfully together; so these persons may surely perform and keep the vow and covenant betwixt them made, whereof this ring given and received is a token and pledge: and may ever remain in perfect love and peace together; and live according to thy laws; through Jesus Christ our Lord. Amen.

Then shall the Priest join their right hands together, and say.

¶ Those whom God hath joined together, let no man put asunder.

Then shall the minister speak unto the people.

FORASMUCH as *N.* and *N.* have consented together in holy wedlock, and have witnessed the same here before God and this company; and thereto have given and pledged their troth either to other, and have declared the same by giving and receiving gold and silver, and by joining of hands: I pronounce that they be man and wife together: In the name of the Father, of the Son, and of the Holy Ghost. Amen.

And the Minister shall add this blessing.

¶ God the Father bless you. ✠ God the Son keep you: God the Holy Ghost lighten your understanding: The Lord mercifully with his favour look upon you, and so fill you with all spiritual benediction, and grace, that you may have remission of your sins in this life, and in the world to come life everlasting. Amen.

Then shall they go into the quire, and the ministers or clerks shall say or sing this Psalm following.

BLESSED are all they that fear the Lord, and walk in his ways. *Beati omnes* cxxviii.

---

lived faithfully together, so these persons may surely perform and keep the vow and covenant betwixt them made, (whereof this Ring given and received is a token and pledge,) and may ever remain in perfect love and peace together, and live according to thy laws; through Jesus Christ our Lord. *Amen.*

¶ *Then shall the Priest join their right hands together, and say,*

Those whom God hath joined together let no man put asunder.

¶ *Then shall the Minister speak unto the people.*

FORASMUCH as *M.* and *N.* have consented together in holy wedlock, and have witnessed the same before God and this company, and thereto have given and pledged their troth either to other, and have declared the same by giving and receiving of a Ring, and by joining of hands; I pronounce that they be Man and Wife together, In the Name of the Father, and of the Son, and of the Holy Ghost. Amen.

¶ *And the Minister shall add this Blessing.*

GOD the Father, God the Son, God the Holy Ghost, bless, preserve, and keep you; the Lord mercifully with his favour look upon you; and so fill you with all spiritual benediction and grace, that ye may so live together in this life, that in the world to come ye may have life everlasting. *Amen.*

¶ *Then the Minister or Clerks, going to the Lord's Table, shall say or sing this Psalm following.*

Beati omnes. Psalm cxxviii.

BLESSED are all they that fear the Lord: and walk in his ways.

For thou shalt eat the labour of thy hands. O well is thee, and happy shalt thou be.

Thy wife shall be as the fruitful vine, upon the walls of thy house.

Thy children like the olive branches round about thy table.

Lo, thus shall the man be blessed that feareth the Lord.

The Lord from out of Sion shall bless thee: that thou shalt see Hierusalem in prosperity all thy life long.

Yea, that thou shalt see thy children's children: and peace upon Israel.

Glory to the Father, &c.

As it was in the beginning, &c.

Or else this Psalm following.

Deus misereatur nostri. Psalm lxvii.

God be merciful unto us, and bless us, and shew us the light of his countenance: and be merciful unto us.

That thy way may be known upon the earth, thy saving health among all nations.

Let the people praise thee (O God) yea, let all people praise thee.

O let the nations rejoice and be glad, for thou shalt judge the flock righteously, and govern the nations upon the earth.

Let the people praise thee (O God) let all the people praise thee.

Then shall the earth bring forth her increase: and God, even our own God, shall give us his blessing.

God shall bless us, and all the ends of the world shall fear him.

Glory to the Father, &c.

As it was in the, &c.

For thou shalt eat the labour of thine hands: O well is thee, and happy shalt thou be.

Thy wife shall be as the fruitful vine: upon the walls of thine house:

Thy children like the olive-branches: round about thy table.

Lo, thus shall the man be blessed: that feareth the Lord.

The Lord from out of Sion shall so bless thee: that thou shalt see Jerusalem in prosperity all thy life long;

Yea, that thou shalt see thy children's children: and peace upon Israel.

Glory be to the Father, and to the Son: and to the Holy Ghost;

As it was in the beginning, is now, and ever shall be: world without end. Amen.

¶ *Or this Psalm.*

Deus misereatur. Psalm lxvii.

GOD be merciful unto us, and bless us: and shew us the light of his countenance, and be merciful unto us.

That thy way may be known upon earth: thy saving health among all nations.

Let the people praise thee, O God: yea, let all the people praise thee.

O let the nations rejoice and be glad: for thou shalt judge the folk righteously, and govern the nations upon earth.

Let the people praise thee, O God: yea, let all the people praise thee.

Then shall the earth bring forth her increase: and God, even our own God, shall give us his blessing.

God shall bless us: and all the ends of the world shall fear him.

Glory be to the Father, and to the Son: and to the Holy Ghost;

As it was in the beginning, is now, and ever shall be: world without end. Amen.

The Psalm ended, and the man and woman kneeling afore the altar, the priest standing at the altar, and turning his face toward them, shall say,

Lord, have mercy upon us.

Answer. Christ have mercy upon us.

Minister. Lord, have mercy upon us.

¶ Our father, which art in heaven, &c.

And lead us not into temptation.

Answer. But deliver us from evil. Amen.

Minister. O Lord, save thy servant, and thy handmaid.

Answer. Which put their trust in thee.

Minister. O Lord, send them help from thy holy place.

Answer. And evermore defend them.

Minister. Be unto them a tower of strength.

Answer. From the face of their enemy.

Minister. O Lord, hear my prayer.

Answer. And let my cry come unto thee.

The Minister. Let us pray.

O God of Abraham, God of Isaac, God of Jacob, bless these thy servants, and sow the seed of eternal life in their minds, that whatsoever in thy holy word they shall profitably learn, they may in deed fulfil the same. Look, O Lord, mercifully upon them from heaven, and bless them: And as thou didst send thy Angel Raphael to Thobie and Sara, the daughter of Raguel, to their great comfort; so vouchsafe to send thy blessing upon these thy servants, that they

¶ *The Psalm ended, and the Man and the Woman kneeling before the Lord's Table, the Priest standing at the Table, and turning his face towards them, shall say,*

Lord, have mercy upon us.

Answer. Christ have mercy upon us.

Minister. Lord, have mercy upon us.

OUR Father, which art in heaven, Hallowed be thy Name. Thy kingdom come. Thy will be done in earth, As it is in heaven. Give us this day our daily bread. And forgive us our trespasses, As we forgive them that trespass against us. And lead us not into temptation; But deliver us from evil. Amen.

Minister. O Lord, save thy servant, and thy hand-maid;

Answer. Who put their trust in thee.

Minister. O Lord, send them help from thy holy place;

Answer. And evermore defend them.

Minister. Be unto them a tower of strength.

Answer. From the face of their enemy.

Minister. O Lord, hear our prayer.

Answer. And let our cry come unto thee.

Minister.

O GOD of Abraham, God of Isaac, God of Jacob, bless these thy servants, and sow the seed of eternal life in their hearts; that whatsoever in thy holy Word they shall profitably learn, they may in deed fulfil the same. Look O Lord, mercifully upon them from heaven, and bless them. And as thou didst send thy blessing upon Abraham and Sarah, to their great comfort, so vouchsafe to send thy blessing upon these thy ser-

obeying thy will, and alway being in safety under thy protection, may abide in thy love unto their lives' end: through Jesu Christ our Lord. Amen.

This prayer following shall be omitted where the woman is past child-birth.

O MERCIFUL Lord, and heavenly Father, by whose gracious gift mankind is increased: We beseech thee, assist with thy blessing these two persons, that they may both be fruitful in procreation of children; and also live together so long in godly love and honesty, that they may see their childer's children unto the third and fourth generation, unto thy praise and honour: through Jesus Christ our Lord. Amen.

O God, which by thy mighty power hast made all things of nought, which also after other things set in order didst appoint that out of man (created after thine own image and similitude) woman should take her beginning: and, knitting them together, didst teach, that it should never be lawful to put asunder those, whom thou by matrimony hadst made one. O God, which hast consecrated the state of matrimony to such an excellent mystery, that in it is signified and represented the spiritual marriage and unity betwixt Christ and his church: Look mercifully upon these thy servants, that both this man may love his wife, according to thy word, (as Christ did love his spouse the church, who gave himself for it, loving and cherishing it even as his own flesh;) and also that this woman may be loving and amiable to her husband as Rachael, wise as Rebecca, faithful and obedient as Sara; and in all quietness, sobriety, and peace, be a follower of holy and godly matrons. O Lord, bless them both,

vants; that they obeying thy will and alway being in safety under thy protection, may abide in thy love unto their lives' end; through Jesus Christ our Lord. *Amen.*

¶ *This Prayer next following shall be omitted, where the Woman is past child-bearing.*

O MERCIFUL Lord, and heavenly Father, by whose gracious gift mankind is increased; We beseech thee, assist with thy blessing these two persons, that they may both be fruitful in procreation of children, and also live together so long in godly love and honesty, that they may see their children christianly and virtuously brought up, to thy praise and honour; through Jesus Christ our Lord. *Amen.*

O GOD, who by thy mighty power hast made all things of nothing; who also (after other things set in order) didst appoint, that out of man (created after thine own image and similitude) woman should take her beginning; and, knitting them together, didst teach that it should never be lawful to put asunder those whom thou by Matrimony hadst made one: O God, who hast consecrated the state of Matrimony to such an excellent mystery, that it is signified and represented the spiritual marriage and unity betwixt Christ and his Church; Look mercifully upon these thy servants, that both this man may love his wife, according to thy Word, (as Christ didst love his spouse the Church, who gave himself for it, loving and cherishing it even as his own flesh,) and also that this woman may be

loving and amiable, faithful and obedient to her husband; and in all quietness, sobriety, and peace, be a follower of holy and godly matrons. O Lord, bless them both, and grant them to inherit thy everlasting kingdom, through Jesus Christ our Lord. Amen.

Then shall the Priest bless the man and the woman, saying,

ALMIGHTY God, which at the beginning did create our first parents Adam and Eve, and did sanctify and join them together in marriage: Pour upon you the riches of his grace, sanctify and ✠ bless you, that ye may please him both in body and soul, and live together in holy love unto your lives' end. Amen.

Then shall be said after the gospel a sermon, wherein ordinarily (so oft as there is any marriage) the office of man and wife shall be declared according to holy scripture. Or if there be no sermon, the minister shall read this that followeth.

ALL ye which be married, or which intend to take the holy estate of matrimony upon you: hear what holy scripture doth say, as touching the duty of husbands toward their wives, and wives toward their husbands.

Saint Paul (in his Epistle to the Ephesians the fifth chapter) doth give this commandment to all married men.

Ye husbands, love your wives, even as Christ loved the church, and hath given himself for it, to sanctify it, purging it in the fountain of water, through the word, that he might make it unto himself a glorious congregation, not having spot, or wrinkle, or any such thing; but that it should be holy and blameless. So men are bound to love their own wives as their own bodies: he that loveth his own wife, loveth himself. For never did any man hate his own flesh, but nourisheth, and cherisheth it, even as the Lord doth the congregation; for we are members of his body, of his flesh, and of his bones. For this cause shall a man

and grant them to inherit thy everlasting kingdom; through Jesus Christ our Lord. *Amen.*

¶ *Then shall the Priest say,*

ALMIGHTY God, who at the beginning did create our first parents, Adam and Eve, and did sanctify and join them together in marriage; Pour upon you the riches of his grace, sanctify and bless you, that ye may please him both in body and soul, and live together in holy love unto your lives' end. *Amen.*

¶ *After which, if there be no sermon declaring the duties of Man and Wife, the Minister shall read as followeth.*

ALL ye that are married, or that intend to take the holy estate of Matrimony upon you, hear what the holy Scripture doth say as touching the duty of husbands towards their wives, and wives towards their husbands.

Saint Paul in his Epistle to the Ephesians, the fifth Chapter, doth give this commandment to all married men: Husbands, love your wives, even as Christ also loved the Church, and gave himself for it, that he might sanctify and cleanse it with the washing of water, by the Word; that he might present it to himself a glorious Church, not having spot, or wrinkle, or any such thing; but that it should be holy, and without blemish. So ought men to love their wives as their own bodies. He that loveth his wife loveth himself: for no man ever yet hated his own flesh, but nourisheth and cherisheth it, even as the Lord the Church: for we are members of his body, of his flesh, and of his bones. For this cause shall a man leave his father and mother, and shall be joined

leave father and mother, and shall be joined unto his wife, and they two shall be one flesh. This mystery is great, but I speak of Christ and of the congregation. Nevertheless, let every one of you so love his own wife, even as himself.

Likewise the same Saint Paul (writing to the Colossians) speaketh thus to all men that be married: Ye men, love your wives and be not bitter unto them. Coloss. iii.

Hear also what saint Peter the apostle of Christ, (which was himself a married man) saith unto all men that are married. Ye husbands, dwell with your wives according to knowledge: giving honour unto the wife, as unto the weaker vessel, and as heirs together of the grace of life, so that your prayers be not hindered. 1 Pet. iii.

Hitherto ye have heard the duty of the husband toward the wife. Now likewise, ye wives, hear and learn your duty toward your husbands, even as it is plainly set forth in holy scripture.

Saint Paul (in the forenamed Epistle to the Ephesians) teacheth you thus: Ye women subject yourselves unto your own husbands as unto the Lord: for the husband is the wife's head, even as Christ is the head of the church: And he also is the Saviour of the whole body. Therefore as the church, or congregation, is subject unto Christ: so likewise let the wives also be in subjection unto their own husbands in all things. And again he saith: Let the wife reverence her husband. And in his Epistle to the Colossians Saint Paul giveth you this short lesson: Ye wives, submit yourselves unto your own husbands, as it is convenient in the Lord. Ephes. v. Coloss. iii.

unto his wife; and they two shall be one flesh. This is a great mystery; but I speak concerning Christ and the Church. Nevertheless, let every one of you in particular, so love his wife, even as himself.

Likewise the same Saint Paul, writing to the Colossians, speaketh thus to all men that are married; Husbands, love your wives, and be not bitter against them.

Hear also what Saint Peter, the Apostle of Christ, who was himself a married man, saith unto them that are married; Ye husbands, dwell with your wives according to knowledge; giving honour unto the wife, as unto the weaker vessel, and as being heirs together of the grace of life, that your prayers be not hindered.

Hitherto ye have heard the duty of the husband toward the wife. Now likewise, ye wives, hear and learn your duties toward your husbands, even as it is plainly set forth in holy Scripture.

Saint Paul, in the aforenamed Epistle to the Ephesians, teacheth you thus; Wives, submit yourselves unto your own husbands, as unto the Lord. For the husband is the head of the wife, even as Christ is the head of the Church: and he is the Saviour of the body. Therefore as the Church is subject unto Christ, so let the wives be to their own husbands in every thing. And again he saith, Let the wife see that she reverence her husband.

And in his Epistle to the Colossians, Saint Paul giveth you this short lesson; Wives, submit yourselves unto your own husbands, as it is fit in the Lord.

Saint Peter also doth instruct you very godly, thus saying: Let wives be subject to their own husbands, so that if any obey not the word, they may be won without the word, by the conversation of the wives; while they behold your chaste conversation, coupled with fear: whose apparel let it not be outward, with broided hair, and trimming about with gold, either in putting on of gorgeous apparel: But let the hid man, which is in the heart, be without all corruption, so that the spirit be mild and quiet, which is a precious thing in the sight of God. For after this manner (in the old time) did the holy women, which trusted in God, apparel themselves, being subject to their own husbands: as Sara obeyed Abraham calling him lord, whose daughters ye are made, doing well and being not dismayed with any fear.

1 Pet. iii.

The new married persons (the same day of their marriage) must receive the holy communion.

Saint Peter also doth instruct you very well, thus saying; Ye wives, be in subjection to your own husbands; that, if any obey not the Word, they also may without the Word be won by the conversation of the wives; while they behold your chaste conversation coupled with fear. Whose adorning, let it not be that outward adorning of plaiting the hair, and of wearing gold, or of putting on of apparel; but let it be the hidden man of the heart, in that which is not corruptible; even the ornament of a meek and quiet spirit, which is in the sight of God of great price. For after this manner in the old time the holy women also, who trusted in God, adorned themselves, being in subjection unto their own husbands; even as Sarah obeyed Abraham, calling him lord; whose daughters ye are as long as ye do well, and are not afraid with any amazement.

¶ *It is convenient that the new-married persons should receive the holy Communion at the time of their Marriage or at the first opportunity after their Marriage.*

THE ORDER FOR THE

VISITATION OF THE SICK,

AND THE COMMUNION OF THE SAME.

¶ *The Priest entering into the sick person's house, shall say,*

PEACE be in this house, and to all that dwell in it.

When he cometh into the sick man's presence, he shall say this Psalm.

HEAR my prayer, (O Lord,) and consider my desire: hearken unto me for thy truth and righteousness' sake. *Domine exaudi.* Psalm cxliii.

And enter not into judgement with thy servant: for in thy sight shall no man living be justified.

For the enemy hath persecuted my soul; he hath smitten my life down to the ground: he hath laid me in the darkness, as the men that have been long dead.

Therefore is my spirit vexed within me: and my heart within me is desolate.

Yet do I remember the time past; I muse upon all thy works: yea, I exercise myself in the works of thy hands.

I stretch forth mine hands unto thee: my soul gaspeth unto thee as a thirsty land.

Hear me, (O lord,) and that soon, for my spirit waxeth faint: hide not thy face from me, lest I be like unto them that go down into the pit.

O let me hear thy loving-kindness betimes in the morning, for in thee is my trust; shew thou me the way that I should walk in, for I lift up my soul unto thee.

THE ORDER FOR THE

VISITATION OF THE SICK.

¶ *When any person is sick, notice shall be given thereof to the Minister of the Parish; who, coming into the sick person's house, shall say,*

PEACE be to this house, and to all that dwell in it.

¶ *When he cometh into the sick man's presence he shall say,*

Deliver me, (O lord,) from mine enemies: for I fly unto thee to hide me.

Teach me to do the thing that pleaseth thee, for thou art my god, let thy loving spirit lead me forth unto the land of righteousness.

Quicken me, (O lord,) for thy name's sake, and for thy righteousness' sake bring my soul out of trouble.

And of thy goodness slay mine enemies; and destroy all them that vex my soul; for I am thy servant.

Glory to the father, and to the son, &c.

As it was in the beginning, &c.

¶ *With this anthem.*

REMEMBER not, Lord, our iniquities, nor the iniquities of our forefathers. Spare us, good Lord, spare thy people, whom thou hast redeemed with thy most precious blood, and be not angry with us for ever.

Lord, have mercy upon us.
Christ, have mercy upon us.
Lord, have mercy upon us.
Our Father, which art in heaven, &c.

And lead us not into temptation.

Answer. But deliver us from evil. Amen.

The Minister. O Lord, save thy servant.

Answer. Which putteth his trust in thee.

Minister. Send him help from thy holy place.

Answer. And evermore mightily defend him.

kneeling down,

REMEMBER not, Lord, our iniquities, nor the iniquities of our forefathers: Spare us, good Lord, spare thy people, whom thou hast redeemed with thy most precious blood, and be not angry with us for ever.

Answer. Spare us, good Lord.

¶ *Then the Minister shall say,*

Let us pray.

Lord, have mercy upon us.
Christ, have mercy upon us.
Lord, have mercy upon us.

OUR Father, which art in heaven, Hallowed be thy Name. Thy kingdom come. Thy will be done in earth, As it is in heaven. Give us this day our daily bread. And forgive us our trespasses, As we forgive them that trespass against us. And lead us not into temptation: But deliver us from evil. Amen.

Minister. O Lord, save thy servant;

Answer. Which putteth *his* trust in thee.

Minister. Send *him* help from thy holy place;

Answer. And evermore mightily defend *him*.

Minister. Let the enemy have none advantage of him.
Answer. Nor the wicked approach to hurt him.
Minister. Be unto him, O Lord, a strong tower.
Answer. From the face of his enemy.
Minister. Lord, hear my prayer.
Answer. And let my cry come unto thee.

Minister. Let us pray.

O Lord, look down from heaven, behold, visit, and relieve this thy servant: Look upon him with the eyes of thy mercy, give him comfort, and sure confidence in thee: Defend him from the danger of the enemy, and keep him in perpetual peace, and safety: through Jesus Christ our Lord. Amen.

Hear us, Almighty and most merciful God and Saviour: extend thy accustomed goodness to this thy servant, which is grieved with sickness: Visit him, O Lord, as thou didst visit Peter's wife's mother and the Captain's servant. And as thou preservedst Thobie and Sara by thy Angel from danger: So restore unto this sick person his former health, (if it be thy will,) or else give him grace so to take thy correction, that after this painful life ended, he may dwell with thee in life everlasting. Amen.

Then shall the Minister exhort the sick person after this form, or other like.

Dearly beloved, know this, that Almighty God is the Lord over

Minister. Let the enemy have no advantage of *him*.
Answer. Nor the wicked approach to hurt *him*,
Minister, Be unto *him*, O Lord, a strong tower.
Answer. From the face of *his* enemy.
Minister. O Lord, hear our prayers.
Answer. And let our cry come unto thee.

Minister.

O LORD, look down from heaven, behold, visit, and relieve this thy servant. Look upon *him* with the eyes of thy mercy, give *him* comfort and sure confidence in thee, defend *him* from the danger of the enemy, and keep *him* in perpetual peace and safety; through Jesus Christ our Lord. *Amen.*

HEAR us, Almighty and most merciful God and Saviour; extend thy accustomed goodness to this thy servant who is grieved with sickness. Sanctify, we beseech thee, this thy fatherly correction to *him*; that the sense of *his* weakness may add strength to *his* faith, and seriousness to *his* repentance: That, if it shall be thy good pleasure to restore *him* to *his* former health, *he* may lead the residue of *his* life in thy fear, and to thy glory: or else, give *him* grace so to take thy visitation, that, after this painful life ended, *he* may dwell with thee in life everlasting; through Jesus Christ our Lord. *Amen.*

¶ *Then shall the Minister exhort the sick person after this form, or other like.*

DEARLY beloved, know this, that Almighty God is the

life, and death, and over all things to them pertaining, as youth, strength, health, age, weakness, and sickness. Wherefore, whatsoever your sickness is, know you certainly, that it is God's visitation. And for what cause soever this sickness is sent unto you; whether it be to try your patience for the example of other, and that your faith may be found, in the day of the Lord, laudable, glorious, and honourable, to the increase of glory, and endless felicity: or else it be sent unto you to correct and amend in you, whatsoever doth offend the eyes of our heavenly Father: know you certainly, that if you truly repent you of your sins, and bear your sickness patiently, trusting in God's mercy, for his dear Son Jesus Christ's sake, and render unto him humble thanks for his fatherly visitation, submitting yourself wholly to his will; it shall turn to your profit, and help you forward in the right way that leadeth unto everlasting life*. Take therefore in good worth the chastement of the Lord: for whom the Lord loveth he chastiseth. Yea, (as Saint Paul saith,) he scourgeth every son, which he receiveth: if you endure chastisement, he offereth himself unto you as unto his own children. What son is he that the father chastiseth not? If ye be not under correction (whereof all the true children are partakers), then are ye bastards, and not children.

* If the person visited be very sick, then the Curate may end his exhortation at this place.

Therefore seeing that when our carnal fathers do correct us, we reverently obey them, shall we not now much rather be obedient to our spiritual Father, and so live? And they for a few days do chastise us after their own pleasure: but he doth chastise us for our profit, to the intent he may make us par-

Lord of life, and death, and of all things to them pertaining, as youth, strength, health, age, weakness, and sickness. Wherefore, whatsoever your sickness is, know you certainly, that it is God's visitation. And for what cause soever this sickness is sent unto you; whether it be to try your patience for the example of others, and that your faith may be found, in the day of the Lord, laudable, glorious, and honourable, to the increase of glory, and endless felicity; or else it be sent unto you to correct and amend in you, whatsoever doth offend the eyes of your heavenly Father; know you certainly, that if you truly repent you of your sins, and bear your sickness patiently, trusting in God's mercy, for his dear Son Jesus Christ's sake, and render unto him humble thanks for his fatherly visitation, submitting yourself wholly unto his will, it shall turn to your profit, and help you forward in the right way that leadeth unto everlasting life.

¶ *If the person visited be very sick, then the Curate may end his exhortation in this place, or else proceed.*

TAKE therefore in good part the chastisement of the Lord: For (as Saint Paul saith in the twelfth Chapter to the Hebrews) whom the Lord loveth he chasteneth, and scourgeth every son whom he receiveth. If ye endure chastening, God dealeth with you as with sons; for what son is he whom the father chasteneth not? But if ye be without chastisement, whereof all are partakers, then are ye bastards, and not sons. Furthermore, we have had fathers of our flesh, which corrected us, and we gave them reverence: shall we not much rather be in subjection unto the Father of spirits, and live? For they verily for a few days chastened us after their own pleasure;

takers of his holiness. These words, good brother, are God's words, and written in holy scripture for our comfort and instruction, that we should patiently and with thanksgiving bear our heavenly Father's correction, whensoever by any manner of adversity it shall please his gracious goodness to visit us. And there should be no greater comfort to christian persons, than to be made like unto Christ, by suffering patiently adversities, troubles, and sicknesses. For he himself went not up to joy, but first he suffered pain: he entered not into his glory, before he was crucified. So truly our way to eternal joy is to suffer here with Christ, and our door to enter into eternal life is gladly to die with Christ, that we may rise again from death, and dwell with him in everlasting life. Now therefore taking your sickness, which is thus profitable for you, patiently: I exhort you in the name of God, to remember the profession which you made unto God in your Baptism. And forasmuch as after this life there is account to be given unto the righteous Judge, of whom all must be judged without respect of persons: I require you to examine yourself and your state, both toward God and man, so that accusing and condemning yourself for your own faults, you may find mercy at our heavenly Father's hand, for Christ's sake, and not be accused and condemned in that fearful judgment. Therefore I shall shortly rehearse the articles of our faith, that ye may know whether you do believe as a christian man should believe or no.

Here the minister shall rehearse the articles of the faith, saying thus.

Dost thou believe in God the Father Almighty?

And so forth, as it is in Baptism.

but he for our profit, that we might be partakers of his holiness. These words, good *brother*, are written in holy Scripture for our comfort and instruction; that we should patiently, and with thanksgiving, bear our heavenly Father's correction, whensoever by any manner of adversity it shall please his gracious goodness to visit us. And there should be no greater comfort to Christian persons, than to be made like unto Christ, by suffering patiently adversities, troubles, and sicknesses. For he himself went not up to joy, but first he suffered pain; he entered not into his glory before he was crucified. So truly our way to eternal joy is to suffer here with Christ; and our door to enter into eternal life is gladly to die with Christ; that we may rise again from death, and dwell with him in everlasting life. Now therefore, taking your sickness, which is thus profitable for you, patiently, I exhort you, in the Name of God, to remember the profession which you made unto God in your Baptism. And forasmuch as after this life there is an account to be given unto the righteous Judge, by whom all must be judged without respect of persons, I require you to examine yourself and your estate, both toward God and man; so that, accusing and condemning yourself for your own faults, you may find mercy at our heavenly Father's hand for Christ's sake, and not be accused and condemned in that fearful judgement. Therefore I shall rehearse to you the Articles of our Faith, that you may know whether you do believe as a Christian man should, or no.

¶ *Here the Minister shall rehearse the Articles of the Faith, saying thus,*

DOST thou believe in God the Father Almighty, Maker of heaven and earth?

Then shall the Minister examine whether he be in charity with all the world: Exhorting him to forgive from the bottom of his heart all persons that have offended him: and if he have offended other to ask them forgiveness: and where he hath done injury or wrong to any man, that he make amends to his uttermost power. And if he have not afore disposed his goods, let him then make his will. (But men must be oft admonished that they set an order for their temporal goods and lands when they be in health.) And also to declare his debts, what he oweth, and what is owing unto him: for discharging of his conscience, and quietness of his executors. The minister may not forget nor omit to move the sick person (and that most earnestly) to liberality toward the poor.*

* This may be done before the minister begin his prayers as he shall see cause.

¶ *Here shall the sick person make a special confession, if he feel his conscience troubled with any weighty matter. After which confession, the Priest shall absolve him after this form.*

And the same form of absolution shall be used in all private confessions.

And in Jesus Christ his only-begotten Son our Lord? And that he was conceived by the Holy Ghost, born of the Virgin Mary; that he suffered under Pontius Pilate, was crucified, dead, and buried; that he went down into hell, and also did rise again the third day; that he ascended into heaven, and sitteth at the right hand of God the Father Almighty; and from thence shall come again at the end of the world, to judge the quick and the dead?

And dost thou believe in the Holy Ghost; the holy Catholick Church; the Communion of Saints; the Remission of sins; the Resurrection of the flesh; and everlasting life after death?

¶ *The sick person shall answer,*

All this I stedfastly believe.

¶ *Then shall the Minister examine whether he repent him truly of his sins, and be in charity with all the world; exhorting him to forgive, from the bottom of his heart, all persons that have offended him; and if he hath offended any other, to ask them forgiveness; and where he hath done injury or wrong to any man, that he make amends to the uttermost of his power. And if he hath not before disposed of his goods, let him then be admonished to make his Will, and to declare his Debts, what he oweth, and what is owing unto him; for the better discharging of his conscience, and the quietness of his Executors. But men should often be put in remembrance to take order for the settling of their temporal estates, whilst they are in health.*

¶ *These words before rehearsed may be said before the Minister begin his Prayer, as he shall see cause.*

¶ *The Minister should not omit earnestly to move such sick persons as are of ability to be liberal to the poor.*

¶ *Here shall the sick person be moved to make a special Confession of his sins, if he feel his conscience troubled with any weighty matter. After which Confession, the Priest shall absolve him (if he humbly and heartily desire it) after this sort.*

OUR Lord Jesus Christ, who hath left power to his Church to absolve all sinners, which truly repent and believe in him, of his great mercy forgive thee thine offences: and by his authority committed to me, I absolve thee from all thy sins, in the name of the Father, and of the Son, and of the Holy Ghost. Amen.

And then the Priest shall say the Collect following.

Let us pray.

O MOST merciful God, which according to the multitude of thy mercies dost so put away the sins of those which truly repent, that thou rememberest them no more: open thy eye of mercy upon this thy servant, who most earnestly desireth pardon and forgiveness: Renew in him, most loving Father, whatsoever hath been decayed by the fraud and malice of the devil, or by his own carnal will, and frailness: preserve and continue this sick member in the unity of thy Church, consider his contrition, accept his tears, assuage his pain, as shall be seen to thee most expedient for him. And forasmuch as he putteth his full trust only in thy mercy: Impute not unto him his former sins, but take him unto thy favour: through the merits of thy most dearly beloved Son Jesus Christ. Amen.

Then the Minister shall say this Psalm.

In te Domine speravi. Psal. 71.

IN thee, O Lord, have I put my trust, let me never be put to confusion, but rid me, and deliver me, into thy righteousness: incline thine ear unto me, and save me.

Be thou my strong hold, (where-

OUR Lord Jesus Christ, who hath left power to his Church to absolve all sinners who truly repent and believe in him, of his great mercy forgive thee thine offences: And by his authority committed to me, I absolve thee from all thy sins, In the Name of the Father, and of the Son, and of the Holy Ghost. Amen.

¶ *And then the Priest shall say the Collect following.*

Let us pray.

O MOST merciful God, who, according to the multitude of thy mercies, dost so put away the sins of those who truly repent, that thou rememberest them no more; Open thine eye of mercy upon this thy servant, who most earnestly desireth pardon and forgiveness. Renew in *him*, most loving Father, whatsoever hath been decayed by the fraud and malice of the devil, or by *his* own carnal will and frailness; preserve and continue this sick member in the unity of the Church; consider *his* contrition, accept *his* tears, asswage *his* pain, as shall seem to thee most expedient for *him*. And forasmuch as *he* putteth *his* full trust only in thy mercy, impute not unto *him his* former sins, but strengthen *him* with thy blessed Spirit; and when thou art pleased to take *him* hence, take *him* unto thy favour, through the merits of thy most dearly beloved Son Jesus Christ our Lord. *Amen.*

¶ *Then shall the Minister say this Psalm.*

In te, Domine, speravi. Psal. lxxi.

IN thee, O Lord, have I put my trust; let me never be put to confusion: but rid me, and deliver me in thy righteousness; incline thine ear unto me, and save me.

Be thou my strong hold, whereunto I may alway resort) thou hast promised to help me: for thou art my house of defence, and my castle.

Deliver me (O my God) out of the hand of the ungodly, out of the hand of the unrighteous and cruel man.

For thou (O Lord God) art the thing that I long for, thou art my hope, even from my youth.

Through thee have I been holden up ever since I was born, thou art heth at took me out of my mother's womb; my praise shall be always of thee.

I am become as it were a monster unto many: but my sure trust is in thee.

O let my mouth be filled with thy praise (that I may sing of thy glory) and honour all the day long.

Cast me not away in the time of age, forsake me not when my strength faileth me.

For mine enemies speak against me: and they that lay wait for my soul take their counsel together, saying: God hath forsaken him; persecute him, and take him, for there is none to deliver him.

Go not far from me, O God: my God, haste thee to help me.

Let them be confounded and perish that are against my soul: let them be covered with shame and dishonour that seek to do me evil.

As for me, I will patiently abide alway, and will praise thee more and more.

My mouth shall daily speak of thy righteousness and salvation, for I know no end thereof.

I will go forth in the strength of the Lord God: and will make mention of thy righteousness only.

Thou (O God) hast taught me from my youth up until now, therefore will I tell of thy wondrous works.

Forsake me not (O God) in mine

unto I may alway resort: thou hast promised to help me; for thou art my house of defence, and my castle.

Deliver me, O my God, out of the hand of the ungodly: out of the hand of the unrighteous and cruel man.

For thou, O Lord God, art the thing that I long for: thou art my hope, even from my youth.

Through thee have I been holden up ever since I was born: thou art he that took me out of my mother's womb; my praise shall alway be of thee.

I am become as it were a monster unto many: but my sure trust is in thee.

O let my mouth be filled with thy praise: that I may sing of thy glory and honour all the day long.

Cast me not away in the time of age: forsake me not when my strength faileth me.

For my enemies speak against me, and they that lay wait for my soul take their counsel together, saying: God hath forsaken him, persecute him, and take him; for there is none to deliver him.

Go not far from me, O God my God, haste thee to help me.

Let them be confounded and perish that are against my soul: let them be covered with shame and dishonour that seek to do me evil.

As for me, I will patiently abide alway: and will praise thee more and more.

My mouth shall daily speak of thy righteousness and salvation, for I know no end thereof.

I will go forth in the strength of the Lord God: and will make mention of thy righteousness only.

Thou, O God hast taught me from my youth up until now: therefore will I tell of thy wondrous works.

Forsake me not, O God, in mine

1549	1886
old age, when I am gray-headed, until I have shewed thy strength unto this generation, and thy power to all them that are yet for to come.	old age, when I am gray-headed: until I have shewed thy strength unto this generation, and thy power to all them that are yet for to come.
Thy righteousness (O God) is very high, and great things are they that thou hast done: O God, who is like unto thee?	Thy righteousness, O God, is very high, and great things are they that thou hast done: O God, who is like unto thee?
O what great troubles and adversities hast thou shewed me! and yet didst thou turn and refresh me: yea, and broughtest me from the deep of the earth again.	
Thou hast brought me to great honour, and comforted me on every side.	
Therefore will I praise thee and thy faithfulness (O God) playing upon an instrument of musick, unto thee will I sing upon the harp, O thou holy one of Israel.	
My lips will be fain when I sing unto thee: and so will my soul whom thou hast delivered.	
My tongue also shall talk of thy righteousness all the day long, for they are confounded and brought unto shame that seek to do me evil.	
Glory to the Father, &c.	Glory be to the Father, and to the Son: and to the Holy Ghost;
As it was in the beginning, &c.	As it was in the beginning, is now, and ever shall be: world without end. Amen.
Adding this Anthem.	¶ *Adding this.*
O SAVIOUR of the world, save us, which by thy cross and precious blood hast redeemed us, help us we beseech thee, O God.	O SAVIOUR of the world, who by thy Cross and precious Blood hast redeemed us, Save us, and help us, we humbly beseech thee, O Lord.
Then shall the minister say,	¶ *Then shall the Minister say,*
THE Almighty Lord, which is a most strong tower to all them that put their trust in him, to whom all things in heaven, in earth, and under earth, do bow and obey: be now and evermore thy defence, and make thee know and feel, that	THE Almighty Lord, who is a most strong tower to all them that put their trust in him, to whom all things in heaven, in earth, and under the earth, do bow and obey, be now and evermore thy defence: and make thee know

there is no other name under heaven given to man, in whom and through whom thou mayest receive health and salvation, but only the name of our Lord Jesus Christ. Amen.

¶ *If the sick person desire to be anointed, then shall the Priest anoint him upon the forehead or breast only, making the sign of the cross, saying thus,*

As with this visible oil thy body outwardly is anointed: so our heavenly Father, Almighty God, grant of his infinite goodness, that thy soul inwardly may be anointed with the Holy Ghost, who is the Spirit of all strength, comfort, relief, and gladness: and vouchsafe for his great mercy (if it be his blessed will) to restore unto thee thy bodily health, and strength, to serve him; and send thee release of all thy pains, troubles, and diseases, both in body and mind. And howsoever his goodness (by his divine and unsearchable providence) shall dispose of thee: we, his unworthy ministers and servants, humbly beseech the eternal majesty to do with thee according to the multitude of his innumerable mercies, and to pardon thee all thy sins and offences, committed by all thy bodily senses, passions, and carnal affections: who also vouchsafe mercifully to grant unto thee ghostly strength, by his Holy Spirit, to withstand and overcome all temptations and assaults of thine adversary, that in no wise he prevail against thee, but that thou mayest have perfect victory and triumph against the devil, sin, and death, through Christ our Lord: Who by his death hath overcomed the prince of death, and with the Father and the Holy Ghost evermore liveth and reigneth God, world without end. Amen.

How long wilt thou forget me, (O Lord,) for ever? how long wilt thou

and feel, that there is none other Name under heaven given to man, in whom, and through whom, thou mayest receive health and salvation, but only the Name of our Lord Jesus Christ. Amen.

hide thy face from me? how long shall I seek counsel in my soul? and be so vexed in mine heart? how long shall mine enemy triumph over me? Consider, and hear me, (O lord my God): lighten mine eyes, that I sleep not in death. Lest mine enemy say, I have prevailed against him: for if I be cast down, they that trouble me will rejoice at it. But my trust is in thy mercy: and my heart is joyful in thy salvation. I will sing of the lord, because he hath dealt so lovingly with me: yea, I will praise the Name of the Lord the most Highest. Glory to the, &c. As it was in the, &c.

Usque quo, Domine. Psalm xiii.

¶ *And after that shall say,*

UNTO God's gracious mercy and protection we commit thee. The Lord bless thee, and keep thee. The Lord make his face to shine upon thee, and be gracious unto thee. The Lord lift up his countenance upon thee, and give thee peace, both now and evermore. *Amen.*

A Prayer for a sick child.

O ALMIGHTY God, and merciful Father, to whom alone belong the issues of life and death; Look down from heaven, we humbly beseech thee, with the eyes of mercy upon this child now lying upon the bed of sickness: Visit *him*, O Lord, with thy salvation; deliver *him* in thy good appointed time from *his* bodily pain, and save *his* soul for thy mercies' sake: That, if it shall be thy pleasure to prolong *his* days here on earth, *he* may live to thee, and be an instrument of thy glory, by serving thee faithfully, and doing good in *his* generation; or else receive *him* into those heavenly habitations, where the souls of them that sleep in the Lord Jesus enjoy perpetual rest and felicity. Grant this, O Lord, for thy mercies' sake, in the same thy Son our Lord Jesus Christ, who liveth and reigneth with thee and the Holy Ghost, ever one God, world without end. *Amen.*

A Prayer for a sick person, when there appeareth small hope of recovery.

O FATHER of mercies, and God of all comfort, our only help in time of need; We fly unto thee for succour in behalf of this thy servant, here lying under thy hand in great weakness of body. Look graciously upon *him*, O Lord; and the more the outward man decayeth, strengthen *him*, we beseech thee, so much the more continually with thy grace and holy Spirit in the inner man. Give *him* unfeigned repentance for all the errors of *his* life past, and stedfast faith in thy Son Jesus; that *his* sins may be done away by thy mercy, and *his* pardon sealed in heaven, before *he* go hence, and be no more seen. We know, O Lord, that there is no word impossible with thee; and that, if thou wilt, thou canst even yet raise *him* up, and grant *him* a longer continuance amongst us: Yet, forasmuch as in all appearance the time of *his* dissolution draweth near, so fit and prepare *him*, we beseech thee, against the hour of death, that after *his* departure hence in peace, and in thy favour, *his* soul may be received into thine everlasting kingdom, through the merits and mediation of Jesus Christ, thine only Son, our Lord and Saviour. *Amen.*

A commendatory Prayer for a sick person at the point of departure.

O ALMIGHTY God, with whom do live the spirits of just men made perfect, after they are delivered from their earthly prisons; We humbly commend the soul of this thy servant, our dear *brother*, into thy hands, as into the hands of a faithful Creator, and most merciful Saviour; most humbly beseeching thee, that it may be precious in thy sight. Wash it, we pray thee, in the blood of that immaculate Lamb that was slain to take away the sins of the world; that whatsoever defilements it may have contracted in the midst of this miserable and naughty world, through the lusts of the flesh, or the wiles of Satan, being purged and done away, it may be presented pure and without spot before thee. And teach us who survive, in this and other like daily spectacles of mortality, to see how frail and uncertain our own condition is; and so to number our days, that we may seriously apply our hearts to that holy and heavenly wisdom, whilst we live here, which may in the end bring us to life everlasting, through the merits of Jesus Christ thine only Son our Lord. *Amen.*

A Prayer for persons troubled in mind or in conscience.

O BLESSED Lord, the Father of mercies, and the God of all comforts; We beseech thee, look down in pity and compassion upon this thy afflicted servant. Thou writest bitter things against *him*, and makest *him* to possess *his* former iniquities; thy wrath lieth hard upon *him*, and *his* soul is full of trouble: But, O merciful God, who hast written thy holy Word for our learning, that we, through patience and comfort of thy holy scriptures, might have hope; give *him* a right understanding of *himself*, and of thy threats and promises; that *he* may neither cast away *his* confidence in thee, nor place it any where but in thee. Give *him* strength against all *his* temptations, and heal all *his* distempers. Break not the bruised reed, nor quench the smoking flax. Shut not up thy tender mercies in displeasure; but make *him* to hear of joy and gladness, that the bones which thou hast broken may rejoice. Deliver *him* from fear of the enemy, and lift up the light of thy countenance upon *him*, and give *him* peace, through the merits and mediation of Jesus Christ our Lord. *Amen.*

THE COMMUNION OF THE SICK.

Forasmuch as all mortal men be subject to many sudden perils, diseases, and sicknesses, and ever uncertain what time they shall depart out of this life : Therefore to the intent they may be always in a readiness to die, whensoever it shall please Almighty God to call them, the curates shall diligently from time to time, but specially in the plague time, exhort their parishioners to the oft receiving (in the church) of the holy Communion of the body and blood of our Saviour Christ : which if they do, they shall have no cause, in their sudden visitation, to be unquieted for lack of the same. But if the sick person be not able to come to the church, and yet is desirous to receive the Communion in his house, then he must give knowledge over night, or else early in the morning to the curate, signifying also how many be appointed to communicate with him.

And if the same day there be a celebration of the Holy Communion in the church, then shall the Priest reserve (at the open Communion) so much of the sacrament of the body and blood, as shall serve the sick person, and so many as shall communicate with him (if there be any) ; and so soon as he conveniently may, after the open Communion ended in the church, shall go and minister the same, first to those that are appointed to communicate with the sick (if there be any), and last of all to the sick person himself. But before the Curate distribute the holy Communion, the appointed general confession *must be made in the name of the communicants, the curate adding the* absolution with the comfortable sentences of scripture *following in the open Communion : and after the communion ended, the Collect.*

ALMIGHTY and everliving God, we most heartily thank thee, &c.

¶ *But if the day be not appointed for the open communion in the church, then (upon convenient warning given) the curate shall come and visit the sick person afore noon. And having a convenient place in the sick man's house (where he may reverently celebrate) with all things necessary for the same, and not being otherwise letted with the public service or any other just impediment ; he shall there celebrate the holy communion after such form and sort as hereafter is appointed.*

THE COMMUNION OF THE SICK.

¶ *Forasmuch as all mortal men be subject to many sudden perils, diseases, and sicknesses, and ever uncertain what time they shall depart out of this life ; therefore to the intent they may be always in a readiness to die, whensoever it shall please Almighty God to call them, the Curates shall diligently from time to time (but especially in the time of pestilence, or other infectious sickness) exhort their Parishioners to the often receiving of the holy Communion of the Body and Blood of our Saviour Christ, when it shall be publickly administered in the Church ; that so doing, they may, in case of sudden visitation, have the less cause to be disquieted for lack of the same. But if the sick person be not able to come to the Church, and yet is desirous to receive the Communion in his house ; then he must give timely notice to the Curate, signifying also how many there are to communicate with him, (which shall be three, or two at the least,)*

and having a convenient place in the sick man's house, with all things necessary so prepared, that the Curate may reverently minister, he shall there celebrate the Holy Communion, beginning with the Collect, Epistle, and Gospel, here following.

THE CELEBRATION
of the Holy Communion for the Sick.

O PRAISE the Lord, all ye nations, laud him, all ye people: for his merciful kindness is confirmed toward us, and the truth of the Lord endureth for ever.

Glory be to the Father, and to the Son, &c.

Lord, have mercy upon us.
Christ, have mercy upon us.
Lord, have mercy upon us.
Without any more repetition.

The Priest. The Lord be with you.

Answer. And with thy spirit.

Let us pray.

ALMIGHTY everliving God, maker of mankind, which dost correct those whom thou dost love, and chastisest every one whom thou dost receive: we beseech thee to have mercy upon this thy servant visited with thy hand, and to grant that he may take his sickness patiently, and recover his bodily health (if it be thy gracious will), and whensoever his soul shall depart from the body, it may without spot be presented unto thee: through Jesus Christ our Lord. Amen.

The Epistle.

MY son, despise not the correction of the Lord, neither faint when thou art rebuked of him: for whom the Lord loveth, him he correcteth, yea and he scourgeth every son, whom he receiveth. Heb. xii.

The Gospel.

VERILY, verily I say unto you, He that heareth my word, and be-

The Collect.

ALMIGHTY, everliving God, Maker of mankind, who dost correct those whom thou dost love, and chastise every one whom thou dost receive; We beseech thee to have mercy upon this thy servant visited with thine hand, and grant that *he* may take *his* sickness patiently, and recover *his* bodily health, (if it be thy gracious will;) and whensoever *his* soul shall depart from the body, it may be without spot presented unto thee; through Jesus Christ our Lord. *Amen.*

The Epistle. Hebr. xii. 5.

MY son, despise not thou the chastening of the Lord, nor faint when thou art rebuked of him. For whom the Lord loveth he chasteneth: and scourgeth every son whom he receiveth.

The Gospel. St. John v. 24.

VERILY, verily I say unto you, He that heareth my word,

lieveth on him that sent me, hath everlasting life, and shall not come unto damnation, but he passeth from death unto life. John v.

The Preface.

The Lord be with you.

Answer. And with thy spirit.

¶ Lift up your hearts, &c.

Unto the end of the Canon.

¶ *At the time of the distribution of the holy sacrament, the Priest shall first receive the Communion himself, and after minister to them that be appointed to Communicate with the sick (if there be any), and then to the sick person. And the sick person shall always desire some, either of his own house, or else of his neighbours, to receive the holy Communion with him; for that shall be to him a singular great comfort, and of their part a great token of charity.*

¶ *And if there be more sick persons to be visited the same day that the Curate doth celebrate in any sick man's house; then shall the curate (there) reserve so much of the sacrament of the body and blood, as shall serve the other sick persons, and such as be appointed to communicate with them (if there be any); and shall immediately carry it, and minister it unto them.*

¶ *But if any man either by reason of extremity of sickness, or for lack of warning given in due time to the curate, or by any other just impediment, do not receive the sacrament of Christ's body and blood; then the curate shall instruct him, that if he do truly repent him of his sins, and stedfastly believe that Jesus Christ hath suffered death upon the cross for him, and shed his blood for his redemption, earnestly remembering the benefits he hath thereby, and giving him hearty thanks therefore; he doth eat and drink spiritually the body and blood of our Saviour Christ, profitably to his soul's health, although he do not receive the sacrament with his mouth.*

¶ *When the sick person is visited and receiveth the holy Commnnion all at one time: then the priest for more expedition shall use this order at the visitation.*

The Anthem.

Remember not, Lord, &c.

and believeth on him that sent me, hath everlasting life, and shall not come into condemnation; but is passed from death unto life.

¶ *After which the Priest shall proceed according to the form before prescribed for the holy Communion, beginning at these words* [Ye that do truly *&c.*]

¶ *At the time of the distribution of the holy Sacrament, the Priest shall first receive the Communion himself, and after minister unto them that are appointed to communicate with the sick, and last of all to the sick person.*

¶ *But if a man, either by reason of extremity of sickness, or for want of warning in due time to the Curate, or for lack of company to receive with him, or by any other just impediment, do not receive the Sacrament of Christ's Body and Blood, the Curate shall instruct him, that if he do truly repent him of his sins, and stedfastly believe that Jesus Christ hath suffered death upon the Cross for him, and shed his Blood for his redemption, earnestly remembering the benefits he hath thereby, and giving him hearty thanks therefore, he doth eat and drink the Body and Blood of our Saviour Christ profitably to his Soul's health, although he do not receive the Sacrament with his mouth.*

¶ *When the sick person is visited, and receiveth the holy Communion all at one time, then the Priest, for more expedition, shall cut off the form of the Visitation at the Psalm* [In thee, O Lord, have I put my trust, *&c.*] *and go straight to the Communion.*

Lord, have mercy upon us.
Christ, have mercy upon us.
Lord, have mercy upon us.

¶ Our Father which art in heaven, &c.

And lead us not into temptation.

Answer. But deliver us from evil. Amen.

Let us pray.

O Lord, look down from heaven, &c.

With the first part of the exhortation and all other things unto the Psalm,

In thee, O Lord, have I put my trust, &c.

And if the sick desire to be anointed, then shall the Priest use the appointed prayer without any Psalm.

¶ *In the time of the Plague, Sweat, or such other like contagious times of sickness or diseases, when none of the Parish or neighbours can be gotten to communicate with the sick in their houses, for fear of the infection, upon special request of the diseased, the Minister may only communicate with him.*

THE ORDER FOR THE

BURIAL OF THE DEAD.

The priest meeting the corpse at the church stile, shall say: Or else the priests and clerks shall sing, and so go either into the church, or towards the grave.

I AM the resurrection and the life (saith the Lord): he that believeth in me, yea though he were dead, yet shall he live. And whosoever liveth and believeth in me, shall not die for ever. John xi.

I KNOW that my Redeemer liveth, and that I shall rise out of the earth in the last day, and shall be covered again with my skin, and shall see God in my flesh: yea and I myself shall behold him, not with other but with these same eyes. Job xix.

WE brought nothing into this world, neither may we carry any thing out of this world. The Lord giveth, and the Lord taketh away. Even as it pleaseth the Lord, so cometh things to pass: blessed be the name of the Lord. 1 Tim. vi. Job i.

When they come at the grave, whiles the corpse is made ready to be laid into the earth, the priest shall say, or else the priests and clerks shall sing.

MAN that is born of a woman, hath but a short time to live, and is full of misery: he cometh up and is cut down like a flower; he flieth as it were a shadow, and never continueth in one stay. Job. ix.

¶ In the midst of life we be in death: of whom may we seek for

THE ORDER FOR

THE BURIAL OF THE DEAD.

¶ *Here is to be noted, that the Office ensuing is not to be used for any that die unbaptized, or excommunicate, or have laid violent hands upon themselves.*

¶ *The Priest and Clerks meeting the Corpse at the entrance of the Church-yard, and going before it, either into the Church, or towards the Grave, shall say, or sing,*

I AM the resurrection and the life, saith the Lord: he that believeth in me, though he were dead, yet shall he live: and whosoever liveth and believeth in me shall never die. *St. John* xi. 25, 26.

I KNOW that my Redeemer liveth, and that he shall stand at the latter day upon the earth. And though after my skin worms destroy this body, yet in my flesh shall I see God: whom I shall see for myself, and mine eyes shall behold, and not another. *Job* xix. 25, 26, 27.

WE brought nothing into this world, and it is certain we can carry nothing out. The Lord gave, and the Lord hath taken away; blessed be the Name of the Lord. 1 *Tim.* vi. 7. *Job.* i. 21.

succour, but of thee, O Lord, which for our sins justly art moved? Yet O Lord God most holy, O Lord most mighty, O holy and most merciful Saviour, deliver us not into the bitter pains of eternal death. Thou knowest, Lord, the secrets of our hearts: shut not up thy merciful eyes to our prayers: But spare us, Lord most holy, O God most mighty, O holy and merciful Saviour, thou most worthy Judge eternal, suffer us not at our last hour for any pains of death to fall from thee.

Then the priest casting earth upon the corpse, shall say,

I COMMEND thy soul to God the Father Almighty, and thy body to the ground, earth to earth, ashes to ashes, dust to dust, in sure and certain hope of resurrection to eternal life, through our Lord Jesus Christ, who shall change our vile body, that it may be like to his glorious body, according to the mighty working whereby he is able to subdue all things to himself.

Then shall be said or sung,

I HEARD a voice from heaven, saying unto me: Write, blessed are the dead which die in Lord. Even so saith the Spirit, that they rest from their labours. Apoc. xiv.

Let us pray.

WE commend into thy hands of mercy, most merciful Father, the soul of this our brother departed, *N.* And his body we commit to the earth, beseeching thine infinite goodness, to give us grace to live in thy fear and love, and to die in thy favour: that when the judgment shall come which thou hast committed to thy well beloved Son, both this our brother, and we, may be found acceptable in thy sight, and receive that blessing, which thy well beloved Son shall then pronounce to all that love and fear thee, saying, Come, ye blessed children of my Father: Receive the kingdom prepared for you before the beginning of the world. Grant this, merciful Father, for the honour of Jesu Christ our only Saviour, Mediator, and Advocate. Amen.

This prayer shall also be added.

ALMIGHTY God, we give thee hearty thanks for this thy servant, whom thou hast delivered from the miseries of this wretched world, from the body of death and all temptation; and, as we trust, hast brought his soul, which he committed into thy holy hands, into sure consolation and rest: Grant, we beseech thee, that at the day of judgment his soul and all the souls of thy elect, departed out of this life, may with us, and we with them, fully receive thy promises, and be made perfit altogether, thorough the glorious resurrection of thy Son Jesus Christ our Lord.

These psalms with other suffrages following are to be said in the church, either before or after the burial of the corpse.

Dilexi, quoniam. Psalm cxvi.

I AM well pleased that the Lord hath heard the voice of my prayer.

That he hath inclined his ear unto me, therefore will I call upon him as long as I live.

The snares of death compassed me round about, and the pains of hell gat hold upon me: I shall find trouble and heaviness, and I shall call upon the name of the Lord, (O Lord), I beseech thee deliver my soul.

Gracious is the Lord, and righteous, yea, our God is merciful.

The Lord preserveth the simple: I was in misery, and he helped me.

¶ *After they are come into the Church, shall be read one or both of these Psalms following.*

Turn again then unto thy rest, O my Soul, for the Lord hath rewarded thee.

And why? thou hast delivered my soul from death, mine eyes from tears, and my feet from falling.

I will walk before the Lord, in the land of the living.

I believed, and therefore will I speak: but I was sore troubled. I said in my haste: all men are liars.

What reward shall I give unto the Lord for all the benefits that he hath done unto me?

I will receive the cup of salvation, and call upon the Name of the Lord.

I will pay my vows now in the presence of all his people: right dear in the sight of Lord is the death of his Saints.

Behold (O Lord) how that I am thy servant; I am thy servant, and the son of thy handmaid, thou hast broken my bonds in sunder.

I will offer to thee the sacrifice of thanksgiving, and will call upon the Name of the Lord.

I will pay my vows unto the Lord, in the sight of all his people, in the courts of the Lord's house, even in the midst of thee, O Hierusalem.

Glory be to the Father, &c.

As it was in the beginning, &c.

Lauda, anima, mea. Psal. cxlvi. ☛ *Note that this Psalm is to be said after the other that followeth.*

PRAISE the Lord, (O my soul), while I live will I praise the Lord: yea, as long as I have any being, I will sing praises unto my God.

O put not your trust in princes, nor in any child of man, for there is no help in them.

For when the breath of man goeth forth, he shall turn again to his earth, and then all his thoughts perish.

Blessed is he that hath the God of Jacob for his help: and whose hope is in the Lord his God.

Which made heaven and earth, the sea, and all that therein is: which keepeth his promise for ever.

Which helpeth them to right that suffer wrong, which feedeth the hungry.

The Lord looseth men out of prison, the Lord giveth sight to the blind.

The Lord helpeth them up that are fallen, the Lord careth for the righteous.

The Lord careth for the strangers, he defendeth the fatherless and widow: as for the way of the ungodly, he turneth it upside down.

The Lord thy God, O Sion, shall be King for evermore, and throughout all generations.

Glory be to the Father, &c.

As it was in the beginning, &c.

Domine, probasti. Psalm cxxxix.

O Lord, thou hast searched me out, and known me.

Thou knowest my down-sitting, and mine uprising: thou understandest my thoughts long before.

Thou art about my path, and about my bed, and spiest out all my ways.

For lo, there is not a word in my tongue, but thou (O Lord) knowest it altogether.

Thou hast fashioned me, behind and before, and laid thine hand upon me.

Such knowledge is too wonderful and excellent for me; I cannot attain unto it.

Whither shall I go then from thy Spirit? or whither shall I go then from thy presence?

If I climb up into heaven, thou art there: if I go down to hell, thou art there also.

If I take the wings of the morning, and remain in the uttermost parts of the sea;

Even there also shall thy hand lead me, and thy right hand shall hold me.

If I say: peradventure the darkness shall cover me, then shall my night be turned to day.

Yea, the darkness is no darkness with thee: but the night is all clear as the day, the darkness and light to thee are both alike.

For my reins are thine, thou hast covered me in my mother's womb: I will give thanks unto thee, for I am fearfully and wonderfully made: marvellous are thy works, and that my soul knoweth right well.

My bones are not hid from thee, though I be made secretly, and fashioned beneath in the earth.

Thine eyes did see my substance, yet being unperfect: and in thy book were all my members written;

Which day by day were fashioned, when as yet there was none of them.

How dear are thy counsels unto me, O God? O how great is the sum of them?

If I tell them they are more in number than the sand: when I wake up, I am present with thee.

Wilt thou not slay the wicked, O God? depart from me, ye bloodthirsty men.

For they speak unrighteously against thee: and thine enemies take thy Name in vain.

Do not I hate them, O Lord, that hate thee: and am not I grieved with those that rise up against thee?

Yea, I hate them right sore? even as though they were mine enemies.

Try me, O God, and seek the ground of mine heart: prove me, and examine my thoughts.

Look well if there be any way of wickedness in me, and lead me in the way everlasting.

Glory be to the Father, &c.

As it was in the beginning, &c.

Dixi, custodiam. Psal. xxxix.

I SAID, I will take heed to my ways: that I offend not in my tongue.

I will keep my mouth as it were with a bridle: while the ungodly is in my sight.

I held my tongue, and spake nothing: I kept silence, yea, even from good words; but it was pain and grief to me.

My heart was hot within me, and while I was thus musing the fire kindled: and at the last I spake with my tongue;

Lord, let me know mine end, and the number of my days: that I may be certified how long I have to live.

Behold, thou hast made my days as it were a span long: and mine age is even as nothing in respect of thee; and verily every man living is altogether vanity.

For man walketh in a vain shadow, and disquieteth himself in vain: he heapeth up riches, and cannot tell who shall gather them.

And now, Lord, what is my hope: truly my hope is even in thee.

Deliver me from all mine offences: and make me not a rebuke unto the foolish.

I became dumb, and opened not my mouth: for it was thy doing.

Take thy plague away from me: I am even consumed by means of thy heavy hand.

When thou with rebukes dost chasten man for sin, thou makest his beauty to consume away, like as it were a moth fretting a garment: every man therefore is but vanity.

Hear my prayer, O Lord, and with thine ears consider my calling: hold not thy peace at my tears.

For I am a stranger with thee: and a sojourner, as all my fathers were.

O spare me a little, that I may recover my strength: before I go hence, and be no more seen.

Glory be to the Father, and to the Son: and to the Holy Ghost;

As it was in the beginning, is now, and ever shall be: world without end. Amen.

Domine, refugium. Psal. xc.

LORD, thou hast been our refuge: from one generation to another.

Before the mountains were brought forth, or ever the earth and the world were made: thou art God from everlasting, and world without end.

Thou turnest man to destruction: again thou sayest, Come again, ye children of men.

For a thousand years in thy sight are but as yesterday: seeing that is past as a watch in the night.

As soon as thou scatterest them, they are even as a sleep: and fade away suddenly like the grass.

In the morning it is green, and groweth up: but in the evening it is cut down, dried up, and withered.

For we consume away in thy displeasure: and are afraid at thy wrathful indignation.

Thou hast set our misdeeds before thee: and our secret sins in the light of thy countenance.

For when thou art angry all our days are gone: we bring our years to an end, as it were a tale that is told.

The days of our age are threescore years and ten; and though men be so strong, that they come to fourscore years: yet is their strength then but labour and sorrow; so soon passeth it away, and we are gone.

But who regardeth the power of thy wrath: for even thereafter as a man feareth, so is thy displeasure.

O teach us to number our days:

Then shall follow this lesson, taken out of the fifteenth chapter to the Corinthians, the first Epistle.

CHRIST is risen from the dead, and become the first fruits of them that slept. For by a man came death, and by a man came the resurrection of the dead. For as by Adam all die, even so by Christ shall all be made alive, but every man in his own order. The first is Christ, then they that are Christ's, at his coming. Then cometh the end, when he hath delivered up the kingdom to God the Father, when he hath put down all rule and all authority and power. For he must reign till he hath put all his enemies under his feet. The last enemy that shall be destroyed is death. For he hath put all things under his feet. But when he saith all things are put under him, it is manifest that he is excepted, which did put all things under him. When all things are

1 Cor. 15.

that we may apply our hearts unto wisdom.

Turn thee again, O Lord, at the last: and be gracious unto thy servants.

O satisfy us with thy mercy, and that soon: so shall we rejoice and be glad all the days of our life.

Comfort us again now after the time that thou hast plagued us: and for the years wherein we have suffered adversity.

Shew thy servants thy work: and their children thy glory.

And the glorious Majesty of the Lord our God be upon us: prosper thou the work of our hands upon us, O prosper thou our handy-work.

Glory be to the Father, and to the Son: and to the Holy Ghost;

As it was in the beginning, is now, and ever shall be: world without end. Amen.

¶ *Then shall follow the Lesson taken out of the fifteenth Chapter of the former Epistle of Saint Paul to the Corinthians.*

1 Cor. xv. 20.

NOW is Christ risen from the dead, and become the first-fruits of them that slept. For since by man came death, by man came also the resurrection of the dead. For as in Adam all die, even so in Christ shall all be made alive. But every man in his own order: Christ the first-fruits; afterward they that are Christ's, at his coming. Then cometh the end, when he shall have delivered up the kingdom to God, even the Father; when he shall have put down all rule, and all authority, and power. For he must reign, till he hath put all enemies under his feet. The last enemy that shall be destroyed is death. For he hath put all things under his feet. But when he saith, all things are put under him, it is manifest that he is excepted, which did put all things

subdued unto him, then shall the Son also himself be subject unto him that put all things under him, that God may be all in all. Else what do they which are baptized over the dead, if the dead rise not at all? Why are they then baptized over them? yea and why stand we alway then in jeopardy? By our rejoicing, which I have in Christ Jesu our Lord, I die daily. That I have fought with beasts at Ephesus after the manner of men, what advantageth it me, if the dead rise not again? Let us eat, and drink, for to-morrow we shall die. Be ye not deceived: evil words corrupt good manners. Awake truly out of sleep, and sin not. For some have not the knowledge of God. I speak this to your shame. But some man will say: How arise the dead? with what body shall they come? Thou fool, that which thou sowest is not quickened, except it die. And what sowest thou? Thou sowest not that body that shall be; but bare corn as of wheat, or of some other: but God giveth it a body at his pleasure, to every seed his own body. All flesh is not one manner of flesh: but there is one manner of flesh of men, another manner of flesh of beasts, another of fishes, another of birds. There are also celestial bodies, aud there are bodies terrestrial. But the glory of the celestial is one, and the glory of the terrestrial is another. There is one manner glory of the sun, and another glory of the moon, and another glory of the stars. For one star differeth from another in glory. So is the resurrection of the dead. It is sown in corruption, it riseth again in incorruption. It is sown in dishonour, it riseth again in honour. It is sown in weakness, it riseth again in power. It is sown a natural body, it riseth again a spiritual body. There is a natural body, and there is a spiritual body:

under him. And when all things shall be subdued unto him, then shall the Son also himself be subject unto him that put all things under him, that God may be all in all. Else what shall they do which are baptized for the dead, if the dead rise not at all? Why are they then baptized for the dead? and why stand we in jeopardy every hour? I protest by your rejoicing, which I have in Christ Jesus our Lord, I die daily. If after the manner of men I have fought with beasts at Ephesus, what advantageth it me, if the dead rise not? Let us eat and drink, for to-morrow we die. Be not deceived: evil communications corrupt good manners. Awake to righteousness, and sin not; for some have not the knowledge of God. I speak this to your shame. But some man will say, how are the dead raised up? and with what body do they come? Thou fool, that which thou sowest is not quickened, except it die. And that which thou sowest, thou sowest not that body that shall be, but bare grain, it may chance of wheat, or of some other grain: But God giveth it a body, as it hath pleased him, and to every seed his own body. All flesh is not the same flesh; but there is one kind of flesh of men, another flesh of beasts, another of fishes, and another of birds. There are also celestial bodies, and bodies terrestrial; but the glory of the celestial is one, and the glory of the terrestrial is another. There is one glory of the sun, and another glory of the moon, and another glory of the stars; for one star differeth from another star in glory. So also is the resurrection of the dead; It is sown in corruption; it is raised in incorruption: It is sown in dishonour; it is raised in glory: It is sown in weakness; it is raised in power: It is sown a natural

as it is also written: The first man Adam was made a living soul, and the last Adam was made a quickening Spirit. Howbeit, that is not first which is spiritual: but that which is natural, and then that which is spiritual. The first man is of the earth, earthy: the second man is the Lord from heaven (heavenly). As is the earthy, such are they that are earthy. And as is the heavenly, such are they that are heavenly. And as we have borne the image of the earthy, so shall we bear the image of the heavenly. This say I, brethren, that flesh and blood cannot inherit the kingdom of God: neither doth corruption inherit uncorruption. Behold, I shew you a mystery. We shall not all sleep: but we shall all be changed and that in a moment, in the twinkling of an eye by the last trump. For the trump shall blow and the dead shall rise incorruptible, and we shall be changed. For this corruptible must put on incorruption: and this mortal must put on immortality. When this corruptible hath put on incorruption, and this mortal hath put on immortality: then shall be brought to pass the saying that is written: Death is swallowed up in victory: Death, where is thy sting? Hell, where is thy victory? The sting of death is sin: and the strength of sin is the law. But thanks be unto God which hath given us victory, through our Lord Jesus Christ. Therefore, my dear brethren, be ye stedfast, and unmoveable, always rich in the work of the Lord, forasmuch as ye know that your labour is not in vain in the Lord.

The lesson ended, then shall the Priest say

Lord, have mercy upon us.
Christ, have mercy upon us.

body; it is raised a spiritual body. There is a natural body, and there is a spiritual body. And so it is written, The first man Adam was made a living soul; the last Adam was made a quickening spirit. Howbeit, that was not first which is spiritual, but that which is natural: and afterward that which is spiritual. The first man is of the earth, earthy: the second man is the Lord from heaven. As is the earthy, such are they that are earthy: and as is the heavenly, such are they also that are heavenly. And as we have borne the image of the earthy, we shall also bear the image of the heavenly. Now this I say, brethren, that flesh and blood cannot inherit the kingdom of God; neither doth corruption inherit incorruption. Behold, I shew you a mystery: We shall not all sleep, but we shall all be changed, in a moment, in the twinkling of an eye, at the last trump, (for the trumpet shall sound,) and the dead shall be raised incorruptible, and we shall be changed. For this corruptible must put on incorruption, and this mortal must put on immortality. So when this corruptible shall have put on incorruption, and this mortal shall have put on immortality; then shall be brought to pass the saying that is written, Death is swallowed up in victory. O death, where is thy sting? O grave, where is thy victory? The sting of death is sin, and the strength of sin is the law. But thanks be to God, which giveth us the victory through our Lord Jesus Christ. Therefore, my beloved brethren, be ye stedfast, unmoveable, always abounding in the work of the Lord, forasmuch as ye know that your labour is not in vain in the Lord.

Lord, have mercy upon us.

Our Father which art in heaven, &c.

And lead us not into temptation.

Answer. But deliver us from evil. Amen.

Priest. Enter not (O Lord) into judgment with thy servant.

Answer. For in thy sight no living creature shall be justified.

Priest. From the gates of hell.

Answer. Deliver their souls, O Lord.

Priest. I believe to see the goodness of the Lord.

Answer. In the land of the living.

Priest. O Lord, graciously hear my prayer.

Answer. And let my cry come unto thee.

Let us pray.

O LORD, with whom do live the spirits of them that be dead: and in whom the souls of them that be elected, after they be delivered from the burden of the flesh, be in joy and felicity (Grant unto this thy servant, that the sins which he committed in this world be not imputed unto him, but that he, escaping the gates of hell, and pains of eternal darkness, may ever dwell in the region of light, with Abraham, Isaac, and Jacob, in the place where is no weeping, sorrow, nor heaviness; and when that dreadful day of the general resurrection shall come, make him to rise also with the just and righteous, and receive this body again to glory, then made pure and incorruptible: set him on the right hand of thy Son Jesus Christ, among thy holy and elect, that then he may hear with them these most sweet and comfortable words:) Come to me, ye blessed of my Father, possess the kingdom which hath been prepared for you from the beginning of the world: Grant this, we beseech thee, O merciful Father, through Jesus Christ our Mediator and Redeemer. Amen.

¶ *When they come to the grave, while the Corpse is made ready to be laid into the earth, the Priest shall say, or the Priest and Clerks shall sing:*

MAN that is born of a woman hath but a short time to live, and is full of misery. He cometh up, and is cut down, like a flower; he fleeth as it were a shadow, and never continueth in one stay.

In the midst of life we are in death: of whom may we seek for succour, but of thee, O Lord, who for our sins art justly displeased?

Yet, O Lord God most holy, O Lord most mighty, O holy and most merciful Saviour, deliver us not into the bitter pains of eternal death.

Thou knowest, Lord, the secrets of our hearts, shut not thy merciful ears to our prayer; but spare us, Lord most holy, O God most mighty, O holy and merciful Saviour, thou most worthy Judge eternal, suffer us not, at our last hour, for any pains of death, to fall from thee.

¶ *Then, while the earth shall be cast upon the Body by some standing by, the Priest shall say,*

FORASMUCH as it hath pleased Almighty God of his great mercy to take unto himself the soul of our dear *brother* here departed, we therefore commit *his* body to the ground; earth to earth, ashes to ashes, dust to dust; in sure and certain hope of the Resurrection to eternal life, through our Lord Jesus Christ; who shall change our vile body, that it may be like unto his glorious body, according to the mighty working, whereby he is able to subdue all things to himself.

¶ *Then shall be said or sung,*

I HEARD a voice from heaven, saying unto me, Write, From henceforth blessed are the dead which die in the Lord: even so saith the Spirit; for they rest from their labours.

¶ *Then the Priest shall say,*

Lord, have mercy upon us.
Christ have mercy upon us.
Lord, have mercy upon us.

OUR Father, which art in heaven, Hallowed be thy Name. Thy kingdom come. Thy will be done in earth, As it is in heaven. Give us this day our daily bread. And forgive us our trespasses, As we forgive them that trespass against us. And lead us not into temptation; But deliver us from evil. Amen.

Priest.

ALMIGHTY God, with whom do live the spirits of them that depart hence in the Lord, and with whom the souls of the faithful, after they are delivered from the burden of the flesh, are in joy and felicity; We give thee hearty thanks, for that it hath pleased thee to deliver this our *brother* out of the miseries of this sinful world; beseeching thee, that it may please thee, of thy gracious goodness, shortly to accomplish the number of thine elect, and to hasten thy kingdom; that we, with all those that are departed in the true faith of thy holy Name, may have our perfect consummation and bliss, both in body and soul, in thy eternal and everlasting glory; through Jesus Christ our Lord. *Amen.*

The Collect.

O MERCIFUL God, the Father of our Lord Jesus Christ,

who is the resurrection and the life; in whom whosoever believeth shall live, though he die; and whosoever liveth, and believeth in him, shall not die eternally; who also hath taught us, by his holy Apostle Saint Paul, not to be sorry, as men without hope, for them that sleep in him; We meekly beseech thee, O Father to raise us from the death of sin unto the life of righteousness: that, when we shall depart this life, we may rest in him, as our hope is this our *brother* doth; and that, at the general resurrection in the last day, we may be found acceptable in thy sight; and receive that blessing, which thy well-beloved Son shall then pronounce to all that love and fear thee, saying, Come ye blessed children of my Father, receive the kingdom prepared for you from the beginning of the world: Grant this, we beseech thee, O merciful Father, through Jesus Christ, our Mediator and Redeemer. *Amen.*

THE grace of our Lord Jesus Christ, and the love of God, and the fellowship of the Holy Ghost, be with us all evermore. *Amen.*

THE CELEBRATION

of the holy communion when there is a burial of the dead.

Quemadmodum Psalm xlii.

LIKE as the hart desireth the water-brooks, so longeth my soul after thee, O God.

My soul is athirst for God, yea, even for the living God: when shall I come to appear before the presence of God?

My tears have been my meat day and night, while they daily say unto me, Where is now thy God?

Now when I think thereupon, I pour out my heart by myself: for I went with the multitude, and brought them forth unto the house of God, in the voice of praise and thanksgiving, among such as keep holy-day.

Why art thou so full of heaviness, (O my soul): and why art thou so unquiet within me?

Put thy trnst in God, for I will yet give him thanks for the help of his countenance.

My God, my soul is vexed within me: therefore will I remember thee concerning the land of Jordan, and the little hill of Hermonim.

One deep calleth another, because of thy noise of thy water-pipes, all thy waves and storms are gone over me.

The Lord hath granted his loving-kindness on the day-time, and in the night-season did I sing of him, and made my prayer unto the God of my life.

I will say unto the God of my strength, why hast thou forgotten me? why go I thus heavily, while the enemy oppresseth me?

My bones are smitten asunder, while mine enemies (that trouble me) cast me in the teeth, namely, while they say daily unto me: where is now thy God?

Why art thou so vexed, (O my soul) and why art thou so disquieted within me?

O put thy trust in God, for I will yet thank him which is the help of my countenance, and my God.

Glory to the Father, &c.

As it was in the beginning, &c.

The Collect.

O MERCIFUL God the Father of our Lord Jesu Christ, who is the resurrection and the life: In whom whosoever believeth shall live, though he die: and whosoever liveth, and believeth in him, shall not die eternally: who also hath taught us (by his holy Apostle Paul) not to be sorry as men without hope for them that sleep in him: We meekly beseech thee (O Father) to raise us from the death of sin unto the life of righteousness, that when we shall depart this life, we may sleep in him (as our hope is this our brother doth), and at the general resurrection in the last day both we and this our brother departed, receiving again our bodies, and rising again in thy most gracious favour, may with all thine elect Saints obtain eternal joy. Grant this, O Lord God, by the means of our Advocate Jesus Christ: which with thee and the Holy Ghost, liveth and reigneth one God for ever. Amen.

The Epistle.

I WOULD not, brethren, that ye should be ignorant concerning them which are fallen asleep, that ye sorrow not, as other do, which have no hope. For if we believe that Jesus died and rose again: even so them also which sleep by Jesus, will God bring again with him. For this say we unto you in the word of the Lord, that we which shall live, and shall remain in the coming of the Lord, shall not come ere they which sleep. For the Lord himself shall descend from heaven with a shout, and the voice of the archangel, and trump of God: and the dead in Christ shall rise first: Then we which shall live (even we shall remain) shall be caught up with them also in the clouds, to meet the Lord in the air: and so shall we ever be with the Lord. Wherefore comfort yourselves one another with these words.

1 Thess. iv.

¶ *The Gospel.*

Jesus said to his disciples and to the Jews: All that the Father giveth me shall come to me: and he that cometh to

John vi.

me I shall not cast away. For I came down from heaven: not to do that I will, but that he will, which hath sent me. And this is the Father's will which hath sent me, that of all which he hath given me, I shall lose nothing: but raise them up again at the last day. And this is the will of him that sent me: that every one which seeth the son and believeth on him, have everlasting life: and I will raise him up at the last day.

THE ORDER OF THE PURIFICATION OF WOMEN.

The woman shall come into the church, and there shall kneel down in some convenient place, nigh unto the quire door: and the Priest standing by her shall say these words, or such like, as the case shall require.

FORASMUCH as it hath pleased Almighty God of his goodness to give you safe deliverance, and your child baptism, and hath preserved you in the great danger of child-birth: ye shall therefore give hearty thanks unto God, and pray.

Then shall the Priest say this Psalm.

THE THANKSGIVING OF WOMEN AFTER CHILD-BIRTH, COMMONLY CALLED, THE CHURCHING OF WOMEN.

¶ *The Woman, at the usual time after her Delivery, shall come into the Church decently apparelled, and there shall kneel down in some convenient place, as hath been accustomed, or as the Ordinary shall direct: And then the Priest shall say unto her,*

FORASMUCH as it hath pleased Almighty God of his goodness to give you safe deliverance, and hath preserved you in the great danger of Child-birth; you shall therefore give hearty thanks unto God, and say,

(¶ *Then shall the Priest say the* cxvi*th Psalm.)*

Dilexi quoniam.

I AM well pleased: that the Lord hath heard the voice of my prayer;

That he hath inclined his ear unto me: therefore will I call upon him as long as I live.

The snares of death compassed me round about: and the pains of hell gat hold upon me.

I found trouble and heaviness, and I called upon the Name of the Lord: O Lord, I beseech thee, deliver my soul.

Gracious is the Lord, and righteous: yea, our God is merciful.

The Lord preserveth the simple: I was in misery, and he helped me.

Turn again then unto thy rest, O my soul: for the Lord hath rewarded thee.

And why? thou hast delivered my soul from death: mine eyes from tears, and my feet from falling.

I will walk before the Lord: in the land of the living.

I believed, and therefore will I speak; but I was sore troubled: I said in my haste, All men are liars.

What reward shall I give unto the Lord: for all the benefits that he hath done unto me?

I will receive the cup of salvation: and call upon the Name of the Lord.

I will pay my vows now in the presence of all his people: in the courts of the Lord's house, even in the midst of thee, O Jerusalem. Praise the Lord.

Glory be to the Father, and to the Son: and to the Holy Ghost;

As it was in the beginning, is now, and ever shall be: world without end. Amen.

I HAVE lifted up mine eyes unto the hills, from whence cometh my help? *Levavi oculos.* Psalm cxxi.

My help cometh even from the Lord, which hath made heaven and earth.

He will not suffer thy foot to be moved, and he that keepeth thee will not sleep.

Behold, he that keepeth Israel, shall neither slumber nor sleep.

The Lord himself is thy keeper, the Lord is thy defence upon thy right hand.

So that the sun shall not burn thee by day, neither the moon by night.

The Lord shall preserve thee from all evil, yea, it is even he that shall keep thy soul.

The Lord shall preserve thy going out, and thy coming in, from this time forth for evermore.

Glory to the Father, &c.

As it was in the beginning, &c.

Or, Psalm cxxvii. *Nisi Dominus.*

EXCEPT the Lord build the house: their labour is but lost that build it.

Except the Lord keep the city: the watchman waketh but in vain.

It is but lost labour that ye

Lord, have mercy upon us.
Christ, have mercy upon us.
Lord, have mercy upon us.

¶ Our Father, which art in heaven, &c.

And lead us not into temptation.

Answer. But deliver us from evil. Amen.

Priest. O Lord, save this woman thy servant.

Answer. Which putteth her trust in thee.

Priest. Be thou to her a strong tower.

Answer. From the face of her enemy.

Priest. Lord, hear our prayer.

Answer. And let our cry come to thee.

Priest. ¶ Let us pray.

O ALMIGHTY God, which hast delivered this woman thy servant

haste to rise up early, and so late take rest, and eat the bread of carefulness: for so he giveth his beloved sleep.

Lo, children and the fruit of the womb: are an heritage and gift that cometh of the Lord.

Like as the arrows in the hand of the giant: even so are the young children.

Happy is the man that hath his quiver full of them: they shall not be ashamed when they speak with their enemies in the gate.

Glory be to the Father, and to the Son: and to the Holy Ghost;

As it was in the beginning, is now, and ever shall be: world without end. Amen.

¶ *Then the Priest shall say,*

Let us pray.

Lord, have mercy upon us.
Christ, have mercy upon us.
Lord, have mercy upon us.

OUR Father, which art in heaven, Hallowed be thy Name. Thy kingdom come. Thy will be done in earth, As it is in heaven. Give us this day our daily bread. And forgive us our trespasses, As we forgive them that trespass against us. And lead us not into temptation; But deliver us from evil: For thine is the kingdom, The power and the glory, For ever and ever. Amen.

Minister. O Lord, save this woman thy servant.

Answer. Who putteth her trust in thee.

Minister. Be thou to her a strong tower;

Answer. From the face of her enemy.

Minister. Lord, hear our prayer.

Answer. And let our cry come unto thee.

Minister. Let us pray.

O ALMIGHTY God, we give thee humble thanks for that

from the great pain and peril of childbirth: Grant, we beseech thee (most merciful Father), that she through thy help may both faithfully live, and walk in her vocation according to thy will in this life present; and also may be partaker of everlasting glory in the life to come: through Jesus Christ our Lord. Amen.

The woman that is purified, must offer her chrisom, and other accustomed offerings. And if there be a Communion, it is convenient that she receive the holy Communion.

thou hast vouchsafed to deliver this woman thy servant from the great pain and peril of Child-birth; Grant, we beseech thee, most merciful Father, that she, through thy help, may both faithfully live, and walk according to thy will, in this life present: and also may be partaker of everlasting glory in the life to come; through Jesus Christ our Lord. *Amen.*

¶ *The Woman, that cometh to give her Thanks, must offer accustomed Offerings; and, if there be a Communion, it is convenient that she receive the holy Communion.*

THE FIRST DAY OF LENT

COMMONLY CALLED

ASH-WEDNESDAY.

¶ *After Matins ended, the people being called together by the ringing of a bell, and assembled in the church, the English Litany shall be said after the accustomed manner: which ended, the Priest shall go into the pulpit, and say thus:*

BRETHREN, in the primitive church there was a godly discipline, that at the beginning of Lent such persons as were notorious sinners, were put to open penance, and punished in this world, that their souls might be saved in the day of the Lord; and that other admonished by their example, might be more afraid to offend. In the stead whereof, until the said discipline may be restored again, (which thing is much to be wished,) it is thought good, that at this time (in your presence) should be read the general sentences of God's cursing against impenitent sinners, gathered out of the xxviith chapter of Deuteronomy, and other places of scripture: and that ye should answer to every sentence, Amen. To the intent that you being admonished of the great indignation of God against sinners, may the rather be called to earnest and true repentance, and may walk more warily in these dangerous days, fleeing from such vices, for the which ye affirm with your own mouths the curse of God to be due.

¶ CURSED is the man that maketh any carved or molten image, an abomination to the Lord, the work

A COMMINATION

OR DENOUNCING OF GOD'S ANGER AND JUDGEMENTS AGAINST SINNERS, WITH CERTAIN PRAYERS, TO BE USED ON THE FIRST DAY OF LENT, AND AT OTHER TIMES, AS THE ORDINARY SHALL APPOINT.

¶ *After Morning Prayer, the Litany ended according to the accustomed manner, the Priest shall, in the Reading-Pew or Pulpit, say,*

BRETHREN, in the Primitive Church there was a godly discipline, that, at the beginning of Lent, such persons as stood convicted of notorious sin were put to open penance, and punished in this world, that their souls might be saved in the day of the Lord; and that others, admonished by their example, might be the more afraid to offend.

Instead whereof, (until the said discipline may be restored again, which is much to be wished,) it is thought good that at this time (in the presence of you all) should be read the general sentences of God's cursing against impenitent sinners, gathered out of the seven and twentieth Chapter of Deuteronomy, and other places of Scripture; and that ye should answer to every Sentence, *Amen:* To the intent that, being admonished of the great indignation of God against sinners, ye may the rather be moved to earnest and true repentance; and may walk more warily in these dangerous days; fleeing from such vices, for which ye affirm with your own mouths the curse of God to be due.

CURSED is the man that maketh any carved or molten image, to worship it.

of the hands of the craftsman, and putteth it in a secret place to worship it.

And the people shall answer and say,

Amen.

Minister. Cursed is he that curseth his father, and mother.

Answer. Amen.

Minister. Cursed is he that removeth away the mark of his neighbour's land.

Answer. Amen.

Minister. Cursed is he that maketh the blind to go out of his way.

Answer. Amen.

Minister. Cursed is he that letteth in judgment the right of the stranger, of them that be fatherless, and of widows.

Answer. Amen.

Minister. Cursed is he that smiteth his neighbour secretly.

Answer. Amen.

Minister. Cursed is he that lieth with his neighbour's wife.

Answer. Amen.

Minister. Cursed is he that taketh reward to slay the soul of innocent blood.

Answer. Amen.

Minister. Cursed is he that putteth his trust in man, and taketh man for his defence, and in his heart goeth from the Lord.

Answer. Amen.

Minister. Cursed are the unmerciful, the fornicators and advouterers, the covetous persons, the worshippers of images, slanderers, drunkards, and extortioners.

Answer. Amen.

The Minister. Now seeing that all they be accursed (as the prophet David beareth witness) which do err and go astray from the commandments of God, let us (remembering the dreadful judgment hanging over

Psal. cxviii.

¶ *And the people shall answer and say,* Amen.

Minister. Cursed is he that curseth his father or mother.

Answer. Amen.

Minister. Cursed is he that removeth his neighbour's landmark.

Answer. Amen.

Minister. Cursed is he that maketh the blind to go out of his way.

Answer. Amen.

Minister. Cursed is he that perverteth the judgement of the stranger, the fatherless, and widow.

Answer. Amen.

Minister. Cursed is he that smiteth his neighbour secretly.

Answer. Amen.

Minister. Cursed is he that lieth with his neighbour's wife.

Answer. Amen.

Minister. Cursed is he that taketh reward to slay the innocent.

Answer. Amen.

Minister. Cursed is he that putteth his trust in man, and taketh man for his defence, and in his heart goeth from the Lord.

Answer. Amen.

Minister. Cursed are the unmerciful, fornicators, and adulterers, covetous persons, idolaters, slanderers, drunkards, and extortioners.

Answer. Amen.

Minister.

NOW seeing that all they are accursed (as the prophet David beareth witness) who do err and go astray from the commandments of God; let us (remembering the dreadful judgement hanging over our heads, and always

our heads, and being always at hand) return unto our Lord God, with all contrition and meekness of heart, bewailing and lamenting our sinful life, knowledging and confessing our offences, and seeking to bring forth worthy fruits of penance. For even now is the axe put unto the root of the trees, so that every tree which bringeth not forth good fruit, is hewn down and cast into the fire. It is a fearful thing to fall into the hands of the living God: he shall pour down rain upon the sinners, snares, fire and brimstone, storm and tempest: this shall be their portion to drink. For lo, the Lord is coming out of his place, to visit the wickedness of such as dwell upon the earth. But who may abide the day of his coming? Who shall be able to endure when he appeareth? His fan is in his hand, and he will purge his floor, and gather his wheat into the barn, but he will burn the chaff with unquenchable fire. The day of the Lord cometh as a thief upon the night; and when men shall say peace, and all things are safe, then shall sudden destruction come upon them, as sorrow cometh upon a a woman travailing with child, and they shall not escape: then shall appear the wrath of God in the day of vengeance, which obstinate sinners, through the stubbornness of their heart, have heaped unto themself, which despised the goodness, patience, and long-sufferance of God, when he called them continually to repentance. Then shall they call upon me (saith the Lord), but I will not hear: they shall seek me early, but they shall not find me, and that because they hated know-

Mat. iii. Hebru. x. Psal. x. Esai. xxvi. Mal. iii. Mat. iii 1 Thess. v. Rom. ii. Proverb. i.

ready to fall upon us) return unto our Lord God, with all contrition and meekness of heart, bewailing and lamenting our sinful life, acknowledging and confessing our offences, and seeking to bring forth worthy fruits of penance. For now is the ax put unto the root of the trees, so that every tree that bringeth not forth good fruit is hewn down, and cast into the fire. It is a fearful thing to fall into the hands of the living God: he shall pour down rain upon the sinners, snares, fire and brimstone, storm and tempest; this shall be their portion to drink. For lo, the Lord is come out of his place to visit the wickedness of such as dwell upon the earth. But who may abide the day of his coming? Who shall be able to endure when he appeareth? His fan is in his hand, and he will purge his floor, and gather his wheat into the barn; but he will burn the chaff with unquenchable fire. The day of the Lord cometh as a thief in the night: and when men shall say, Peace, and all things are safe, then shall sudden destruction come upon them, as sorrow cometh upon a woman travailing with child, and they shall not escape. Then shall appear the wrath of God in the day of vengeance, which obstinate sinners, through the stubbornness of their heart, have heaped unto themselves; which despised the goodness, patience, and long-sufferance of God, when he calleth them continually to repentance. Then shall they call upon me, (saith the Lord,) but I will not hear; they shall seek me early, but they shall not find me; and that, because they hated knowledge, and received not the fear of the Lord, but abhorred my counsel, and despised my correction. Then shall it be too late to knock when the door shall be shut; and too late to cry

ledge, and received not the fear of the Lord, but abhorred my counsel and despised my correction: then shall it be too late to knock, when the door shall be shut, and too late to cry for mercy, when it is the time of justice. O terrible voice of most just judgment, which shall be pronounced upon them, when it shall be said unto them, Go ye cursed into the fire everlasting, Math. xxv. which is prepared for the devil and his angels. Therefore, brethren, take we heed betime, while the day of salvation lasteth, for the night cometh when 2 Cor. vi. John ix. none can work: but let us, while we have the light, believe in the light, and walk as the children of the light, that we be not cast into the utter darkness, Mat. xxv. where is weeping and gnashing of teeth. Let us not abuse the goodness of God, which calleth us mercifully to amendment, and of his endless pity promiseth us forgiveness of that which is past, if (with a whole mind and a true heart) we return unto him: for though our sins be red as scarlet, they shall Esai. i. Esech. xviii. be as white as snow; and though they be like purple, yet shall they be as white as wool. Turn you clean (saith the Lord) from all your wickedness, and your sin shall not be your destruction. Cast away from you all your ungodliness that ye have done, make you new hearts, and a new spirit: wherefore will ye die, O ye house of Israel, seeing I have no pleasure in the death of him that dieth? saith the Lord God. Turn you then, and you shall live. Although we have sinned, yet have we an Advocate 1 John ii. with the Father, Jesus Christ the righteous, and he it is that obtaineth grace for our sins; for he was wounded for our offences, and

for mercy when it is the time of justice. O terrible voice of most just judgement, which shall be pronounced upon them, when it shall be said unto them, Go, ye cursed, into the fire everlasting, which is prepared for the devil and his angels. Therefore, brethren, take we heed betime, while the day of salvation lasteth; for the night cometh, when none can work. But let us, while we have the light, believe in the light, and walk as children of the light; that we be not cast into utter darkness, where is weeping and gnashing of teeth. Let us not abuse the goodness of God, who calleth us mercifully to amendment, and of his endless pity promiseth us forgiveness of that which is past, if with a perfect and true heart we return unto him. For though our sins be as red as scarlet, they shall be made white as snow; and though they be like purple, yet they shall be made white as wool. Turn ye (saith the Lord) from all your wickedness, and your sin shall not be your destruction: Cast away from you all your ungodliness that ye have done: Make you new hearts, and a new spirit: Wherefore will ye die, O ye house of Israel, seeing that I have no pleasure in the death of him that dieth, saith the Lord God? Turn ye then, and ye shall live. Although we have sinned, yet have we an Advocate with the Father, Jesus Christ the righteous; and he is the propitiation for our sins. For he was wounded for our offences, and smitten for our wickedness. Let us therefore return unto him, who is the merciful receiver of all true penitent sinners; assuring ourselves that he is ready to receive us, and most willing to pardon us, if we come unto him with faithful repentance; if we submit ourselves unto him, and from henceforth walk in his

smitten for our wickedness: let us therefore return unto him, who is the merciful receiver of all true penitent sinners, assuring ourself that he is ready to receive us, and most willing to pardon us, if we come to him with faithful repentance: if we will submit ourselves unto him, and from henceforth walk in his ways: if we will take his easy yoke and light burden upon us to follow him in lowliness, patience, and charity, and be ordered by the governance of his holy Spirit, seeking always his glory, and serving him duly in our vocation with thanksgiving. This if we do, Christ will deliver us from the curse of the law, and from the extreme malediction which shall light upon them that shall be set on the left hand: and he will set us on his right hand, and give us the blessed benediction of his Father, commanding us to take possession of his glorious kingdom; unto the which he vouchsafe to bring us all, for his infinite mercy. Amen.

Esai. liii. Math. xi. Math. xxv.

¶ *Then shall they all kneel upon their knees: and the Priest and Clerks kneeling (where they are accustomed to say the Litany) shall say this psalm.*

HAVE mercy upon me, (O God,) after thy great goodness: according to the multitude of thy mercies, do away mine offences.

Miserere mei Deus. Psal. li.

Wash me throughly from my wickedness, and cleanse me from my sin.

For I knowledge my faults, and my sin is ever before me.

Against thee only have I sinned, and done this evil in thy sight: that thou mightest be justified in thy saying, and clear when thou art judged.

ways; if we will take his easy yoke, and light burden upon us, to follow him in lowliness, patience, and charity, and be ordered by the governance of his Holy Spirit; seeking always his glory, and serving him duly in our vocation with thanksgiving: This if we do, Christ will deliver us from the curse of the law, and from the extreme malediction which shall light upon them that shall be set on the left hand; and he will set us on his right hand, and give us the gracious benediction of his Father, commanding us to take possession of his glorious kingdom: Unto which he vouchsafe to bring us all, for his infinite mercy. Amen.

¶ *Then shall they all kneel upon their knees, and the Priest and Clerks kneeling (in the place where they are accustomed to say the Litany) shall say this Psalm.*

Miserere mei, Deus. Psal. li.

HAVE mercy upon me, O God, after thy great goodness: according to the multitude of thy mercies do away mine offences.

Wash me throughly from my wickedness: and cleanse me from my sin.

For I acknowledge my faults: and my sin is ever before me.

Against thee only have I sinned, and done this evil in thy sight: that thou mightest be justified in thy saying, and clear when thou art judged.

Behold, I was shapen in wickedness, and in sin hath my mother conceived me.

But lo, thou requirest truth in the inward parts, and shalt make me to understand wisdom secretly.

Thou shalt purge me with hyssop, and I shall be clean: thou shalt wash me, and I shall be whiter than snow.

Thou shalt make me hear of joy and gladness, that the bones which thou hast broken may rejoice.

Turn thy face from my sins, and put out all my misdeeds.

Make me a clean heart, (O God) and renew a right spirit within me.

Cast me not away from thy presence, and take not thy holy Spirit from me.

O give me the comfort of thy help again, and stablish me with thy free spirit.

Then shall I teach thy ways unto the wicked, and sinners shall be converted unto thee.

Deliver me from blood-guiltiness, (O God,) thou that art the God of my health: and my tongue shall sing of thy righteousness.

Thou shalt open my lips, (O Lord) and my mouth shall shew thy praise.

For thou desirest no sacrifice, else would I give it thee: but thou delightest not in burnt-offering.

The sacrifice of God is a troubled spirit, a broken and contrite heart, (O God,) shalt thou not despise.

O be favourable and gracious unto Sion, build thou the walls of Jerusalem.

Then shalt thou be pleased with the sacrifice of righteousness, with the burnt-offerings and oblations: then shall they offer youug bullocks upon thine altar.

Glory to the Father, &c.

As it was in the beginning, &c.

Behold, I was shapen in wickedness: and in sin hath my mother conceived me.

But lo, thou requirest truth in the inward parts: and shalt make me to understand wisdom secretly.

Thou shalt purge me with hyssop, and I shall be clean: thou shalt wash me, and I shall be whiter than snow.

Thou shalt make me hear of joy and gladness: that the bones which thou hast broken may rejoice.

Turn thy face away from my sins: and put out all my misdeeds.

Make me a clean heart, O God: and renew a right spirit within me.

Cast me not away from thy presence: and take not thy holy Spirit from me.

O give me the comfort of thy help again: and stablish me with thy free Spirit.

Then shall I teach thy ways unto the wicked: and sinners shall be converted unto thee.

Deliver me from blood-guiltiness, O God, thou that art the God of my health: and my tongue shall sing of thy righteousness.

Thou shalt open my lips, O Lord: and my mouth shall shew thy praise.

For thou desirest no sacrifice, else would I give it thee: but thou delightest not in burnt-offerings.

The sacrifice of God is a troubled spirit: a broken and contrite heart, O God, shalt thou not despise.

O be favourable and gracious unto Sion: build thou the walls of Jerusalem.

Then shalt thou be pleased with the sacrifice of righteousness, with the burnt-offerings and oblations: then shall they offer young bullocks upon thine altar.

Glory be to the Father, and to the Son: and to the Holy Ghost;

Answer. As it was in the beginning, is now, and ever shall be: world without end. Amen.

¶ Lord, have mercy upon us.
¶ Christ, have mercy upon us.
¶ Lord, have mercy upon us.

Our Father which art in heaven, &c.

And lead us not into temptation.

Answer. But deliver us from evil. Amen.

Minister. O Lord save thy servants.

Answer. Which put their trust in thee.

Minister. Send unto them help from above.

Answer. And evermore mightily defend them.

Minister. Help us, O God our Saviour.

Answer. And for the glory of thy name's sake deliver us, be merciful unto us sinners for thy name's sake.

Minister. O Lord, hear my prayer.

Answer. And let my cry come to thee.

Let us pray.

O Lord, we beseech thee mercifully hear our prayers, and spare all those which confess their sins to thee, that they whose consciences by sin are accused, by thy merciful pardon may be absolved, through Christ our Lord. Amen.

O most mighty God and merciful Father, which hast compassion of all men, and hatest nothing that thou hast made: which wouldest not the death of a sinner, but that he should rather turn from sin and be saved: mercifully forgive us our trespasses, receive and comfort us, which be grieved and wearied with the burden of

Lord, have mercy upon us.
Christ, have mercy upon us.
Lord, have mercy upon us.

OUR Father which art in heaven, Hallowed be thy Name. Thy kingdom come. Thy will be done in earth, As it is in heaven. Give us this day our daily bread. And forgive us our trespasses, As we forgive them that trespass against us. And lead us not into temptation; But deliver us from evil. Amen.

Minister. O Lord, save thy servants;

Answer. That put their trust in thee.

Minister. Send unto them help from above.

Answer. And evermore mightily defend them.

Minister. Help us, O God, our Saviour.

Answer. And for the glory of thy Name deliver us; be merciful to us sinners, for thy Name's sake.

Minister. O Lord hear our prayer.

Answer. And let our cry come unto thee.

Minister. Let us pray.

O LORD, we beseech thee mercifully hear our prayers, and spare all those who confess their sins unto thee; that they whose consciences by sin are accused, by thy merciful pardon may be absolved; through Christ our Lord. *Amen.*

O MOST mighty God, and merciful Father, who hast compassion upon all men, and hatest nothing that thou hast made; who wouldest not the death of a sinner, but that he should rather turn from his sin, and be saved; Mercifully forgive us our trespasses; receive and comfort us, who are grieved and wearied with the bur-

our sin. Thy property is to have mercy, to thee only it appertaineth to forgive sins: spare us therefore, good Lord, spare thy people whom thou hast redeemed. Enter not into judgment with thy servants, which be vile earth, and miserable sinners: But so turn thy ire from us, which meekly knowledge our vileness, and truly repent us of our faults: so make haste to help us in this world, that we may ever live with thee in the world to come: through Jesus Christ our Lord. Amen.

Then shall this anthem be said or sung.

TURN thou us, good Lord, and so shall we be turned: be favourable (O Lord) be favourable to thy people, which turn to thee in weeping, fasting, and praying: for thou art a merciful God, full of compassion, long suffering, and of a great pity: Thou sparest when we deserve punishment, and in thy wrath thinkest upon mercy. Spare thy people, good Lord, spare them, and let not thine heritage be brought to confusion: Hear us (O Lord) for thy mercy is great, and after the multitude of thy mercies look upon us.

den of our sins. Thy property is always to have mercy; to thee only it appertaineth to forgive sins. Spare us therefore, good Lord, spare thy people, whom thou hast redeemed; enter not into judgement with thy servants, who are vile earth, and miserable sinners; but so turn thine anger from us, who meekly acknowledge our vileness, and truly repent us of our faults, and so make haste to help us in this world, that we may ever live with thee in the world to come; through Jesus Christ our Lord. *Amen.*

¶ *Then shall the people say this that followeth, after the Minister.*

TURN thou us, O good Lord, and so shall we be turned. Be favourable, O Lord, Be favourable to thy people, Who turn to thee in weeping, fasting, and praying. For thou art a merciful God, Full of compassion, Long-suffering, and of great pity. Thou sparest when we deserve punishment, And in thy wrath thinkest upon mercy. Spare thy people good Lord, spare them, And let not thine heritage be brought to confusion. Hear us, O Lord, for thy mercy is great, And after the multitude of thy mercies look upon us; Through the merits and mediation of thy blessed Son, Jesus Christ our Lord. Amen.

¶ *Then the Minister alone shall say,*

THE Lord bless us, and keep us; the Lord lift up the light of his countenance upon us, and give us peace, now and for evermore. *Amen.*

OF CEREMONIES,

WHY SOME BE ABOLISHED AND SOME RETAINED. (n)

(n) This Explanation is printed in this volume after the Preface, p. 14, that it may be compared with the Explanation of the present Book of Common Prayer (1886).

Certain notes for the more plain explication and decent ministration of things contained in this book. (o)

(o) These Notes have been already printed in this volume, p. 51.

FINIS.

Imprinted at London in Fletestrete, at the sign of the Sunne over against the conduyte, by Edvvarde VVhitchurche the seventh daye of Marche, the year of our Lorde 1549.

THE

PSALMS OF DAVID. (p)

Day I. Morning Prayer.

Psalm I.

Beatus vir, qui non abiit.

Blessed is the man......

(p) THE PSALTER is not printed in this volume, as it did not form a part of the First Prayer Book of Edward VI., but was printed separately.

FORMS OF PRAYER

TO BE

USED AT SEA. (q)

(q) The Prayers to be used at Sea are not printed in this volume, as they had no place in First Prayer Book of Edward VI.

The forme
and maner of makyng
and consecratyng
Archebishoppes
Bishoppes
Priestes
and
Deacons
M.D.XLIX. (r)

THE FORM AND MANNER
OF
MAKING ORDAINING AND
CONSECRATING
OF
BISHOPS, PRIESTS, AND
DEACONS,
ACCORDING TO THE ORDER OF
The Church of England.

(r) The Ordinal was not issued till 1550, but has been considered a part of First Prayer Book of Edward VI.

1549	1886
THE PREFACE.	THE PREFACE.
IT is evident unto all men, diligently reading holy scripture, and ancient authors, that from the Apostles' time there hath been these orders of Ministers in Christ's church: Bishops, Priests, and Deacons: which Offices were evermore had in such reverent estimation, that no man by his own private authority might presume to execute any of them, except he were first called, tried, examined, and known to have such qualities as were requisite for the same; and also, by public prayer, with imposition of hands, approved, and admitted thereunto. And therefore, to the intent these orders should be continued, and reverently used, and esteemed, in this Church of England, it is requisite, that no man (not being at this present Bishop, Priest, or Deacon) shall execute any of them, except he be called, tried, examined and admitted, according to the form hereafter following.	*IT is evident unto all men diligently reading the Holy Scripture and ancient Authors, that from the Apostles' time there have been these Orders of Ministers in Christ's Church; Bishops, Priests, and Deacons. Which Offices were evermore had in such reverend Estimation, that no man might presume to execute any of them, except he were first called, tried, examined, and known to have such qualities as are requisite for the same; and also by publick Prayer, with Imposition of Hands, were approved and admitted thereunto by lawful Authority. And therefore, to the intent that these Orders may be continued, and reverently used and esteemed, in the Church of* England; *no man shall be accounted or taken to be a lawful Bishop, Priest, or Deacon in the Church of* England, *or suffered to execute any of the said Functions, except he be called, tried, examined, and admitted thereunto, according to the Form hereafter following, or hath had formerly Episcopal Consecration, or Ordination.*
And none shall be admitted a Deacon, except he be twenty-one years of age at the least. And every man which is to be admitted a Priest, shall be full twenty-four years old. And every man which is to be consecrated a Bishop, shall be fully thirty years of age.	*And none shall be admitted a Deacon, except he be Twenty-three years of age, unless he have a Faculty. And every man which is to be admitted a Priest shall be full Four-and-Twenty years old. And every man which is to be ordained or consecrated Bishop, shall be fully Thirty years of age.*
And the Bishop knowing, either by himself, or by sufficient testimony, any person to be a man of virtuous conversation, and without crime, and after examination and trial, finding him learned in the	*And the Bishop, knowing either by himself, or by sufficient testimony, any Person to be a man of virtuous conversation, and without crime; and, after examination and trial, finding him learned in the Latin*

Latin tongue, and sufficiently instructed in holy scripture, may upon a Sunday or holy day, in the face of the church, admit him a Deacon, in such manner and form, as hereafter followeth.

Tongue, and sufficiently instructed in holy Scripture, may at the times appointed in the Canon, or else, on urgent occasion, upon some other Sunday or Holy-day, in the face of the Church, admit him a Deacon, in such manner and form as hereafter followeth.

THE

FORM AND MANNER OF ORDERING OF DEACONS.

¶ *First, when the day appointed by the Bishop is come, there shall be an exhortation, declaring the duty and office of such as come to be admitted Ministers, how necessary such orders are in the church of Christ, and also, how the people ought to esteem them in their vocation.*

¶ *After the exhortation ended, the Archdeacon, or his deputy, shall present such as come to be admitted, to the Bishop; every one of them, that are presented, having upon him a plain Albe: and the Archdeacon, or his deputy, shall say these words.*

REVEREND Father in GOD, I present unto you these persons present, to be admitted Deacons.

¶ *The Bishop.* Take heed that the persons whom ye present unto us, be apt and meet, for their learning, and Godly conversation, to exercise their ministry duly, to the honour of God, and edifying of his Church.

The Archdeacon shall answer.

I have enquired of them, and also examined them, and think them so to be.

¶ *And then the Bishop shall say unto the people,*

BRETHREN, if there be any of you, who knoweth any impediment, or notable crime, in any of these persons presented to be ordered Deacons, for the which he ought not to be admitted to the same, let him come forth, in the name of

THE FORM AND MANNER OF MAKING OF DEACONS.

¶ *When the day appointed by the Bishop is come, after Morning Prayer is ended, there shall be a Sermon or Exhortation, declaring the Duty and Office of such as come to be admitted Deacons; how necessary that Order is in the Church of Christ, and also, how the people ought to esteem them in their Office.*

¶ *First the Archdeacon, or his Deputy, shall present unto the Bishop (sitting in his chair near to the holy Table) such as desire to be ordained Deacons, (each of them being decently habited,) saying these words,*

REVEREND Father in God, I present unto you these persons present, to be admitted Deacons.

The Bishop.

TAKE heed that the persons, whom ye present unto us, be apt and meet, for their learning and godly conversation, to exercise their Ministry duly, to the honour of God, and the edifying of his his Church.

¶ *The Archdeacon shall answer,*

I HAVE enquired of them, and also examined them, and think them so to be.

¶ *Then the Bishop shall say unto the people:*

BRETHREN, if there be any of you who knoweth any Impediment, or notable Crime, in any of these persons presented to be ordered Deacons, for the which he ought not to be admitted to that Office, let him come forth in

God, and shew what the crime, or impediment is.

¶ *And if any great crime or impediment be objected, the Bishop shall surcease from ordering that person, until such time as the party accused shall try himself clear of that crime.*

Then the Bishop, commending such as shall be found meet to be ordered, to the prayers of the Congregation, with the Clerks, and people present, shall say or sing the Litany as followeth.

The Litany and Suffrages.

O God the Father of heaven: have mercy upon us miserable sinners.

O God the Father of heaven: have mercy upon us miserable sinners.

O God the Son, Redeemer of the world: have mercy upon us miserable sinners.

O God the Son, Redeemer of the world: have mercy upon us miserable sinners.

O God the Holy Ghost, proceeding from the Father and the Son: have mercy upon us miserable sinners.

O God the Holy Ghost, proceeding from the Father and the Son: have mercy upon us miserable sinners.

O holy, blessed, and glorious Trinity, three persons and one God: have mercy upon us miserable sinners.

O holy, blessed, and glorious Trinity, three persons and one God: have mercy upon us miserable sinners.

Remember not, Lord, our offences, nor the offences of our forefathers, neither take thou vengeance of our sins: spare us, good Lord, spare thy people, whom thou hast redeemed with thy most precious blood, and be not angry with us for ever.

Spare us, good Lord.

the Name of God, and shew what the Crime or Impediment is.

¶ *And if any great Crime or Impediment be objected, the Bishop shall surcease from Ordering that person, until such time as the party accused shall be found clear of that Crime.*

¶ *Then the Bishop (commending such as shall be found meet to be Ordered to the Prayers of the Congregation) shall, with the Clergy and people present, sing or say the Litany, with the Prayers as followeth.*

The Litany and Suffrages.

O GOD the Father, of heaven: have mercy upon us miserable sinners.

O God the Father, of heaven: have mercy upon us miserable sinners.

O God the Son, Redeemer of the world: have mercy upon us miserable sinners.

O God the Son, Redeemer of the world: have mercy upon us miserable sinners.

O God the Holy Ghost, proceeding from the Father and the Son: have mercy upon us miserable sinners.

O God the Holy Ghost, proceeding from the Father and the Son: have mercy upon us miserable sinners.

O holy, blessed, and glorious Trinity, three Persons and one God: have mercy upon us miserable sinners.

O holy, blessed, and glorious Trinity, three Persons and one God: have mercy upon us miserable sinners.

Remember not, Lord, our offences, nor the offences of our forefathers; neither take thou vengeance of our sins; spare us, good Lord, spare thy people, whom thou hast redeemed with thy most precious blood, and be not angry with us for ever.

Spare us, good Lord.

1549	1886
From all evil and mischief, from sin, from the crafts and assaults of the devil, from thy wrath, and from everlasting damnation. *Good Lord, deliver us.*	From all evil and mischief; from sin, from the crafts and assaults of the devil; from thy wrath, and from everlasting damnation, *Good Lord, deliver us.*
From blindness of heart, from pride, vainglory, and hypocrisy, from envy, hatred, and malice, and all uncharitableness. *Good Lord, deliver us.*	From all blindness of heart; from pride, vain-glory, and hypocrisy; from envy, hatred, and malice, and all uncharitableness, *Good Lord, deliver us.*
From fornication, and all deadly sin; and from all the deceits of the world, the flesh, and the devil. *Good Lord, deliver us.*	From fornication, and all other deadly sin; and from all the deceits of the world, the flesh, and the devil, *Good Lord, deliver us.*
From Lightning and Tempest, from Plague, Pestilence, and Famine, from Battle and murther, and from sudden death. *Good Lord, deliver us.*	From lightning and tempest; from plague, pestilence, and famine; from battle and murder, and from sudden death, *Good Lord, deliver us.*
From all sedition and privy conspiracy, from the tyranny of the Bishop of Rome, and all his detestable enormities, from all false doctrine and heresy, from hardness of heart, and contempt of thy word and commandment. *Good Lord, deliver us.*	From all sedition, privy conspiracy, and rebellion; from all false doctrine, heresy, and schism; from hardness of heart, and contempt of thy Word and Commandment, *Good Lord, deliver us.*
By the mystery of thy holy incarnation, by thy holy nativity and Circumcision, by thy baptism, fasting, and temptation. *Good Lord, deliver us.*	By the mystery of thy holy Incarnation; by thy holy Nativity and Circumcision; by thy Baptism, Fasting, and Temptation, *Good Lord, deliver us.*
By thine agony and bloody sweat, by thy Cross and passion, by thy precious death and burial, by thy glorious resurrection and ascension, by the coming of the Holy Ghost. *Good Lord, deliver us.*	By thine Agony and bloody Sweat; by thy Cross and Passion; by thy precious Death and Burial; by thy glorious Resurrection and Ascension; and by the coming of the Holy Ghost, *Good Lord, deliver us.*
In all time of our tribulation, in all time of our wealth, in the hour of death, in the day of judgment. *Good Lord, deliver us.*	In all time of our tribulation; in all time of our wealth; in the hour of death, and in the day of judgement, *Good Lord, deliver us,*
We sinners do beseech thee to hear us (O Lord God), and that it may please thee to rule and govern thy holy church universal in the right way. *We beseech thee to hear us good Lord.*	We sinners do beseech thee to hear us, O Lord God; and that it may please thee to rule and govern thy holy Church universal in the right way; *We beseech thee to hear us, good Lord.*

1549	1886
That it may please thee, to keep EDWARD the VI, thy servant, our King and governor.	That it may please thee to keep and strengthen in the true worshipping of thee, in righteousness and holiness of life, thy Servant *VICTORIA*, our most gracious Queen and Governour;
We beseech thee to hear us good Lord.	*We beseech thee to hear us, good Lord.*
That it may please thee, to rule his heart in thy faith, fear and love, that he may always, have affiance in thee, and ever seek thy honour and glory.	That it may please thee to rule her heart in thy faith, fear, and love, and that she may evermore have affiance in thee, and ever seek thy honour and glory;
We beseech thee to hear us, good Lord.	*We beseech thee to hear us, good Lord.*
That it may please thee to be his defender and keeper, giving him the victory over all his enemies.	That it may please thee to be her defender, and keeper, giving her the victory over all her enemies.
We beseech thee to hear us, good Lord.	*We beseech thee to hear us, good Lord.*
	That it may please thee to bless and preserve *Albert Edward* Prince of *Wales*, the Princess of *Wales*, and all the Royal Family;
	We beseech thee to hear us, good Lord.
That it may please thee, to illuminate all Bishops, Pastors, and ministers of the church, with true knowledge, and understanding of thy word, and that both by their preaching and living they may set it forth, and shew it accordingly.	That it may please thee to illuminate all Bishops, Priests, and Deacons, with true knowledge and understanding of thy Word; and that both by their preaching and living they may set it forth, and shew it accordingly;
We beseech thee to hear us, good Lord.	*We beseech thee to hear us, good Lord.*
That it may please thee to bless these men, and send thy grace upon them, that they may duly execute the office, now to be committed unto them, to the edifying of thy Church, and to thy honour, praise, and glory.	That it may please thee to bless these thy servants, now to be admitted to the Order of Deacons, [*or Priests*] and to pour thy grace upon them; that they may duly execute their Office, to the edifying of thy Church, and the glory of thy holy Name;
We beseech thee to hear us, good Lord.	*We beseech thee to hear us, good Lord.*
That it may please thee to endue the lords of the council, and all the nobility, with grace, wisdom, and understanding.	That it may please thee to endue the Lords of the Council, and all the Nobility, with grace, wisdom, and understanding;
We beseech thee to hear us, good Lord.	*We beseech thee to hear us, good Lord.*

That it may please thee, to bless and keep the Magistrates, giving them grace to execute justice, and to maintain truth.

We beseech thee to hear us, good Lord.

That it may please thee, to bless and keep all thy people.

We beseech thee to hear us, good Lord.

That it may please thee, to give to all nations, unity, peace, and concord.

We beseech thee to hear us, good Lord.

That it may please thee, to give us an heart, to love and dread thee, and diligently to live after thy commandments.

We beseech thee to hear us good Lord.

That it may please thee, to give all thy people increase of grace, to hear meekly thy word, and to receive it with pure affection, and to bring forth the fruits of the Spirit.

We beseech thee to hear us, good Lord.

That it may please thee, to bring into the way of truth all such as have erred and are deceived.

We beseech thee to hear us, good Lord.

That it may please thee, to strengthen such as do stand, and to comfort and help the weak-hearted, and to raise them up that fall, and finally to beat down Sathan under our feet.

We beseech thee to hear us, good Lord.

That it may please thee, to succour, help and comfort, all that be in danger, necessity and tribulation.

We beseech thee to hear us, good Lord.

That it may please thee, to preserve all that travel by land, or by water, all women labouring

That it may please thee to bless and keep the Magistrates, giving them grace to execute justice, and to maintain truth;

We beseech thee to hear us, good Lord.

That it may please thee to bless and keep all thy people;

We beseech thee to hear us, good Lord.

That it may please thee to give to all nations unity, peace, and concord;

We beseech thee to hear us, good Lord.

That it may please thee to give us an heart to love and dread thee, and diligently to live after thy commandments;

We beseech thee to hear us, good Lord.

That it may please thee to give to all thy people increase of grace to hear meekly thy Word, and to receive it with pure affection, and to bring forth the fruits of the Spirit;

We beseech thee to hear us, good Lord.

That it may please thee to bring into the way of truth all such as have erred, and are deceived;

We beseech thee to hear us, good Lord.

That it may please thee to strengthen such as do stand; and to comfort and help the weak-hearted; and to raise up them that fall; and finally to beat down Satan under our feet;

We beseech thee to hear us, good Lord.

That it may please thee to succour, help, and comfort, all that are in danger, necessity, and tribulation;

We beseech thee to hear us, good Lord.

That it may please thee to preserve all that travel by land or by water, all women labouring of child, all sick persons, and young children, and to shew thy pity upon all prisoners and captives.

We beseech thee to hear us good Lord.

That it may please thee, to defend and provide for the fatherless children and widows, and all that be desolate and oppressed.

We beseech thee to hear us, good Lord.

That it may please thee, to have mercy upon all men.

We beseech thee to hear us, good Lord.

That it may please thee, to forgive our enemies, persecutors, and slanderers, and to turn their hearts.

We beseech thee to hear us, good Lord.

That it may please thee, to give and preserve to our use the kindly fruits of the earth, so as in due time we may enjoy them.

We beseech thee to hear us, good Lord.

That it may please thee, to give us true repentance, to forgive us all our sins, negligences, and ignorances, and to endue us with the grace of thy holy Spirit to amend our lives, according to thy holy word.

We beseech thee to hear us, good Lord.

Son of GOD: we beseech thee to hear us.

Son of God: we beseech thee to hear us.

O Lamb of God, that takest away the sins of the world.

Grant us thy peace.

O Lamb of God, that takest away the sins of the world.

Have mercy upon us.

O Christ, hear us.

O Christ, hear us.

Lord, have mercy upon us.

Lord, have mercy upon us.

of child, all sick persons, and young children; and to shew thy pity upon all prisoners and captives;

We beseech thee to hear us, good Lord.

That it may please thee to defend, and provide for, the fatherless children and widows, and all that are desolate and oppressed;

We beseech thee to hear us, good Lord.

That it may please thee to have mercy upon all men;

We beseech thee to hear us, good Lord.

That it may please thee to forgive our enemies, persecutors, and slanderers, and to turn their hearts;

We beseech thee to hear us, good Lord.

That it may please thee to give and preserve to our use the kindly fruits of the earth, so as in due time we may enjoy them;

We beseech thee to hear us, good Lord.

That it may please thee to give us true repentance; to forgive us all our sins, negligences, and ignorances; and to endue us with the grace of thy Holy Spirit to amend our lives according to thy holy Word.

We beseech thee to hear us, good Lord.

Son of God: we beseech thee to hear us.

Son of God: we beseech thee to hear us.

O Lamb of God: that takest away the sins of the world;

Grant us thy peace.

O Lamb of God: that takest away the sins of the world;

Have mercy upon us.

O Christ, hear us.

O Christ, hear us.

Lord, have mercy upon us.

Lord, have mercy upon us.

Christ, have mercy upon us.
Christ, have mercy upon us.
Lord, have mercy upon us.
Lord, have mercy upon us.

Our Father, which art in heaven.

With the residue of the Pater Noster.

And lead us not into temptation.
But deliver us from evil.

The Versicle. O Lord, deal not with us after our sins.

The Answer. Neither reward us after our iniquities.

Let us pray.

O God merciful Father, that despisest not the sighing of a contrite heart, nor the desire of such as be sorrowful, mercifully assist our prayers that we make before thee, in all our troubles and adversities, whensoever they oppress us: and graciously hear us, that those evils, which the craft and subtilty of the Devil, or man, worketh against us, be brought to nought, and by the providence of thy goodness they may be dispersed, that we thy servants, being hurt by no persecutions, may evermore give thanks unto thee, in thy holy Church: Through Jesu Christ our Lord.

O Lord, arise, help us, and deliver us, for thy name's sake.

O God, we have heard with our ears, and our fathers have declared unto us, the noble works, that thou didst in their days, and in the old time before them.

O Lord, arise, help us, and deliver us, for thine honour.

Christ, have mercy upon us.
Christ, have mercy upon us.
Lord, have mercy upon us.
Lord, have mercy upon us.

¶ *Then shall the Priest, and the people with him, say the Lord's Prayer.*

OUR Father, which art in heaven, Hallowed be thy Name. Thy kingdom come. Thy will be done in earth, As it is in heaven. Give us this day our daily bread. And forgive us our trespasses, As we forgive them that trespass against us. And lead us not into temptation; But deliver us from evil. Amen.

Priest. O Lord, deal not with us after our sins.

Answer. Neither reward us after our iniquities.

Let us pray.

O GOD, merciful Father, that despisest not the sighing of a contrite heart, nor the desire of such as be sorrowful; Mercifully assist our prayers that we make before thee in all our troubles and adversities, whensoever they oppress us; and graciously hear us, that those evils, which the craft and subtility of the devil or man worketh against us, be brought to nought; and by the providence of thy goodness they may be dispersed; that we thy servants, being hurt by no persecutions, may evermore give thanks unto thee in thy holy Church; through Jesus Christ our Lord.

O Lord, arise, help us, and deliver us for thy Name's sake.

O GOD, we have heard with our ears, and our fathers have declared unto us the noble works that thou didst in their days, and in the old time before them.

O Lord, arise, help us, and deliver us for thine honour.

Glory be to the Father, the Son, and to the Holy Ghost: as it was in the beginning, is now, and ever shall be, world without end. Amen.

From our enemies defend us, O Christ.

Graciously look upon our afflictions.

Pitifully behold the dolor of our heart.

Mercifully forgive the sins of thy people.

Favourably with mercy hear our prayers.

O Son of David, have mercy upon us.

Both now and ever vouchsafe to hear us, O Christ.

Graciously hear us, O Christ.

Graciously hear us, O Lord Christ.

¶ *The Versicle.* O Lord, let thy mercy be shewed upon us.

The Answer. As we do put our trust in thee.

¶ Let us pray.

We humbly beseech thee, O Father, mercifully to look upon our infirmities, and for the glory of thy name's sake, turn from us all those evils, that we most righteously have deserved: And grant that in all our troubles we may put our whole trust and confidence in thy mercy, and evermore serve thee, in pureness of living, to thy honour and glory, through our only mediator and advocate Jesus Christ our Lord. Amen.

Almighty God, which hast given us grace at this time with one accord to make our supplications unto thee, and dost promise, that when two or three be gathered in thy name, thou wilt grant their requests: fulfil now, O Lord, the desires and petitions of thy servants, as may be most expedient

Glory be to the Father, and to the Son: and to the Holy Ghost;

Answer. As it was in the beginning, is now, and ever shall be: world without end. Amen.

From our enemies defend us, O O Christ.

Graciously look upon our afflictions.

Pitifully behold the sorrows of our hearts.

Mercifully forgive the sins of thy people.

Favourably with mercy hear our prayers.

O Son of David, have mercy upon us.

Both now and ever vouchsafe to hear us, O Christ.

Graciously hear us, O Christ; graciously hear us, O Lord Christ.

Priest. O Lord, let thy mercy be shewed upon us;

Answer. As we do put our trust in thee.

Let us pray.

We humbly beseech thee, O Father, mercifully to look upon our infirmities; and for the glory of thy Name turn from us all those evils that we most righteously have deserved; and grant that in all our troubles we may put our whole trust and confidence in thy mercy, and evermore serve thee in holiness and pureness of living, to thy honour and glory; through our only Mediator and Advocate, Jesus Christ our Lord. *Amen.*

for them, granting us in this world knowledge of thy truth, and in the world to come life everlasting. Amen.

ALMIGHTY God, which by thy divine providence hast appointed diverse Orders of Ministers in the church, and didst inspire thine holy Apostles to choose unto this Order of Deacons thy first Martyr saint Stephin, with other: mercifully behold these thy servants, now called to the like Office and ministration; replenish them so with the truth of thy doctrine, and innocency of life, that, both by word and good example, they may faithfully serve thee in this Office, to the glory of thy name, and profit of the congregation, through the merits of our Saviour Jesu Christ, who liveth and reigneth with thee, and the holy Ghost, now and ever. Amen.

Then shall be sung or said, the Communion of the day, saving the Epistle shall be read out of Timothy, as followeth.

LIKEWISE must the ministers be honest not double-tongued, nor given unto much wine, neither greedy of filthy lucre, but holding the mystery of the faith, with a pure conscience. And let them first be proved, and then let them minister so that no man be able to reprove them. Even so must their wives be honest, not evil speakers, but sober, and faithful in all things. Let the Deacons be the husbands of one wife, and such as rule their children well, and their own households. For they that minister well get themselves a good degree, and a great liberty in the faith which is in Christ Jesu.

These things write I unto thee

¶ *Then shall be sung or said the Service for the Communion, with the Collect, Epistle, and Gospel, as followeth.*

The Collect.

ALMIGHTY God, who by thy Divine providence hast appointed divers Orders of Ministers in thy Church, and didst inspire thine Apostles to choose into the Order of Deacons the first Martyr Saint Stephen, with others; Mercifully behold these thy servants now called to the like Office and Administration; replenish them so with the truth of thy Doctrine, and adorn them with innocency of life, that, both by word and good example, they may faithfully serve thee in this Office, to the glory of thy Name, and the edification of thy Church; through the merits of our Saviour Jesus Christ, who liveth and reigneth with thee and the Holy Ghost, now and for ever. *Amen.*

The Epistle. 1 Tim. iii. 8.

LIKEWISE must the Deacons be grave, not double tongued, not given to much wine, not greedy of filthy lucre, holding the mystery of the faith in a pure conscience. And let these also first be proved; then let them use the Office of a Deacon, being found blameless. Even so must their wives be grave, not slanderers, sober, faithful in all things. Let the Deacons be the husbands of one wife, ruling their children and their own houses well. For they that have used the Office of a Deacon well purchase to themselves a good degree, and great boldness in the faith which is in Christ Jesus.

trusting to come shortly unto thee; but and if I tarry long, that then thou mayest yet have knowledge, how thou oughtest to behave thyself in the house of God, which is the congregation of the living God, the pillar and ground of truth. And without doubt great is that mystery of godliness. God was shewed in the flesh, was justified in the spirit, was seen among the angels, was preached unto the Gentiles, was believed on in the world, and received up in glory.

Or else this, out of the sixth of the Acts.

THEN the twelve called the multitude of the disciples together, and said: It is not meet that we should leave the Word of God, and serve tables. Wherefore, brethren, look ye out among you seven men of honest report, and full of the holy Ghost and wisdom, to whom we may commit this business. But we will give ourselves continually to prayer, and to the administration of the Word. And that saying pleased the whole multitude. And they chose Stephen, a man full of faith, and full of the holy Ghost, and Philip, and Prochorus, and Nicanor, and Timon, and Permenas, and Nicolas a convert of Antioch. These they set before the Apostles: and, when they had prayed, they laid their hands on them. And the Word of God increased, and the number of the disciples multiplied in Jerusalem greatly, and a great company of the Priests, were obedient unto the faith.

¶ *And before the Gospel, the Bishop sitting in a Chair, shall cause the Oath of the King's Supremacy, and against the usurped power and authority of the Bishop of Rome, to be ministered unto every of them, that are to be ordered.*

Or else this, out of the sixth of the Acts of the Apostles.

Acts vi. 2.

THEN the twelve called the multitude of the disciples unto them, and said, It is not reason that we should leave the Word of God, and serve tables. Wherefore. brethren, look ye out among you seven men of honest report, full of the Holy Ghost and wisdom, whom we may appoint over this business. But we will give ourselves continually to prayer, and to the ministry of the Word. And the saying pleased the whole multitude. And they chose Stephen, a man full of faith, and of the holy Ghost, and Philip, and Prochorus, and Nicanor, and Timon, and Parmenas, and Nicolas a proselyte of Antioch; whom they set before the Apostles; and, when they had prayed, they laid their hands on them. And the Word of God increased, and the number of the disciples multiplied in Jerusalem greatly, and a great company of the Priests were obedient to the faith.

¶ *The Oath of the* Kings Supremacy.

I FROM henceforth shall utterly renounce, refuse, relinquish, and forsake the Bishop of Rome, and his authority, power, and jurisdiction. And I shall never consent nor agree, that the Bishop of Rome shall practice, exercise, or have, any manner of authority, jurisdiction, or power within this realm, or any other the king's dominions, but shall resist the same at all times to the uttermost of my power And I from henceforth will accept, repute, and take the King's Majesty to be the only supreme head in earth, of the church of England: And to my cunning, wit, and uttermost of my power, without guile, fraud, or other undue mean, I will observe, keep, maintain and defend, the whole effects and contents of all and singular acts and statutes made, and to be made within this realm, in derogation, extirpation, and extinguishment of the Bishop of Rome, and his authority, and all other acts and statutes, made or to be made, in reformation and corroboration of the King's power, of the supreme head in earth, of the church of England: and this I will do against all manner of persons, of what estate, dignity or degree, or condition they be, and in no wise do nor attempt, nor to my power suffer to be done or attempted, directly, or indirectly, any thing or things, privily or apertly, to the let, hinderance, damage, or derogation thereof, or any part thereof, by any manner of means, or for any manner of pretence. And in case any other be made, or hath been made, by me, to any person or persons, in maintenance, defence, or favour of the Bishop of Rome, or his authority, jurisdiction, or power, I repute the same as vain and annihilate, so help me GOD, all saints and the holy Evangelist.

Then shall the Bishop examine every one of them, that are to be ordered, in the presence of the people, after this manner following.

Do you trust that you are inwardly moved by the Holy Ghost to take upon you this Office and ministration to serve GOD, for the promoting of his glory, and the edifying of his people?

Answer. I trust so.

The Bishop. Do ye think, that ye truly be called, according to the will of our Lord Jesus Christ, and the due order of this realm to the ministry of the church?

Answer. I think so.

The Bishop. Do ye unfeignedly believe all the Canonical scriptures, of the old and new Testament?

Answer. I do believe.

The Bishop. Will you diligently read the same unto the people assembled in the church where you shall be appointed to serve?

Answer. I will.

The Bishop. It pertaineth to the office of a Deacon to assist the Priest in divine service, and specially when he ministereth the holy Communion, and help him in the distribution thereof, and to read holy scriptures and Homilies in the congregation, and instruct the youth in the Catechism, and also to baptize and preach if he be commanded by the Bishop. And furthermore, it is his office to search for the sick, poor, and impotent people of the parish, and to intimate

¶ *And before the Gospel, the Bishop, sitting in his chair, shall examine every one of them that are to be Ordered, in the presence of the people, after this manner following.*

DO you trust that you are inwardly moved by the Holy Ghost to take upon you this Office and Ministration, to serve God for the promoting of his glory, and the edifying of his people?

Answer. I trust so.

The Bishop.

DO you think that you are truly called, according to the will of our Lord Jesus Christ, and the due Order of this Realm, to the Ministry of the Church?

Answer. I think so.

The Bishop.

DO you unfeignedly believe all the Canonical Scriptures of the Old and New Testament?

Answer. I do believe them.

The Bishop.

WILL you diligently read the same unto the people assembled in the Church where you shall be appointed to serve?

Answer. I will.

The Bishop.

IT appertaineth to the Office of a Deacon, in the Church where he shall be appointed to serve, to assist the Priest in Divine Service, and specially when he ministereth the holy Communion, and to help him in the distribution thereof, and to read holy Scriptures and Homilies in the Church; and to instruct the youth in the Catechism; in the absence of the Priest to baptize infants, and to preach, if he be admitted thereto by the Bishop. And furthermore, it is his Office,

their estates, names, and places where they dwell to the Curate, that by his exhortation they may be relieved by the parish or other convenient alms: will you do this gladly and willingly?

Answer. I will do so by the help of God.

The Bishop. Will you apply all your diligence to frame and fashion your own lives, and the lives of all your family according to the doctrine of Christ, and to make both yourselves and them, as much as in you lieth, wholesome examples of the flock of Christ?

Answer. I will do so, the Lord being my helper.

The Bishop. Will you reverently obey your ordinary and other chief Ministers of the Church, and them to whom the government and charge is committed over you, following with a glad mind and will their godly admonitions?

Answer. I will thus endeavour myself, the Lord being my helper.

¶ *Then the Bishop laying his hands severally upon the head of every one of them, shall say.*

Take thou authority to execute the office of a Deacon in the Church of God committed unto thee: in the name of the Father, the Son, and the Holy Ghost. Amen.

Then shall the Bishop deliver to every one of them the new Testament, saying.

Take thou authority to read the Gospel in the Church of God, and to preach the same, if thou be thereunto ordinarily commanded.

---

where provision is so made, to search for the sick, poor, and impotent people of the Parish, to intimate their estates, names, and places where they dwell, unto the Curate, that by his exhortation they may be relieved with the alms of the Parishioners, or others. Will you do this gladly and willingly?

Answer. I will so do, by the help of God.

The Bishop.

WILL you apply all your diligence to frame and fashion your own lives, and the lives of your families, according to the Doctrine of Christ; and to make both yourselves and them, as much as in you lieth, wholesome examples of the flock of Christ?

Answer. I will so do, the Lord being my helper.

The Bishop.

WILL you reverently obey your Ordinary, and other chief Ministers of the Church, and them to whom the charge and government over you is committed, following with a glad mind and will their godly admonitions?

Answer. I will endeavour myself, the Lord being my helper.

¶ *Then the Bishop laying his Hands severally upon the Head of every one of them, humbly kneeling before him, shall say,*

TAKE thou Authority to execute the Office of a Deacon in the Church of God committed unto thee; In the Name of the Father, and of the Son, and of the Holy Ghost. Amen.

¶ *Then shall the Bishop deliver to every one of them the New Testament, saying,*

TAKE thou Authority to read the Gospel in the Church of God, and to preach the same, if thou be thereto licensed by the Bishop himself.

Then one of them, appointed by the Bishop, putting on a tunicle, shall read the Gospel of that day.

Then shall the Bishop proceed to the Communion, and all that be ordered, shall tarry and receive the holy communion the same day with the Bishop.

The Communion ended, after the last collect and immediately before the benediction, shall be said this Collect following.

ALMIGHTY God, giver of all good things, which of thy great goodness hast vouchsafed to accept and take these thy servants unto the office of Deacons in thy church: make them, we beseech thee, O Lord, to be modest, humble, and constant in their ministration, and to have a ready will to observe all spiritual discipline, that they having always the testimony of a good conscience, and continuing ever stable and strong in thy Son Christ, may so well use themselves in this inferior office, that they may be found worthy to be called unto the higher ministries in thy Church, through the same thy Son our Saviour Christ, to whom be glory and honour world without end. Amen.

¶ *Then one of them, appointed by the Bishop, shall read the Gospel.*

St. Luke xii. 35.

LET your loins be girded about, and your lights burning; and ye yourselves like unto men that wait for their Lord, when he will return from the wedding; that, when he cometh and knocketh, they may open unto him immediately. Blessed are those servants, whom the Lord when he cometh shall find watching. Verily I say unto you, that he shall gird himself, and make them to sit down to meat, and will come forth and serve them. And if he shall come in the second watch, or come in the third watch, and find them so, blessed are those servants.

¶ *Then shall the Bishop proceed in the Communion, and all that are Ordered shall tarry, and receive the holy communion the same day with the Bishop.*

¶ *The Communion ended, after the last Collect, and immediately before the Benediction, shall be said these Collects following.*

ALMIGHTY God, giver of all good things, who of thy great goodness hast vouchsafed to accept and take these thy servants unto the Office of Deacons in thy Church; Make them, we beseech thee, O Lord, to be modest, humble, and constant in their Ministration, to have a ready will to observe all spiritual Discipline; that they having always the testimony of a good conscience, and continuing ever stable and strong in thy Son Christ, may so well behave themselves in this inferior Office, that they may be found worthy to be called unto the higher Ministries in thy Church; through the same thy Son our Saviour Jesus Christ, to whom be glory and honour world without end. *Amen.*

PREVENT us, O Lord, in all our doings with thy most gracious favour, and further us with

¶ *And here it must be shewed unto the Deacon, that he must continue in that office of a Deacon the spacc of a whole year at the least (except for reasonable causes it be otherwise seen to his ordinary) to the intent he may be perfect, and well expert in the things appertaining to the Ecclesiastical administration, in executing whereof if he be found faithful and diligent, he may be admitted by his diocesan to the order of Priesthood.*

thy continual help; that in all our works begun, continued, and ended in thee, we may glorify thy holy Name, and finally by thy mercy obtain everlasting life; through Jesus Christ our Lord. *Amen.*

THE peace of God, which passeth all understanding, keep your hearts and minds in the knowledge and love of God, and of his Son Jesus Christ our Lord: And the Blessing of God Almighty, the Father, the Son, and the Holy Ghost, be amongst you, and remain with you always. *Amen.*

¶ *And here it must be declared vnto the Deacon, that he must continue in that Office of a Deaeon the space of a whole year (except for reasonable causes it shall otherwise seem good unto the Bishop) to the intent he may be perfect, and well expert in the things appertaining to the Ecclesiastical Administration. In executing whereof if he be found faithful and diligent, he may be admitted by his Diocesan to the Order of Priesthood, at the times appointed in the Canon; or else, on urgent occasion, upon some other Sunday, or Holy-day, in the face of the Church, in such manner and form as hereafter followeth.*

THE FORM

OF

ORDERING OF PRIESTS.

THE FORM AND MANNER

OF

ORDERING OF PRIESTS.

¶ *When the day appointed by the Bishop is come, after Morning Prayer is ended, there shall be a Sermon or Exhortation, declaring the Duty and Office of such as come to be admitted Priests; how necessary that Order is in the Church of Christ, and also how the people ought to esteem them in their Office.*

¶ *First the Archdeacon, or, in his absence, one appointed in his stead, shall present unto the Bishop (sitting in his chair near to the holy Table) all them that shall receive the Order of Priesthood that day (each of them being decently habited) and say,*

REVEREND Father in God, I present unto you these persons present, to be admitted to the Order of Priesthood.

The Bishop.

TAKE heed that the persons, whom ye present unto us, be apt and meet, for their learning and godly conversation, to exercise their Ministry duly, to the honour of God, and the edifying of his Church.

¶ *The Archdeacon shall answer,*

I HAVE enquired of them, and also examined them, and think them so to be.

¶ *Then the Bishop shall say unto the people;*

GOOD people, these are they whom we purpose, God willing, to receive this day unto the holy Office of Priesthood: For after due examination we find not to the contrary, but that they be lawfully called to their Function and Ministry, and that they be persons meet for the same. But yet if there be any of you, who knoweth any Impediment, or no-

When the exhortation is ended, then shall be sung, for the Introit to the Communion, this Psalm.

Expectans expectavi Dominum. Psalm xl.

Or else this Psalm.

Memento Domine David. Psalm cxxxii.

Or else this Psalm.

Laudate nomen Domini. Psalm cxxxv.

Then shall be read for the Epistle this out of the xx. Chapter of the Acts of the Apostles.

FROM Mileto Paul sent messengers to Ephesus, and called the elders of the congregation, which when they were come to him, he said unto them, Ye know, that from the first day that I came into Asia, after what manner I have been with you at all seasons, serv-

table Crime, in any of them, for the which he ought not to be received into this holy Ministry, let him come forth in the Name of God, and shew what the Crime or Impediment is.

¶ *And if any great crime or Impediment be objected, the Bishop shall surcease from Ordering that person, until such time as the party accused shall be found clear of that Crime.*

¶ *Then the Bishop (commending such as shall be found meet to be Ordered to the Prayers of the Congregation) shall, with the Clergy and people present, sing or say the Litany, with the Prayers, as is before appointed in the Form of Ordering Deacons; save only, that, in the Proper Suffrage there added, the word* [Deacons] *shall be omitted, and the word* [Priests] *inserted instead of it.*

¶ *Then shall be sung or said the Service for the Communion, with the Collect, Epistle, and Gospel, as followeth.*

The Collect.

ALMIGHTY God, giver of all good things, who by thy Holy Spirit hast appointed divers Orders of Ministers in the Church; Mercifully behold these thy servants now called to the Office of Priesthood; and replenish them so with the truth of thy doctrine, and adorn them with innocency of life, that, both by word and good example, they may faithfully serve thee in this Office, to the glory of thy Name, and the edification of thy Church; through the merits of our Saviour Jesus Christ, who liveth and reigneth with thee and the Holy Ghost, world without end. *Amen.*

ing the Lord with all humbleness of mind, and with many tears and temptations which happened unto me by the laying await of the Jews; because I would keep back nothing that was profitable unto you, but to shew you, and teach you openly throughout every house: witnessing both to the Jews, and also to the Greeks, the repentance that is towards God, and the faith which is toward our Lord Jesus Christ. And now behold, I go bound in the spirit unto Jerusalem, not knowing the things that shall come on me there; but that the Holy Ghost witnesseth in every city, saying, that bonds and trouble abide me. But none of these things move me, neither is my life dear unto myself, that I might fulfil my course with joy, and the ministration of the word which I have received of the Lord Jesu, to testify the Gospel of the grace of God. And now behold, I am sure that henceforth ye all, through whom I have gone preaching the kingdom of God, shall see my face no more. Wherefore I take you to record this day, that I am pure from the blood of all men. For I have spared no labour, but have shewed you all the counsel of God. Take heed therefore unto yourselves, and to all the flock amongst whom the Holy Ghost hath made you Overseers, to rule the congregation of God, which he hath purchased with his blood. For I am sure of this, that after my departing shall grievous wolves enter in among you, not sparing the flock. Moreover of your own selves shall men arise speaking perverse things, to draw disciples after them. Therefore awake and remember, that by the space of three years, I ceased not to warn every one of you night and day with tears. And now, brethren, I commend you to God, and to the word of his grace, which is able to build further, and to give you an inheritance among all them which are sanctified. I have desired no man's silver, gold, or vesture; Yea, you know yourselves, that these hands have ministered unto my necessities, and to them that were with me. I have shewed you all things, how that so labouring ye ought to receive the weak; and to remember the words of the Lord Jesu, how that he said, It is more blessed to give than to receive.

Or else this third Chapter of the first Epistle to Timothy.

THIS is a true saying, If any man desire the Office of a Bishop, he desireth an honest work. A Bishop therefore must be blameless, the husband of one wife, vigilant, sober, discreet, a keeper of hospitality, apt to teach; not given to overmuch wine, no fighter, not greedy of filthy lucre, but gentle, abhorring fighting, abhorring covetous-

The Epistle. Ephes. iv. 7.

UNTO every one of us is given grace, according to the measure of the gift of Christ. Wherefor he saith, When he ascended up on high, he led captivity captive, and gave gifts unto men. (Now that he ascended, what is it but that he also descended first into the lower parts of the earth? He that descended is the same also that ascended up far above all heavens, that he might fill all things.) And he gave some Apostles, and some Prophets, and some Evangelists, and some Pastors and Teachers; for the perfecting of the Saints, for the work of the Ministry, for the edifying of the Body of Christ; till we all come in the unity of the faith, and of the knowledge of the Son of God, unto a perfect man, unto the measure of the stature of the fulness of Christ.

ness; one that ruleth well his own house, one that hath children in subjection with all reverence. (For if a man cannot rule his own house, how shall he care for the congregation of God?) He may not be a young scholar, lest he swell and fall into the judgement of the evil speaker. He must also have a good report of them which are without; lest he fall into rebuke and snare of the evil speaker.

Likewise must the ministers be honest not double-tongued, not given unto much wine, neither greedy of filthy lucre; but holding the mystery of the faith with a pure conscience; and let them first be proved, and then let them minister so that no man be able to reprove them.

Even so must their wives be honest; not evil-speakers, but sober and faithful in all things. Let the deacons be the husbands of one wife, and such as rule their children well and their own households, for they that minister well get themselves a good degree and great liberty in the faith which is in Christ Jesu.

These things write I unto thee, trusting to come shortly unto thee, but, and if I tarry long, that then thou mayest have yet knowledge how thou oughtest to behave thy self in the house of God, which is the congregation of the living God, the Pillar and ground of truth. And without doubt great is that mystery of Godliness. God was shewed in the flesh, was Justified in the Spirit, was seen among the Angels, was preached unto the Gentiles, was believed on in the world, and received up in glory.

After this shall be read for the Gospel a piece of the last Chapter of Matthew, as followeth.

JESUS came and spake unto them, saying: All power is given unto me in heaven and in earth. Go ye therefore and teach all nations, baptizing them In the name of the father, and of the son, and of the holy ghost. Teaching them to observe all things, whatsoever I have commanded you. And lo, I am with you alway, even until the end of the world.

Or else this that followeth, of the x. Chapter of John.

VERILY, verily I say unto you, He that entereth not in by the door into the sheep-fold, but climbeth up some other way, the same is a thief and a murtherer. But he that entereth in by the door is the Shepherd of the sheep. To him the porter openeth, and the sheep heareth his voice, and he calleth his own sheep by name, and leadeth them out. And when he hath sent forth his own sheep he goeth before them, and the sheep follow him, for they know his voice. A stranger will they not follow, but will flee from him; for they know not the voice of strangers. This Proverb spake Jesus unto them, but they understood not what things they were which he spake unto them. Then said Jesus unto them again, Verily, verily I say unto you, I am the door of the sheep. All (even as many as come before me) are thieves and murtherers: but the

¶ *After this shall be read for the Gospel part of the ninth Chapter of Saint* Matthew, *as followeth.*

St. Matth. ix. 36.

WHEN Jesus saw the multitudes, he was moved with compassion on them, because they fainted, and were scattered abroad as sheep having no shepherd, Then saith he unto his disciples, The harvest truly is plenteous, but the labourers are few. Pray ye therefore the Lord of the harvest, that he will send forth labourers into his harvest.

¶ *Or else this that followeth, out of the tenth Chapter of Saint* John.

St. John x. 1.

VERILY, verily I say unto you, He that entereth not by the door into the sheep-fold, but climbeth up some other way, the same is a thief and a robber. But he that entereth in by the door is the Shepherd of the sheep. To him the porter openeth, and the sheep hear his voice; aud he calleth his own sheep by name, and leadeth them out. And when he putteth forth his own sheep he goeth before them, and the sheep follow him; for they know his voice. And a stranger will they not fcllow, but will flee from him; for they know not the voice of strangers. This parable spake Jesus unto them, but they understood not what things they were which he spake unto them. Then said Jesus unto them again, Verily, verily I say unto you, I am the door of the sheep. All that ever came before me are thieves and robbers; but the sheep did not sheep did not hear them. I am the door, by me if any man enter in, he shall be safe, and go in and out, and find pasture. A thief cometh not but for to steal, kill, and to destroy. I am come that they might have life, and that they might have it more abundantly. I am the good Shepherd: a good Shepherd giveth his life for the sheep. An hired servant, and he which is not the Shepherd (neither the sheep are his own) seeth the wolf coming, and leaveth the sheep, and fleeth, and the wolf catcheth aud scattereth the sheep. The hired servant fleeth, because he is an hired servant, and careth not for the sheep. I am the good Shepherd and know my sheep, and am known of mine. As my Father knoweth me, even so know I also my Father. And I give my life for the sheep. And other sheep I have, which are not of this fold. Them also must I bring, and they shall hear my voice, and there shall be one fold, and one Shepherd.

Or else this, of the xx. chapter of John.

THE same day at night, which was the first day of the Sabboths, when the doors were shut (where the disciples were assembled together for fear of the Jews) came Jesus and stood in the midst, and saith unto them, Peace be unto you. And when he had so said, he shewed unto them his hands and his side. Then were the disciples glad, when they saw the Lord. Then said Jesus unto them again, Peace be unto you. As my Father sent me, even so send I you also. And when he had said these words, he breathed on them, and said unto them, Receive ye the holy ghost: whosesoever sins ye remit, they are remitted unto them: and whosesoever sins ye retain, they are retained.

hear them. I am the door; by me if any man enter in, he shall be saved, and shall go in and out, and find pasture. The thief cometh not but for to steal, and to kill, and to destroy: I am come that they might have life, and that they might have it more abundantly. I am the good Shepherd: the good Shepherd giveth his life for the sheep. But he that is an hireling, and not the Shepherd, whose own the sheep are not, seeth the wolf coming, and leaveth the sheep, and fleeth; and the wolf catcheth them, and scattereth the sheep. The hireling fleeth, because he is an hireling, and careth not for the sheep. I am the good Shepherd, and know my sheep, and am known of mine. As the Father knoweth me, even so know I the Father; and I lay down my life for the sheep. And other sheep I have, which are not of this fold: them also I must bring, and they shall hear my voice; and there shall be one fold, and one Shepherd.

When the Gospel is ended, then shall be said or sung.

COME Holy Ghost eternal God, proceeding from above,
Both from the Father and the Son, the God of peace and love:
Visit our minds, and into us thy heavenly grace inspire,
That in all truth and Godliness we may have true desire.

Thou art the very comforter, in all woe and distress,
The heavenly gift of God most high, which no tongue can express,
The fountain and the lively spring of joy celestial,
The fire so bright, the love so clear, and unction spiritual.

Thou in thy gifts art manifold, whereby Christ's Church doth stand,
In faithful hearts writing thy law, the finger of God's hand:
According to thy promise made, thou givest speech of grace,
That through thy help, the praise of God may sound in every place.

O Holy Ghost, into our wits send down thy heavenly light,
Kindle our hearts with fervent love, to serve God day and night,
Strength and stablish all our weakness, so feeble and so frail,
That neither flesh, the world, nor devil, against us do prevail.

Put back our enemy far from us, and grant us to obtain
Peace in our hearts with God and man, without grudge or disdain.
And grant, O Lord, that thou being our leader and our guide,
We may eschew the snares of sin, and from thee never slide.

To us such plenty of thy grace, good Lord, grant, we thee pray,
That thou Lord mayest be our comfort, at the last dreadful day.

Of all strife and dissension, O Lord, dissolve the bands,
And make the knots of peace and love throughout all Christian lands.

Grant us, O Lord, through thee to know the Father most of might,
That of his dear beloved Son we may attain the sight:
And that with perfit faith also we may acknowledge thee,
The Spirit of them both, alway one God in persons three.

Laud and praise be to the Father, and to the Son equal,
And to the Holy Spirit also, one God coeternal:
And pray we that the only Son vouchsafe his Spirit to send
To all that do profess his name, unto the world's end. Amen.

And then the Archdeacon shall present unto the Bishop all them that shall receive the order of Priesthood that day, every of them having upon him a plain Albe: The Archdeacon saying,

REVEREND father in God, I present unto you these persons present, to be admitted to the Order of Priesthood, ***cum interrogatione et responsione, ut in Ordine Diaconatus.***

And then the Bishop shall say to the people.

GOOD people, these be they whom we purpose, God willing, to receive this day unto the holy office of Priesthood. For after due examination, we find not the contrary, but that they be lawfully called to their function and ministry, and that they be persons meet for the same. But yet if there be any of you, which knoweth any impediment, or notable crime in any of them, for the which he ought not to be received to this holy ministry, now in the name of God declare the same.

¶ *And if any great crime or impediment be objected, &c.*, ut supra in Ordine Diaconatus usque ad finem Litaniæ cum hac Collecta.

ALMIGHTY God, giver of all good things, which by thy Holy Spirit hast appointed diverse orders of Ministers in thy church: mercifully behold these thy servants, now called to the Office of Priesthood, and replenish them so with the truth of thy doctrine, and innocency of life, that both by word and good example they may faithfully serve thee in this office, to the glory of thy name, and profit of the congregation, through the merits of our Saviour Jesu Christ, who liveth and reigneth, with thee and the Holy Ghost, world without end. Amen.

¶ *Then the Bishop shall minister unto every of them the oath, concerning the King's Supremacy, as it is set out in the Order of Deacons. And that done, he shall say unto them, which are appointed to receive the said Office, as hereafter followeth.*

You have heard, brethren, as well in your private examination, as in the exhortation, and in the holy lessons taken out of the Gospel, and of the writings of the Apostles, of what dignity, and of how great importance this office is, (whereunto ye be called). And now we exhort you, in the name of our Lord Jesus Christ, to have in remembrance, into how high a dignity, and to how chargeable an office ye be called, that is to say, to be the Messengers, the Watchmen, the Pastors, and the Stewards of the Lord, to teach, to premonish, to feed, and provide for the Lord's family: to seek for Christ's Sheep, that be dispersed abroad, and for his children, which be in the midst of this naughty world, to be saved through Christ for ever. Have always therefore printed in your remembrance, how great a treasure is committed to your charge: for they be the Sheep of Christ, which

¶ *Then the Bishop, sitting in his chair, shall say unto them as hereafter followeth.*

YOU have heard, Brethren, as well in your private examination, as in the exhortation which was now made to you, and in the holy Lessons taken out of the Gospel, and the writings of the Apostles, of what dignity, and of how great importance this Office is, whereunto ye be called. And now again we exhort you, in the Name of our Lord Jesus Christ, that you have in remembrance, into how high a Dignity, and to how weighty an Office and Charge ye are called: that is to say, to be Messengers, Watchmen, and Stewards of the Lord; to teach, and to premonish, to feed and provide for the Lord's family; to seek for Christ's sheep, that are dispersed abroad, and for his children who are in the midst of this naughty world, that they may be saved through Christ for ever.

Have always therefore printed in your remembrance, how great

he bought by his death, and for whom he shed his blood. The Church and congregation, whom you must serve, is his spouse and his body. And if it shall chance the same Church, or any member thereof, to take any hurt or hinderance by reason of your negligence, ye know the greatness of the fault, and also of the horrible punishment which will ensue. Wherefore, consider with yourselves the end of your ministry, towards the children of God, toward the spouse and body of Christ, and see that ye never cease your labour, your care and diligence, until you have done all that lieth in you, according to your bounden duty, to bring all such as are, or shall be committed to your charge, unto that agreement in faith, and knowledge of God, and to that ripeness, and perfectness of age in Christ, that there be no place left among them, either for error in religion, or for viciousness in life.

Then forasmuch as your office is both of so great excellency, and of so great difficulty, ye see with how great care and study ye ought to apply yourselves, as well that you may shew yourselves kind to that Lord, who hath placed you in so high a dignity, as also to beware, that neither you yourselves offend, neither be occasion that other offend. Howbeit ye cannot have a mind and a will thereto of yourselves, for that power and ability is given of God alone. Therefore ye see how ye ought and have need, earnestly to pray for his Holy Spirit. And seeing that ye cannot, by any other means, compass the doing of so weighty a work, pertaining to the salvation of man, but with doctrine and exhortation, taken out of holy Scripture and

a treasure is committed to your charge. For they are the sheep of Christ, which he bought with his death, and for whom he shed his blood. The Church and Congregation whom you must serve, is his Spouse, and his Body. And if it shall happen the same Church, or any Member thereof, to take any hurt or hindrance by reason of your negligence, ye know the greatness of the fault, and also the horrible punishment that will ensue. Wherefore consider with yourselves the end of your Ministry towards the children of God, towards the Spouse and Body of Christ; and see that you never cease your labour, your care and diligence, until you have done all that lieth in you, according to your bounden duty, to bring all such as are or shall be committed to your charge, unto that agreement in the faith and knowledge of God, and to that ripeness and perfectness of age in Christ, that there be no place left among you, either for error in religion, or for viciousness in life.

Forasmuch then as your Office is both of so great excellency, and of so great difficulty, ye see with how great care and study ye ought to apply yourselves, as well that ye may shew yourselves dutiful and thankful unto that Lord, who hath placed you in so high a Dignity; as also to beware, that neither you yourselves offend, nor be occasion that others offend. Howbeit, ye cannot have a mind and will thereto of yourselves; for that will and ability is given of God alone: therefore ye ought, and have need, to pray earnestly for his holy Spirit. And seeing that you cannot by any other means compass the doing of so weighty a work, pertaining to the salvation of man, but with doctrine and exhortation taken out of the holy Scriptures, with a life agreeable unto the same, you perceive how studious ye ought to be in reading and learning the holy scriptures, and in framing the manners, both of yourselves, and of them that specially pertain unto you, according to the rule of the same scriptures. And for this selfsame cause, ye see how you ought to forsake and set aside (as much as you may) all worldly cares and studies.

We have a good hope, that you have well weighed and pondered these things with yourselves, long before this time, and that you have clearly determined by God's grace, to give yourselves wholly to this vocation, whereunto it hath pleased God to call you, so that (as much as lieth in you) you apply yourselves wholly to this one thing, and draw all your cares and studies this way, and to this end. And that you will continually pray for the heavenly assistance of the Holy Ghost, from God the Father, by the mediation of our only Mediator and Saviour Jesus Christ, that by daily reading and weighing of the scriptures ye may wax riper and stronger in your Ministry: and that ye may so endeavour yourselves, from time to time, to sanctify the lives of you and yours, and to fashion them, after the rule and doctrine of Christ, and that ye may be wholesome and godly examples and patterns for the rest of the congregation to follow: and that this present congregation of Christ, here assembled, may also understand your minds and wills, in these things.

¶ AND that this your promise shall more move you to do your duties, ye shall answer plainly to these things, which we in the name of the Congregation shall demand of you, touching the same.

Do you think in your heart, that you be truly called, according

and with a life agreeable to the same; consider how studious ye ought to be in reading and learning the Scriptures, and in framing the manners both of yourselves, and of them that specially pertain unto you, according to the rule of the same Scriptures: and for this self-same cause, how ye ought to forsake and set aside (as much as you may) all worldly cares and studies.

We have good hope that you have well weighed and pondered these things with yourselves long before this time; and that you have clearly determined, by God's grace, to give yourselves wholly to this Office, whereunto it hath pleased God to call you: so that, as much as lieth in you, you will apply yourselves wholly to this one thing, and draw all your cares and studies this way; and that you will continually pray to God the Father, by the Mediation of our only Saviour Jesus Christ, for the heavenly assistance of the Holy Ghost; that, by daily reading and weighing of the Scriptures, ye may wax riper and stronger in your Ministry; and that ye may so endeavour yourselves, from time to time, to sanctify the lives of you and yours, and to fashion them after the Rule and Doctrine of Christ, that ye may be wholesome and godly examples and patterns for the people to follow.

And now, that this present Congregation of Christ here assembled may also understand your minds and wills in these things, and that this your promise may the more move you to do your duties, ye shall answer plainly to these things, which we, in the Name of God, and of his Church, shall demand of you touching the same.

DO you think in your heart, that you be truly called, acto the will of our Lord Jesus Christ, and the order of this Church of England, to the ministry of Priesthood?

Answer. I think it.

The Bishop. Be you persuaded that the holy scriptures contain sufficiently all doctrine, required of necessity for eternal salvation, through faith in Jesu Christ? And are you determined with the said scriptures to instruct the people committed to your charge, and to teach nothing as required of necessity to eternal salvation, but that you shall be persuaded, may be concluded, and proved by the scripture?

Answer. I am so persuaded, and have so determined by God's grace.

The Bishop. Will you then give your faithful diligence always, so to minister the doctrine, and Sacraments, and the discipline of Christ, as the Lord hath commanded, and as this realm hath received the same, according to the commandments of God, so that ye may teach the people committed to your cure and charge with all diligence to keep and observe the same?

Answer. I will so do, by the help of the Lord.

The Bishop. Will you be ready with all faithful diligence to banish and drive away all erroneous and strange doctrines contrary to God's word, and to use both public and private monitions and exhortations, as well to the sick as to the whole, within your cures, as need shall require and occasion be given?

cording to the will of our Lord Jesus Christ, and the order of this Church of *England*, to the Order and Ministry of Priesthood?

Answer. I think it.

The Bishop.

ARE you persuaded that the holy Scriptures contain sufficiently all Doctrine required of necessity for eternal salvation through faith in Jesus Christ? and are you determined, out of the said Scriptures to instruct the people committed to your charge, and to teach nothing, as required of necessity to eternal salvation, but that which you shall be persuaded may be concluded and proved by the Scripture?

Answer. I am so persuaded, and have so determined by God's grace.

The Bishop.

WILL you then give your faithful diligence always so to minister the Doctrine and Sacraments, and the Discipline of Christ, as the Lord hath commanded, and as this Church and Realm hath received the same, according to the Commandments of God; so that you may teach the people committed to your Cure and Charge with all diligence to keep and observe the same?

Answer. I will do so, by the help of the Lord.

The Bishop.

WILL you be ready, with all faithful diligence, to banish and drive away all erroneous and strange doctrines contrary to God's word; and to use both publick and private monitions and exhortations, as well to the sick as to the whole, within your Cures, as need shall require, and occasion shall be given?

Answer. I will, the Lord being my helper.

The Bishop. Will you be diligent in prayers and in reading of the holy scriptures, and in such studies as help to the knowledge of the same, laying aside the study of the world and the flesh?

Answer. I will endeavour myself so to do, the Lord being my helper.

The Bishop. Will you be diligent to frame and fashion your own selves and your families according to the doctrine of Christ, and to make both yourselves and them (as much as in you lieth) wholesome examples and spectacles to the flock of Christ?

Answer. I will so apply myself, the Lord being my helper.

The Bishop. Will you maintain and set forwards (as much as lieth in you) quietness, peace, and love amongst all Christian people, and specially amongst them that are or shall be committed to your charge?

Answer. I will so do, the Lord being my helper.

The Bishop. Will you reverently obey your ordinary, and other chief ministers, unto whom the government and charge is committed over you, following with a glad mind and will their godly admonition, and submitting yourselves to their godly judgments?

Answer. I will so do, the Lord being my helper.

¶ *Then shall the Bishop say,*

ALMIGHTY God, who hath given you this will to do all these things,

Answer. I will, the Lord being my helper.

The Bishop.

WILL you be diligent in prayers, and in reading of the holy Scriptures, and in such studies as help to the knowledge of the same, laying aside the study of the world and the flesh?

Answer. I will endeavour myself so to do, the Lord being my helper.

The Bishop.

WILL you be diligent to frame and fashion your own selves, and your families, according to the Doctrine of Christ; and to make both yourselves and them, as much as in you lieth, wholesome examples and patterns to the flock of Christ?

Answer. I will apply myself thereto, the Lord being my helper.

The Bishop.

WILL you maintain and set forwards, as much as lieth in you, quietness, peace, and love, among all Christian people, and especially among them that are or shall be committed to your charge?

Answer. I will so do, the Lord being my helper.

The Bishop.

WILL you reverently obey your Ordinary and other chief Ministers, unto whom is committed the charge and government over you; following with a glad mind and will their godly admonitions, and submitting yourselves to their godly judgements?

Answer. I will do so, the Lord being my helper.

¶ *Then shall the Bishop standing up, say,*

ALMIGHTY God, who hath given you this will to do all

grant also unto you strength and power to perform the same, that he may accomplish his work which he hath begun in you, until the time he shall come at the latter day to judge the quick and the dead.

¶ *After this the congregation shall be desired secretly in their prayers to make humble supplications to God for the foresaid things, for the which prayers there shall be a certain space kept in silence.*

This done, the Bishop shall pray in this wise.

The Lord be with you.
Answer. And with thy spirit.

¶ Let us pray.

Almighty God and heavenly Father, which of thy infinite love and goodness towards us, hast given to us thy only and most dear beloved Son Jesus Christ, to be our redeemer and author of everlasting life: who after he had made perfect our redemption by his death, and was ascended into heaven, sent abroad into the world his Apostles, Prophets, Evangelists, Doctors, and Pastors, by whose labour and ministry he gathered together a great flock in all parts of the world, to set forth the eternal praise of thy holy name: For these so great benefits of thy eternal goodness, and for that thou hast vouchsafed to call these thy servants here present to the same office and ministry of the salvation of mankind, we render unto thee most hearty thanks, we worship and praise thee; and we humbly beseech thee by the same thy Son, to grant unto all us which either here or elsewhere call upon thy name, that we may shew ourselves thankful to thee for these and all other thy benefits, and that we may daily increase and go forwards in the knowledge and faith of thee, and thy Son, by the Holy Spirit. So that as well by these

these things; Grant also unto you strength and power to perform the same; that he may accomplish his work which he hath begun in you; through Jesus Christ our Lord. *Amen.*

thy ministers, as by them to whom they shall be appointed ministers, thy holy name may be always glorified, and thy blessed kingdom enlarged: through the same thy Son our Lord Jesus Christ, which liveth and reigneth with thee in the unity of the same Holy Spirit world without end. Amen.

¶ *After this, the Congregation shall be desired, secretly in their Prayers, to make their humble supplications to God for all these things: for the which Prayers there shall be silence kept for a space.*

¶ *After which shall be sung or said by the Bishop (the persons to be Ordained Priests all kneeling)* Veni, Creator Spiritus: *the Bishop beginning, and the Priests, and others that are present, answering by verses, as followeth,*

COME, Holy Ghost, our souls inspire,
And lighten with celestial fire.
Thou the anointing Spirit art,
Who dost thy seven-fold gifts impart.

Thy blessed Unction from above,
Is comfort, life, and fire of love.
Enable with perpetual light
The dulness of our blinded sight.

Anoint and cheer our soiled face
With the abundance of thy grace.
Keep far our foes, give peace at home:
Where thou art guide, no ill can come.

Teach us to know the Father, Son,
And thee, of both, to be but One.
That, through the ages all along,
This may be our endless song:

Praise to thy eternal merit,
Father, Son, and Holy Spirit.

Or this:

COME, Holy Ghost, eternal God,
Proceeding from above,
Both from the Father and the Son,
The God of peace and love;

Visit our minds, into our hearts
  Thy heavenly grace inspire;
That truth and godliness we may
  Pursue with full desire.

Thou art the very Comforter
  In grief and all distress;
The heav'nly gift of God most high,
  No tongue can it express;

The fountain and the living spring
  Of joy celestial;
The fire so bright, the love so sweet,
  The Unction spiritual.

Thou in thy gifts art manifold,
  By them Christ's Church doth stand:
In faithful hearts thou writ'st thy law,
  The finger of God's hand.

According to thy promise, Lord,
  Thou givest speech with grace;
That through thy help God's praises may
  Resound in every place.

O Holy Ghost, into our minds
  Send down thy heav'nly light;
Kindle our hearts with fervent zeal,
  To serve God day and night.

Our weakness strengthen and confirm,
  (For, Lord, thou know'st us frail;)
That neither devil, world, nor flesh,
  Against us may prevail.

Put back our enemy far from us,
  And help us to obtain
Peace in our hearts with God and man,
  (The best, the truest gain;)

And grant that thou being, O Lord,
  Our leader and our guide,
We may escape the snares of sin,
  And never from thee slide.

Such measures of thy powerful grace
  Grant, Lord, to us, we pray;
That thou may'st be our Comforter
  At the last dreadful day.

Of strife and of dissention
  Dissolve, O Lord, the bands,
And knit the knots of peace and love
  Throughout all Christian lands.

Grant us the grace that we may know
  The Father of all might,
That we of his beloved Son
  May gain the blissful sight;

And that we may with perfect faith
  Ever acknowledge thee,
The Spirit of Father, and of Son,
  One God in Persons Three.

To God the Father laud and praise,
  And to his blessed Son,
And to the Holy Spirit of grace,
  Co-equal Three in One.

And pray we, that our only Lord
  Would please his Spirit to send
On all that shall profess his Name,
  From hence to the world's end.
  Amen.

¶ *That done, the Bishop shall pray in this wise, and say,*

Let us pray.

ALMIGHTY God, and heavenly Father, who, of thine infinite love and goodness towards us, hast given to us thy only and most dearly beloved Son Jesus Christ, to be our Redeemer, and the Author of everlasting life; who, after he had made perfect our redemption by his death, and was ascended into heaven, sent abroad into the world his Apostles, Prophets, Evangelists, Doctors, and Pastors; by whose labour and ministry he gathered together a great flock in all the parts of the world, to set forth the eternal praise of thy holy Name: For these so great benefits of thy eternal goodness, and for that thou hast vouchsafed to call these thy servants here present to the same Office and Ministry appointed for the salvation of mankind, we render unto thee most hearty thanks, we praise and wor-thee; and we humbly beseech thee, by the same thy blessed Son, to grant unto all, which either here or elsewhere call upon thy holy Name, that we may continue to shew ourselves thankful unto thee for these and all other thy benefits; and that we may daily increase and go forwards in the knowledge and faith of thee and thy Son, by the Holy Spirit. So that as well by these thy Ministers, as by them over whom they shall be appointed thy Ministers, thy holy Name may be for ever glorified, and thy blessed kingdom enlarged; through the same thy Son Jesus Christ our Lord, who liveth and reigneth with thee in the unity of the same Holy Spirit, world without end. *Amen.*

¶ *When this prayer is done, the Bishop with the Priests present shall lay their hands severally upon the head of every one that receiveth orders. The receivers humbly kneeling upon their knees, and the Bishop saying:*

RECEIVE the Holy Ghost: whose sins thou dost forgive, they are forgiven: and whose sins thou dost retain, they are retained: and be thou a faithful dispenser of the word of God, and of his holy sacraments. In the name of the Father, and of the Son, and of the Holy Ghost. Amen.

¶ *When this prayer is done, the Bishop with the Priests present shall lay their hands severally upon the head of every one that receiveth the Order of Priesthood; the Receivers humbly kneeling upon their knees, and the Bishop saying,*

RECEIVE the holy Ghost for the Office and work of a Priest in the Church of God, now committed unto thee by the Imposition of our hands. Whose sins thou dost forgive, they are forgiven; and whose sins thou dost retain, they are retained. And be thou a faithful Dispenser of the Word of God, and of his holy Sacraments; In the Name of the Father, and of the Son, and of the Holy Ghost. Amen.

The Bishop shall deliver to every one of them the Bible in the one hand, and the Chalice or cup with the bread, in the other hand, and say,

TAKE thou authority to preach the word of God, and to minister the holy Sacraments in this Congregation.

¶ *Then the Bishop shall deliver to every one of them kneeling, the Bible into his hand, saying,*

TAKE thou Authority to preach the Word of God, and to minister the holy Sacraments in the Congregation, where thou shalt be lawfully appointed thereunto.

¶ *When this is done, the Congregation shall sing the Creed, and also they shall go to the*

¶ *When this is done, the* Nicene *Creed shall be sung or said; and the Bishop shall after*

Communion, which all they that receive orders shall take together, and remain in the same place where the hands were laid upon them, until such time as they have received the Communion.

¶ *The Communion being done, after the last Collect, and immediately before the benediction, shall be said this Collect:*

Most merciful Father, we beseech thee, so to send upon these thy Servants thy heavenly blessing, that they may be clad about with all justice, and that thy word spoken by their mouths may have such success, that it may never be spoken in vain. Grant also that we may have grace to hear and receive the same as thy most holy word and the mean of our salvation, that in all our words and deeds we may seek thy glory and the increase of thy kingdom, through Jesus Christ our Lord. Amen.

¶ *If the orders of Deacon and Priesthood be given both upon one day, then shall the Psalm for the Introit and other things at the holy Communion be used as they are appointed at the ordering of Priests. Saving that for the Epistle, the whole iii. chapter of the first to Timothy shall be read, as it is*

that go on in the Service of the Communion, which all they that receive Orders shall take together, and remain in the same place where Hands were laid upon them, until such time as they have received the Communion.

¶ *The Communion being done, after the last Collect, and immediately before the Benediction, shall be said these Collects.*

MOST merciful Father, we beseech thee to send upon these thy servants thy heavenly blessing; that they may be clothed with righteousness, and that thy Word spoken by their mouths may have such success, that it may never be spoken in vain. Grant also, that we may have grace to hear and receive what they shall deliver out of thy most holy Word, or agreeable to the same, as the means of our salvation; that in all our words and deeds we may seek thy glory, and the increase of thy kingdom; through Jesus Christ our Lord. *Amen.*

PREVENT us, O Lord, in all our doings, with thy most gracious favour, and further us with thy continual help; that in all our works begun, continued, and ended in thee, we may glorify thy holy Name, and finally by thy mercy obtain everlasting life; through Jesus Christ our Lord. *Amen.*

THE peace of God, which passeth all understanding, keep your hearts and minds in the knowledge and love of God, and of his Son Jesus Christ our Lord; And the blessing of God Almighty, the Father, the Son, and the Holy Ghost, be amongst you, and remain with you always. *Amen.*

¶ *And if on the same day the Order of Deacons be given to some, and the Order of Priesthood to others; the Deacons shall be first presented, and then the Priests; and it shall suffice that the Litany be once said for both. The Collects shall both be used; first, that for Deacons, then that for Priests.*

set out before in the order of Priests. And immediately after the Epistle, the Deacons shall be ordered. And it shall suffice the Litany to be said once.

The Epistle shall be Ephes. iv. 7—13, *as before in this Office. Immediately after which, they that are to be made Deacons shall be examined, and Ordained, as is above prescribed. Then one of them having read the Gospel (which shall be either out of* St. Matth. ix. 36—38, *as before in this Office; or else* St. Luke xii. 35—38, *as before in the Form for the Ordering of Deacons,) they that are to be made Priests shall likewise be examined, and Ordained, as is in this Office before appointed.*

THE FORM OF CONSECRATING OF AN ARCHBISHOP OR BISHOP.

The Psalm for the Introit at the Communion, as at the Ordering of Priests.

The Epistle.

THIS is a true saying, If a man desire the office of a Bishop, he desireth an honest work. A Bishop therefore must be blameless, the husband of one wife, diligent, sober, discreet, a keeper of hospitality, apt to teach, not given to overmuch wine, no fighter, not greedy of filthy lucre, but gentle, abhorring fighting, abhorring covetousness, one that ruleth well his own house; one that hath children in subjection with all reverence. For if a man cannot rule his own house, how

1 Tim. iii.

THE FORM OF ORDAINING OR CONSECRATING OF AN ARCHBISHOP OR BISHOP;

WHICH IS ALWAYS TO BE PERFORMED UPON SOME SUNDAY OR HOLY-DAY.

¶ *When all things are duly prepared in the Church, and set in order, after Morning Prayer is ended, the Archbishop or (some other Bishop appointed) shall begin the Communion Service; in which this shall be*

The Collect.

ALMIGHTY God, who by thy Son Jesus Christ didst give to thy holy Apostles many excellent gifts, and didst charge them to feed thy flock; Give grace, we beseech thee, to all Bishops, the Pastors of thy Church, that they may diligently preach thy Word, and duly administer the godly Discipline thereof; and grant to the people, that they may obediently follow the same; that all may receive the crown of everlasting glory; through Jesus Christ our Lord. *Amen.*

¶ *And another Bishop shall read the Epistle.*

1 Tim. iii. 1.

THIS is a true saying, If a man desire the Office of a Bishop, he desireth a good work. A Bishop then must be blameless, the husband of one wife, vigilant, sober, of good behaviour, given to hospitality, apt to teach; not given to wine, no striker, not greedy of filthy lucre, but patient, not a brawler, not covetous; one that ruleth well his own house, having his children in subjection with all gravity; (For if a man know not how to rule his own house, how shall he take care of the Church

shall he care for the congregation of God? he may not be a young scholar, lest he swell, and fall into the judgment of the evil speaker. He must also have a good report of them which are without, lest he fall into rebuke and snare of the evil speaker.

of God?) Not a novice, lest being lifted up with pride he fall into the condemnation of the devil. Moreover, he must have a good report of them which are without; lest he fall into reproach, and the snare of the devil.

Or this.

For the Epistle. Acts xx. 17.

FROM Miletus Paul sent to Ephesus, and called the elders of the Church. And when they were come to him, he said unto them, Ye know, from the first day that I came into Asia, after what manner I have been with you at all seasons, serving the Lord with all humility of mind, and with many tears and temptations which befel me by the lying in wait of the Jews: And how I kept back nothing that was profitable unto you, but have shewed you, and have taught you publickly, and from house to house, testifying both to the Jews, and also to the Greeks, repentance toward God, and faith toward our Lord Jesus Christ. And now behold, I go bound in the spirit unto Jerusalem, not knowing the things that shall befal me there; save that the Holy Ghost witnesseth in every city, saying, That bonds and afflictions abide me. But none of these things move me, neither count I my life dear unto myself, so that I might finish my course with joy, and the ministry which I have received of the Lord Jesus, to testify the Gospel of the grace of God. And now behold, I know that ye all, among whom I have gone preaching the kingdom of God, shall see my face no more. Wherefore I take you to record this day, that I am pure from the blood of all men. For I have not shunned to declare unto you all the counsel of God. Take heed therefore unto yourselves, and to all the flock over the which the Holy Ghost hath made you Overseers, to feed the Church of God, which he hath purchased with his own blood. For I know this, that after my departing shall grievous wolves enter in among you, not sparing the flock. Also of your own selves shall men arise speaking perverse things, to draw away disciples after them. Therefore watch, and remember, that by the space of three years, I ceased not to warn every one night and day with tears. And now, brethren, I commend you to God, and to the word of his grace, which is able to build you up, and to give you an inheritance among all them which are sanctified. I have coveted no man's silver, or gold, or apparel; yea, ye yourselves know, that these hands have ministered unto my necessities, and to them that were with me. I have shewed you all things, how that so labouring ye ought to support the weak; and to remember the words of the Lord Jesus, how he said, It is more blessed to give than to receive.

The Gospel.

JESUS said to Simon Peter, Simon Johanna, lovest thou me more than these? He said unto him, Yea, Lord, thou knowest that I love thee. He said unto him, Feed my lambs. He said to him again the second time: Simon Johanna, lovest thou me? He said unto him, Yea, Lord, thou knowest that I love thee. He said unto him, Feed my sheep. He said unto him the third time, Simon Johanna, lovest thou me? Peter was sorry because he said unto him the third time, Lovest thou me? and he said unto him: Lord, thou knowest all

John xxi.

¶ *Then another Bishop shall read the Gospel.*

St. John xxi. 15.

JESUS saith to Simon Peter, Simon, son of Jonas, lovest thou me more than these? He saith unto him, Yea, Lord, thou knowest that I love thee. He saith unto him, Feed my lambs. He saith to him again the second time, Simon, Son of Jonas, lovest thou me? He saith unto him, Yea, Lord, thou knowest that I love thee. He saith unto him, Feed my sheep. He saith unto him the third time, Simon, son of Jonas, lovest thou me? Peter was grieved because he said unto him the third time, Lovest thou

things, thou knowest that I love thee. Jesus said unto him, Feed my sheep.

¶ *Or else out of the x. Chapter of John, as before in the order of Priests.*

¶ *After the Gospel and Credo ended, first the elected Bishop, having upon him a surplice and a cope, shall be presented by two Bishops (being also in surplices and copes, and having their pastoral staves in their hands) unto the Archbishop of the Province, or to some other Bishop appointed by his commission: the Bishops that present, saying:*

MOST reverend Father in God, we present unto you this godly

me? And he said unto him, Lord, thou knowest all things; thou knowest that I love thee. Jesus saith unto him, Feed my sheep.

Or else this. St. John xx. 19.

THE same day at evening, being the first day of the week, when the doors were shut where the disciples were assembled for fear of the Jews, came Jesus, and stood in the midst, and saith unto them, Peace be unto you. And when he had so said, he shewed unto them his hands and his side. Then were the disciples glad, when they saw the Lord. Then saith Jesus to them again, Peace be unto you: as my Father hath sent me, even so send I you. And when he had said this, he breathed on them, and saith unto them, Receive ye the holy Ghost. Whosesoever sins ye remit, they are remitted unto them; and whosesoever sins ye retain, they are retained.

Or this. St. Matt. xxviii. 18.

JESUS came and spake unto them, saying, All power is given unto me in heaven and in earth. Go ye therefore and teach all nations, baptizing them In the Name of the Father, and of the Son, and of the Holy Ghost; teaching them to observe all things whatsoever I have commanded you: and lo, I am with you alway, even unto the end of the world.

¶ *After the Gospel, and the* Nicene *Creed, and the Sermon are ended, the Elected Bishop (vested with his Rochet) shall be presented by two Bishops unto the Archbishop of that province (or to some other Bishop appointed by lawful commission) the Archbishop sitting in his chair near the holy Table, and the Bishops that present him saying,*

MOST Reverend Father in God, we present unto you this

and well learned man to be consecrated Bishop.

¶ *And then the King's mandate to the Archbishop for the Consecration shall be read. And the oath touching the knowledging of the King's supremacy shall be ministered to the person elected, as it is set out in the order of Deacons. And then shall be ministered also the Oath of due obedience unto the Archbishop as followeth.*

¶ *THE OATH OF DUE OBEDIENCE to the Archbishop.*

In the Name of GOD, Amen. I, *N.* chosen Bishop of the church and see of *N.* do profess and promise all due reverence and obedience to the Archbishop and to the Metropolitical church of *N.* and to their successors, so help me God and his holy Gospel.

¶ *Then the Archbishop shall move the congregation present to pray, saying thus to them.*

Brethren, it is written in the Gospel of Saint Luke, that our Saviour Christ continued the whole night in prayer or ever that he did choose and send forth his xii. Apostles. It is written also in the Acts of the Apostles, that the disciples which were at Antioch did fast and pray or ever they laid hands upon or sent forth Paul and Barnabas. Let us therefore, following the example of our Saviour Christ and his Apostles, first fall to prayer or that we admit and send forth this person presented unto us, to the work whereunto we trust the Holy Ghost hath called him.

¶ *And then shall be said the Litany as afore in the order of Deacons. And after this place: That it may please thee to illuminate all Bishops &c. he shall say.*

godly and well-learned man to be Ordained and Consecrated Bishop.

¶ *Then shall the Archbishop demand the Queen's Mandate for the Consecration, and cause it to be read. And then shall be ministered unto them the Oath of due Obedience to the Archbishop, as followeth.*

The Oath of due Obedience to the Archbishop.

In the Name of God. Amen. I *N.* chosen Bishop of the Church and See of *N.* do profess and promise all due reverence and obedience to the Archbishop and to the Metropolitical Church of *N.* and to their Successors: So help me God, through Jesus Christ.

¶ *This Oath shall not be made at the Consecration of an Archbishop.*

¶ *Then the Archbishop shall move the Congregation present to pray, saying thus to them:*

Brethren, it is written in the Gospel of Saint Luke, That our Saviour Christ continued the whole night in prayer, before he did choose and send forth his twelve Apostles. It is written also in the Acts of the Apostles, That the Disciples who were at Antioch did fast and pray, before they laid hands on Paul and Barnabas, and sent them forth. Let us therefore, following the example of our Saviour Christ, and his Apostles, first fall to prayer, before we admit, and send forth this person presented unto us, to the work whereunto we trust the Holy Ghost hath called him.

¶ *And then shall be said the Litany, as before in the Form of Ordering Deacons, save only, that after this place* That it may please thee to illuminate all Bishops, &c. *the proper Suffrage there following shall be omitted, and this inserted instead of it;*

THAT it may please thee to bless this our brother elected, and to send thy grace upon him, that he may duly execute the office whereunto he is called, to the edifying of thy church, and to the honour, praise and glory of thy name.

Answer. We beseech thee to hear us, good Lord.

Concluding the Litany in the end with this prayer:

ALMIGHTY God, giver of all good things, which by thy Holy Spirit hast appointed divers orders of Ministers in thy Church: mercifully behold this thy servant now called to the work and ministry of a Bishop, and replenish him so with the truth of thy doctrine and innocency of life, that both by word and deed he may faithfully serve thee in this office, to the glory of thy name, and profit of thy congregation: through the merits of our Saviour Jesu Christ, who liveth and reigneth with thee and the Holy Ghost, world without end. Amen.

Then the Archbishop sitting in a chair, shall say this to him that is to be consecrated.

BROTHER, forasmuch as holy Scripture and the old Canons commandeth that we should not be hasty in laying on hands and admitting of any person to the government of the congregation of Christ, which he hath purchased with no less price than the effusion of his own blood, afore that I admit you to this administration whereunto ye are called, I will examine you in certain articles, to the end the Congregation present may have a trial and bear witness how ye be minded to behave yourself in the church of God.

Are you persuaded that you be truly called to this ministration

THAT it may please thee to bless this our Brother elected, and to send thy grace upon him, that he may duly execute the Office whereunto he is called, to the edifying of thy Church, and to the honour, praise, and glory of thy Name;

Answer. *We beseech thee to hear us, good Lord.*

¶ *Then shall be said this prayer following.*

ALMIGHTY God, giver of all good things, who by thy Holy Spirit hast appointed divers Orders of Ministers in thy Church; Mercifully behold this thy servant now called to the Work and Ministry of a Bishop; and replenish him so with the truth of thy doctrine, and adorn him with innocency of life, that, both by word and deed, he may faithfully serve thee in this Office, to the glory of thy Name, and the edifying and well-governing of thy Church; through the merits of our Saviour Jesus Christ, who liveth and reigneth with thee and the Holy Ghost, world without end. *Amen.*

¶ *Then the Archbishop, sitting in his chair, shall say to him that is to be Consecrated,*

BROTHER, forasmuch as the holy Scripture and the ancient Canons command, that we should not be hasty in laying on hands, and admitting any person to Government in the Church of Christ, which he hath purchased with no less price than the effusion of his own blood; before I admit you to this Administration, I will examine you in certain Articles, to the end that the Congregation present may have a trial, and bear witness, how you be minded to behave yourself in the Church of God.

ARE you persuaded that you be truly called to this Ministra-

according to the will of our Lord Jesus Christ and the order of this realm?

Answer. I am so persuaded.

The Archbishop. Are you persuaded that the holy Scriptures contain sufficiently all doctrine required of necessity for eternal salvation through the faith in Jesu Christ? And are you determined with the same holy Scriptures to instruct the people committed to your charge, and to teach or maintain nothing, as required of necessity to eternal salvation, but that you shall be persuaded may be concluded and proved by the same?

Answer. I am so persuaded and determined by God's grace.

The Archbishop. Will you then faithfully exercise yourself in the said holy Scriptures, and call upon God by prayer for the true understanding of the same, so as ye may be able by them to teach and exhort with wholesome doctrine, and to withstand and convince the gainsayers?

Answer. I will so do, by the help of God.

The Archbishop. Be you ready with all faithful diligence to banish and drive away all erroneous and strange doctrine contrary to God's word, and both privately and openly to call upon and encourage other to the same?

Answer. I am ready, the Lord being my helper.

The Archbishop. Will you deny all ungodliness, and worldly lusts, and live soberly, righteously, and

tion, according to the will of our Lord Jesus Christ, and the order of this Realm?

Answer. I am so persuaded.

The Archbishop.

ARE you persuaded that the holy Scriptures contain sufficiently all Doctrine required of necessity for eternal salvation through faith in Jesus Christ? And are you determined out of the same holy Scriptures to instruct the people committed to your charge; and to teach or maintain nothing as required of necessity to eternal salvation, but that which you shall be persuaded may be concluded and proved by the same?

Answer. I am so persuaded, and determined, by God's grace.

The Archbishop.

WILL you then faithfully exercise yourself in the same holy Scriptures, and call upon God by prayer, for the true understanding of the same; so as you may be able by them to teach and exhort with wholesome Doctrine, and to withstand and convince the gainsayers?

Answer. I will so do, by the help of God.

The Archbishop.

ARE you ready, with all faithful diligence, to banish and drive away all erroneous and strange doctrine contrary to God's Word; and both privately and openly to call upon and encourage others to the same?

Answer. I am ready, the Lord being my helper.

The Archbishop.

WILL you deny all ungodliness and worldly lusts, and live soberly, righteously, and god-

Godly in this world, that you may shew yourself in all things an example of good works unto other, that the adversary may be ashamed, having nothing to lay against you?

Answer. I will so do, the Lord being my helper.

The Archbishop. Will you maintain and set forward, (as much as shall lie in you) quietness, peace, and love, among all men? And such as be unquiet, disobedient, and criminous within your diocese, correct and punish, according to such authority, as ye have by God's word, and as to you shall be committed, by the ordinance of this realm?

Answer. I will so do, by the help of God.

The Archbishop. Will you shew yourself gentle, and be merciful for Christ's sake, to poor and needy people, and to all strangers destitute of help?

Answer. I will so shew myself by God's grace.

The Archbishop. Almighty God our heavenly Father, who hath given you a good will to do all these things, grant also unto you strength and power, to perform the same, that he accomplishing in you the good work which he hath begun, ye may be found perfect, and irreprehensible at the latter day, through Jesu Christ our Lord. Amen.

ly in this present world; that you may shew yourself in all things an example of good works unto others, that the adversary may be ashamed, having nothing to say against you?

Answer. I will so do, the Lord being my helper.

The Archbishop.

WILL you maintain and set forward, as much as shall lie in you, quietness, love, and peace among all men; and such as be unquiet, disobedient, and criminous, within your Diocese, correct and punish, according to such authority as you have by God's Word, and as to you shall be committed by the Ordinance of this Realm?

Answer. I will so do, by the help of God.

The Archbishop.

WILL you be faithful in Ordaining sending, or laying hands upon others?

Answer. I will so be, by the help of God.

The Archbishop.

WILL you shew yourself gentle, and be merciful for Christ's sake to poor and needy people, and to all strangers destitute of help?

Answer. I will so shew myself, by God's help.

¶ *Then the Archbishop standing up shall say.*

ALMIGHTY God, our heavenly Father, who hath given you a good will to do all these things, Grant also unto you strength and power to perform the same; that, he accomplishing in you the good work which he hath begun, you may be found perfect and irreprehensible at the latter day; through Jesus Christ our Lord. *Amen*.

Then shall be sung or said Come Holy Ghost, *&c., as it is set out in the Order of Priests.*

¶ *Then shall the Bishop elect put on the rest of the Episcopal habit; and kneeling down,* Veni, Creator Spiritus, *shall be sung or said over him, the Archbishop beginning, and the Bishops, with others that are present, answering by verses, as followeth.*

COME, Holy Ghost, our souls inspire,
And lighten with celestial fire.
Thou the anointing Spirit art,
Who dost thy seven-fold gifts impart.

Thy blessed Unction from above,
Is comfort, life, and fire of love.
Enable with perpetual light
The dulness of our blinded sight.

Anoint and cheer our soiled face
With the abundance of thy grace.
Keep far our foes, give peace at home:
Where thou art guide, no ill can come.

Teach us to know the Father, Son,
And thee, of both, to be but One.
That, through the ages all along,
This may be our endless song;

Praise to thy eternal merit,
Father, Son, and Holy Spirit.

Or this:

COME, Holy Ghost, eternal God,
Proceeding from above, &c.

As before in the Form for Ordering Priests.

That ended, the Archbishop shall say,

The Lord be with you.
Answer. And with thy spirit.

¶ *That ended, the Archbishop shall say,*

Lord, hear our prayer.
Answer. And let our cry come unto thee.

¶ Let us pray.

ALMIGHTY God and most merciful Father, which of thy infinite goodness, hast given to us thy only and most dear beloved Son Jesus Christ, to be our redeemer and author of everlasting life, who after that he had made perfect our redemption by his death, and was ascended into heaven, poured down

Let us pray.

ALMIGHTY God, and most merciful Father, who of thine infinite goodness hast given thine only and dearly beloved Son Jesus Christ, to be our Redeemer, and the Author of everlasting life; who, after that he had made perfect our Redemption by his death, and was ascended into heaven, poured his gifts abundantly upon men, making some Apostles, some Prophets, some Evangelists, some Pastors and Doctors, to the edifying and making perfect of his congregation: Grant, we beseech thee, to this thy servant such grace, that he may be evermore ready to spread abroad thy Gospel, and glad tidings of reconcilement to God, and to use the authority given unto him, not to destroy, but to save, not to hurt, but to help, so that he as a faithful and wise servant, giving to thy family meat in due season, may at the last day be received into joy, through Jesu Christ our Lord, who with thee and the Holy Ghost liveth and reigneth one God, world without end. Amen.

Then the Archbishop and Bishops present shall lay their hands upon the head of the elect Bishop, the Archbishop saying,

TAKE the Holy Ghost, and remember that thou stir up the grace of God, which is in thee, by imposition of hands: for God hath not given us the spirit of fear, but of power, and love, and of soberness.

Then the Archbishop shall lay the Bible upon his neck, saying,

GIVE heed unto reading, exhortation and doctrine, think upon those things contained in this book, be diligent in them, that the increase coming thereby may be manifest unto all men. Take heed unto thyself, and unto teaching, and be diligent in doing them, for by doing this thou shalt save thyself and them that hear thee, through Jesus Christ our Lord.

down his gifts abundantly upon men, making some Apostles, some Prophets, some Evangelists, some Pastors and Doctors, to the edifying and making perfect his Church; Grant, we beseech thee, to this thy servant such grace, that he may evermore be ready to spread abroad thy Gospel, the glad tidings of reconciliation with thee; and use the authority given him, not to destruction, but to salvation; not to hurt, but to help; so that as a wise and faithful servant, giving to thy family their portion in due season, he may at last be received into everlasting joy; through Jesus Christ our Lord, who, with thee and the Holy Ghost liveth and reigneth, one God, world without end. *Amen.*

¶ *Then the Archbishop and Bishops present shall lay their hands upon the head of the elected Bishop kneeling before them upon his knees, the Archbishop saying,*

RECEIVE the holy Ghost, for the Office and Work of a Bishop in the Church of God, now committed unto thee by the Imposition of our hands; In the Name of the Father, and of the Son, and of the Holy Ghost. Amen. And remember that thou stir up the grace of God which is given thee by this Imposition of our hands: for God hath not given us the spirit of fear, but of power, and love, and soberness.

¶ *Then the Archbishop shall deliver him the Bible, saying,*

GIVE heed unto reading, exhortation, and doctrine. Think upon the things contained in this Book. Be diligent in them, that the increase coming thereby may be manifest unto all men. Take heed unto thyself, and to doctrine, and be diligent in doing them: for by so doing thou shalt both save thyself and them that hear thee.

Then shall the Archbishop put into his hand the pastoral staff, saying:

Be to the flock of Christ a shepherd, not a wolf, feed them, devour them not, hold up the weak, heal the sick, bind together the broken, bring again the outcasts, seek the lost: Be so merciful that you be not too remiss, so minister discipline, that ye forget not mercy, that when the chief Shepherd shall come, ye may receive the immarcessible Crown of glory, through Jesus Christ our Lord.

¶ *Then the Archbishop shall proceed to the Communion, with whom the new consecrated Bishop shall also communicate. And after the last Collect, immediately afore the benediction, shall be said this prayer:*

Most merciful Father, we beseech thee to send down upon this thy servant thy heavenly blessing, and so endue him with thy Holy Spirit, that he preaching thy word, may not only be earnest to reprove, beseech, and rebuke with all patience and Doctrine, but also may be to such as believe an wholesome example in word, in conversation, in love, in faith, in chastity, and purity, that faithfully fulfilling his course, at the latter day he may receive the crown of righteousness, laid up by the Lord, the righteous Judge, who liveth and reigneth, one God with the Father and Holy Ghost, world without end. Amen.

Be to the flock of Christ a shepherd, not a wolf; feed them, devour them not. Hold up the weak, heal the sick, bind up the broken, bring again the outcasts, seek the lost. Be so merciful, that you be not too remiss; so minister discipline, that you forget not mercy: that when the chief Shepherd shall appear you may receive the never-fading crown of glory; through Jesus Christ our Lord. *Amen.*

¶ *Then the Archbishop shall proceed in the Communion-Service; with whom the new Consecrated Bishop (with others) shall also communicate.*

¶ *And for the last Collect, immediately before the Benediction, shall be said these Prayers.*

MOST merciful Father, we beseech thee to send down upon this thy servant thy heavenly blessing; and so endue him with thy holy Spirit, that he, preaching thy Word, may not only be earnest to reprove, beseech, and rebuke with all patience and doctrine; but also may be to such as believe a wholesome example, in word, in conversation, in love, in faith, in chastity, and in purity; that, faithfully fulfilling his course, at the latter day he may receive the crown of righteousness laid up by the Lord the righteous Judge, who liveth and reigneth one God with the Father and the Holy Ghost, world without end. *Amen.*

PREVENT us, O Lord, in all our doings, with thy most gracious favour, and further us with thy continual help; that in all our works begun, continued, and ended in thee, we may glorify thy holy Name, and finally by thy mercy obtain everlasting life; through Jesus Christ our Lord. *Amen.*

RICHARDVS GRAFTON

typographus Regius excudebat.

Mense Martii

A.M.D.XLIX

Cum priuilegio ad imprimendum solum.

THE peace of God, which passeth all understanding, keep your hearts and minds in the knowledge and love of God, and of his Son Jesus Christ our Lord: And the blessing of God Almighty, the Father, the Son, and the Holy Ghost be amongst you, and remain with you always. *Amen.*

A FORM OF

PRAYER WITH THANKSGIVING

TO BE USED UPON THE

TWENTIETH DAY OF JUNE. (s)

(s) This Form of Prayer is not printed here, as there was no corresponding Service in Edward's Book.

ARTICLES OF RELIGION. (t)

(t) The Articles are not printed in this volume, as they have no part in the First Prayer Book of Edward VI.

A TABLE OF KINDRED AND AFFINITY,

WHEREIN WHOSOEVER ARE RELATED ARE FORBIDDEN IN SCRIPTURE AND OUR LAWS TO MARRY TOGETHER.

A Man may not marry his

1 GRANDMOTHER,
2 Grandfather's Wife,
3 Wife's Grandmother.

4 Father's Sister,
5 Mother's Sister,
6 Father's Brother's Wife.

7 Mother's Brother's Wife,
8 Wife's Father's Sister,
9 Wife's Mother's Sister.

10 Mother,
11 Step-Mother,
12 Wife's Mother.

13 Daughter,
14 Wife's Daughter,
15 Son's Wife.

16 Sister,
17 Wife's Sister,
18 Brother's Wife.

19 Son's Daughter,
20 Daughter's Daughter,
21 Son's Son's Wife.

22 Daughter's Son's Wife,
23 Wife's Son's Daughter,
24 Wife's Daughter's Daughter.

25 Brother's Daughter,
26 Sister's Daughter,
27 Brother's Son's Wife.

28 Sister's Son's Wife,
29 Wife's Brother's Daughter,
30 Wife's Sister's Daughter.

A TABLE
OF
KINDRED AND AFFINITY,
CONTINUED.

A Woman may not marry with her

1 GRANDFATHER,
2 Grandmother's Husband,
3 Husband's Grandfather.

4 Father's Brother,
5 Mother's Brother,
6 Father's Sister's Husband.

7 Mother's Sister's Husband,
8 Husband's Father's Brother,
9 Husband's Mother's Brother.

10 Father,
11 Step-Father,
12 Husband's Father.

13 Son,
14 Husband's Son,
15 Daughter's Husband.

16 Brother,
17 Husband's Brother,
18 Sister's Husband.

19 Son's Son,
20 Daughter's Son,
21 Son's Daughter's Husband.

22 Daughter's Daughter's Husband,
23 Husband's Son's Son,
24 Husband's Daughter's Son.

25 Brother's Son,
26 Sister's Son,
27 Brother's Daughter's Husband.

28 Sister's Daughter's Husband.
29 Husband's Brother's Son,
30 Husband's Sister's Son.

THE END.

APPENDICES.

Appendix I.

Tabular View of Morning and Evening Prayer.

Appendix II.

Tabular View of Office for Holy Communion.

Appendix III.

Exhortations to Holy Communion Compared.

Appendix IV.

Prayer of Consecration Compared.

APPENDIX 1.

TABULAR VIEW OF ORDER FOR MORNING AND EVENING PRAYER.

1549]	[1886
MATINS.	MORNING PRAYER.
	Sentences of Holy Scripture.
	Exhortation.
	Confession.
	Absolution.
Lord's Prayer by Priest, with Answer, 'Deliver us &c.'	Lord's Prayer by Priest and People.
'O Lord open thou my lips' and Answer.	'O Lord open thou our lips' and Answer.
'O Lord make speed to save me' and Answer.	'O God make speed to save us' and Answer.
'Gloria Patri' by Priest.	'Gloria Patri' and Answer.
'Praise ye the Lord.'	'Praise ye the Lord' and Answer.
Venite.	Venite.
Psalms in order, with Gloria Patri.	Psalms in order, with Gloria Patri.
First Lesson.	First Lesson.
Te Deum, or Benedicite (in Lent).	Te Deum, or Benedicite.
Second Lesson.	Second Lesson.
Benedictus.	Benedictus, or Jubilate.
Lesser Litany.	
Apostles' Creed by Minister.	Apostles' Creed by Minister and People.
Lord's Prayer by Minister, with Answer by People, 'Deliver us &c.'	
Versicles.	
Salutation. 'The Lord be with you, &c.'	Salutation. 'The Lord be with you, &c.'

	Lesser Litany.
	Lord's Prayer by Minister, Clerks, and People.
	Versicles.
Collect of the Day.	Collect of the Day.
„ for Peace.	„ for Peace.
„ for Grace.	„ for Grace.
	Anthem (in Quires).
	Prayer for Queen.
	„ Royal Family.
	„ Clergy and People.
	Prayer of St. Chrysostom. II. Cor. xiii.
EVENSONG.	**EVENING PRAYER.**
As at Matins, (except that Psalms follow immediately after 'Praise ye the Lord, &c.') to First Lesson.	As at Morning Prayer, (except that Psalms follow immediately after 'Praise ye, &c.') to First Lesson.
Magnificat.	Magnificat, or Cantate.
Second Lesson.	Second Lesson.
Nunc Dimittis.	Nunc Dimittis, or Deus Misereatur.
As at Matins to	As at Morning Prayer to
2nd Collect of Peace.	2nd Collect for Peace.
3rd „ of aid against Perils.	3rd „ for aid against all Perils.
	Anthem (in Quires).
	Prayer for Queen, &c., as at Morning Prayer.

APPENDIX II.

TABULAR VIEW OF OFFICE FOR THE HOLY COMMUNION.

1549]	[1886
FIRST PRAYER BOOK OF EDWARD VI.	THE PRESENT BOOK OF COMMON PRAYER.
THE SUPPER OF THE LORD AND THE HOLY COMMUNION, COMMONLY CALLED THE MASS.	THE ORDER OF THE ADMINISTRATION OF THE LORD'S SUPPER OR HOLY COMMUNION.
The priest, standing humbly afore the middle of the Altar, shall say, &c.	*The priest, standing at the North side of the Table, shall say, &c.*
The Lord's Prayer.	The Lord's Prayer.
Collect for Purity.	Collect for Purity.
Introit.	
'Lord have mercy upon us,' &c.	
Gloria in Excelsis.	
'The Lord be with you,' and Answer.	
	The Ten Commandments, with prayer following, 'Lord have mercy upon us and incline &c.'
One of two Collects for the King.	One of two Collects for the Queen.
The Collect of the Day.	The Collect of the Day.
The Epistle.	The Epistle.
The Holy Gospel.	The Holy Gospel.
The Nicene Creed.	The Nicene Creed.
Sermon or Homily.	Sermon or Homily.

The Exhortation (to those minded to receive).	
The Exhortation (if people negligent).	
The Offertory.	The Offertory.
	The Alms presented and placed upon the Holy Table.
The Bread and Wine (with a little pure and clean water put thereto) set upon the Altar.	The Bread and Wine placed upon the Table.
Sursum Corda.	
Preface.	
Ter Sanctus.	
The PRAYER OF CONSECRATION, commencing with the	
Prayer for 'the whole State of Christ's Church,' which includes	Prayer for 'the whole State of Christ's Church militant here in earth,' which includes
	Prayer for acceptance of alms and oblations.
Prayer for the living.	Prayer for the living.
Thanksgiving for the dead.	Thanksgiving for the dead.
Prayer for the Dead.	
The Invocation of the Holy Spirit upon the Elements (the sign of the Cross being used).	
The Words of Institution.	
The prayer of Oblation of the elements as a Memorial, and of ourselves as a living Sacrifice.	
The Lord's Prayer.	
The Salutation: 'The peace of the Lord be always with you,' and Answer.	
A Commemoration of the Sacrifice of Christ as the Paschal Lamb.	
	The Exhortation (on Sunday before).
	The Exhortation (if people negligent).
	The Exhortation (at time of Communion).
The Invitation.	The Invitation.
The Confession.	The Confession.

1549	1886
The Absolution.	The Absolution.
The Comfortable Words.	The Comfortable Words.
	Sursum Corda.
	Preface.
	Ter Sanctus.
The prayer of Humble Access.	The Prayer of Humble Access.
	The PRAYER OF CONSECRATION with the Words of Institution, and breaking of Bread, and laying of hands on Bread and on vessels containing Wine.
COMMUNION.	COMMUNION.
Words of Administration, one clause; 'the people to receive the Sacrament of Christ's body in their mouths at the priest's hand.'	Words of Administration, two clauses; 'the Bread to be delivered to the people into their hands.'
Agnus Dei.	
The Post Communion. Anthem.	
	The Lord's Prayer.
	The Oblation of ourselves as a living Sacrifice, or
The Thanksgiving.	The Thanksgiving.
	Gloria in Excelsis.
The Blessing.	The Blessing.

APPENDIX III.

THE EXHORTATIONS TO HOLY COMMUNION COMPARED.

i.

1549]

¶ *After the Creed ended, shall follow the Sermon or Homily, or some portion of one of the Homilies, as they shall be hereafter divided: wherein if the people be not exhorted to the worthy receiving of the holy Sacrament of the body and blood of our Saviour Christ, then shall the Curate give this exhortation, to those that be minded to receive the same.*

Dearly beloved in the Lord, ye that mind to come to the holy Communion of the body and blood of our Saviour Christ, must consider what St. Paul writeth to the Corinthians, how he exhorteth all persons diligently to try and examine themselves, before they presume to eat of that bread and drink of that cup: for as the benefit is great, if with a truly penitent heart, and lively faith, we receive that holy Sacrament; (for then we spiritually eat the flesh of Christ, and drink his blood, then we dwell in Christ and Christ in us, we be made one with Christ and Christ with us;) so is the danger great, if we receive the same unworthily; for then we become guilty of the body and blood of Christ our Saviour, we eat and drink our own damnation, not considering the Lord's body. We kindle God's wrath over us, we provoke him to plague us with divers diseases and sundry kinds of death.

[1886

¶ *At the time of the celebration of the Communion, the Communicants being conveniently placed for the receiving of the holy Sacrament, the Priest shall say this Exhortation.* (1)

DEARLY beloved in the Lord, ye that mind to come to the holy Communion of the Body and Blood of our Saviour Christ, must consider how Saint Paul exhorteth all persons diligently to try and examine themselves, before they presume to eat of that Bread, and drink of that Cup. For as the benefit is great, if with a true penitent heart and lively faith we receive that holy Sacrament; (for then we spiritually eat the flesh of Christ, and drink his blood; then we dwell in Christ, and Christ in us; we are one with Christ, and Christ with us;) so is the danger great, if we receive the same unworthily. For then we are guilty of the Body and Blood of Christ our Saviour; we eat and drink our own damnation, not considering the Lord's body; we kindle God's wrath against us; we provoke him to plague us with divers diseases and sundry kinds of death.

(1) This Exhortation in 1886 comes immediately before the Invitation.

Therefore if any here be a blasphemer, advouterer, or be in malice, or envy, or in any other grievous crime (except he be truly sorry therefore, and earnestly minded to leave the same vices, and do trust himself to be reconciled to Almighty God, and in charity with all the world), let him bewail his sins, and not come to that holy table; lest after the taking of that most blessed bread, the devil enter into him, as he did into Judas, to fill him full of all iniquity, and to bring him to destruction, both of body and soul. (2)

Judge therefore yourselves(brethren) that ye be not judged of the Lord. Let your minds be without desire to sin, repent you truly for your sins past, have an earnest and lively faith in Christ our Saviour, be in perfect charity with all men; so shall ye be meet partakers of those holy mysteries. And above all things: ye must give most humble and hearty thanks to God the Father, the Son, and the Holy Ghost, for the redemption of the world by the death and passion of our Saviour Christ, both God and man, who did humble himself even to the death upon the cross, for us miserable sinners, which lay in darkness and shadow of death, that he might make us the children of God, and exalt us to everlasting life. And to the end that we should alway remember the exceeding love of our Master, and only Saviour Jesu Christ, thus dying for us, and the innumerable benefits which (by his precious blood-shedding) he hath obtained to us, he hath left in those holy mysteries, as a pledge of his love, and a continual, remembrance of the same, his own blessed body, and precious blood, for us to feed upon spiritually, to our endless

(2) This Paragraph forms part of the first Exhortation in giving warning of Celebration, in present book, 1886—(see note 4.)

Judge therefore yourselves, brethren, that ye be not judged of the Lord; repent you truly for your sins past; have a lively and stedfast faith in Christ our Saviour; amend your lives, and be in perfect charity with all men; so shall ye be meet partakers of those holy mysteries. And above all things ye must give most humble and hearty thanks to God, the Father, the Son, and the Holy Ghost, for the redemption of the world by the death and passion of our Saviour Christ, both God and man; who did humble himself, even to the death upon the Cross, for us, miserable sinners, who lay in darkness and the shadow of death; that he might make us the children of God, and exalt us to everlasting life. And to the end that we should alway remember the exceeding great love of our Master, and only Saviour, Jesus Christ, thus dying for us, and the innumerable benefits which by his precious blood-shedding he hath obtained to us; he hath instituted and ordained holy mysteries, as pledges of his love, and for a continual remembrance of his death, to our great and endless comfort.

comfort and consolation. To him therefore, with the Father and the Holy Ghost, let us give (as we are most bounden) continual thanks, submitting ourselves wholly to his holy will and pleasure, and studying to serve him in true holiness and righteousness, all the days of our life. Amen.

¶ *In Cathedral churches or other places, where there is daily Communion, it shall be sufficient to read this exhortation above written, once in a month. And in parish churches, upon the week days it may be left unsaid.*

To him therefore, with the Father and the Holy Ghost, let us give (as we are most bounden) continual thanks; submitting ourselves wholly to his holy will and pleasure, and studying to serve him in true holiness and righteousness all the days of our life. *Amen.*

ii.

¶ *And if upon the Sunday or holyday, the people be negligent to come to the Communion: Then shall the Priest earnestly exhort his parishioners, to dispose themselves to the receiving of the holy communion more diligently, saying these or like words unto them.* (3)

DEAR friends, and you especially upon whose souls I have cure and charge, on next, I do intend by God's grace, to offer to all such as shall be godly disposed, the most comfortable Sacrament of the body and blood of Christ, to be taken of them in the remembrance of his most fruitful and glorious Passion: by the which passion we have obtained remission of our sins, and be made partakers of the kingdom of heaven, whereof we be assured and ascertained, if we come to the said Sacrament with hearty repentance for our offences, stedfast faith in God's mercy, and earnest mind to obey God's will, and to offend no more. Wherefore our duty is to come to these holy mysteries, with most hearty thanks to be given to Almighty GOD for his infinite mercy and benefits given and bestowed upon us his unworthy servants, for whom he hath not only given his body to death, and

(3) In present Prayer Book there is a third Exhortation ('*if the people be negligent*') which has not a parallel in 1549.

¶ *When the Minister giveth warning for the celebration of the holy Communion, (which he shall always do upon the Sunday, or some Holy-day, immediately preceding,) after the Sermon or Homily ended, he shall read this Exhortation following*

DEARLY beloved, on——day next I purpose, through God's assistance, to administer to all such as shall be religiously and devoutly disposed the most comfortable Sacrament of the Body and Blood of Christ; to be by them received in remembrance of his meritorious Cross and Passion; whereby alone we obtain remission of our sins, and are made partakers of the Kingdom of heaven.

Wherefore it is our duty to render most humble and hearty thanks to Almighty God our heavenly Father, for that he hath given his Son our Saviour Jesus Christ, not only to die for us, but also to be our spiritual food and sustenance in that holy Sacrament.

shed his blood, but also doth vouchsafe in a Sacrament and mystery to give us his said body and blood to feed upon spiritually. The which Sacrament being so divine and holy a thing, and so comfortable to them which receive it worthily, and so dangerous to them that will presume to take the same unworthily: My duty is to exhort you in the mean season, to consider the greatness of the thing, and to search and examine your own consciences, and that not lightly nor after the manner of dissimulers with GOD: but as they which should come to a most Godly and heavenly banquet, not to come but in the marriage garment required of God in scripture; that you may (so much as lieth in you) be found worthy to come to such a table.

The ways and means thereto is, First, that you be truly repentant of your former evil life, and that you confess with an unfeigned heart to Almighty God your sins and unkindness towards his Majesty committed, either by will, word, or deed, infirmity or ignorance: and that with inward sorrow and tears you bewail your offences, and require of Almighty God mercy and pardon, promising to him (from the bottom of your hearts) the amendment of your former life.

And amongst all others, I am commanded of God, especially to move and exhort you to reconcile yourselves to your neighbours, whom you have offended, or who hath offended you, putting out of your hearts all hatred and malice against them, and to be in love and charity with all the world, and to forgive other as you would that God should forgive you. And if any man have done wrong to any other, let him make satisfaction, and due restitution of all lands and goods, wrongfully taken away or withholden, before he come to God's

Which being so divine and comfortable a thing to them who receive it worthily, and so dangerous to them that will presume to receive it unworthily; my duty is to exhort you in the mean season to consider the dignity of that holy mystery, and the great peril of the unworthy receiving thereof; and so to search and examine your own consciences, (and that not lightly, and after the manner of dissemblers with God; but so) that ye may come holy and clean to such a heavenly Feast, in the marriage-garment required by God in holy Scripture, and be received as worthy partakers of that holy Table.

The way and means thereto is; First, to examine your lives and conversations by the rule of God's commandments; and whereinsoever ye shall perceive yourselves to have offended, either by will, word, or deed, there to bewail your own sinfulness, and to confess yourselves to Almighty God, with full purpose of amendment of life.

And if ye shall perceive your offences to be such as are not only against God, but also against your neighbours; then ye shall reconcile yourselves unto them; being ready to make restitution and satisfaction, according to the uttermost of your powers, for all injuries and wrongs done by you to any other; and being likewise ready to forgive others that have offended you, as ye would have forgiveness of your offences at God's hand:

board, or at the least be in full mind and purpose so to do, as soon as he is able; or else let him not come to this holy table, thinking to deceive God, who seeth all men's hearts.

For neither the absolution of the priest can anything avail them, nor the receiving of this holy sacrament doth anything but increase their damnation.

And if there be any of you, whose conscience is troubled and grieved in any thing, lacking comfort or counsel, let him come to me, or to some other discreet and learned priest, taught in the law of God, and confess and open his sin and grief secretly, that he may receive such ghostly counsel, advice, and comfort, that his conscience may be relieved, and that of us (as of the ministers of GOD and of the the church) he may receive comfort and absolution, to the satisfaction of his mind, and avoiding of all scruple and doubtfulness: requiring such as shall be satisfied with a general confession, not to be offended with them that do use, to their further satisfying, the auricular and secret confession to the priest; nor those also which think needful or convenient, for the quietness of their own consciences, particularly to open their sins to the priest, to be offended

for otherwise the receiving of the holy Communion doth nothing else but increase your damnation.

Therefore if any of you be a blasphemer of God, an hinderer or slanderer of his Word, an adulterer, or be in malice, or envy, or in any other grievous crime, repent you of your sins, or else come not to that holy Table: lest, after the taking of that holy Sacrament, the devil enter into you, as he entered into Judas, and fill you full of all iniquities, and bring you to destruction both of body and soul. (4)

And because it is requisite, that no man should come to the holy Communion, but with a full trust in God's mercy, and with a quiet conscience; therefore if there be any of you, who by this means cannot quiet his own conscience herein, but requireth further comfort or counsel, let him come to me, or to some other discreet and learned Minister of God's Word, and open his grief; that by the ministry of God's holy Word he may receive the benefit of absolution, together with ghostly counsel and advice, to the quieting of his conscience, and avoiding of all scruple and doubtfulness.

(4) This Paragraph forms part of the Exhortation at time of receiving in 1549—(see note 2.)

with them that are satisfied with their humble confession to GOD, and the general confession to the church. But in all things to follow and keep the rule of charity, and every man to be satisfied with his own conscience, not judging other men's minds or consciences; where as he hath no warrant of God's word to the same.

APPENDIX IV.

THE PRAYER OF CONSECRATION COMPARED

1549]	[1886
Let us pray for the whole state of Christ's church.	Let us pray for the whole state of Christ's Church militant here in earth.
¶ *Then the Priest, turning him to the Altar, shall say or sing, plainly and distinctly, this prayer following:*	
ALMIGHTY and everliving God, which by thy holy Apostle hast taught us to make prayers and supplications, and to give thanks for all men: We humbly beseech thee most mercifully	ALMIGHTY and everliving God, who by thy holy Apostle hast taught us to make prayers, and supplications, and to give thanks, for all men; We humbly beseech thee most mercifully [* *to accept our alms and oblations, and*] to receive these our prayers, which we
	* *If there be no alms or oblations, then shall the words* [of accepting our alms and oblations] *be left out unsaid.*
to receive these our prayers, which we offer unto thy divine Majesty, beseeching thee to inspire continually the universal church with the spirit of truth, unity, and concord: And grant that all they that do confess thy holy name, may agree in the truth of thy holy word, and live in unity and godly love. Specially we beseech thee to save and defend thy	offer unto thy Divine Majesty; beseeching thee to inspire continually the universal Church with the spirit of truth, unity, and concord: And grant, that all they that do confess thy holy Name may agree in the truth of thy holy Word, and live in unity, and godly love. We beseech thee also to save and defend all Christian Kings, Princes, and Governours; and specially thy
servant Edward our King, that under him we may be Godly and quietly governed. And grant unto his whole council, and to all that be put in authority under him, that they may truly and indifferently minister justice, to the punishment of wickedness and vice, and to the maintenance of God's true religion and virtue. Give grace (O heavenly Father) to all Bishops, Pastors, and Curates, that they may both by their life and doctrine set forth thy	servant *VICTORIA* our Queen; that under her we may be godly and quietly governed: And grant unto her whole Council, and to all that are put in authority under her, that they may truly and indifferently minister justice, to the punishment of wickedness and vice, and to the maintenance of thy true religion, and virtue. Give grace, O heavenly Father, to all Bishops, and Curates, that they may both by their life and doctrine set forth thy true

1549	1886
true and lively word, and rightly and duly administer thy holy Sacraments: and to all thy people give thy heavenly grace, that with meek heart and due reverence they may hear and receive thy holy word, truly serving thee in holiness and righteousness all the days of their life.	and lively Word, and rightly and duly administer thy holy Sacraments: And to all thy people give thy heavenly grace; and especially to this congregation here present; that, with meek heart and due reverence, they may hear, and receive thy holy word; truly serving thee in holiness and righteousness all the days of their life.
And we most humbly beseech thee of thy goodness (O Lord) to comfort and succour all them, which in this transitory life be in trouble, sorrow, need, sickness, or any other adversity.	And we most humbly beseech thee of thy goodness, O Lord, to comfort and succour all them, who in this transitory life are in trouble, sorrow, need, sickness, or any other adversity.
And especially we commend unto thy merciful goodness this congregation which is here assembled in thy name, to celebrate the commemoration of the most glorious death of thy Son:	
And here we do give unto thee most high praise, and hearty thanks, for the wonderful grace and virtue, declared in all thy saints, from the beginning of the world: And chiefly in the glorious and most blessed virgin Mary, mother of thy Son Jesu Christ our Lord and God, and in the holy Patriarchs, Prophets, Apostles and Martyrs,	And we also bless thy holy Name for all thy servants departed this life in thy faith and fear;
whose examples (O Lord) and steadfastness in thy faith, and keeping thy holy commandments, grant us to follow. We commend unto thy mercy (O Lord) all other thy servants, which are departed hence from us, with the sign of faith, and now do rest in the sleep of peace: Grant unto them, we beseech thee, thy mercy, and everlasting peace, and that,	beseeching thee to give us grace so to follow their good examples,
at the day of the general resurrection, we and all they which be of the mystical body of thy Son, may altogether be set on his right hand, and hear that his most joyful voice: Come unto me, O ye that be blessed of my Father, and possess the kingdom, which is prepared for you from the beginning of the world:	that with them we may be partakers of thy heavenly kingdom:

1549

grant this, O Father, for Jesus Christ's sake, our only Mediator and Advocate.

O God heavenly Father, which of thy tender mercy didst give thine only Son Jesu Christ, to suffer death upon the cross for our redemption, who made there (by his one oblation, once offered) a full, perfect, and sufficient sacrifice, oblation, and satisfaction, for the sins of the whole world, and did institute, and in his holy Gospel command us to celebrate, a perpetual memory of that his precious death, until his coming again;

Hear us (O merciful Father) we beseech thee; and with thy holy Spirit and word vouchsafe to bl✠ess and sanc✠tify these thy gifts, and creatures of bread and wine, that they may be unto us the body and blood of thy most dearly beloved Son Jesus Christ.

Here the Priest must take the bread into his hands.

Who, in the same night that he was betrayed, took bread, and when he had blessed, and given thanks, he brake it, and gave it to his disciples, saying: Take, eat, this is my body which is given for you: do this in remembrance of me.

Likewise after supper he took the cup, and when he had given

Here the Priest shall take the cup into his hands.

thanks, he gave it to them, saying: Drink ye all of this, for this

1886

Grant this, O Father, for Jesus Christ's sake, our only Mediator and Advocate. *Amen.*

¶ *When the Priest, standing before the Table, hath so ordered the Bread and Wine, that he may with the more readiness and decency break the Bread before the people, and take the Cup into his hands, he shall say the Prayer of Consecration, as followeth.*

ALMIGHTY God, our heavenly Father, who of thy tender mercy didst give thine only Son Jesus Christ to suffer death upon the cross for our redemption; who made there (by his one oblation of himself once offered) a full, perfect, and sufficient sacrifice, oblation, and satisfaction, for the sins of the whole world; and did institute, and in his holy Gospel command us to continue, a perpetual memory of that his precious death, until his coming again: Hear us, O merciful Father, we most humbly beseech thee;

and grant that we receiving these thy creatures of bread and wine, according to thy Son our Saviour Jesus Christ's holy institution, in remembrance of his death and passion, may be partakers of his most blessed Body and Blood: who in the same night that he was betrayed [a] took Bread; and, when he had given thanks, [b] he brake it, and gave it to his disciples, saying, Take eat, [c] this is my Body which is given for you: Do this in remembrance of me. Likewise after supper he [d] took the Cup; and, when he had given thanks, he gave it to them, saying, Drink

[a] Here the Priest is to take the Paten into his hands:

[b] And here to break the Bread.

[c] And here to lay his hand upon all the Bread.

[d] Here he is to take the Cup into his hand:

is my blood of the new Testament, which is shed for you and for many, for remission of sins: Do this as oft as you shall drink it, in remembrance of me.

These words before rehearsed are to be said turning still to the Altar, without any elevation, or shewing the Sacrament to the people.

WHEREFORE, O Lord and heavenly Father, according to the Institution of thy dearly beloved Son, our Saviour Jesu Christ, we thy humble servants do celebrate, and make here before thy divine Majesty, with these thy holy gifts, the memorial which thy Son hath willed us to make: having in remembrance his blessed passion, mighty ressurrection, and glorious ascension, rendering unto thee most hearty thanks, for the innumerable benefits procured unto us by the same, entirely desiring thy fatherly goodness, mercifully to accept this our Sacrifice of praise and thanksgiving: most humbly beseeching thee to grant, that by the merits and death of thy Son Jesus Christ, and through faith in his blood, we and all thy whole church may obtain remission of our sins, and all other benefits of his passion. And here we offer and present unto thee (O Lord) ourself, our souls, and bodies to be a reasonable, holy, and lively sacrifice unto thee: humbly beseeching thee that whosoever shall be partakers of this holy Communion, may worthily receive the most precious body and blood of thy Son Jesus Christ, and be fulfilled with thy grace and heavenly benediction, and made one body with thy Son Jesus Christ, that he may dwell in them, and they in him.

e And here to lay his hand upon every vessel (be it Chalice or Flagon) in which there is any Wine to be consecrated.

ye all of this; for this [e] is my Blood of the New Testament, which is shed for you and for many for the remission of sins: Do this, as oft as ye shall drink it, in remembrance of me. *Amen.*

¶ *After shall be said as followeth.* (5)

O LORD and heavenly Father,

we thy humble servants

entirely desire thy fatherly goodness mercifully to accept this our sacrifice of praise and thanksgiving; most humbly beseeching thee to grant, that by the merits and death of thy Son Jesus Christ, and through faith in his blood, we and all thy whole Church may obtain remission of our sins, and all other benefits of his passion. And here we offer and present unto thee, O Lord, ourselves, our souls and bodies, to be a reasonable, holy, and lively sacrifice unto thee; humbly beseeching thee,

(5) This is a Post Communion prayer in present Prayer Book.

And although we be unworthy (through our manifold sins) to offer unto thee any Sacrifice: Yet we beseech thee to accept this our bounden duty and service, and command these our prayers and supplications, by the ministry of thy holy Angels, to be brought up into thy holy Tabernacle before the sight of thy divine Majesty; not weighing our merits, but pardoning our offences, through Christ our Lord; by whom, and with whom, in the unity of the holy Ghost, all honour and glory be unto thee, O Father Almighty, world without end. Amen.

Let us pray.

As our Saviour Christ hath commanded and taught us, we are bold to say. Our Father, which art in heaven, hallowed be thy name. Thy kingdom come. Thy will be done in earth, as it is in heaven, Give us this day our daily bread. And forgive us our trespasses, as we forgive them that trespass against us. And lead us not into temptation.

The Answer But deliver us from evil. Amen.

Then shall the Priest say,

The peace of the Lord be alway with you.

The Clerks. And with thy spirit.

The Priest. Christ our paschal Lamb is offered up for us, once for all, when he bare our sins on his body upon the cross, for he is the very Lamb of God, that taketh away the sins of the world: wherefore let us keep a joyful and holy feast with the Lord.

that all we, who are partakers of this holy Communion, may be fulfilled with thy grace and heavenly benediction.

And although we be unworthy, through our manifold sins, to offer unto thee any sacrifice, yet we beseech thee to accept this our bounden duty and service:

not weighing our merits, but pardoning our offences, through Jesus Christ our Lord: by whom, and with whom, in the unity of the Holy Ghost, all honour and glory be unto thee, O Father Almighty, world without end. *Amen.*

¶ *Then shall the Priest say the Lord's Prayer, the people repeating after him every petition.* (6)

OUR Father, which art in heaven, Hallowed be thy Name. Thy kingdom come. Thy will be done in earth, As it is in heaven. Give us this day our daily bread. And forgive us our trespasses, As we forgive them that trespass against us. And lead us not into temptation; But deliver us from evil; For thine is the kingdom, The power, and the glory, For ever and ever. Amen.

(6) The Lord's Prayer in 1886 comes after Communion.

INDEX.

	1549 PAGE.	1886 PAGE.
Absolution, Form of Private	259	
Agnus Dei. sung at Communion time	186	
Albe	51, 155, 193, 310, 333	
Alms, Presenting of		167
Altar	155, 167, 178, 180	
Anointing of Sick	268	
Baptism by Affusion	206	206
Baptism by Immersion	205	205
Benedicite, for Te Deum, in Lent	57	
Bread for Holy Communion	194	194
Bread, Breaking of, in Prayer of Consecration		182
Bread and Wine placed on Holy Table	167	167
Bread and Wine consecrated, remaining not to be carried out of the Church		194
Burial of Dead, Communion at	286	
Ceremonies, Of	14	14
Chalice	167, 343	183
Chrisom	207	
Christmas-Day, a second Introit, Collect, &c.	98	
Confession, Auricular	164	
Consecration of Bread and Wine	180	182
Consecration of Water	218	205
Cope	51, 155, 193, 249	
Corporas	167	
Cross, Sign of, in Prayer of Consecration	180	
Cross, Sign of, in Baptism	200, 218	206, 209, 216
Cross, Sign of, in Confirmation	240	
Cross, Sign of, in Matrimony	247	
Declaration on Kneeling		196
Delivery of Bread into mouth	195	
Delivery of Bread into hands		185

	1549 — PAGE.	1886 — PAGE.
Departed, Commemoration of	179	168, 285
Departed, Prayer for...	179, 283	
Easter Day, a second Introit, Collect, &c.	118	
Evensong	66	22
Exorcism in Baptism	201	
Gestures	51	
God's Board	185	
Habit of Bishop Elect at Consecration	349	349
Habit of Deacon Candidate	310	
Habit of Priest Candidate...	333	
Introits	95	
Invocation of Holy Ghost upon Elements ...	180	
Litany	79	
Lord's Prayer	62	
Magdalene, St. Mary, Collect, Epistle, &c.... ...	148	
Mass	154	
Matins	52	22
Nicene Creed	159	159
North side of Holy Table		155
Notes respecting 'Decent Ministration'... ...	51	
Oath of Supremacy	320	
Oblations		168
Ornaments Rubric...		51
Pastoral Staff	51, 349	
Prayer for Church Militant	178	167
Prayer of Consecration	179	182
Prayer for Departed	179, 283	
Priest, Position of, at Holy Communion...	155, 178	155, 182

	1549 — PAGE.	1886 — PAGE.
Reservation of Sacrament	...268	
Rochet...	51	349
Rome, Bishop of	80, 312, 320	
Sacraments Of, in Catechism		235
Spousage, Tokens of	...246	
Table		155, 167
Table, Holy		167, 186
Table, Lord's		175, 181, 182
Table, Position of		155
Table, Fair linen covering of		155
Ten Commandments	...233	156, 233
Ter Sanctus...	177	177
Trine Immersion	...205	
Tunicle	155, 323	
Vestment	155	
Vestment Rubrics...	51, 154, 193	
Water, Mixing of, with Wine	167	
Water for Baptism...	...217	198
Withdrawal of Non-Communicants...	167	
Words of Administration	...185, 186	185, 186

PRESTON:
PRINTED BY H. OAKEY, CAXTON HOUSE, 36, FISHERGATE.

www.ingramcontent.com/pod-product-compliance
Lightning Source LLC
Chambersburg PA
CBHW050846300426
44111CB00010B/1153
9783337200879